Fantastic Mr Dahl

MICHAEL ROSEN

PUFFIN

PUFFIN BOOKS

Published by the Penguin Group
Penguin Books Ltd, 80 Strand, London WC2R 0RL, England
Penguin Group (USA) Inc., 375 Hudson Street, New York, New York 10014, USA
Penguin Group (Canada), 90 Eglinton Avenue East, Suite 700, Toronto, Ontario, Canada M4P 2Y3
(a division of Pearson Penguin Canada Inc.)
Penguin Ireland, 25 St Stephen's Green, Dublin 2, Ireland (a division of Penguin Books Ltd)
Penguin Group (Australia), 250 Camberwell Road, Camberwell, Victoria 3124, Australia
(a division of Pearson Australia Group Pty Ltd)
Penguin Books India Pvt Ltd, 11 Community Centre, Panchsheel Park, New Delhi – 110 017, India
Penguin Group (NZ), 67 Apollo Drive, Rosedale, Auckland 0632, New Zealand
(a division of Pearson New Zealand Ltd)
Penguin Books (South Africa) (Pty) Ltd, Block D, Rosebank Office Park, 181 Jan Smuts Avenue,
Parktown North, Gauteng 2193, South Africa

Penguin Books Ltd, Registered Offices: 80 Strand, London WC2R 0RL, England

puffinbooks.com

First published 2012

001 – 10 9 8 7 6 5 4 3 2 1

Text copyright © Michael Rosen, 2012
Illustrations copyright © Quentin Blake, 2012
Additional illustrations by Rowan Clifford, 2012
Archive photographs copyright © Roald Dahl Nominee Ltd, 2012
All rights reserved

The moral right of the author and illustrators has been asserted

Printed in Great Britain by Clays Ltd, St Ives plc

British Library Cataloguing in Publication Data
A CIP catalogue record for this book is available from the British Library

ISBN: 978-0-141-32213-1

www.greenpenguin.co.uk

MIX
Paper from
responsible sources
FSC™ C018179
www.fsc.org

Penguin Books is committed to a sustainable
future for our business, our readers and our
planet. This book is made from paper certified
by the Forest Stewardship Council.

Roald Dahl's motto

My candle burns at both ends;
It will not last the night;
But ah, my foes, and oh, my friends –
It gives a lovely light!
– Edna St Vincent Millay

Contents

*For Emma, Elsie and Emile
and for Joe, who was there for
Roald to talk to*

Introduction

I first met Roald Dahl in a television studio in 1980. He was already very famous, though perhaps not quite as mega-famous as he is today. He'd written *James and the Giant Peach*, *Charlie and the Chocolate Factory*, *Fantastic Mr Fox* and *Danny the Champion of the World*. But now he had a new book out. And so did I. We were both appearing in the same TV programme because someone thought that we were writing similar kinds of stories. To tell the truth, I was quite excited. I was going to meet a writer whose books millions of children loved. But there was someone else with me who was even more excited than I was. This was my son Joe, who was about five years old.

In TV studios, there's often a little room away from all the cameras, where you wait until it's your turn to be filmed. It's called the green room – even though it's not usually green. Joe and I sat on one side of this particular green room and Roald Dahl was on the other. I noticed that he didn't really look at me even though I looked at him and tried to say hello. Instead, every now and then, Roald Dahl looked across at Joe. This went on for some time. After a bit, Roald caught Joe's attention and said to him in quite a stern way, 'Come here.'

Joe looked at me and I nodded. So he went over and stood in front of Roald Dahl. And, as everyone will tell you, Roald was very big – even when he was sitting down. Big legs, big body, even a big head. For a little boy, he must have seemed huge. A real giant.

Then, in a big, booming voice, Roald Dahl said to Joe, 'What's that growing on your father's face?'

Joe looked across the room at me and then back at Roald Dahl. In a small voice, he said, 'A beard?'

'Exactly!' said Roald Dahl. 'And it's disgusting!'

Joe looked unsure. Was this a joke or was it serious? He smiled, but only a little.

Roald Dahl went on, 'It's probably got this morning's breakfast in it. And last night's dinner. And old bits of rubbish, any old stuff that he's come across. You might even find a bicycle wheel in it.'

Joe looked back again at me and my beard. I could see on his face that there was a part of him that believed what he had just heard. After all, Roald Dahl hadn't asked Joe what he thought *might* be in my beard. He'd just told him in that firm, very sure voice what was actually, really and very definitely in my beard.

And that's what Roald Dahl was like. When he spoke, he did sound very, very certain – even if what he was saying was extraordinary, amazing, weird, fantastical or downright crazy.

Soon after that, Roald and I were called into the studio – me to talk about my book about a giant flea that lived in the London Underground and Roald Dahl to talk about . . . can you guess? *The Twits,* of course.

It's all a long time ago now, but I seem to remember that the interviewer asked us what we thought were the 'ingredients' of a good story for children.

'Above all,' Roald Dahl told the interviewer, 'it must be FUNNY.'

Afterwards, we returned to the green room, picked up our coats and went home. I think he said goodbye to me. He certainly said goodbye to little Joe, and had a few words of wisdom for him too. He leaned towards my son and said, 'And don't forget what I said about your father's beard.'

This book is about one of the world's greatest storytellers. Roald Dahl tells the story of his life in *Boy* and *Going Solo*. And, like Roald Dahl did, I want to tell you about things that happened to him that were deeply interesting and, more often than not, utterly, utterly amazing. But, most of all, I want to look closely at his writing.

I'm a writer and when I meet children, they often ask me how I got into writing. Why did I start? Where do I get my ideas from? Where do I write? How long does it take me to finish a book or a poem? What's my next book about?

In this book, I'm going to try to answer these questions about Roald Dahl's writing, along with one more. A little like the TV interviewer, I'd like to discover the special ingredients that, when mixed together, made Roald Dahl such an amazing a writer of children's books.

Now, a warning: it's impossible to write the whole, true story of anything. We always leave things out. We quite often put things in. Sometimes, no matter how hard we try not to, we change things. We tell the story in our own way, which might not be the same way that someone else would tell it. This book is my point of view. I'm looking at all the things I've read and heard about Roald Dahl, and choosing some of them to tell you about, in my particular way.

Writing often looks simple, clear and truthful, but it's always more complicated than it seems. This book is about that. It's about writing.

Duckworth Butterflies – Roald Dahl's house at St Peter's

Roald Dahl in his St Peter's school uniform

The Boy

Else, Roald and Alfhild

Chapter 1

Homesick

To understand how Roald Dahl became such a fantastic writer, I think it's important to find out what he was like as a boy. Let's picture him, aged about nine years old when he first went to boarding school.

It was called St Peter's, and it was a long way from home, near the seaside town of Weston-super-Mare in Somerset, England. There were about seventy boys there, aged between eight and thirteen. No girls. St Peter's didn't really look like a school. It was more like the kind of spooky house you find in ghost stories, with dark, pointed windows and ivy creeping all over the outside walls.

The boys were grouped into 'houses', which meant that they lived together in different parts of the school. Each house had a name: Duckworth Butterflies, Duckworth Grasshoppers, Crawford Butterflies and Crawford Grasshoppers. And Roald was a Duckworth Butterfly. The four houses were like teams. They competed against each other in sports, schoolwork and almost everything. So, really, Roald belonged not just to a school but to a house within that school.

Most of Roald's teachers had fought in the First World War, which would have been a terrible, terrifying, scary time for them. They would nearly all have seen and heard awful, frightening things; they would all have been saddened by knowing someone who had been killed. Some of them would have been badly injured. In one of his letters home, Roald told his mother about a new teacher:

'Mr Jopp, he has only got one hand, he was in the air force.'

Some of these teachers were fierce. Some of them did odd, crazy things, like chasing the boys around on school trolleys! Many of them were keen on teaching the boys to love the finest things in life, such as great art, great stories, so that they would go on to do great things when they grew up. They did this by giving them inspiring lectures, showing them inspiring films and reading them inspiring stories.

The boys slept in dormitories, which were like old, cold classrooms with iron beds in them. Roald was not allowed to go to the toilet at night, so under his bed he had a kind of potty called a bedpan. There was no bathroom. He and the other boys washed in front of everyone else in the dormitory, using basins of cold water. Brrrr! If Roald woke up in the night, he could hear all the other boys breathing. Sometimes he could hear boys crying. Sometimes this was a place where he planned great tricks, like climbing out of the windows or hiding sweets and cakes. But sometimes this was a place where boys ganged up on other boys.

Nearly everybody Roald Dahl knew at school was male, apart from one or two teachers, his housemaster's wife and Matron, who was a sort of replacement mother while the boys were away from home. Some schoolboys really liked their matron. Others didn't. Not at all. Roald was one of those. In his first autobiography *Boy*, he says:

Looking back on it now, there seems little doubt that the Matron disliked small boys very much indeed. She never smiled at us or said anything nice, and when for example the lint stuck to the cut on your kneecap, you were not allowed to take it off yourself bit by bit so that it didn't hurt. She would always whip it off with a flourish, muttering, 'Don't be such a ridiculous little baby!'

When he first went to boarding school, Roald was very homesick. He slept in his bed the wrong way round, with his head near the window, so that he could look out across the Bristol Channel towards Llandaff, his home town in Wales, on the other side of the water. Once he was so homesick that he pretended to be seriously ill with appendicitis, which wasn't just an illness that would get him out of school for a couple of weeks, but an illness that meant a surgeon would slice him open and whip out his appendix. He wanted to go home *that* badly. In *Boy*, Roald says that the school sent him home, but the family doctor soon figured out that Roald was just pretending and so he and the doctor struck a deal: the doctor wouldn't say anything about Roald fibbing and would confirm that he had a real stomach infection – but only if Roald went back to the school.

I should say here that anyone writing about Roald Dahl's life has to be very, very careful about one thing. Roald sometimes told stories that were *not* completely and utterly true. As he once wrote, 'I don't lie. I merely make the truth a little more interesting . . . I don't break my word – I merely bend it slightly.'

So, did Roald *really* strike a deal with the doctor? Did he *really* fool Matron and his teachers that he had appendicitis? We'll never know for certain. My guess is that *something* like that happened, but as he told the story he added bits to it. And I think this because – *shhh* – I do the same thing when I write!

But what we *do* know is that Roald Dahl was

definitely homesick. In *Boy,* he says that for the whole of the first term he was homesick. He talks of the people looking after him – the headmaster, teachers and Matron – as if they were a mix of tyrants, dictators, swindlers and cranks.

Harald Dahl, 1863–1920

However you might be surprised about the sort of home he was homesick for, because his family was quite EXTRAORDINARY.

Although Roald had an English accent, his parents came from Norway. Before Roald was born, his father, Harald Dahl, decided to leave Norway and seek his fortune. He set up a new business in the thriving coal industry of South Wales. His mother, before she married Harald, was called Sofie Magdalene Hesselberg. Roald wasn't their first baby. Before him there were Astri and Alfhild. And, before that, Harald had had

Astri Dahl, 1912–20

two children with his first wife. They were called Ellen and Louis. Harald's first wife, whom he had loved very much, had died. So, Roald was number five and number six was Else. But then two terrible things happened. First, Astri died and then, soon after, Roald's father died too. Roald's mother was expecting a baby when her husband died. This was another daughter – Asta. And all this happened by the time Roald was still only three years old.

That's an awful lot of information to absorb in one go, but I think it's important to know about a person's background if you are to understand them. It's events like these that go to shape who a person is, and how he or she thinks. (If you'd like to see Roald Dahl's family tree, it's on page 20.)

Roald would have remembered very little of the tragedies, because he was so young when they happened. He must have grown up relying on his mother for stories about his father and his older sister. He would have heard stories *about* these people instead of having them as *real* people to know and to touch. And he would have had to imagine what they were like from the stories he had heard about them. This must have been a lot of work for his imagination. If we're looking for the different ingredients that made Roald Dahl into a storyteller, I think learning to imagine and learning to listen to stories are two of the most important.

And there's something else. These family stories weren't told to Roald in the language he used at school. They were told in Norwegian. Back then, he was bilingual – he could think and talk in two different languages – and there was hardly anyone he met in Britain who could speak his home language of Norwegian. He grew up knowing a sort of secret language, and it was in that secret language he would have learned about his father.

For those of us who speak just one language, how we speak and how we write are kind of invisible. We just do it. We don't have to think too much about which words to use, or why we use one word or another. And we don't have to think too much about how we say things. But people who are bilingual hop between their two languages and doing that hopping often stirs up questions about the words we use and why and how we use them.

Roald's mother was a very important person in his life. She was right at the heart of the Dahl family. She was the one who kept things and people together. And she told stories. But she was also

Roald Dahl's mother

Roald, aged 6

the person who sent Roald away to school. So she was responsible for making him happy *and* making him feel homesick and sad.

Much later in his life, Roald often told interviewers that he thought children were quite able to love and hate their parents at the same time and that was why in his stories he wrote about parents or other grown-ups who are beastly, alongside others who are lovely. There are Matilda's parents and Miss Honey in *Matilda*. Or how about the witches and Grandmamma in *The Witches*? Roald Dahl was one of the first writers who created this mixture of good and bad parents in his children's books. You can find it in fairy tales like *Hansel and Gretel* and *Snow White and the Seven Dwarfs* but before Roald Dahl it was quite rare to find these beastly and lovely characters side by side in stories.

So that's what Roald Dahl's life was like when he was nine years old. I think it's quite unusual. You may recognize some bits of it. I hope you don't recognize others. But the good bits and the sad bits and the downright bizarre bits form the background of one of my favourite writers. And I think, together, they start to give an idea of why he went on to write such amazing books.

I'm going to end this chapter with a little story of my own.

When I think of Roald Dahl's childhood, I'm reminded of someone I knew very, very well: my own father. When my father was a little boy, about the same age as Roald, his parents split up and he never saw his dad again. So he also lost his dad. Like Roald, he was brought up in a household mostly full of women — his mother, his sister and his aunts. And, some of the time, there was a different language spoken at home. His mother told him they were different and that other people didn't believe the same things. This was sometimes a strange and uncomfortable feeling.

My dad said that all through his childhood, whenever he felt sad or angry or uncomfortable or different, he would dream that his father would suddenly turn up and make things better. He would stare at the photos of his father and listen to his mother's stories about him, about how good and clever he was. But it was always just the photos. No dad turned up. So my dad said that he had a secret inner life where he and his imaginary father lived.

My dad wasn't sent away to a boarding school, but his mother used to have to go into hospital for several weeks at a time, and, while she was away, he used to have nightmares in which she would die and he would have to live with the relatives he didn't like and who, he thought, didn't like him. And people around him told stories, some of them about ghosts and spirits called 'dybbuks' and a giant clay man called 'the Golem' who smashes up a whole city. Meanwhile, there was another place, another country, where his grandfather and some of his other relations came from, where it was said there were dangerous men on horses called 'Cossacks'. . .

And there the similarity ends, because my dad didn't grow up to be a famous writer like Roald Dahl. But he did become a storyteller and he did write about his own life. He also did a lot of other kinds of writing: he turned this inner life into thoughts about how best to teach and talk to children so that they would enjoy listening, reading and acting out stories. He kept thinking about the child he once was, imagining that quite a few of the children he was teaching were a bit like him, and wondering what kinds of stories and poems he and they might like. He wrote about languages other than English and he looked closely at how children speak and write.

So, when I think about Roald Dahl's childhood, I can't help but think how there were some things about both Roald and my father and their lives that were quite similar, and how perhaps that led them both to do things in life that were quite similar too.

I think that a childhood can sometimes last a lifetime.

The Family Tree

Harald Dahl

Marie   Astri   Alf

Roald

Louis Ellen

Olivia Tessa   Theo Ophelia   Lucy

Sofie Magdalene Hesselberg
Mormor

Else   Asta

Patricia
Neal

Liccy

Neisha   Charlotte   Lorina

Llandaff Cathedral

Chapter 2
School Days

Harald Dahl

Harald Dahl, Roald's father, was a man who worked very hard for his living. He was a shipbroker. This didn't mean that he broke ships. It meant that he supplied boats to people who wanted to sell their goods to other countries and who needed to transport their goods there, by sea. Harald must have been a great success at his job, because by the time he died, when Roald was only three, he left a lot of money and property to his family. In today's money, they would have been worth a colossal £5 million.

This must have been a relief to Roald's mother, Sofie. Neither she nor any of her children would need to go without food or new clothes. Mrs Dahl could afford to employ servants – or help, as they were known – to do the washing, cleaning and cooking, and to look after the children. Roald and his sisters could probably have the toys they wanted, they had a big house and garden to live and play in, and went on lots of nice holidays too – sometimes in Wales or often in Norway with their relatives. And one thing his mother could certainly afford was to send Roald to expensive schools.

First, there was the kindergarten, or nursery, at Elmtree House in Llandaff, near Cardiff, where he went when he was six years old, in 1922. He was there for just one year. Then he went to Llandaff Cathedral School for two years. His next school was St Peter's, the boarding school in Weston-super-Mare, where he stayed until 1929, when he was thirteen. After that it was off to Repton, a famous public school not far from Derby in the Midlands, which he left in 1934, aged eighteen.

Thanks to Roald and his mother, we can travel back in time and find out more about his schooldays. This is because he kept his school reports and his mother kept the letters that he sent home to her. *Thank goodness*. That's a lot of valuable information about a boy who became a world-famous author.

One of the first glimpses we get of Roald's schooldays is at Elmtree House. Here, Roald was looked after and taught by two sisters, Mrs Corfield and Miss Tucker. He remembered his teachers as being 'sweet and smiling'.

Things were very different at his next school:

Llandaff Cathedral School. It stood next door to the – you've guessed it – cathedral. (In fact, it's still there, if you want to see where Roald went to school.) There was a proper headmaster in this place. And it was steeped in tradition – full of stories about itself, stretching back hundreds of years. Roald's two years at the school became full of stories for him too, especially the famous one he tells in *Boy* about the time he and his friends played a trick on a woman they thought was utterly, completely, totally horrible – Mrs Pratchett. She ran the local sweet shop and Roald's little gang from the cathedral school came to hate her . . .

She never smiled. She never welcomed us when we went in, and the only times she spoke were when she said things like, 'I'm watchin' you so keep yer thievin' fingers off them chocolates!' Or 'I don't want you in 'ere just to look around! Either you forks out or you gets out!'

But by far the most loathsome thing about Mrs Pratchett was the filth that clung around her. Her apron was grey and greasy. Her blouse had bits of breakfast all over it, toast-crumbs and tea stains and splotches of dried egg-yolk. It was her hands, however, that disturbed us most. They were disgusting. They were black with dirt and grime. They looked as though they had been putting lumps of coal on the fire all day long. And do not forget please that it was these very hands and fingers that she plunged into the sweet-jars when we asked for a pennyworth of Treacle Toffee or Wine Gums or Nut Clusters or whatever . . .

The other thing we hated Mrs Pratchett for was her meanness. Unless you spent a whole sixpence all in one go, she wouldn't give you a bag. Instead you got your sweets twisted up in a small piece of newspaper which she tore off a pile of old Daily Mirrors lying on the counter.

And *then* Roald says that he and his friends found a dead mouse under the floorboards, which gave him a wonderfully wicked idea.

'Why don't we,' I said, 'slip it into one of Mrs Pratchett's jars of sweets? Then when she puts her dirty hand in to grab a handful, she'll grab a stinky dead mouse instead.'

But how would they put the mouse into the sweet jar *without* Mrs Pratchett seeing? This called for a fiendishly clever plot. The 'Great Mouse Plot', in fact.

We were strutting a little as we entered the shop. We were the victors now and Mrs Pratchett was the victim. She stood behind the counter and her small malignant pig-eyes watched us suspiciously as we came forward.

'One Sherbet Sucker, please,' Thwaites said to her, holding out his penny.

I kept to the rear of the group, and when I saw Mrs Pratchett turn her head away for a couple of seconds to fish a Sherbet Sucker out of the box, I lifted the heavy glass lid of the Gobstopper jar and dropped the mouse in. Then I replaced the lid as silently as possible. My heart was thumping like mad and my hands had gone all sweaty.

'And one Bootlace, please,' I heard Thwaites saying.

When I turned round, I saw Mrs Pratchett holding out the Bootlace in her filthy fingers.

'I don't want all the lot of you troopin' in 'ere if only one of you is buyin',' she screamed at us. 'Now beat it! Go on, get out!'

As soon as we were outside, we broke into a run. 'Did you do it?' they shouted at me.

'Of course I did!' I said.

'Well done you!' they cried. 'What a super show!'

I felt like a hero. I was a hero. It was marvellous to be so popular.

Every time I read that story, I think about one thing: the word 'trick'. Here is Roald Dahl, less than nine years old, and what is he doing? Coming up with a trick! And that reminds me of the books he wrote. They are full of tricks, cunning plans and naughty jokes. If the story about the mouse and the sweet-shop lady is true (and we can never be absolutely, totally sure about that), and it really was Roald who came up with the 'Great Mouse Plot', then I think he had already begun to invent ways of writing.

Why?

Because if you plot and plan a trick, you need to think ahead and imagine 'What would happen if . . . ?' If you're someone who loves to imagine 'What would happen if . . . ?', such as 'What would happen if my best friend turned into cat . . . ?' then you're well on the way to being a writer. Roald wrote the story of what happened in the 'Great Mouse Plot' many, many years after it happened. But, in a way, he 'wrote' it when he and his friends looked at the dead mouse and imagined what they were going to do with it. He wasn't really writing it, of course, but he was thinking ahead, planning and imagining . . .

When I read the 'Great Mouse Plot', it made me wonder what kind of writer Roald Dahl was. When you write stories, you have to do all you can to grab your readers' attention. How does Roald do this here?

First of all, he tells us about Mrs Pratchett. But he doesn't just say 'Mrs Pratchett was horrible' and then move straight on to the plot. Instead, he shows us what's horrible about how she *looks*, the things she *says* and one key thing about her *character*, her meanness. In fact, he gives us such a thorough picture that we can start to imagine things about her that Roald Dahl does *not* tell us, like what she might think of this group of boys coming into her shop. Does she think *they* are horrible? But why would she think that? What might they have done? What *else* is Dahl not telling us?

I also noticed that Roald does what can be called 'inside-outside'. This is where a writer tells some of the story as if he were a fly on the wall, watching everyone from the outside, but at other times he goes 'inside' a character to tell the story from their point of view. This keeps our minds busy, flipping to and fro between outside and inside. One moment we're *looking* at what's going on and the next we're *listening*. Just like this. We *hear* Roald say to his friends, 'Then when she puts her dirty hand in to grab a handful, she'll grab a stinky dead mouse instead . . .' And he *describes* the scene: 'We were strutting a little as we entered the shop.' This mix of listening and looking also makes us want to follow the story and to enjoy getting the whole picture.

At first glance, the 'Great Mouse Plot' might look one-dimensional. This means that the story is not complicated: in this case, that it's just about goodies and baddies – Mrs Pratchett is a baddy and the boys are getting their own back on her. 'Serves her right!' we might say. And that's all there is to it. But, if you are a really good storyteller, you can turn a one-dimensional story into something that readers will wonder about. I think that good writing will always give you a chance to look at things from different points of view, rather as if you were seeing a scene first from the front and then from behind, or first from inside one person's head and then from inside another person's.

One thing that none of them – not Roald, nor his friends – seems to have thought about was what would happen to them if their terrible mouse crime were found out. And this was . . . PUNISHMENT.

I'm sure you know about punishment. You probably know of people – even you! – who have been sent out of the classroom . . . or made to stay in at breaktime . . . or been given a detention . . . or sent to see the head teacher . . . or even been excluded from school altogether. What's absolutely NOT allowed is for anyone in school to hit you. But when I was at school and, before that, when Roald was at school, teachers were allowed to punish children by hitting them. They could use all sorts of things – their bare hands, sticks, belts, rulers, blackboard rubbers, shoes – and they could hit a child in all sorts of places – round the face, across the hand or on their backside. Sometimes they did it when they were angry, while we were sitting at our desks. Sometimes we were called out to the front of the class and they did it in front of everyone. Sometimes they just threw things at us. When I was at secondary school I had one teacher who used to yank my hair, pulling my head down to the desk. Then he'd let go. But, before I could lift my head up, the teacher would turn his hand into a fist and then punch the back of my head. Another one – a very nice man, actually – walloped me round the face.

Caning was one thing that bothered Roald Dahl more than any other about school. It leaps out of the pages of his books. He wanted all of his readers to know he HATED being caned. He says that plenty of his teachers were 'cane-happy', but there was one particular way of dishing out this punishment that always felt very serious and solemn. This was when you were called to the headmaster's office. Just imagine standing nervously on his carpet, perhaps daring to look around his office at the old photos and books, the chairs and the desk while you waited. Aside from your own parents, the headmaster was probably the most important person you knew, and this special, clever and important person had chosen you for this extra-special thing: to beat you because you had misbehaved. And there was always something you had to do before you were beaten: you had to make some part of yourself available so that he could hit it. Every boy knew by heart the words 'Hold out your hand' or 'Bend over'. These were words that were said over and over again, and they set in motion a series of moves that always happened in the same way, with the same quiet, solemn tone to it all.

The teachers told themselves that they were trying to make you a better person. It happened to me at primary school because I and some other boys ran after a ball into the girls' playground, then booed a teacher who tried to take the ball. And, Roald tells us, this kind of punishment happened to him and his friends at school. In fact, he spent a good deal of one book, *Matilda*, showing us one teacher in particular, Miss Trunchbull, who loved beating children. He made her so horrible and so cruel that many people – and, I've noticed, especially children – laugh. One part that people laugh at a lot is when she throws a boy out of the window.

This doesn't mean that Roald thought the beating stuff didn't matter. Just the opposite, in fact. He thought it mattered a great deal. He hated it so much that one of the ways he could deal with his feelings was to turn it into a story and exaggerate it, making it so big that readers end up thinking it's funny. Writers for children had made punishment funny before – in the Billy Bunter books and in comics like *The Beano*. What's really unusual and special about Roald is that he was one of the first writers for children to get us all thinking that this sort of punishment was both funny and wrong *at the same time*.

But the point about the beating is that it was supposed to hurt. It hurt Roald and it hurt his friends in the 'Great Mouse Plot'. They secretly showed each other their wounds. In a school where children were regularly beaten, it wasn't spoken about in public, but *everyone* spoke about it in private. Some children made secret plans on how to make it hurt less (like stuffing a book down your trousers). Then there were stories about what you could put on your skin before and after (vinegar, turps, olive oil). There were also mind-games people talked about, ways of making yourself think it didn't hurt so much or ways of showing the teacher you didn't care. There were even stories of children who hit the teacher back! And there was the big, big deal about what to tell your parents, what they would say when you told them and what they actually did . . .

This is what Roald's mother did. She saw the marks that the cane had made on Roald's skin — the scarlet stripes, as he called them — and she took him away from Llandaff Cathedral School at once.

Roald Dahl's Schools

Elmtree House, 1922–23
Kindergarten
Age 6–7
Llandaff, Cardiff, Wales

NOW CLOSED

Llandaff Cathedral School, 1923–5
Preparatory school
Age 7–9
Llandaff, Cardiff, Wales

STILL OPEN

St Peter's School, 1925–9
Preparatory school
Age 9–13
Weston-super-Mare,
Somerset, England

CLOSED

ST. PETER'S, WESTON-SUPER-MARE.

Then and NOW

Repton, 1929–34
Independent school
Age 13–17
Repton, Derbyshire, England

THE PRIORY HOUSE,
REPTON,
DERBY.

Porta Vaca Cupe

Dear Mama
Thanks awfully
and your letters. We
last night. We frijed
hieny beans over the
cream. Those bis
Last night we
there is abou
a Sonald &

March 23rd 1930.

Dear Mama,

Thanks awfully for your letter, and the parcel, a
one of egg had a crack around it, exactly the same as au
none of the slime had come out, and I had two of th
were excellent, in the form of poached eggs on toa
At the beginning of the week we had another hea
now the weather is beginning starting to look mor
There have been a lot of sports last week, notably th
high jumping; the two from each of the ten houses n
said I had to jump for Priory, and I don't kno
With Henderson, and Bell we also won the sen
very shaky, though, jumping in front of most of th
glad when it was over.
Yester

Dear Mama

I am having a lovely time here. 23th Spt

& We play foot ball every day here. The beads
the beds have no springs. Will you send my
stamp album, and quite a lot of swops.
The masters are very nice. I've
got all my clothes now, & and a belt,
and, tie, and a school Jersy.

love from

Boy

Chapter 3

Letters

The next thing that happened to Roald was that the amazing Mrs Dahl, who'd just rescued him from the local school, packed him off to boarding school instead. As you know from the first chapter, St Peter's was on the other side of the Bristol Channel – a big stretch of water where the River Severn becomes the sea. Roald travelled with his mother to school on a paddle steamer that chugged across the water, going the rest of the way by taxi. And then she left him there.

Roald was nine years old and he was on his own. Here's the very first letter that he wrote home from St Peter's in 1925. It makes me wonder what I would have written to my mother in his situation. What do you think of it? I've left in the spelling mistakes because they're funny!

Dear Mama   23rd Sept

I am having a lovely time here. We play football every day here. The beds have no springs. Will you send my stamp album, and quite a lot of swops. The masters are very nice. I've got all my clothes now, and a belt, and, tie, and a school Jersey.

Love from
Boy

At first glance it might look a bit dull – and maybe not a letter from the future Fantastic Mr Dahl. Where are the jokes? Where's the story about a horrible, crazy teacher or some awful boy at the school? It doesn't tell us very much about the young Roald . . . or does it? Let's look at the letter again, this time as if we're detectives searching for clues. Because it's a valuable piece of evidence.

First, he calls his mother **Mama**, which reminds us that Roald had strong ties to another country: Norway. Then he says that he's having a **lovely time**. Hmm, I wonder! Later, he did have some really good times at St Peter's, but I can't help thinking that the very first moments wouldn't have been *lovely*. And, in *Boy*, he tells us very clearly and strongly that his first moments were anything but.

'I had never spent a single night away from our large family before,' he says. *'I was left standing there beside my brand new trunk and my brand new tuck-box. I began to cry.'*

So why does he tell Mama that he's having a lovely time? Maybe his teacher had told him what to write but I like to think he's making sure at first that she doesn't worry about him. Don't you?

Then he tells Mama that they play **football** every day. This didn't mean that he and the other boys were just kicking a ball about in the playground. Instead, it would have been an organized game on the school field. Roald grew to really like sport and as a newcomer he must have already spotted that it was a big deal at St Peter's.

He goes on to tell Mama that the **beds have no springs**. When I was nine, the springs were broken on my bed and I was always complaining to my parents about it and moaning that my brother's bed was more comfortable than mine! Maybe, in a way, I was getting all moany and whingy about the fact that having a lumpy bed proved that my parents didn't care enough about me to get me a nice comfy bed! Is young Roald trying to send Mama a message that he doesn't think she's done enough to make sure he's comfy at night?

Then it's on to **stamps**. All his life, Roald was a great collector. If you go to the Roald Dahl Museum and Story Centre in Great Missenden you can see some of the things he collected, including a ball he made out of the silver wrapping gathered from the many chocolate bars he ate! Squirrels collect nuts. They bury them in the ground so that when winter comes and there's no food they can go round digging them up. I think writers are a bit like that. We collect stuff so that when we're searching for inspiration we can look at our collections and – hey presto! – ideas might pop into our heads. It would have been very easy for Roald to collect stamps – he had foreign relatives who would have sent letters and parcels covered in exciting stamps, with pictures of intriguing foreign places, kings, queens and famous people. This might have impressed all the boys Roald was meeting. What's more, he had 'swops'. These were double copies (or more) of any stamp, which could be swapped with other boys' stamps in order to make his collection even better. A great future in both collecting and looking good among his friends was opening up straight away, so long as Mama sent them.

Next Roald tells his mother that the **masters are very nice**. I doubt it. In 1925 the masters of private boarding schools were all sorts of things, but on the whole I've never heard them called 'nice'. Is Roald trying to reassure Mama it's not like the other school where he got beaten really badly? When young children see anxious looks on their parents' faces, some think that it's their job to get rid of that worry, even if it means making up a little story to do so. Perhaps Roald was trying to convince her that everything was all right, *even when it wasn't*. Anyone who learns how to do that is well on their way to becoming a storyteller!

Finally, Roald finishes the letter with his nickname, '**Boy**'. In his new world, where everyone called him 'Roald', it must have been a relief to use a name that no one else at school knew about. 'Boy' was his home name and must have reminded him and his mother of how much they loved each other.

Love from
~~Boy~~ Boy

In *Boy* Roald says their letters were censored. This meant each boy had to show his letter to a teacher so that he could point out any spelling mistakes. But, secretly, Roald thought that the teachers were checking up on them, making sure that the boys didn't complain to their parents about the food or being badly treated.

Here's Roald's second letter, which was written only two days later:

Dear Mama

Thank you for the stamps. I've swoped quite a lot. I played football yesterday, and scored one goal. We went for a walk today but it was not a very long one. I am going to write to Bestemama and Bestepapa and tante Ellen. I doant think I want eny moor stamps. I've got my straw hat. I had it yesterday. I hope Mike will get better soon. Thank Else, and Alfhild, and baby for thire letters. I can understand your writing very well. I am very glad you found my boat.

I like this letter a lot. I like the way Roald includes his Norwegian relatives – Bestemama and Bestepapa are his mother's parents, Roald's grandparents. I like the way he remembers that Mike's ill (I think Mike could be a pet but I'm not entirely sure); the way he reassures Mama that he can decipher her handwriting, so can understand her letters; the way that he is telling her how glad he is that she's looking after his things back home; and I also like his occasionally dodgy spelling.

I enjoy the fact that the letter hints that Mama has sent him a whacking great pile of stamps – too many by the sound of it – so he doesn't need 'eny moor'. And now he's got what might have struck Mama as being one of the most English things ever: a straw hat. It would have been a boater – a hard, flat straw hat with a ribbon around it.

It occurs to me that this letter is strong on empathy – that's the ability to understand and feel what other people feel. All writers need empathy. They need to be able to imagine what other people think and feel so that they can write about them, and they need to be able to guess what readers would like to know. In Roald's letter, I can hear loudly and clearly that he's trying to figure out what Mama would like to hear, and he's trying to think about his relatives and Mike. Funnily enough, some people have said that Roald Dahl the writer was sometimes short of empathy, that he made too many people in his books into people we just hate or despise. Think of George's grandmother in *George's Marvellous Medicine*, Miss Trunchbull and Matilda's parents in *Matilda*, the landowner in *Danny the Champion of the World*, the witches in *The Witches*, Boggis in *Fantastic Mr Fox* and even the crocodile in *The Enormous Crocodile*. But saying that these characters are just hateful or that they prove Roald the writer didn't show empathy misses the point, I think. As he was writing, Roald Dahl was always asking himself what kinds of things children would like reading about. (He also thought a good deal about why they might enjoy them too.) He was showing empathy for children by inventing characters and scenes that they would enjoy. Anyway, apart from that, he was also someone who did more than show us horrible people being defeated; he also tried to show people's kindness and love or their kind and loving deeds – there's Miss Honey in *Matilda*, Grandmamma in *The Witches*, Danny and his father in *Danny the Champion of the World* and even Mr Fox in *Fantastic Mr Fox*. That needs empathy too.

In the four years Roald was at St Peter's he had a big advantage when it came to sport and that was his height. Because he was taller than the other boys – one school report called him 'overgrown' – he was a useful player in the rugby team. He did well at boxing and also enjoyed cricket and football. In his letters, he talks a lot about his sporting achievements, telling Mama things like:

'*I hit two sixes . . . One hit the pavilion with a tremendous crash and just missed a window.*'

Oops.

But sometimes his studies didn't go very well. 'He imagines he is doing badly and consequently does badly,' said one teacher's report. At that school, if you did badly, it meant that you were kept in the same class for another year, with younger pupils. The danger of being kept back a year must have bothered Roald quite a lot, because some of his letters are just lists of where he is in each class for the different subjects, like the one opposite, written in November 1926.

There are several letters like this. I get the feeling that Roald, his mother and the school cared a great deal about learning, study, tests and marks.

Dear Mama

This is my order,

French = 6th

Latin = 3rd

grammar and composition = 5th

General Knolidge = 1st

Geometry = 1st

Divinity = 2nd

History = 5th

Arithmetic = 1st

Algebra = 1st

Geography = 3rd

There are 14 boys in the form.

I am first in the three maths.

Love from

Roald

One of his old school friends, Douglas, noticed that there was something quite different about Roald and said, 'He was very much an immigrant from Norway. I was an immigrant from Turkey . . . we were both foreigners.' This seems to have brought them together. The two boys used to walk together on school trips into the local town of Weston-super-Mare, talking about the school's 'stupid or unnecessary rules', as they put it. But they didn't just whinge. They liked playing with the English language too, making up word games. And this reminds me of *The BFG*. Every time I read it, I think that *The BFG* is a book written by someone who liked having fun with words, with how they sound and how you can make up new ones.

Douglas also says that his friend was brilliant at conkers and in one letter Roald told his mother that he was the school champion because he had 'the highest conker in the school – 273'. This meant that Roald's conker had won a phizz-whizzing 273 times!

In his letters, Roald also talked about collecting things from the great outdoors, like birds' eggs (this is absolutely forbidden now – do not do it unless you actually want to be arrested). Altogether, he collected 172, all carefully laid out in a special glass cabinet with ten drawers, ranging from the eggs of a little tiny bird like the wren up to the eggs of big birds like gulls and crows.

But, besides collecting and conkers, there was something else that Roald was becoming good at: writing.

His letters start to fill up with loving descriptions of the things he sees and finds. And he spends pages telling his mother the latest fabulous things he has just learned in school – especially anything to do with animals and birds. He and the other boys were shown films that fired his imagination. In one, a pilot flew to the Cape of Good Hope in South Africa (it may not seem like a world-shattering event now, but this was in the very early days of flying) and in another he learned about climbing Mount Everest. They watched a film about a long-distance car journey to India and Tibet, and another showing ants fighting a centipede and flipping a woodlouse on its back.

Roald Dahl was a writer of extremes – he liked writing about amazing, odd, extraordinary and exaggerated things. When reading some of his letters, I can't help feeling that he was always on the lookout for bizarre events. There was the trip to the caves in Cheddar Gorge near his school, when Roald and the others were crammed into an open-top coach called a charabanc. Once in Weston-super-Mare there was a gas explosion, which started a terrible fire that burned down three shops – Roald went the next day to inspect the damage. Perhaps Mama liked to hear about them. Perhaps he liked to write about them. But, if something worth writing about happened, then that's what he did.

It's not surprising that if there was anything to do with storytelling at school, Roald loved it. In November 1925 he wrote to his mother about a lecture on 'bird legends' and he tells her the Aesop fable of how the wren became king of the birds, and another of how the blackbird got black feathers and a yellow beak.

One of Roald's favourite speakers was Major Cottam, who seems to have been quite a showman. The Major features quite often in Roald's letters, reading and reciting, and that conjures up for me an interesting picture: a man with a military background – I wonder, did he wear his uniform? – acting out stories and poems to groups of the boys, fascinating them, making them laugh, fall silent and be thoroughly amazed as he brought great books to life.

Last night about seven o'clock Major Cottam recited 'The Merchant of Venice' on the field under the trees, he was awfuly funny, and then he recited a little Sweedish poem and then a famous poem from Kiplin, 'Gounga-Dedn', it was awfuly funny, he acts as well while he is reciting.

Just before Christmas in 1926, when he's ten, Roald writes:

On friday we had a topping lecture in Esqimaux, all the slides were coloured, it was very interesting. And today we are having a cinamatograph on Dr Banardos Homes . . .

We had a special treat last night, we all hung up our stockings, and when it was dark matron came in dressed up as father Xmas, and put things in our stockings, I got a kind of musical box and a soldier on a horse in mine. The same night she hung up hers outside her door and we all put things in it, it was full in the end. We start Exams next Tuesday and they go on till Thursday. I AM COMING HOME NEXT FRIDAY ON THE 17TH OF DECEMBER, BY the 1.36 (one thirty six) train, please meet me.

So, if Matron dressed up as Father Christmas, maybe she wasn't quite as bad as he made out in *Boy* . . . ? And I like the capital letters too. Is he reminding Mama to be there? Is it possible that she sometimes forgot to meet him?

Another topic that really seemed to interest Roald was anything to do with illness and accidents, and all the different medicines and cures too. Here's a letter he wrote on 6 October 1929:

My headaches have quite gone now. I had one all the first week of the term, and I thought I would try 'Mistol'. So I did, I fairley poured it down for two days and it developed into a bad cold which I soon got rid of with that worthy muck. And now if I ever get the slightest head, I take a go of Mistol and it goes. What do you think it was? Hayfever perhaps. There are now a lot of colds about, and several boys in the sick room, so I think there will be flu soon, (there might not be of course), but after all that I have nearly finished my bottle of mistol, so please send me another, because I don't want flu this term, for the Common Entrance is on the 12th November.

It sounds as if young Roald has already learned — or thinks that he's learned — to take control. Today, children don't dose themselves up with medicine because that would be very dangerous. But back then Roald was pouring it down his throat. He figures that the medicine is making him better and keeping the flu away. It wasn't doing anything of the sort. That's just his imagination. But a belief in special, magic potions is very handy if you want to write books. And I can't stop myself thinking about a certain George and some *marvellous medicine* . . . can you?

Roald Dahl was also developing an eye for detail. During a royal visit to Weston-super-Mare, what interested him most was the fact that a train ran over someone and a local shopkeeper became so excited that he fired six shots into the air and terrified the royals!

When he writes to his sister Alfhild, he says:

> The barber is a very funny man, his name is Mr Lundy, when I went to have my hair cut last Monday, a lot of spiders came out from under the cupboard and he stepped on them and there was a nasty squashy mess on the floor.

In the Drill Display we have a Pyramid, there are a lot a boys standing in the shape of a star fish and some boys in the middle and a boy standing on one of the boys shoulders with his hands out, it looks very nice.

No one becomes a writer overnight. Just as actors rehearse their parts over and over again before we see them in plays and films, and sports people practise their movements, strokes, aims and tackles, so writers practise their writing – perhaps without even realizing it. It doesn't seem as if ten-year-old Roald knew that he was going to be a writer, but nevertheless he was practising and not just in lessons.

His letters home were giving him the chance to see what sounded good and what worked. He was finding out what sorts of things grabbed his mother's and his sisters' attention. And he was learning what made them laugh. Many years later, Roald discovered that his mother had secretly kept every single one of his letters to her. Isn't that amazing? I think this shows how proud she was of her young son, and how much she missed him.

And there's something else a young writer needs to do: read lots of different books. Before he went to St Peter's, Roald had read Beatrix Potter's stories.

He liked *Winnie-the-Pooh* by A. A. Milne, *The Secret Garden* by Frances Hodgson Burnett and the fairytales of Hans Christian Andersen, such as *The Snow Queen*. He also liked Hilaire Belloc's *Cautionary Verses*, which he learned off by heart. If you compare Roald Dahl's *Dirty Beasts* and *Revolting Rhymes* with *Cautionary Verses*, you can see that in some ways he wrote in Hilaire Belloc's style.

At St Peter's, he began to read Shakespeare's plays, novels by Charles Dickens and Robert Louis Stevenson's *Treasure Island*. And he loved rollicking adventure stories by authors with wonderful names like H. Rider Haggard. Roald and his friend Douglas moved on to ghost stories and they were soon reading and talking about the scary stories of Edgar Allan Poe. It's clear that he and his fellow pupils were expected to read a lot and read very widely.

Many times he wrote home to tell his mother about the exams he had to do. On one occasion, he challenged her to answer one of the exam questions.

He says that he got most of these right:

In what books do the following carecters occur and give the authors:-

Beccey Sharp

Sam Weller

Beetle

Mowgli
Israel Hands
Athos
Jean Val Sican

Complete the following proverbs:-

A little learning . . .
A Rolling stone . . .
Bird in the Hand . . .
A sticth in time . . .

One job that a writer has to do is to help their readers see and feel what things are like. And one way of doing this is by using metaphors and similes. When talking about the charabanc that took them to the caves in Cheddar Gorge, Roald wrote that they were packed in *'like sardins in a tin'*, which is a simile. And here are the closing words that Roald wrote in his very last letter home from St Peter's:

Please excuse this bad writing, but
I am writing it in Prep, under rather
bad conditions, also, an excuse is that
someone is singing downstairs, and the
noise closely resembles that of a flys'
kneecap, rattled about in a bilious
buttercup, both having kidny trouble
and lumbago.

These sound to me like the words of a boy who loves
language. This is a boy who is trying hard – maybe
a little too hard – to think up similes that sound
weird, funny and amazing. And this is a boy who is
thoroughly enjoying doing it.

Roald Dahl's Letters

Jan 19ᵗʰ 1926

Dear Mama
I got to school
all right. Please send
my music book as quick
as posible. Don't forget
to tell Smiths to send
"Bubles".

Love from
Boy

POST CARD

Mrs Dahl

Cumberland Lodge
Llandaff
Nr Cardiff

St Peter's
Weston-super-mare.

Jan. 27ᵗʰ 1928.

Dear Mama
Thank you very much for the cake etc.
I got the book the day before yesterday, quite a
nice edition. How are the chicks? hope they'll all
live. By the way, you said she would'nt get
any.

Here are a few more of Roald Dahl's letters to his mother from St Peter's.

St Peter's

Weston-super-mare.

March 24th 1926.

Dear Else

    I will soon be coming home, I am coming by train next Wedensday. There is a craze for darts and gliders, nearly every one has got one, I have got one topping one, it glides like anything, a boy called Huntly-Wood made it for me. I have got five quarter-

stars, I got one of them to day, it was for writing from Mr Francis. I think the French Play was very good, and very funny as well, I could not understand much of it, but I think every one liked it.

Love from

BOY

RD 13/1/1/44

St Peter's.

Oct. 13th 1929.

Weston-super-mare

Dear Mama

    Thanks awfully for the Roller skates, they are topphole. Were they the largest pair? at full stretch they fit toppingly, but if my feet grow much more they wont fit. We skate on the yard; we had a top fine time last night after tea; You see, the chaps who haven't got pairs, pull you. At one time I had eight chaps pulling me with a long rope, at a terrific lick, and, I sat down in the middle of it; my bottom is all polbue now! We also have "trains"; You get about ten chaps to pull, and with a long rope, and all the roller-skaters hang on to each other, and go around; but if one chap falls all the ones behind him come on top of him! The yard is

getting quite smooth now.

Last Wednesday we played a school called "Clarence" and beat them on 5-1. So far we have played 3 matches and won them all; I hope we have as good a term as the Rugger.

Last Sunday we had a lantern lecture on light-houses; the man, gave pictures of the Wolf; the Lizard, the Bishops Rock, and Longships at Landsend, all of which we saw last hols.

By the way, I had a birthday present from Marali yesterday. I was a thing called a "Yo Yah", which runs up and down on a string, but is very hard to work. It is very fascinating, but she confessed that it was bought at Woolworths; and she said that it was the craze there. I'll show you when I get home. Can you send me another tube of Gensop' toothpaste please

love from Roald

RD 13/1/3/

The beach at Nevlunghavn

Chapter 4

Holidays

Roald Dahl aged eight

Roald didn't just come across stories at school. For him, the holidays were crammed with strange and wonderful events too. By the time he was eleven, his mother and sisters had moved from Wales to a house in Bexley in Kent, about fifteen miles from London. It sounds a beautiful place, with a tennis court and grounds so huge that his mother had a gardener to look after them. In the house, there was even a special room for playing billiards.

In the 1920s many people as rich as the Dahls were very keen on behaving 'properly'. They had perfect manners, they wore the right clothes for every occasion, they spoke very politely and never ever said rude words or made rude noises. A lot of attention was paid to being clean – clean rooms, clean clothes, clean hair, clean face, clean hands – and any kind of shouting or running was strictly reserved for sport. Every day followed a special schedule, with breakfast, lunch and tea happening exactly on time. Boys were supposed to behave in one kind of a way and girls in another. There were also things that were 'proper' to read and see (and a lot of things that weren't). It was as if there were invisible rules. And people who didn't stick to the rules were frowned upon.

Did the Dahl family behave like this at home? Not at all. It seems as if Roald's mother didn't mind the children running about all over the place. She didn't appear to be bothered about them saying rude words, climbing trees or doing naughty and dangerous things. They were unconventional – they weren't like other people and they didn't stick to the rules. One story that the Dahl family liked to tell was how young Roald got himself an airgun, persuaded his sister to climb up a tree and then shot at her! In January 1928 he wrote to his mother, 'Please can you send my blank cartridge revolver, everybody here has one, including Highton and no one minds.' Years later, Roald told the story of how he once rigged up a kind of chariot on a wire so that he could water-bomb passers-by with water from old soup tins.

There weren't many mums like Mrs Dahl. It rather looks as if she thought that being naughty and wild was absolutely fine and part of how a child learns.

Maybe this is one of the reasons that Roald and Mama got on so well. In one of his letters, Roald even tells her this: 'We've got a new Matron called Miss Farmer in place of Miss Turner who left last term, one night in the washing room, having inspected a boy called Ford, she KISSED HIM.'

One thing we know about Roald Dahl, both from his books and from real life, was that he was quite naughty and wild himself. Most of us are held back by invisible rules, but Roald wasn't. Something gave him the confidence to say, write and do things that plenty of other people thought were shocking – think what the BFG did when he visited the Queen! I believe that it was Mrs Dahl who helped to give him this confidence.

'Stinky snozzcumbers,' the BFG said.

The school holidays weren't just spent at home. At Easter, the Dahls would pack their bags and go away. One place they went to was Tenby in South Wales. This is a beautiful Victorian seaside town, with an old harbour and long sandy beaches. Here, Roald could collect his eggs and starfish and go donkey riding. There was an island just off the coast with an ancient monastery on it and Roald would take a boat out to explore. Mrs Dahl used to rent a house overlooking the harbour for the family to stay in.

But for the Dahls there was an even more magical place: Norway. In *Boy*, Roald lovingly tells the story of how a great group of them travelled for several days to get there.

We were always an enormous party. There were my three sisters and my ancient half-sister (that's four), and my half-brother and me (that's six), and my mother (that's seven), and Nanny (that's eight) and in addition to these, there were never less than two others who were some sort of anonymous ancient friends of the ancient half-sister (that's ten altogether).

And, as Roald reminds us, they all spoke Norwegian.

Bestepapa Hesselberg

In a way, he says, 'going to Norway every summer was like going home'.

After a long, long journey, this large family group, with all their trunks and bags, would first visit the house in Oslo where Mrs Dahl's father and mother – Bestepapa and Bestemama – and her two sisters lived. Here, they ate old-style Norwegian food, with piles of fresh fish and home-made ice cream with little chips of crisp burnt toffee mixed into it, while the grown-ups drank and toasted each other over and over again, calling out, '*Skaal!*'

Next, they were off to the seaside! The Norwegian coastline is a magical place full of islands and fjords – long, narrow inlets where the mountainsides are steep and the water is very, very deep. In summer, the water is stunningly blue and the mountain slopes are covered in dark green pine forests. If ever you get the chance to visit the coast of Norway, you will see how beautiful and mysterious it is.

The fjords were full of fish and Roald loved to spend hours and hours in a boat, often with Louis, his half-brother, fishing and sunbathing. When he was older,

Mrs Dahl got hold of an old motorboat. It was 'a small and not very seaworthy white wooden vessel which sat far too low in the water and was powered by an unreliable one-cylinder engine'. It doesn't sound very safe, does it? But Roald and the

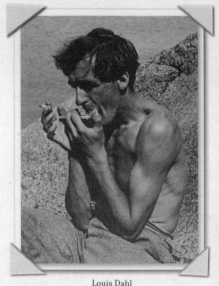

Louis Dahl

others headed up the fjord, hunting for different islands where they could go rock-pooling, fishing, swimming, diving and exploring, looking at the 'wooden skeletons of shipwrecked boats', feeding off wild strawberries and mussels and watching the 'shaggy, long-haired goats'. Sometimes, the sea was rough and it became pretty dangerous for the little party in this not-very-good boat. But Roald lived to tell the tale.

At night, Roald's mother told stories – sometimes made up, sometimes myths, legends and fairy tales, sometimes the stories of famous Norwegian writers who wrote about the kind of lonely, difficult lives people and animals had in this landscape of forests, mountains, rivers and fjords. She told of Norse gods who fought with giants in battles that lasted for days and weeks on end. There were tales of boys who outwitted wicked trolls, and of giant insects and giant frogs and cloud monsters, and of the hare who laughed till his jaws cracked and the tabby cat who ate too much. It was fantastic, magical, amazing, weird, scary, exciting stuff.

All this must have helped Roald Dahl to feel wonderfully different, in a good way. He was experiencing both a very proper English education *and* traditional Norwegian life. He doesn't seem to have known anyone outside his family who shared this particular mix of cultures. Being different can

Fishing on the Oslofjord

be very important for a writer. It can make you want to write about what it feels like to be you. It can make you want to write about the things that everyone else takes for granted, but which you see in a different way. Sometimes, it just makes you want to tell people about strange, different places and ways of life. Next time you think of the Big Friendly Giant, you might want to read some of the wonderful Norse myths or look at pictures of the coast of Norway and think about a young boy in his boat, far out on the fjord, looking down into the clear water, thinking, wondering, dreaming, planning and collecting.

Time is something that every writer needs. Time to think, wonder, dream, plan and collect. And Roald Dahl had plenty of that.

Roald, Alfhild, Else – Norway, 1924

Roald Dahl and Food

As well as chocolate, Roald Dahl loved to eat (and drink) many other things too. Here are just a few of them.

Roald Dahl's favourite foods of all time

Norwegian prawns
Lobster
Caviar
Scrumptious roast beef

Roald Dahl's favourite pudding

'*Krokaan* is simply a kind of crispy, crunchy toffee made from butter, sugar and almonds, and quite apart from the fact that its taste is so beguiling, it makes a most satisfying crunchy noise when you chew it. Ice cream, whatever flavour it is, is invariably a soft and silent meal, but when you fill it with krokaan chips, it suddenly becomes something that goes crunch when you chew instead of just floating silently down your throat.'

Roald Dahl's favourite soup

'*Chłodnik* is a cold Polish soup with a beetroot base and a number of other special ingredients, including chunks of lobster. It is the greatest soup that I have ever tasted, ice-cold, creamy and with a flavour so subtle and enticing that you feel you want to go on eating it forever.'

Roald Dahl's favourite family breakfast

Hot-house Eggs
Cut a circle out of a slice of bread. Pop the bread into a frying pan and cook on both sides in a little butter. Crack the egg into the hole in the bread – the white will spill over the edges very slightly to glue the egg in place. Flip the whole thing over and cook briefly on the other side.

'We always called it Hot-house Eggs,' said Roald Dahl. 'Don't ask me why.'

Roald Dahl's favourite workday lunch

Gin and tonic
Norwegian prawns with mayonnaise and lettuce
Kit Kat

A favourite supper of Roald Dahl's

Plump grilled Dover sole straight out of the Atlantic
Faintly green Portuguese wine
Almond tart

School dinners at Repton

Chapter 5

Teenage Years

In 1930 the teenage Roald Dahl was a new boy all over again, at Repton – the big, old public school for boys near Derby. There was a uniform, of course. But now it sounds more like fancy dress – striped trousers, a waistcoat, a long jacket called a tailcoat, a shirt with a stiff collar that had to be fixed to the shirt with special metal studs, very shiny black shoes and, finally, a boater. It must have taken a *long* time to get dressed.

Roald's house was called The Priory and about fifty boys lived there, with twelve from each year. Unlike at St Peter's, it really *was* a house, separate from the school in the town of Repton. The housemaster, Mr Jenkyns – the boys called him 'Binks' – and his family lived there too. Roald liked him a lot.

For the younger boys at this school and many like it, the real terror was in the way their lives were run by the older boys. At Repton, they ran a system where the oldest boys used the younger boys as their servants or,

Mr and Mrs Jenkyns and the boys from Priory House.
Roald Dahl is on the right of the second row from the front.

as Dahl called them, 'personal slaves'. Their way of keeping the younger boys in line was to beat them over and over again. So a new school-boy started off being a slave who was caned and ended up being a slave-master, beating the next new lot of youngsters coming in. It was a sort of training in bullying. But the schoolmasters of the time thought that it was a training in leadership instead. What do *you* think?

In *Boy*, Roald tells us how much he hated all the bullying and beatings and nastiness. And, if you think the book sounds bad, you'll be stunned to know that when he first wrote *Boy* the descriptions sounded even worse. There, in full gory detail, he told the story of how the older boys once dumped him – fully dressed – into a cold bath and held his head under the water. But here's the strangest thing. In one draft Roald says that, after the beatings, the boys didn't sympathize with each other. Instead, they 'developed a curiously detached attitude to these vile tortures in order to preserve their sanity'. He says, if they had gathered around each other helping each other, 'I think we would all have broken down.'

As we have seen, illness is something that Roald worried about a lot. Whether he was really ill or not isn't totally clear. In his letters home, he was always asking his mother to send him pills, lozenges, ointments and medicines of all kinds. He complains of corns, coughs, colds, headaches, constipation, weak bones . . . and there was even some conversation about him having a weak heart. At school, it was Matron who dealt with any serious illnesses, but when it came to things like cough medicine, the boys looked after themselves. Roald definitely did that. And, because of all his letters home, the view in the Dahl family was that he was not a very well chap.

Roald's teachers had a *lot* to say about him and not all of it good. Unlike his teachers at St Peter's, one thought that he was 'curiously dense and slow', another that he went in for 'fits of childishness' and 'fits of the sulks'. One found him a 'persistent muddler, writing and saying the opposite of what he means'. Other teachers said that he was idle, stupid, obstinate and too pleased with himself. Perhaps he was some of those things or perhaps he was just turning into a teenage rebel. We will never know.

But what we *do* know about is his writing. And sometimes his letters home were fantastic. Here's what he wrote after just a week at Repton:

The chap who takes us in Maths: Major Strickland (Stricker) who is chief of the O.T.C. is terrificly numerous. For instance, he will suddenly turn to you and say, 'Are you a slug, do you leave a long slimey track behind you,' the chap says 'no' and then he says, 'Well you're a fungus, in fact you're wet!' And perhaps he'll make a statement; 'Do you understand,' and then he will repeat it about six times, either getting louder and louder, or softer and softer, in the end developing into a concentrated mumble. He does'nt mind being answered back, but rather likes it; He is also very funny when arguing. For instance, if he cant think of an answer, he'll say, 'Well your . . .' then after the 'your' he will start mumbling, gradually becoming louder and louder, and in the end developing into a low pitched groan. I believe he's half-baked! He's a short man with a face like a field elderberry, and a moustache which closely resemble the African jungle. A voice like a frog, no chest an a pot-belly, no doubt a species of Rumble-hound. Please dont forget the toothpaste and brush.

Love from Roald

Already, I think that Roald wrote just for the fun of it. After all, this piece of writing wasn't for homework or for an exam. It was just to entertain his mother, and whoever else she might show it to. Here is Roald giving his mother some advice:

You seem to have been doing a lot of painting; but when you paint the lav don't paint the seat, leaving it wet and sticky, or some unfortunantely person who has not noticed it, will adhere to it, and unless his bottom is cut off, or unless he chooses to go about with the seat sticking behind him always, he will be doomed to stay where he is . . .

This sounds very typical of the Roald Dahl I knew, and of Roald Dahl's writing – funny, a bit rude, and a bit exaggerated!

Another glimpse of both the masters' odd behaviour and Roald's growing love of exaggerating things comes when he writes:

Mr. Wall is the most bad tempered man on the staff, but otherwise he is very nice. When he looses his temper he goes completly mad, he rushes round the room, tips his desk clean over, with everything on it, kicked all the furniture in the room as hard as he can, and especially his grandfather clock, which is gradually ceasing to exist. He shouts and yells, rushes round the room, and on Wednesday he nearly threw himself out of the window!

Though good marks are still important to him, the school and his mother, he can't resist making a joke of it:

P.S. I got minus 100 marks from our vicious form master last Friday, so I expect I'll be somewhere near bottom at half term.

I think that his mother must have enjoyed his humour and that he tried hard to make her laugh. But I also think that he liked to keep her on the edge of her seat too. Here he is describing the dramatic events when a fire broke out in The Priory:

The flames were enormous and the heat was colossal. The whole place stank of burning . . . and it got in your throat. I coughed all night. However we got to our bedrooms, which the firemen assured us were safe, but to us they looked as though they were being held up by two thin planks. We picked our way gingerly up the stairs (which were black and charcoaly) of course all the electric light had fused long ago. We got into our beds which were brown and nasty and I don't how but I managed to get some sleep. The place looked grimmer than ever by daylight. All the passage was black and in our study absolutely nothing was left.

What I like about this piece of writing is that we can really see and feel what it was like to be there. Roald gives us clear pictures – bedrooms that seem to be 'held up by two thin planks', beds that are 'brown and nasty' and the place looking 'grimmer than ever by daylight'. We also hear about his other senses – we feel the heat, taste the fire in his throat and smell the burning. He takes us on a journey through the scene: we travel with him from watching the fire, up the stairs to the bedrooms, into bed and looking at the study in the daylight. That gives the writing a feeling of movement. There's a changing speed in the story too. We start with lots of busy stuff happening – flames, coughing, firemen – but we end with blackness and nothingness. And he's not afraid to make up a word: *charcoaly*.

Roald entered school poetry competitions and in one poem he wrote a line that I love:

Evening clouds, like frog spawn, spoil the sky.

It turns something very ordinary into something strange and surprising. Not many people would think of comparing evening clouds to frogspawn, but Roald Dahl did. When writers draw our attention to a similarity we may not have noticed before, you can count that as good writing.

He was never afraid of being alone and the other boys noticed that he liked going off in the fields and hills around the school, fishing and collecting birds' eggs. Roald became a hit taking photographs too. Many of his letters were about this or that camera or film. Sometimes he asks his mother to make sure his photos get printed up properly and other times he sent these home, and then his letters are full of explanations about who or what

Photography at Repton

is in which photo. In *Boy*, you can tell that as an adult he was still very proud of how he got to be good at photography, but there's a way that this too is connected to writing. Taking photos carefully, then keeping them and choosing when to show them to people, is like a writer collecting interesting material, storing it up and then deciding when to use it. As you sit about showing people your photos, talking, telling the stories that go with the pictures, you find out what entertains people, what intrigues them, what little exaggerations and jokes you can get away with.

Here he is in that frame of mind in one of his letters:

Playing Fives the other day I knocked a fellows glasses clean off his head with a beautiful sweep of the right arm, because his head unfortunately happened to be in the same place as the ball at that moment. They flew across the floor and shattered into one hundred thousand pieces (which number of course I verified by counting); and so it was one or two days before he could view the world through glass again.

Then there's oodles of information about the biscuits and cakes he likes, and he's especially grateful to his mother for sending him nice ones. This sickly sweet recipe made me think of a very famous chocolate-factory owner:

Yesterday I made some Toffee; dashed good it is too. It cost about 1/10d. 2lbs of sugar. 1/2lb of butter. 2 tins of Nestles condensed milk & some treacle. I have poured it out into greased tin lids, and just cut some out when it is wanted. It is soft of course but dashed good.

Meanwhile, Roald – who was now sixteen years old – had a secret so fabulous that it was surprising he didn't pop with excitement. None of the other boys or masters knew that he had bought a motorbike. He hid it in a barn at a nearby farm and at weekends he would roar through the countryside on his splendid 500cc Ariel. Clad in goggles, helmet, old overcoat and boots, no one recognized him, not even when he rode through Repton, right under the noses of his teachers. I can imagine him leaving school, telling people he's just going for one of his walks . . . making sure no one is following him . . . going to the secret barn . . . climbing on to the bike . . . starting it up . . . hearing the roar of the engine . . . nudging out into the road . . . then speeding past the hedges and trees so that they just become a blur . . . in a world of his own . . . away from school . . . away from everything. It sounds just like one of the stories from his books.

An Ariel 500

It's no surprise that Roald was never made a prefect. A prefect was one of the boys who were in charge, which meant they ruled over the younger ones. The headmaster and housemaster must have seen that Roald wasn't the kind of boy who lived by the rules.

They never knew what he would do next and could see he wasn't someone who would enjoy bossing other boys around. There was even a chance that if they did give him the job of prefect he would do something strange or crazy!

Roald wasn't sad to leave school – quite the opposite, in fact. In *Boy*, he says, 'Without the slightest regret I said goodbye to Repton forever and rode back to Kent on my motorbike.' But, no matter how happy he was to leave Repton, there was one thing that the school gave him and that was the opportunity to develop his writing. Here's something rather wonderful that he wrote while he was there:

Dreams

Once I dreamed of an iceberg. It was a large iceberg which floated on a cold ocean, as if in sleep. A warm mist enveloped all but a thin white line, against which the ocean lapped unceasing. Then, as I lay wondering, the mist slid on, and I saw the iceberg, hard and cold like some great fragment of an icy coast, far away northward.

I awoke, stretched out an arm and pulled up my bed-clothes from the floor. Outside the hoar-frost lay thick on the field, and in the pens the sheep huddled closer for warmth.

Once I dreamed of the tap in our garden. The tap has an old washer, for even Beck, who has never, never used a lever to fit a tyre on the Morris, failed to stop the drip.

And now, as I dreamed, it was dripping as usual, but in the little hole which the water had made, there lay with its leg caught under a smooth brown pebble, a daddy-long-legs.

The drops welled, limpid, on the lip, and fell with a little splash upon the insect below.

I awoke, closed the windows under which I slept and wiped my face on the sheet. Poor daddy-long-legs.

When I dreamed again it was of the Bay of Biscay. All around me I saw the sea, angry as a wounded tiger, sweeping from the North. The waves, like mountains, heaved to and fro, they rose, frowning, paused for a moment then curling savagely, boiled over in a turmoil of green and white — the wounded tiger was showing its teeth.

And all above me hung the wet black clouds, heavy with rain, like airships of paper filled with oil.

I lay on my raft and cursed the Bay of Biscay. I expressed my feelings most aptly in the language I detest, crying with surely as much feeling as Aenias ever cried it: 'Me miserum quanti, mones volucuntur aquarium.' And I began to like Aenias . . .

It was the last morning of the term, and in the bedder they had thought of an excellent way of waking me. Four of them were trying to tip me on to the floor; it had not occurred to them that a quicker way of waking me would have been to shake my shoulder; but nothing occurs to anyone on the last morning.

Luckily I awoke just before my raft sunk, otherwise I should have discovered to my astonishment that the bottom of the Atlantic was made, not of Planktonic or Forameniferic Oooze but of Repton floorboards, less interesting and harder to fall on.

What do you think of this piece of writing? I really like it. I like the way it is not only *about* dreaming but also feels dreamy to read.

A short while before he left Repton for good, Roald had passed exams in English, history, maths, science, French and religious education. He knew that when he reached his twenty-fifth birthday he would start to receive a small but regular amount of money which his father had left in trust for him. But that was years away. Some young men in his position joined the army, navy or air force. Others became priests or ministers of the church or missionaries. But none of these jobs appealed to Roald.

His headmaster said that Roald had 'ambition and a real artistic sense . . . If he can master himself, he will be a leader'. By this he meant that he believed that Roald would do very well one day, particularly through writing, music and art, but only if he got himself organized!

I think Roald's headmaster was pretty much spot on, don't you?

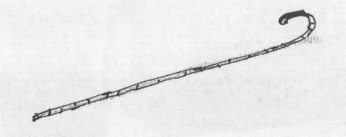

Flying training, Nairobi

The
Man

Roald Dahl, the businessman

Chapter 6

Travels

In July 1934 Roald Dahl's school days had come to an end. He was nearly eighteen years old with his whole future ahead of him. But what was he going to do with his life? He wasn't a writer, not yet. He didn't even seem to think that writing was something he could make into a career.

But there were plenty of things that he loved doing and was good at, such as taking photos, listening to music, bird-spotting, having fun, dreaming up tricks and jokes, travelling, riding his motorbike, inventing gadgets, having adventures, playing cricket and any other game where he could hit a ball with some kind of bat or stick, hanging out with his family – especially his half-brother Louis – and writing, of course. But none of them qualified him for a particular job. And he didn't want to do any more studying, or go to university. This explains why, in his last term at Repton, Roald had applied for – and got – a job with a company that had offices overseas. Because what he really wanted to do was travel the world.

First, Roald had to be trained. And for the next four years, until he was twenty-two, he worked for

Shell Mex House, London

the Shell oil company, sometimes at an oil refinery, but mostly in an office in London. He still lived at home in Bexley. In his spare time, he loved listening to music and reading novels – especially modern American crime novels. He continued taking photos and developed them in a darkroom he'd set up. This was long before digital cameras were invented and developing is a long, slow, painstaking process, with a touch of magic about it. The scene you think you've captured lies hidden and invisible, deep in the heart of the roll of film. Then, when you pour on the right mix of potions and leave them for exactly the right length of time, often in complete darkness or dull red light, the images of those scenes – people's faces, mountains, beaches, cricket teams or whatever – begin to appear on the paper.

Roald started writing short stories and even invented a character called Mr Dippy Dud. It was printed in Shell's company magazine:

Mr Dud is a keen musician, but do not be misled if he's not playing a mouth organ when you see him. He is an equally adept performer on the harmonica, also on the harmonium, euphonium, pandemonium, saxophone, vibraphone, Dictaphone, glockenspiel and catarrh . . . Don't be afraid to tackle anyone you think may be Mr Dud. People who are mistaken for him enter heartily in the fun of the thing, especially town councillors, archdeacons and retired colonels.

At first glance, this may look like a very serious piece of writing, but it's actually a spoof – a piece of writing that pretends to be something that it isn't. Can you see the beginnings of Roald Dahl's writing style? The list of real instruments mixed up with silly ones sounds to me very like the kind of thing that Roald would later write for children.

After four years of footling around in London, Roald's next big adventure began in 1938, when the oil company sent him overseas at last – to East Africa. He travelled there by boat, landing first in Mombasa in Kenya, then going on to the then tiny town of Dar es Salaam in Tanganyika (which is now called Tanzania). He was suddenly surrounded by the wildlife that he'd only read about before, including elephants, leopards, lions and giraffes and snakes. But life in Tanganyika was about to change – in fact, the whole world was about to change – because in September 1939 Britain declared war on Hitler's

Germany. The Second World War had begun.

Roald wrote to the Royal Air Force, saying that he wanted to become a pilot. They agreed to train him. And then he wrote to his mother, telling her how it would be 'very good fun', much better than being in the army, 'marching about in the heat from one place to another', and, what's more, they would teach him how to fly aeroplanes.

Roald Dahl loved gadgets, machines and speed. He loved FUN. He loved spending time on his own – whether that was on his motorbike, in the darkroom, listening to music or aboard a rickety boat on rough seas in Norway. He also seems to have liked the idea of danger. He had no idea just how scary and awful the war was going to be, nor what a terrible loss of life there would be, especially among these young pilots.

So Roald left Dar es Salaam and went to Nairobi in Kenya, where the RAF were going to teach him to fly . . . and immediately hit a big problem. Or rather, a tall problem. With a height of six feet and six inches – or two metres – Roald was too tall to fit into a fighter-plane.

The planes were Tiger Moths, and, compared to modern planes, these aircraft were tiny, weak, fragile things. If ever you look at one in a museum or on the Internet, you'll see that some of them didn't even have canopies – the pilots were exposed to the wind. In most planes there was a kind of windscreen, like on an open-topped car, which protected their faces a little. But Roald's head was higher than the windscreen. This meant that, once he had got up speed and was flying, he could hardly breathe. He got round it, though. He tied a thin cotton cloth over his nose and mouth to stop himself from choking.

Soon he was loving it. He wrote to his mother, 'I've never enjoyed myself so much . . .' Terrible things were happening far, far away in Poland and France, but Roald was like a tourist, flying over the beautiful savannah of Kenya and the Great Rift Valley, amazed by the breathtaking scenes of beauty. In his little plane, he could skim along just above the ground, watching herds of giraffes and wildebeest. He was seeing something that only a handful of people had ever seen. If you are a writer, you often want to feel that you're one of the few to have seen, heard or experienced something, so that when you write you can imagine you're bringing your readers the news. People who got to know Roald Dahl better than I did said the feeling that he was a person who had some news was something he liked very much. He liked having some kind of secret knowledge that he could share with you, or shock you with.

Then things started getting a bit more serious. Roald and his fellow trainee pilots – there were sixteen of them – travelled to Uganda, then on to Cairo and into Iraq. They were being prepared to fight in the hot, dry lands of North Africa, where the war was now being fought too. It was in Iraq that Roald finished his training.

In the mornings, he and the other pilots flew Hawker Harts and Audaxes – planes that were armed with bombs and machine guns. This was not just learning how to fly. This was training for war, learning how to kill. But in the afternoons they could relax, sometimes wandering about the ancient city of Baghdad. It was unbelievably hot, up to 50°C. Daily life was full of flies, sandstorms, scorpions and snakes.

After a few months, Roald Dahl was made a pilot officer, passing his tests with 'Special Distinction'. Out of forty pilots, he came third, and the other two men had already known how to fly before the war. A report said that he had exceptional flying ability. He could swoop and swerve and dive and climb and do the scariest manoeuvre of them all – the loop-the-loop. He was proud to wear his RAF flying badge.

It was now September 1940. Roald had just turned twenty-four years old and what took place next would affect him for the rest of his life. It happened when he was flying a Gloster Gladiator, a little plane that he was taking from the Suez Canal to a secret location in the North African desert. He landed near Alexandria in Egypt on a tiny runway where there were just a few tents and other aeroplanes. He needed more fuel, he was tired and it was getting late. He asked the commanding officer for some directions. The officer phoned ahead and then asked Roald for his map, pointing to a spot in the middle of the desert. Roald was concerned that when he arrived it would be too dark to see and that the runway would be hidden with camouflage.

'You can't miss it,' the officer told him.

But after a while Roald started to get worried. There he was, up in the sky, above the desert. It was getting dark. The wind was blowing the sand about. Below him were rocks, sand, little valleys and humps in the ground – mile after mile after mile, stretching away into the distance. He looked hard for a runway, some tents or other aeroplanes, but he couldn't see a thing. Nothing at all.

And now he was running out of fuel. He didn't even have enough to get him back to Alexandria. What could he do? What would you do?

Roald decided to take a chance. He thought he would be able to land the plane somewhere flat. So he flew towards the ground, slowed down and hoped for the best. But it was no good. The plane hit a rock, dived nose-first into the ground and smashed up. Inside, tangled among the wreckage, was Roald.

His head had crashed against the plane. The fuel then caught light and the aircraft burst into flames. Meanwhile, the guns and bullets on board were whizzing and zinging in all directions. Roald could easily have been hit by one of them.

This is how the authorities wrote about it in the official report:

Pilot Officer Dahl was ferrying an aircraft from No. 102 Maintenance Unit to this unit, but unfortunately not being used to flying aircraft over the desert he made a forced landing two miles west of Mersah Matruh. He made an unsuccessful forced landing and the aircraft burst into flames. The pilot was badly burned and he was conveyed to an Army Field Ambulance station.

Luckily Roald's plane was spotted coming down and two soldiers from a nearby base came out to find him. He was so badly smashed up and burned, and the plane was so badly damaged, that at first they didn't even know he was in the RAF. They took him back to the base, where the army doctors thought he was an Italian pilot – in other words, the enemy! When they realized Roald was in the RAF, they sent him on to the Anglo-Swiss hospital in Alexandria. There the doctors and nurses got to work straight away, treating his burns, his concussion and something that would hurt him for the rest of his life – his back.

At first the doctors thought he might have been permanently blinded in the crash. So did Roald. For several weeks, he couldn't see. He was dizzy and sick and faded in and out of consciousness. Later, when he was better, Roald wrote a short story called 'Beware of the Dog'. I wonder if he was describing what it felt like in those early days after his crash.

The whole world was white and there was nothing in it. It was so white that sometimes it looked black, and after a time it was either white or black, but mostly it was white. He watched it as it turned from white to black, then back to white again, and the white stayed a long time, but the black lasted only a few seconds. He got into the habit of going to sleep during the white periods, of waking up just in time to see the world when it was black. The black was very quick. Sometimes it was only a flash, a flash of black lightning. The white was slow, and in the slowness of it, he always dozed off.

If you look at the first three sentences again, you'll see that he mentions the word 'white' seven times! When we write, we can say something like 'for a lot of the time the world looked white' and leave it at that. Or we can find ways of saying that same thing by repeating a word. This way, the words don't just say what's happening, they start to sound and feel just like the way a person is thinking. The way you write imitates your thoughts. I think it's really interesting that one of the ways Roald became a writer was through trying to write about one of the most awful experiences he ever went through.

So, Roald lay in bed in a strange, dreamlike state, slowly on the mend. But in the middle of it all he heard some news from back home. His mother's house in Bexley had been bombed. His mother and sisters were all right. That was good. But he had lost his precious camera, photos and notebooks. And that wasn't so good. The war was starting to affect everyone and everything Roald knew and loved.

After two months, several operations and hundreds of hours' sleep, Roald started to feel better. His face was remodelled by a plastic surgeon who – as Roald told his mother – 'pulled my nose out of the back of my head and shaped it'. He said that the nose looked 'just as before except that it's a little bent about'. Like in the letters he sent from school, Roald again seemed to be trying to stop his mother from worrying too much about her only son.

After a few more months, he was feeling better still. And the RAF agreed that he was fit and well . . . so they sent him back to the war.

Roald Dahl's Hurricane

Roald Dahl's Jobs

The Businessman

'I enjoyed it, I really did. I began to realize how simple life could be if one had a regular routine to follow with fixed hours and a fixed salary and very little original thinking. The life of a writer is absolute hell compared with the life of a businessman.'

The Fighter Pilot

'I don't think any fighter pilot has ever managed to convey what it is like to be up there in a long-lasting dog-fight . . . It was truly the most breathless and the most exhilarating time I have ever had in my life. I caught glimpses of planes with black smoke pouring from their engines. I saw planes with pieces of metal flying off their fuselages . . . The sky was so full of aircraft that half my time was spent in actually avoiding collisions.'

The Spy

His proper title was Assistant Air Attaché, but REALLY Roald Dahl was a spy. This must have come in very handy indeed when he was writing the screenplay for the James Bond film – *You Only Live Twice*.

The Toilet-seat Warmer!

It's true. This was Roald's job when he was at school. The toilets were in an unheated outhouse and in winter he had to wipe the frost off the toilet seat and then warm up the seat for one of the Boazers (prefects).

The Writer

Do you think this was Roald's favourite job of all? I do.

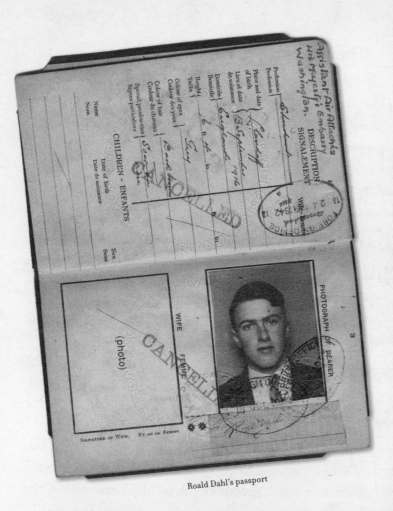

Roald Dahl's passport

Chapter 7

War Hero and Spy

It was March 1941. Roald was twenty-five and an RAF pilot once more, who soared through the sky in a Mark I Hurricane, a modern, fast-flying machine, doing his bit to win the war against Germany and her allies.

The Battle of Britain, a battle fought in the skies in 1940 between the Germans and the British, helped to glamorize all RAF pilots, no matter where they flew. This is partly because the pilots did what very few people in the 1940s had experienced: flying fast and high. Another reason – and it's a sad and awful reason – is that so many of these very young men were shot down in their planes and killed. So, just being alive meant that there was something almost magical about them. If they had survived the many dangers of flying in wartime, surely they could survive anything?

When I was a boy, we imitated these pilots with our toy planes, looping the loop and making ack-ack-ack noises as we shot down the imaginary enemy. In the movies we watched, the men were always handsome, calm and brave. And women always fell in love with them. At school, if one of our teachers had been in the RAF during the war, we knew that he'd been to places and seen things that were more incredible than we could imagine. We also knew that he must be full of stories, just like those in our adventure books and comics, where the pilot sat in his cockpit, his helmet on, enemy planes in the sky behind him, shouting out to his tail gunner, 'Let him have it, Binky!' And then the air would be full of zigzag lines and noises like 'BLAM! BLAM! BLAM!' and the next picture would show a plume of smoke in the sky.

Whether he liked it or not, Roald became one of these hero-like characters. Although he didn't fly in the Battle of Britain itself, he and his fellow pilots – all members of 80 Squadron – fought a series of brave air battles, mostly above Greece. At the time, he wrote about what was happening in letters to his mother and to his friends.

Of all the shocking things that happened, death affected him the most – the deaths of his young friends and the deaths of the young men he had to kill. His way of coping was by trying to be indifferent, or not caring. Whether he managed this or not, I don't know. Perhaps he was very good at pretending that he didn't care. But later in life, as he wrote more and more, at least some of that indifference – real or otherwise – vanished. He had to care about his characters – Matilda, Danny, Sophie and the rest – so that when we read about them in his books we care about them too. On the other hand, he wrote *Dirty Beasts* and *Revolting Rhymes* and one of the reasons why those poems are so funny is that people die or do horrible things to each other in ways that don't really seem to matter. Those poems seem to me to almost laugh at death. Perhaps this is what Roald Dahl learned to do in the midst of all that sadness and loss when he was a pilot during the war. What do you think?

Roald's crash had left him with terrible headaches and, after a year of active service, these headaches grew so bad that he had to be sent home. He had been away from his mother and his sisters for three years. After everything he and they had been through, their reunion must have been a very emotional experience. Many years later, when he was reading aloud the last chapter of his second autobiography, *Going Solo*, to an audience at the National Theatre in London, his daughter Ophelia saw him crying. It seems as if that sadness still remained many years later.

What was left of Roald's old house had been taken over by the British Army. (As the country was at war, the army could do that at any time.) His new home was now a strange, much smaller, older house in a little village called Ludgershall in Buckinghamshire and it was here that he planned to spend time recovering from the war . . . except, he couldn't do that. Just because the RAF had sent Roald back to England didn't mean that they were finished with him. Not yet. There were plenty of jobs on the ground for him, like helping the RAF to find and train more pilots. But this wasn't really what Roald wanted to do.

What happened next was like something out of a James Bond movie. A member of parliament took Roald out for a meal in a tiny, very posh gentlemen's club. It was a strange and secretive meeting in which Roald was offered a job at the British Embassy in Washington, USA. He would be called an Assistant Air Attaché. This hush-hush job offer must have been very exciting for someone like Roald, who loved tricks, plots and plans. But what would he actually be doing?

In March 1942 the USA had only just joined in the war. Most people in Britain had desperately wanted such a big, rich and powerful nation to become involved because they would be able to supply millions of soldiers, planes, boats and tanks. But the Americans were still very divided about the war. Some had always thought that they should join in, while others thought that they definitely shouldn't.

The British government, headed by Winston Churchill, decided that they needed some of their own people in the USA, people whose role would be to keep America on Britain's side in the war. And it was Roald's job to encourage very powerful people in the American government to support Britain, reminding them what the RAF was doing and making sure that stories showing what a terrible time the British people were having got into the American newspapers.

It would also be Roald's job to report back to Churchill and his ministers on the mood of the country – whether the Americans were more or less keen to support Britain, whether there was any gossip from people in high places that Britain needed to know about.

Roald's new job looked like a lot of fun – dinner parties, tennis matches, barbecues, late-night chats with newspaper reporters and long conversations about going up in planes and being brave. But, underneath the glitz and the socializing, it was really all about collecting and sending out information. This job has a name: intelligence. And the fantastically exciting word for it is 'spying'. Roald Dahl had become a spy. He would work for the British government by spying on the USA, a country that was, to a large extent, friends with Britain.

So off he went. He travelled by train to Glasgow in Scotland, where he boarded a ship and headed off across the Atlantic Ocean to Canada. Then he went by train from Montreal to Washington, DC, to stay in the Willard Hotel until he found an apartment.

And that's how Roald added something else to the amazing list that people tend to put after his name – you know the sort of thing: 'Roald Dahl, world-famous bestselling writer, war hero and spy . . .'

Roald was about to begin the next chapter in his life, in a place where things were very different from what he was used to. And, talking of chapters, it really does seem that Roald Dahl was someone whose life was a series of wildly different chapters. It was as if he finished one adventure and then started on another straight away, in a new place and with new people. I don't know if that's something he created for himself or if life just kept happening to him that way. What do you think?

Roald Dahl, trainee pilot, Iraq, 1940

Roald Dahl in his writing hut

The
Writer

Roald Dahl in the RAF

Chapter 8

Gremlins

I once watched a documentary that claimed polar bears survive because they are endlessly curious. It showed a polar bear coming up to a camera and sniffing it and poking it. I think writers are a bit like polar bears. They are forever sniffing out things, listening and remembering, so that they can turn them into stories, which they sell and that helps them make a living, which means that they survive too!

On the way to his top-secret job in North America, Roald met someone called Douglas Bisgood, a wounded pilot like him. Douglas had fought in the Battle of Britain and before that he had been a racing-car driver. As the two men headed across the Atlantic, they joked and gossiped together.

During the war, RAF pilots became famous for inventing their own slang — special words and ways of saying things. For example, a plane was a 'crate' and a crash was a 'prang'. Put that together and they might say, 'Did you hear about Lofty? He pranged his crate . . .' These pilots, who were living life on the edge, never knowing which flight might be their last, also seemed to have invented their own folklore. They made up stories about little mischievous imp-like creatures who lived in and around the planes, often making the aircraft go horribly wrong but sometimes protecting the pilots. They called them 'gremlins'.

For someone on the verge of becoming a writer, this sort of thing is treasure! Roald's mother had once filled his young head with stories of the trolls and giants of Norwegian folklore. Now, on the deck of the SS *Batori*, Roald and Douglas swapped folklore and made up new stories about gremlins. Sounds like good fun to me.

In Washington, Roald found himself far away from the dangerous world of the fighter pilot and far away from hungry, bombed-out, war-torn London. There were massive amounts of food and drink, and lots of parties. He had oodles of time to listen to his beloved music. All he had to do was give speeches about the great work that the RAF was doing and keep his ear to the ground. Roald had to play the part of a handsome, brave, British chap who had done his best to win the war. It wasn't difficult, because he was and he had.

Meanwhile, inside his head, the gremlins were stirring. And Roald couldn't keep them to himself. He wrote to a magazine about his idea:

'The gremlins comprise a very real and considerable part of the conversation of every RAF pilot in the world. Every

pilot knows what a gremlin is and every one of them talks about gremlins every day of their lives.' Gremlins, he said, were *'little types with horns and a long tail, who walk about on the wings of your aircraft boring holes in the fuselage and urinating in your fuse-box'.*

This is the Roald Dahl I recognize – the Roald Dahl who writes about amazing, funny, odd creatures, making it seem as if they're part of everyday life and – guess what – doing something rude!

Next, he got down to writing an actual story. He called the gremlins' wives 'Fifinellas' and their children 'Widgets' or 'Flipperty-Gibbets'. They lived in a 'beautiful green wood far up in the North. They could walk up and down trees in their special suction boots'. Then horrible humans came and chopped down their trees so that they could build factories and roads and airports. So the gremlins took revenge! They attached themselves to planes and caused accidents. They moved mountains so that the planes would fly straight into them. And they made tiny holes in the side of a plane flown by a pilot called Gus. But Gus was wily and inventive. He fed the gremlins postage stamps and played tricks on them. And, in the end, they become friends.

Roald had created a story – a good story. But

what was he to do with it? How could he turn it into a book?

First, believe it or not, he had to show the story to his bosses for their approval because he was still working for the RAF and everything he did, said and wrote belonged to them. Then he sent it to a magazine where it was published for the first time.

Most writers will tell you that they had a lucky break. Perhaps someone sitting at a desk or next to them on a train or at a party was just the right person at just the right time to help. And perhaps this someone not only was able to see something good in the writing but was also in a job where they could help the story to get out there. For Roald, this someone was a friend who knew the famous film-maker Walt Disney. Walt Disney read Roald's gremlin story and cabled back a message saying that he was interested in turning it into a movie.

WOW. How cool is that!

I don't know what Roald did when he heard this. I like to think that he jumped up and down, ran round the block, rang his mother and sisters in England and threw a party. But if he did, he kept it quiet. He was pleased. But he didn't let himself get carried away.

Roald was invited to Hollywood. He took leave from his job and, before he knew it, he was in the most glamorous place on earth, meeting top movie stars, like the great silent-movie actor Charlie Chaplin.

They thought Roald was funny and cute and quite extraordinary, with a really cool accent. They'd read his story. And they loved it. It wasn't long before Disney 'shot a test reel' – that's a try-out bit of film.

But, although *The Gremlins* had become his very first book and it was going to be a Walt Disney movie, Roald wasn't happy. He didn't particularly like the Disney drawings or the toy gremlins you could buy in the shops. And he found out that Walt Disney himself was worrying whether the time had passed for this kind of film about pilots in the war. Eventually, Disney gave up on the project and told Roald that he wasn't going to finish the movie. That was it. The End.

Except it wasn't The End.

Roald Dahl was nearly twenty-seven years old and now ready to become a great writer. All he needed was a place to write, time to write and enough reasons to go on writing.

It was really The Beginning . . .

Things you might **not** know

1. His favourite sound was the piano.

2. His favourite TV programme was the News.

3. His most frightening moment was in his Hurricane plane, 1941, RAF.

4. If he had not been a writer, he would have been a doctor.

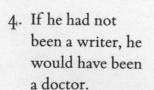

5. He owned a hundred budgerigars.

6. His favourite smell was frying bacon.

7. He loathed Christmas.

8. He loved Easter.

9. In the churchyard at Great Missenden, GIANT footprints lead to his grave.

10. He liked to play Scrabble, but wasn't very good at it because of his ~~apalling~~ ~~appaling~~ terrible spelling!

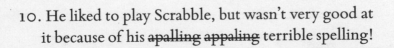

Patricia Neal

Roald

Liccy

Olivia   Tessa   Theo   Ophelia   Lucy

Neisha   Charlotte   Lorina

Roald Dahl's family tree

Chapter 9

Family

In 1946, a few months after the war had ended, Roald returned home to England and, for the next four years, lived with his mother in her house in Buckinghamshire. He began to write short stories for adults and sent them to his agent in America, where they were published. Roald went back to live in New York in 1951 and a year later met a famous actress called Patricia Neal. They fell in love, and in 1953 got married and returned to England to live in Gispy House near to Roald's mother in Great Missenden. But they didn't live there all the time. Instead, the couple travelled to and fro between Britain and the USA so that Pat could act in films, TV programmes and plays. At the same time, they brought up their children, who came along in the following order: Olivia (1955), Tessa (1957), Theo (1960), Ophelia (1964) and Lucy (1965). The childcare was shared between Pat, Roald and a nanny. Sometimes, Pat worked in the USA while Roald stayed in England, at home with the children. Sometimes, they all went to the USA together. Life was very glamorous and exciting.

Meanwhile, Roald was still writing stories for adults. They were full of strange and mysterious goings-on, and characters with nasty or odd ways of thinking and behaving. He loved that kind of fiction, and so did the many Roald Dahl fans who gobbled it up. So, if he was doing well with this type of story, why did he begin writing for children instead? I think that spending so much time around his own children as they grew up might be one of the reasons why Roald became a children's writer.

In his notebook Roald began to jot down ideas and plots for children's stories. On one occasion he stood looking at the fruit in his garden. Why, he wondered, did the apples and pears in his garden stop growing? Why didn't they just go on and on and on growing? And what if, instead of apples or pears, it was a peach? This was how *James and the Giant Peach* started out and in 1961 it became the first of his books for children to be published.

It would be wonderful to imagine

that Roald Dahl's life went on in a magical storybook way, but three tragic events then took place that would have a huge effect on him.

When Theo was four months old, his pram was hit by a taxi in New York City. He suffered terrible head injuries and had to be nursed carefully for years. But, despite many complications, he survived. Roald became very involved with his son's treatment. He worked with a brilliant toymaker and a surgeon to invent a tiny device that would drain the fluid that sometimes builds up after such accidents out of a patient's brain. This became known as the Dahl–Wade–Till valve. Although it was never used on Theo, the valve was used to treat nearly three thousand children all over the world. Somehow, and without any proper training in science or technology, Roald Dahl had become a great inventor.

Roald continued to look after the children when Pat was away filming, as well as working on his next story for children, *Charlie and the Chocolate Factory*. But then in 1962 a second tragedy occurred. Olivia died from complications from measles – she was just seven years old. This was exactly the same age that Roald's sister Astri had been when she died. Perhaps that helped him, perhaps not. It's certainly something he thought about, as he mentions the coincidence of ages in *Boy*.

I can see some of this in close focus. I had a son who

died and the same thing had happened to my father too. He had a son who died before I was born. I've a funny feeling that both Roald and I coped with all the sadness and rage and disbelief in a similar fashion. Roald tried very hard to understand how and why Olivia died. He tried to be scientific about it, writing down in a calm, factual manner the exact sequence of events that led to her death. Afterwards, he was determined to make sure that other children received the measles vaccine.

Eventually, though, the tragedies were too much for Roald and for a long time he was very, very depressed. One way he and Pat found some hope was by helping other children through charity work.

Then the third tragedy hit: Pat became very seriously ill. She suffered a huge stroke. A stroke can mean different things to different people, depending on how severe it is. Some might find that they stop being able to use parts of their body. They might find that they can't speak or walk properly. Pat's stroke looked like it might be one of the worst.

But Roald wasn't going to be beaten. He decided to get Pat better, introducing what looked to some like a military regime – a round of exercises and activity that could never for one day, one hour, one moment stop. Roald was in charge. He gave the orders and it was Pat's job to obey them. This, Roald said, was the only way she could get better.

It sounds like a strange fairy tale, but amazingly and incredibly she did get better. Patricia Neal even went back to acting. It's such a fascinating story that a film was made about it!

Meanwhile, there were four children who needed to be looked after. Friends of the children tell stories about how amazing Roald seemed to them. Here was this incredibly tall, gangly man who was full of hobbies and stories. He was always tinkering about with bits of old furniture, listening to music, talking about art or famous people he knew. And he did unbelievably naughty things. In a restaurant, he might ask what the 'special' was. Then, when the waiter told him, he would say in a loud voice so that the whole restaurant could hear, 'Don't ever get the "special", it's probably last night's leftovers. They only tell you it's the "special" so that they can get rid of it!'

And there was always the chocolate. From his schooldays at Repton, which wasn't far from the Cadbury's factory at Bournville, Roald loved chocolate. So he had a box at the main table in the house that was always packed full of chocolate bars. After every meal, the box was circulated around the table and he would even give a few Smarties to his beloved dog Chopper.

And, talking of chocolate, *Charlie and the Chocolate Factory* was to become his most famous book of all. In America there were plans to turn it into a film. Suddenly everyone was talking about Roald Dahl – but unfortunately not in a good way. Back then, in the 1960s, American Civil Rights activists were trying to make sure black people and white people were treated equally. Many thought that the Oompa-Loompas made black people sound silly, undignified and inferior. Some organizations said that no way should a film version of this book be made. Roald agreed to turn the Oompa-Loompas into white characters, and the film – under the slightly different title of *Willy Wonka and the Chocolate Factory* – went into production.

I don't think Roald Dahl invented the Oompa-Loompas to cause offence. He was not the type of person who would do things like that. But I do think

that perhaps he hadn't realized how certain words, pictures, images and ways of saying things suggest to children that some people are superior and some inferior.

None of this was to stop Roald Dahl from writing and telling stories. Sometimes, he would wake the children – and any of their friends who were staying for a sleepover – and take them for midnight walks down the lane to the arch under the railway, tell them a scary story or two and then march them back to bed.

Then, instead of going to work, like most of the other dads nearby seemed to do, he either pottered about in the house or walked up the garden to his special hut, to write.

By the end of the 1970s Roald had published five more books for children, which were *The Magic Finger, Fantastic Mr Fox, Charlie and the Great Glass Elevator, Danny the Champion of the World* and *The Enormous Crocodile*. At this point in time, Roald and Pat's life together was drifting apart and in 1983 they were divorced. Later that year Roald married

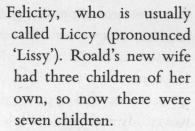

Felicity, who is usually called Liccy (pronounced 'Lissy'). Roald's new wife had three children of her own, so now there were seven children.

In 1977 Roald became a grandfather too. His daughter Tessa had a baby girl: Sophie. She heard the early versions of *The BFG* and the Sophie in the book is named after her. One of the ways Roald got his granddaughter interested in the idea of a big friendly giant who collects dreams was first to tell her the story and then, at night, to climb up a ladder and appear at her bedroom window, just like the BFG!

Can you imagine lying in bed upstairs, when suddenly you see your granddad looking through the window . . . ?

People who visited the Dahl house at this time spoke of how full of people it always seemed to be. It was rowdy and rude, with lots of jokes and noise and music. It rather looks as if Roald had made another Dahl gang, a bit like the family he grew up in.

By the 1980s Roald was world-famous. Millions of people were reading his books, watching his TV programmes and seeing films that he had been involved with. Many people knew that he was often in pain because of his injuries from the plane crash. And some people knew that inside must be hidden away the many things that made him sad.

I once saw him at a big book festival organized by his publisher Puffin Books. It was wonderful to watch hundreds, probably thousands of children trying to get into a hall to hear him read from his latest book. I sneaked in and realized that everyone was listening. And I remember thinking that there was something both sad and funny about his eyebrows. If you lift up your eyebrows, you can do it in a way that makes people laugh, because you look so surprised. And you can also do it in a way that looks sad, as if life has taken you by surprise in a not-very-nice way . . . I remember thinking that Roald Dahl's face and his eyebrows were like this.

Each time a new book came out there was a WHOOP across the world. Children loved them. A few days later, they would be telling each other about the incredible things they'd read – about Bruce Bogtrotter and the enormous chocolate cake from *Matilda* or maybe the amazing whizzpopping scene in front of . . . no . . . surely not . . . the Queen? Not any old imaginary queen, but the real Queen. No way! Yes! Really? Yes!!

Ask any writer what it's like when people are reading and enjoying and talking about your book and they will probably reply that it's one of the best feelings in the world. I certainly think so. And I'm sure Roald Dahl felt the same.

Roald Dahl in his writing hut

Chapter 10

How He Wrote Books

How did Roald Dahl go about writing such fabulously original and funny – and really quite rude – books, one after another?

First, he always did things in the same way. For most of his life, Roald liked writing with a yellow pencil called a Dixon Ticonderoga 1388-2 5/10, medium. (Try saying that quickly!) He wrote on American yellow legal pads, which were sent to him from New York City. It may come as no surprise to learn that yellow was his favourite colour.

Next, he had a special place where he wrote. He and a builder friend built a little brick hut in his garden in Great Missenden. Inside he put things that he liked and he arranged his chair – which had a hole cut in just the right place so that it didn't press on his injured back – to be in the perfect spot, with a special board across the arms of the chair for him to rest his paper on.

When he was writing a book, Roald would walk through the garden to his hut, close the door and no one was allowed to disturb him. Well, that's how it was supposed to be, but you know better than me what children are like! Yes, they would occasionally pop in and out but I imagine the only creatures most likely to see Roald Dahl at work were the cows in the next-door field. If they had peeped through the window, they would have seen Roald scribbling away with his pencil on his yellow paper. Usually, he did his writing only in the morning and in the late afternoon, which would leave him free to do all the other business and fun things during the rest of the day.

Inside his hut, Roald went into a kind of trance. He concentrated so hard that he could whisk himself away to all sorts of different places in his mind – visiting scenes and people and things, both real and

imaginary. It was here that he came up with plots and plans and schemes – the wicked tricks that happen so often in his stories. He had a notebook to capture his ideas and whenever he thought of something, he scribbled it down. Then, later, if he was wondering what to write next, he could comb through his notebook, looking for ideas.

Most writers I know have notebooks. I do. I sometimes think that I have a notebook because I'm afraid that I'll forget things. That's not such a crazy idea, because writing was invented as a way of remembering things. And maybe that's what Roald was doing – trying to hang on to his thoughts and memories. He was always on the lookout for stuff that would surprise his readers, even if it was shocking or disgusting. Sometimes, he was just capturing a bit of language. I imagine that he thought something like this: *I like that . . . I like the way it sounds . . . I like the image it conjures up in my mind . . . I mustn't forget that . . . I'll put that in my ideas book because it might come in handy when I'm trying to describe someone in a story.* I can't tell you if Roald really thought that, but I can tell you that I do.

Like a lot of writers, when Roald was in the middle of writing a book he could be quite twitchy and irritable. Why? To me, it's because the book feels like unfinished business. I am nervous about whether it will work out or not. I worry if I get stuck or if

I think that this book is not turning out as well as the last book. Half of me wants to show the book to other people, the other half thinks that if I show it to someone else, they'll blow away the magic that's making the book happen in the first place or they'll suggest something that will send the story off in totally the wrong direction.

After he'd finished a book and sent it off to the publisher, instead of dancing with relief, Roald would be worried. Sometimes he wondered if he would ever write anything again, and the thought of this made him grumpy. But, as we know, he did go on and on writing, and with the books came stupendous success.

I'm guessing that you've read a few of them (see the whole list on page 160) and I'm also guessing that you have favourite scenes, favourite people and also characters you most like to hate and despise. I hope so, because I think that's part of the fun in reading. But was Roald Dahl trying to say something to us with all with these books?

In *Matilda*, Roald seems to be saying over and over again, 'Don't forget to read books!' But there's a LOT more going on. He paints a picture of a school that is so horrible and a teacher who is so lovely that it's almost as if he's dreaming of the perfect school – one where every teacher is as nice and as kind to children as Miss Honey. And what about Matilda's parents? Is he saying that children deserve better parents than these and that if they don't have them, and if they read and read and read, they can get themselves a better life?

And then there's *Danny the Champion of the World*. I like this book a lot. It's a story about people who don't have very much and people who have too much. There's a father and son who get on really well and together they play an amazing trick that . . . well, I couldn't possibly say. If you've read the book, you'll **KNOW**. If you haven't, go and find a copy at once. You won't be disappointed, I promise. But despite this fabulous, amazing plot that I'm *not* going to tell you about, Roald wrote something else that he would repeat over and over again. Danny's dad was 'sparky' and Roald said that parents should always try to be sparky. What do you think he meant?

When *The Twits* and *George's Marvellous Medicine* and *The Witches* came out, some people started to wonder just how beastly Roald Dahl could get. Were all his books going to be full of incurably horrible characters? And was destroying them the only way to stop them being so despicable? Some people said that too many of these nasty people were women.

Once again, Roald found himself arguing with his critics. He told them that in his books he had horrible women and nice women. And hadn't all stories for children always been like this? In particular, some critics picked out the passage at the beginning of *The Witches* where he says that any woman you meet could turn out to be a witch. Was he trying to make children suspicious of women?

Look at Grandmamma in *The Witches*, he and his defenders said. Look at Sophie in *The BFG*. They were both clever, tender female characters. And he would go on to write about Matilda and Miss Honey in *Matilda* too.

Now, I'll let you into a secret. Did you know that writers don't always get a story right the first time round? It's true. They might try out a storyline and if they or the people who help make the books (the agents, editors and publishers) don't think that the storyline works, they try another one. It's a bit like going to a clothes shop, trying on an outfit, looking in the mirror, deciding if you like what you're wearing, listening to what other people think and then trying on something else. It rarely comes out right the first time. A book is really the end of a long and winding road. Roald wrote several drafts and it often took him over a year to finish a whole story.

Here are some of the storylines that Roald tried out and then scrapped. Which do you prefer — the early storyline or the version that made it into a book?

James and the Giant Peach

The original cast list starred a Hairy-Green Caterpillar and an Earwig. But there was no Old-Green-Grasshopper, no Miss Spider and no Glow-worm either.

The Enormous Crocodile

The crocodile is whirled up into the sky by Trunky the elephant, but instead of hitting the sun he falls safely to earth.

The Twits

Mr and Mrs Twit are stuck upside-down forever.

George's Marvellous Medicine

At the end of the book, Grandma is still incredibly tall.

The Witches

Bruno the mouse became a spy for the British government.

Matilda

Instead of being good, Matilda was the wickedest child in the world. Meanwhile, her parents were really nice and long-suffering. Miss Honey didn't even exist. And there was no Miss Trunchbull either. Instead, there was a teacher called Miss Hayes, who loved betting on horses. Matilda used her special powers to make sure that the horse she wanted to win was first past the post. And that was what kept her from going to prison! In the end this really dreadful Matilda died in a car crash. Oh dear.

Looking at some of Roald's early drafts reminds me that he tried very, very, very hard indeed to make you laugh, make you surprised, make you amazed. Perhaps you think that writing is pretty easy – all you have to do is sit on your backside scribbling a few words down. Well, I'm not going to say it's the hardest thing in the world to do. But I will say that Roald Dahl was a writer who tried hard, day after day after day, to make the stories work. If you really like his books – perhaps love them – then that's because of this hard work. You can't see the hard work, because reading is about fun and enjoyment and interest. And that is part of the magic of writing.

What is it about the way Roald Dahl wrote that makes his books such fun? I think there are LOTS of things he does to entertain his  readers. You might think of totally different things. But that's what is so splendid about books – there are no right answers. Everyone is allowed to have their own ideas about what is and what isn't GREAT.

First, let's peek inside the pages of *Matilda*. Here, the terrible Miss Trunchbull is confronting poor Bruce Bogtrotter:

His plump flabby face had turned grey with fearful apprehension. His stockings hung about his ankles.

'This clot,' boomed the Headmistress, pointing the riding-crop at him like a rapier, 'this black-head, this foul carbuncle, this poisonous pustule that you see before you is none other than a disgusting criminal, a denizen of the underworld, a member of the Mafia!'

'Who, me?' Bruce Bogtrotter said, looking genuinely puzzled.

'A thief!' the Trunchbull screamed. 'A crook! A pirate! A brigand! A rustler!'

'Steady on,' the boy said, 'I mean, dash it all, Headmistress.'

'Do you deny it, you miserable little gumboil? Do you plead not guilty?'

'I don't know what you're talking about,' the boy said, more puzzled than ever.

I love all the different names Miss Trunchbull calls Bruce Bogtrotter. But in real life, people don't usually talk like this. Try it. Pretend you're really angry about something or somebody and make a list of insults. It's actually quite hard. But it's very entertaining. This kind of writing is called exaggeration or hyperbole, which is pronounced 'high-per-bolly' – a word that

I'm sure Roald would have loved.

Flip back a few pages to the very beginning of *Matilda*.

> *It's a funny thing about mothers and fathers. Even when their own child is the most disgusting little blister you could ever imagine, they still think that he or she is wonderful. Some parents go further. They become so blinded by adoration they manage to convince themselves their child has qualities of genius.*
>
> *Well, there is nothing very wrong with all this. It's the way of the world. It is only when the parents begin telling us about the brilliance of their revolting offspring, that we start shouting, 'Bring us a basin! We're going to be sick!'*

A fun thing to do with writing like this is to think about who's speaking. Is it Roald Dahl? Maybe . . . except Matilda is fiction and Roald was absolutely real. In most storybooks, the person telling the story is usually someone pretending to be the author – as if it's a diary or a memoire – or a kind of invisible storyteller who isn't a character, just someone who can magically tell us what's happening.

One of the really intriguing things about Roald

Dahl's books is that he liked to say Roald-Dahl-ish things and do the invisible-storytelling thing, sometimes in the same book, sometimes on the same page. What's more, the Roald-Dahl-ish things are often rude, funny, amazing or totally outrageous.

In this extract, it sounds as if Roald is in the same room, just chatting. It's actually quite hard to write like that, because you have to forget all the stuff you've been told about making sentences long and interesting, with loads of describing words and plenty of connectives – like 'but' and 'and' and 'because' – to join them all together. Instead, you have to make the sentences short and snappy, with very few connectives, because that's how most of us speak when we're just chatting to each other. Look at the very first sentence: 'It's a funny thing about mothers and fathers.' There's no introduction to that sentence. It's almost as if Roald is thinking aloud, or there's been a conversation about mothers and fathers and this is halfway through it. Again, it sounds as if he's just chatting to the reader.

Now for another Roald Dahl trick . . . it's one very small word: we. Roald was brilliant at getting readers on his side. By using the word 'we', it's as if he gets the reader to become his friend, or join his gang while he is telling the story. He doesn't really know that 'we' all think that parents who boast about their children make 'us' sick! He just gets us thinking that we do by saying that we do! When writers do this – especially if it's funny – it can feel kind of cosy. Roald Dahl and others also do it with the word 'you'. I could write, 'Hey, you know how when you're ill and you're lying in bed . . .' and, in one stroke, I've sounded as if I know you, you know me and we're all in the same situation – being ill. If you ever watch stand-up comedians, they do exactly the same thing.

Did you realize that Roald Dahl had squeezed so much into the very beginning of *Matilda*? Put all of these fantastic writing techniques and tricks together and they add up to one thing: a great way to grab someone's attention. It certainly worked for me!

Next, let's dive into *James and the Giant Peach* to one of my very favourite parts, at the end of Chapter Five and beginning of Chapter Six:

> *He picked up the chopper and was just about to start chopping away again when he heard a shout behind him that made him stop and turn.*
>
> *'Sponge! Sponge! Come here at once and look at this!'*
> *'At what?'*
> *'It's a peach!' Aunt Spiker was shouting.*
> *'A what?'*
> *'A peach! Right up there on the highest branch! Can't you see it?'*

'I think you must be mistaken, my dear Spiker. That miserable tree never has any peaches on it.'

'There's one on it now, Sponge! You look for yourself!'

'You're teasing me, Spiker. You're making my mouth water on purpose when there's nothing to put into it. Why, that tree's never even had a blossom on it, let alone a peach. Right up on the highest branch, you say? I can't see a thing. Very funny . . . Ha, ha . . . Good gracious me! Well, I'll be blowed! There really is a peach up there!'

'A nice big one, too!' Aunt Spiker said.

'A beauty, a beauty!' Aunt Sponge cried out.

At this point, James slowly put down his chopper and turned and looked across at the two women who were standing underneath the peach tree.

Something is about to happen, he told himself. Something peculiar is about to happen any moment.

Here, Roald is building suspense. Writing can be a bit like unfolding something, like a game of pass-the-parcel. Slowly, the writer reveals what's happening. But that's only half of what's going on . . . Writers are very cunning people who are not only unfolding and revealing. Just like conjurors and magicians, they are hiding stuff too. Imagine Roald Dahl sitting in his hut. He knows what's coming next. He knows that he's going to tell you about a peach. He knows that he's going to tell you about a GIANT peach. But as he's writing, he's got to keep that wonderful, top-secret information hidden for as long as he can, while making you desperate to know more.

One way of doing this is to reveal details v-e-r-y slowly, bit by bit. Here, Roald does this through the eyes of someone who doesn't believe in the amazing thing that's happening right before her eyes. Aunt Sponge says, '*I think you must be mistaken.*' We are pretty sure that it's *her* who is mistaken, because we have inside knowledge from earlier in the book. We – the readers or listeners or viewers – know more about what's going on than one or all of the characters. And this sometimes makes us so edgy and involved that we want to SHOUT at the character who doesn't know what's going on, just like the audience does at a pantomime.

Then James tells himself, '*Something is about to happen.*' This takes us into the mind of one of the characters, giving us insider knowledge. And, because we know what James is thinking, it's almost as if he knows that we know! It's also a way of building suspense. By taking time to say that 'something is about to happen', it delays for another moment the very thing that is about to happen! It might make us say to ourselves, 'Go on, go on, happen!' It keeps us hooked.

In the first chapter of *James and the Giant Peach*, this happens:

> *. . . one day, James's mother and father went to London to do some shopping, and there a terrible thing happened. Both of them suddenly got eaten up (in full daylight, mind you, and on a crowded street) by an enormous angry rhinoceros which had escaped from the London Zoo.*
>
> *Now this, as you can well imagine, was a rather nasty experience for two such gentle parents.*

Is this sad or funny? I think it's funny. But how can Roald Dahl make it sound as if a child losing his parents is funny? He does this in lots of clever ways: he makes the terrible event happen in a flash; he makes it happen in a totally crazy and impossible way (rhinoceroses don't escape from zoos, and even if they did, they would eat grass, not meat); and then he finishes by saying that it was 'a rather nasty experience', when we know that it would really be a sad and tragic thing.

As the story goes on, Roald introduces Aunt Sponge and Aunt Spiker, James's new guardians:

> *They were selfish and lazy and cruel and right from the beginning they started beating poor James for almost no*

reason at all. They never called him by his real name, but always referred to him as 'you disgusting little beast' or 'you filthy nuisance' or 'you miserable creature', and they certainly never gave him any toys to play with or any picture books to look at. His room was as bare as a prison cell.

Again, Roald makes an awful thing sound funny. James hasn't done anything wrong and he doesn't deserve any punishment, yet here he is being mistreated. At once, I feel sorry for him and hope that this is going to be a story with a happy ending.

But Roald does something else too: he makes sure we are very firmly on James's side. I think this is one of the most important things about his writing. Over and over again, his readers are on the side of the child against horrible adults. For some adults, this makes his books shocking – even rather nasty. For millions of children, it's made them funny, exciting, naughty and even a bit dangerous.

There's one fairy tale that particularly reminds me of *James and the Giant Peach* and that is *Cinderella*. Just like poor Cinderella, James is stuck with two horrible, ugly sisters. When writers write stories, they can't escape from the stories that have been written before, especially the really famous ones like fairy tales. It's almost as if they're haunted by the old stories, so that when they write the ghost of an old story turns up. This can make us feel that we're at home in the story, rather as if we're in a room and recognize the furniture. But it can also mean that the differences between the old story and the new one give us extra surprises and extra fun. I think Roald Dahl knew that very well.

Roald Dahl specialized in the fantastic and the amazing. Nearly all of his books feature odd, bizarre and weird stuff. He even used the word 'fantastic' in the title of one of his books. (And – ahem – so did I.) These fantastic and amazing storylines often involved incredible schemes and plans. One of my absolute favourites appears in *Danny the Champion of the World*:

. . . My father came in and lit the oil-lamp hanging from the ceiling. It was getting dark earlier now. 'All right,' he said. 'What sort of story shall we have tonight?'

'Dad,' I said. 'Wait a minute.'

'What is it?'

'Can I ask you something? I've just had a bit of an idea.'

'Go on,' he said.

'You know that bottle of sleeping pills Doc Spencer gave you when you came back from hospital?'

'I never used them. Don't like the things.'

'Yes, but is there any reason why those wouldn't work on a pheasant?'

My father shook his head sadly from side to side.

'Wait,' I said.

'It's no use, Danny. No pheasant in the world is going to swallow those lousy red capsules. Surely you know that.'

'You're forgetting the raisins, Dad.'

'The raisins? What's that got to do with it?'

'Now listen,' I said. 'Please listen. We take a raisin. We soak it till it swells. Then we make a tiny slit in one side of it with a razor-blade. Then we hollow it out a little. Then we open up one of your red capsules and pour all the powder into the raisin. Then we get a needle and thread and very carefully we sew up the slit . . .'

Out of the corner of my eye, I saw my father's mouth slowly beginning to open.

Here, Roald is building suspense again. At first, the adult doesn't believe what the child is saying. Then, bit by bit, more details are slowly revealed, while at the same time others are kept hidden – the conjuror's trick again. This time, something is being revealed that will make life better for the characters Roald has made us care about. It's a FANTASTIC plan. It's crazy, wild, weird and maybe even IMPOSSIBLE . . .

But hang on a minute. Maybe it is possible? Wouldn't it be brilliant if it were possible?

If a writer can make a reader really want something to be possible, then I think they've done a brilliant job. And Roald Dahl was an absolute master at doing it. On page after page after page. In book after book after book.

I think that's pretty much all I have to say about him. Or very, very nearly all . . .

Postscript

The last time I saw Roald Dahl was at an event in 1988, when he won the Children's Book Award from the Federation of Children's Book Groups for *Matilda*. I was asked to pop over and say hello to him. He was sitting down next to his wife, Liccy, while various people were asking for his autograph and telling him how much they loved his books. I remember that he looked at me and said – almost as if he was talking to all the children's book writers in the world – 'Well, it's over to you now. You're the ones who've got to do the writing now. I've done my bit . . .'

At the time, I thought that this was an odd thing to say. Surely he wasn't going to stop writing now, just when the whole world seemed to be waiting for whatever he wanted to write next? Well, it wasn't quite the end. Roald did write more. But he was very ill and two years later, in 1990, he died. He was seventy-four.

But, of course, that isn't the end. Anyone and everyone can read Roald Dahl's books, or listen to him and others reading them, or stare goggle-eyed at the many film versions, or watch a real live musical at the theatre!

There's even a Roald Dahl Museum and Story

Centre in Great Missenden, Buckinghamshire. It's a marvellous day out, you can find out all sorts of things to do with Roald Dahl's life, and you can even explore his hut with all its original contents. You can go on a 'trail' and see places round the village that he used in his stories, like an old petrol pump which appears in . . . do you know which story? Belonging to someone's father?

Those who want to find out even more about Roald Dahl can arrange to visit the Museum's archive. It's a special store of his handwritten works – stories, poems, letters, scripts, notebooks and scribbled-down notes. The contents are so precious that they have to be kept in a very large, very dry fridge. I've included some things from the archive in this book – the letters he wrote home to his mother and sisters, and the early storylines for his books.

As I've been writing this book, I've been trying to find out what sort of person Roald Dahl was and asking myself what were the ingredients that made him into such a wonderful writer – the Fantastic Mr Dahl.

I hope I've come up with some answers for you.

Acknowledgements

The author and publisher would like to thank Dahl and Dahl Ltd and the Roald Dahl Museum and Story Centre in Great Missenden, Buckinghamshire, for their kind help and assistance, and the following for permission to use the copyright material below:

Additional illustrations from *More About Boy*, copyright © Quentin Blake and Rowan Clifford, 2008; extracts from *Boy*, text and illustrations copyright © Roald Dahl Nominee Ltd, 1984; *The BFG*, text copyright © Roald Dahl Nominee Ltd, 1982; *Danny the Champion of the World*, text copyright © Roald Dahl Nominee Ltd, 1975; 'First Fig', published in *First Figs from Thistles*, published by Harper & Bros., copyright © The Edna St Vincent Millay Society, 1922; *Going Solo*, text copyright © Roald Dahl Nominee Ltd, 1986; *James and the Giant Peach*, text copyright © Roald Dahl Nominee Ltd, 1961; *Matilda*, text copyright © Roald Dahl Nominee Ltd, 1988; *Roald Dahl's Cookbook* by Felicity and Roald Dahl, text copyright © Roald Dahl Nominee Ltd, 1991.

References: *Storyteller: The Life of Roald Dahl* by Donald Sturrock, first published by HarperCollins Publishers, 2010. *D is for Dahl*, first published by Puffin Books, 2004. *More About Boy: Roald Dahl's Tales from Childhood*, first published by Puffin Books, 2008.

Bibliography

Books by Roald Dahl in chronological order

The Gremlins, first published in the USA by Walt Disney/Random House, 1943

James and the Giant Peach, first published in the USA by Alfred A. Knopf, Inc., 1961; published in Great Britain by George Allen and Unwin, 1967

Charlie and the Chocolate Factory, first published in the USA by Alfred A. Knopf, Inc., 1964; published in Great Britain by George Allen and Unwin, 1967

The Magic Finger, first published in the USA by Harper & Row, 1966; published in Great Britain by George Allen and Unwin, 1968

Fantastic Mr Fox, first published by George Allen and Unwin, 1970

Charlie and the Great Glass Elevator, first published in the USA by Alfred A. Knopf, Inc., 1972; published in Great Britain by George Allen and Unwin, 1973

Danny the Champion of the World, first published by Jonathan Cape, 1975

The Wonderful Story of Henry Sugar and Six More, first published by Jonathan Cape, 1977

The Enormous Crocodile, first published by Jonathan Cape, 1978

The Twits, first published by Jonathan Cape, 1980

George's Marvellous Medicine, first published by Jonathan Cape, 1981

The BFG, first published in Great Britain by Jonathan Cape and in the USA by Farrar, Straus and Giroux, 1982

Revolting Rhymes, first published by Jonathan Cape, 1982

The Witches, first published in Great Britain by Jonathan Cape and in the USA by Farrar, Straus and Giroux, 1983

Dirty Beasts, first published in the USA by Farrar, Straus and Giroux, 1983; published in Great Britain by Jonathan Cape, 1984

Boy: Tales of Childhood, first published in Great Britain by Jonathan Cape and in the USA by Farrar, Straus and Giroux, 1984

The Giraffe and the Pelly and Me, first published in Great Britain by Jonathan Cape and in the USA by Farrar, Straus and Giroux, 1985

Going Solo, first published in Great Britain by Jonathan Cape and in the USA by Farrar, Straus and Giroux, 1986

The Complete Adventures of Charlie and Mr Willy Wonka (a bind-up of *Charlie and the Chocolate Factory* and *Charlie and the Great Glass Elevator*), first published by Unwin Hyman, 1987

Matilda, first published by Jonathan Cape, 1988

Rhyme Stew, first published by Jonathan Cape, 1989

Esio Trot, first published in Great Britain by Jonathan Cape and in the USA by Viking Penguin, 1990

These books were completed before his death in 1990, but published posthumously:

The Minpins, first published by Jonathan Cape, 1991

The Vicar Of Nibbleswicke, first published by Random Century Ltd, 1991

My Year, first published by Jonathan Cape, 1993

These books have been carefully collected together from Roald's papers and previously published material:

The Great Automatic Grammatizator and Other Stories, first published by Viking, 1996

The Roald Dahl Treasury, first published by Jonathan Cape, 1997

Skin and Other Stories, first published by Puffin Books 2000

D is for Dahl, first published by Puffin Books, 2004

Songs and Verse, first published by Jonathan Cape, 2005

More about Boy – this special edition was published with new material by Puffin Books, 2008

Spotty Powder and Other Splendiferous Secrets, first published by Puffin Books, 2008

And some of Roald Dahl's novels have been cleverly adapted into plays:

Charlie and the Chocolate Factory: A Play (adapted by Richard George), first published in the USA by Alfred A. Knopf, Inc., 1976; published in Great Britain by Puffin Books, 1979

James and the Giant Peach: A Play (adapted by Richard George), first published by Puffin Books, 1982

Fantastic Mr Fox: A Play (adapted by Sally Reid), first published by Unwin Hyman and Puffin Books, 1987

The BFG: Plays for Children (adapted by David Wood), first published by Puffin Books, 1993

The Witches: Plays for Children (adapted by David Wood), first published by Puffin Books, 2001

The Twits: Plays for Children (adapted by David Wood), first published by Puffin Books, 2003

Danny the Champion of the World: Plays for Children (adapted by David Wood), first published by Puffin Books, 2009

ROALD DAHL DATES

1916 Roald Dahl was born on 13 September in Llandaff in Wales.

1925 Roald was sent to boarding school – St Peter's School in Weston-super-Mare.

1929 Roald went to Repton, another boarding school It was here that he helped to test new chocolate bars for Cadbury's. Favourites included Aero, Crunchie, KitKat, Mars and Smarties.

1934 Roald Dahl left school and went to work for Shell, the big oil company, because he wanted to travel to magical faraway places like Africa and China.

1936 Shell sent him to east Africa. He hated the snakes!

1939 Roald Dahl joined the RAF at the start of the Second World War. He became a fighter pilot, flying Hurricane aeroplanes across the Mediterranean Sea.

1940 His plane crashed in the Western Desert, in north Africa, and he received severe injuries to his head, nose and back.

1942 Roald was sent to the USA to work in the British Embassy (and some say he was also a spy!). His first adult story was published and he wrote his first story for children, about mischievous creatures called Gremlins. Walt Disney started work on turning it into a film and Roald went to Hollywood.

1943 Movie plans ground to a halt, but *The Gremlins* was published in the USA, Britain and Australia. It was Roald's first book.

1953 Roald's book of spine-tingling stories for adults, *Someone Like You*, was published and was a huge success in the USA.

1961 *James and the Giant Peach* was published in the USA, followed by *Charlie and the Chocolate Factory* in 1964. It was an instant hit with children.

1967 *James* and *Charlie* were finally published in Britain and have become two of the most successful and popular children's books ever.

1971 The first *Charlie* film was made as *Willy Wonka and the Chocolate Factory*. Other films followed: *The BFG* and *Danny the Champion of the World* in 1989; *The Witches* in 1990; *James and the Giant Peach* and *Matilda* in 1996; the second *Charlie and the Chocolate Factory*, starring Johnny Depp, came out in 2005.

1978 Roald Dahl's partnership with Quentin Blake began with the publication of *The Enormous Crocodile*.

1990 Roald Dahl died on 23 November, aged seventy-four.

2006 and beyond Roald Dahl Day is celebrated all over the world on 13 September to mark Roald Dahl's birthday. Visit **roalddahlday.info** to join the fun.

ROALD DAHL SAYS

'I think probably kindness is my number one attribute in a human being. I'll put it before any of the things like courage or bravery or generosity or anything else. If you're kind, that's it.'

'I am totally convinced that most grown-ups have completely forgotten what it is like to be a child between the ages of five and ten . . . I can remember exactly what it was like. I am certain I can.'

'When I first thought about writing the book *Charlie and the Chocolate Factory*, I never originally meant to have children in it at all!'

'If I had my way, I would remove January from the calendar altogether and have an extra July instead.'

'You can write about anything for children as long as you've got humour.'

This volume of specially commissioned essays explores the world of Anton Chekhov – one of the most influential and widely performed dramatists in the repertoire and the creation, performance and interpretation of his work. The Companion begins with an examination of Chekhov's life and his Russia and the original productions of his plays at the Moscow Art Theatre. Later film versions and adaptations of Chekhov's works are analysed, with valuable insights also offered in acting Chekhov by Ian McKellen, and directing Chekhov by Trevor Nunn and Leonid Heifetz. The volume also provides essays on 'special topics' such as Chekhov as narrative writer, Chekhov and women, and the Chekhov comedies and stories. Key plays, such as *The Seagull* and *The Cherry Orchard* receive dedicated chapters while lesser known works and genres are also brought to light. The volume concludes with appendices of primary sources, lists of works, illustrations, and a selected bibliography.

CAMBRIDGE COMPANIONS TO LITERATURE

CAMBRIDGE COMPANIONS TO CULTURE

The Cambridge Companion to Modern German Culture
edited by Eva Kolinsky and Wilfried van der Will

The Cambridge Companion to Modern Russian Culture
edited by Nicholas Rzhevsky

The Cambridge Companion to Modern Spanish Culture
edited by David T. Gies

THE CAMBRIDGE
COMPANION TO
CHEKHOV

THE CAMBRIDGE
COMPANION TO
CHEKHOV

EDITED BY

VERA GOTTLIEB

Research Professor in Drama, Goldsmiths College

AND

PAUL ALLAIN

Senior Lecturer in Drama, University of Kent

CAMBRIDGE
UNIVERSITY PRESS

CAMBRIDGE UNIVERSITY PRESS
Cambridge, NewYork, Melbourne, Madrid, Cape Town, Singapore, São Paulo, Delhi

Cambridge University Press
The Edinburgh Building, Cambridge CB2 8RU, UK

Published in the United States of America by Cambridge University Press, New York

www.cambridge.org
Information on this title: www.cambridge.org/9780521589178

First published 1960
Fifth printing 2008

Printed in the United Kingdom at the University Press, Cambridge

A catalogue record for this publication is available from the British Library

Library of Congress cataloging in publication data
The Cambridge companion to Chekhov / edited by Vera Gottlieb and Paul Allain.
p.   cm. – (Cambridge companions to literature)
Includes bibliographical references and index.
ISBN 0 521 58117 6 (hardback) – ISBN 0 521 58917 7 (paperback)
1. Chekhov, Anton Pavlovich, 1860–1904 – Criticism and interpretation.
I. Gottlieb, Vera, 1946– .   II. Allain, Paul.   III. Series.
PG3458.Z8 C36   2000
891.72'3 – dc21   00–055578   CIP

ISBN 978-0-521-58117-2 hardback
ISBN 978-0-521-58917-8 paperback

This book is dedicated to

Stephen Slatter
Paul Slatter
and Johnny

Chekhov's way is the way of Russian freedom, the embodiment of that Russian democracy, true and humane, which never materialised.

Vasily Grossman, *Life and Fate*, 1988

CONTENTS

CONTENTS

ILLUSTRATIONS

to work in the outdated, stereotypical cameo style which is associated with Chekhov and which would have drowned the design in nostalgia . . . The design for *The Seagull* comes from two sources: first, French Impressionism – though more realistic, like the Russian painter Levitan, a friend of Chekhov; and on the other hand, the colored light compositions made of grains of primary colors as in the first color photographs.' – Yannis Kokkos.   265

Illustrations courtesy of Arnold Aronson, Laurence Senelick, Yannis Kokkos, the West Yorkshire Playhouse and the Czech Theatre Institute Catalogue: *In Search of Light*, 1995.

ACKNOWLEDGEMENTS

The editors would like to express particular appreciation to the following: Sergei Volnyets for work done on the translation of the Russian chapters; to Tatiana Shakh-Azizova, friend and colleague, for her work as 'unofficial' Moscow coordinator and advisor; Dr Valentina Ryapolova, whose help included concrete advice on the nuances of translation; to Alexander Akhtyrsky for his help in many different yet essential ways; Professor Edward Braun for acting as a crucial advisor, critic and significantly, translator; to Arnold Aronson and Laurence Senelick for their help over and above their contributions as writers, in obtaining some of the illustrations; to Morag Derby of the Royal National Theatre; the British Film Institute (BFI); the West Yorkshire Playhouse; the Theatre Museum, London; to Hilary Wilson, Administrator of the Drama Department, Goldsmiths College; Elizabeth Goldsmith; and most of all to Joanna Labon, and to Irene Slatter of the Russian Department, University of Durham for support and help.

The Commissioning Editor, Dr Victoria Cooper of Cambridge University Press, deserves special gratitude for her characteristic flexibility, and unfailing sense of humour combined with invaluable critical judgement, *and* for making a potentially complex editorial job not only as painless as possible, but positively enjoyable. We are also indebted to Audrey Cotterell for her copy-editing advice, for her patience and for her help with this book, and to Michelle Williams, of the Production Department of Cambridge University Press, for her tolerance, patience, and positive assistance.

The British Council gave financial and practical support in funding a British–'Soviet' Theatre Conference, held at Goldsmiths College in May 1992, at which some of the contributors first made a commitment to this volume, in particular Anatoly Smeliansky and Tatiana Shakh-Azizova.

Professor Vera Gottlieb is glad to acknowledge the invaluable assistance of the British Academy for the award of a Research Fellowship, which enabled her to work in Moscow on the preparation of this volume.

Vera Gottlieb would also like to express deep appreciation to George Hamilton, Adrian Tookman, David Lipkin, Andrew Platt, and their respective teams at the Royal Free Hospital, London, including Phyl Morris-Vincent, Kate Jones, Leslie Mattin, Mila Constant and the Community team of BP4. Without them, and many others, it may not have been possible to personally fulfil this commitment, but Professor Ted Braun, as friend and colleague, my friend and sister Irene Slatter (a Russian specialist), and Dr Victoria Cooper, with Dr Paul Allain, would have ensured its completion.

NOTES ON CONTRIBUTORS

PAUL ALLAIN is Senior Lecturer in Drama at the University of Kent, Canterbury. He collaborated with the Gardzienice Theatre Association extensively from 1989 to 1993, touring in Britain, Japan and the Ukraine, and is author of *Gardzienice: Polish Theatre in Transition*, 1997. He has worked as Movement Director at the Royal Shakespeare Company and the Royal National Theatre in London. He is writing a monograph on Tadashi Suzuki for Methuen.

ARNOLD ARONSON is Chair of the Theatre Division at Columbia University in New York. He is author of *The History and Theory of Environmental Scenography and American Set Design*, 1981, and served as editor of *Theatre Design and Technology* magazine from 1978 to 1988. He has written extensively on scenography as well as avant-garde theatre and his articles have been published in a wide variety of journals, reference books, and anthologies. He is currently preparing *American Avant-Garde Theatre* for publication by Routledge.

EDWARD BRAUN is Emeritus Professor of Drama and a Senior Research Fellow at the University of Bristol. His compilation of Meyerhold's writings, *Meyerhold on Theatre*, was published in 1969, and his critical study, *The Theatre of Meyerhold*, in 1979. This was followed in 1982 by his analysis of modern theatre practice, *The Director and the Stage*. Since then he has published widely on Russian theatre, including in 1995 a reappraisal of Meyerhold's work entitled *Meyerhold: A Revolution in Theatre*. He has also published a number of articles on television drama, and his current research is concerned with representations of history in drama.

ALEXANDER P. CHUDAKOV, DS (Philology) is Senior Research Associate at the Institute of World Literature and Professor at the Gorky Institute of Literature, Moscow, and author of several works including *The World of Words and Things: from Pushkin to Tolstoy*, 1982; *Chekhov's World: Emergence and Affirmance*, 1986, and *Chekhov's Poetics*, Moscow, 1987.

PHILIP FRENCH was for thirty years a BBC radio producer and has been drama critic of *The New Statesman*, principal book critic of *The Financial Times* and a regular contributor to numerous journals, most notably *The Observer*, where he has written a weekly film column since 1978. His books include *The Movie Moguls*, 1971; *Westerns*, 1977; *Three Honest Men: Edmund Wilson, Lionel Trilling, F.R. Leavis*, 1980; *Malle on Malle*, 1993 and *The Faber Book of Movie Verse*, 1994.

VERA GOTTLIEB is Research Professor in the Drama Department, Goldsmiths College, University of London. Publications include *Chekhov and the Vaudeville*, 1982; *Chekhov in Performance in Russia and Soviet Russia*, 1984; 'Thatcher's Theatre – or After *Equus*', 1989. She has worked as scripts advisor and consultant for the RSC, for Channel 4 and in New York. For Magna Carta Productions, she co-directed and wrote with Robert Gordon *Red Earth*, Hampstead, London, 1984; *Waterloo Road*, Young Vic Studio, London, 1986; she adapted/translated *A Chekhov Quartet*, New End Theatre, London and Chekhov Festival, Yalta and Moscow, 1990, subsequently published 1996. She co-edited *Theatre in a Cool Climate*, 1999.

LEONID Y. HEIFETZ, People's Artist of Russia, is a theatre director and teacher. He is a Professor at the Russian Academy of Theatre Arts, and Chair of the Department of Directing at the Shchukin Drama School. He was Resident Director at the Central Soviet Army Theatre (CSTA), now the Russian Army Theatre (RAT), from 1963 to 1970 (returning there as Chief Director, 1986–94). He was also Resident Director at the Maly Theatre, Moscow (1970–86) and at the MAT from 1986 to 1988. His best-known productions include *The Death of Ivan the Terrible* by Alexei K. Tolstoy, 1966; *Before Sunrise* by Gerhart Hauptmann, 1972; *Fiesco's Plot* by Schiller, 1977, and Shakespeare's *King Lear*, 1979, all at the Maly Theatre. He is also renowned for his production of Dmitry Merezhovsky's *Pavel I*, 1989, as well as Chekhov's *Uncle Vanya*, *The Cherry Orchard* and *Three Sisters*, directed both in Russia and abroad.

THOMAS KILROY is a playwright and novelist. His version of *The Seagull* was produced at the Royal Court in 1981 in a notable production by Max Stafford-Clark. He has been awarded the Guardian Fiction Prize and Heinemann Award. His most recent play, *The Secret Fall of Constance Wilde*, was presented at the Abbey Theatre as part of the 1997 Dublin Theatre Festival, and is opening at the Barbican Centre, London, in September 2000. He is a Fellow of the Royal Society of Literature.

CYNTHIA MARSH is Senior Lecturer in Russian in the Department of Slavonic Studies, University of Nottingham. She has published several books on Russian literature and theatre, including *M.A. Voloshin: Artist-Poet*, 1983, and *File on*

Gorky, 1993, and many articles. She is currently writing a study of Gorky's plays, and working on a project to investigate the impact of Russian theatre on the British repertoire. She has directed most of Chekhov's plays, in both English and Russian.

IAN MCKELLEN is one of Britain's leading film, television and stage actors, and highly experienced in playing Chekhov. His notable film parts include the title role in *Richard III*, which he co-wrote and co-produced, and most recently James Whale in *Gods and Monsters*. He has worked extensively at the Royal Shakespeare Company and the Royal National Theatre as well as with leading regional theatres. He toured with Prospect Theatre for several years and then co-founded the Actors' Company in 1972. He is a member of the Board of the Royal National Theatre, was knighted in 1991 and has received numerous awards for his acting.

TREVOR NUNN became the youngest Artistic Director of the Royal Shakespeare Company in 1968, directing a host of major productions including *Nicholas Nickleby* (winner of five Tony Awards) and the musical, *Les Misérables*, before leaving the RSC in 1986. Subsequent productions have included *Cats*, *Starlight Express*, *Porgy and Bess* and *Arcadia*. He has worked extensively in television and film. He succeeded Sir Richard Eyre as Artistic Director of the Royal National Theatre.

PATRICE PAVIS is Professor of Theatre Studies at the University of Paris, Saint-Denis, Arts Composante, Théâtre. He is editor and commentator on Chekhov's plays for the edition *Le Livre de Poche*. Amongst many other articles and books, he is author of *Performance Analysis*, and of the *Dictionary of the Theatre*, 1998. He has written introductions to *La Mouette*, *Oncle Vania*, *Les Trois Soeurs*, as well as translated *La Cérisaie* with Elena Zahradnikova, for *Le Livre de Poche*. In addition he has written a contemporary version of *The Seagull* (*M(o)uettes*), 1999.

EMMA A. POLOTSKAYA, DS (Philology) works at the Gorky Institute of World Literature, Moscow. Since 1955 she has written and published a number of books and essays on Chekhov. She is an authority on Chekhov's bibliography and textual analysis. Amongst other titles, she is author of *Chekhov: The Evolution of Aesthetic Thought*, 1979, and *Chekhov's Characters*, 1983. She was a member of the prestigious editorial board for the academic edition of *Chekhov's Collected Works and Letters in 30 Volumes*, 1974–83. She has taught at the Literary Institute in Moscow since 1957.

DONALD RAYFIELD was educated at Dulwich College and at Cambridge. He is Professor of Russian and Georgian at Queen Mary and Westfield College, University of London. He has written a number of monographs on Chekhov, including *Chekhov: The Evolution of His Art*, 1975, as well as a biography of the explorer Przhevalsky and a history of Georgian literature. He is currently editing for publication the diaries of Alexey Suvorin, Chekhov's publisher.

LAURENCE SENELICK is Fletcher Professor of Drama and Oratory at Tufts University and Honorary Curator of Russian Drama and Theatre at the Harvard Theatre Collection. His many books include *The Chekhov Theatre: A Century of the Plays in Performance*, 1997; *Anton Chekhov*, 1985; *Mikhail Shchepkin: His Life and Art*, 1984, and *Gordon Craig's Moscow 'Hamlet'*, 1982. Among works edited are *Russian Dramatic Theory from Pushkin to the Symbolists*, 1981; *Russian Satiric Comedy*, 1983, and *National Theatre in Europe 1746–1900*, 1991.

TATIANA K. SHAKH-AZIZOVA works at the State Institute of Arts Studies, Moscow, and is the author of *Chekhov and West European Drama of his Time*, 1966, and of numerous essays on the treatment of Chekhov's theatre on stage and screen. She has worked on several series of television and radio programmes on Chekhov's plays. Other work includes chapters in *The History of the Russian Theatre in 7 volumes*, Moscow, 1977–87, and essays on twentieth-century theatre and the inter-relationships of theatres. She is also a regular theatre critic whose numerous articles include several on the International Chekhov Theatre Festivals in Moscow between 1992 and 1998.

ANATOLY SMELIANSKY, Doctor of Arts, is Associate Artistic Director of the Moscow Art Theatre, 1980–, Associate Head of the Moscow Art Theatre School, 1987–, and Visiting Professor of the Carnegie Mellon University/ Moscow Art Theatre School MFA in Acting Program, 1994–. He has written many articles on Stanislavsky, Bulgakov and Chekhov. His books include *Is Comrade Bulgakov Dead ?*, 1993, and *The Russian Theatre after Stalin*, 1999, as well as a book on Stanislavsky to be published by Cambridge University Press.

CHRONOLOGY

1860   (29 January) Anton Pavlovich Chekhov born in Taganrog, a port in the Crimea (an inlet of the Sea of Azov, itself an inlet of the Black Sea), 600 miles south of Moscow.[1]
Grandfather, a former serf, liberated with the emancipation of 1861. Anton was the third son of shop-owner Pavel Yegorovich Chekhov and Yevgeniya Yakovlevna Chekhova.

1868   Attends Taganrog Grammar School (for Boys) after briefly attending the Greek school.

1873   Creates comic sketches for performance at home. Shows early interest in theatre. Sees local productions of *Hamlet* and Russian classics, Gogol's *The Government Inspector* and Griboyedov's *Woe from Wit* (also translated as *Wit Works Woe*).

1875   Begins his own humorous magazine *Stammerer (Zaika)* for circulation within the family, of comic sketches of Taganrog life.

1876   Father declared bankrupt. Family leaves for Moscow and Chekhov left alone in Taganrog to complete schooling. Works as tutor.

1877   First visit to Moscow, where his family is in hardship. He has to return to Taganrog to finish schooling.

1878   Writes full-length untitled play subsequently known as *Fatherlessness*, then *Platonov*, which was neither performed nor published in his lifetime. Writes two vaudevilles which were also unpublished.

1879   Begins regular submission of short stories to the humorous magazine *Dragonfly*. Moves to Moscow permanently and assumes father's place as head of family. Enrols at School of Medicine, Moscow University, in August.

1880   First sketch published in *Dragonfly*: 'Letter from the Don Landowner Stepan Vladimirovitch N. to His Learned Neighbour Dr Frederik'. More pieces accepted under various pseudonyms, such as 'Antosha Chekhonte' or 'My Brother's Brother'. Meets landscape painter Isaac Levitan, who becomes a close friend.

1881   Sarah Bernhardt performs in Moscow. Chekhov considers her acting 'artificial'.

1882   Increasingly dependent on writing to support family, while continuing with medical studies.

1883   Writes many pieces for popular magazine *Splinters (Oskolki)*.

1884   Publication of first book of selected pieces, *Tales of Melpomene*. Has now published more than 200 pieces. Graduates in medicine. Shows first symptoms of tuberculosis.

1885–86   More than 100 new short stories, many for *St Petersburg Gazette (Peterburgskaya gazeta)*. First story published under his own name, and first in *New Time (Novoye vremya)*. An influential letter from established novelist Grigorovich encourages him to take writing more seriously. First collection of selected tales is published, *Motley Tales* (1886). In the same year he meets A.S. Suvorin, owner of *New Time*, which is the beginning of a long friendship with Suvorin as his publisher. It is a friendship not without serious differences over politics, such as over the Dreyfus Case.

1887   Second book of selected stories published, *In the Twilight*. First publication of vaudeville, *Swan Song*. Initial version of *Ivanov* written at request of owner of the privately owned Korsh Theatre, Moscow. *Ivanov* premièred there, 19 November, to mixed reception.

1888   Story 'The Steppe' published in the serious journal *Northern Herald (Severny vestnik)*. Plays *Swan Song* premièred at Korsh Theatre, 19 February, and *The Bear*, written in February, staged in October. Begins work on *The Wood-Demon* (considered by most critics to have developed into *Uncle Vanya*). Writes one-act farce *The Proposal*. Receives Pushkin Prize for 'In the Twilight'. First meeting with Stanislavsky.

1889   Favourable reception of revised *Ivanov*, at the Imperial Alexandrinsky Theatre, St Petersburg, 31 January. Writes and publishes stories including 'The Princess', 'A Dreary Story', and the one-act plays *The Wedding* and *A Tragic Role*. Works on *The Wood-Demon*: first draft rejected by the Alexandrinsky Theatre; revised version performed at another private theatre, the Abramov Theatre, Moscow, on 27 December and unanimously condemned. Taken off after first performance. Brother Nikolai dies of tuberculosis.

1890   'Gusev' published. Leaves Moscow on 21 April and travels across Siberia by train, horse-drawn vehicle and river-boat, to investigate conditions on penal island of Sakhalin: compiles census there. Returns to Moscow in early December via Hong Kong, Singapore and Ceylon.

1891   'The Duel' and 'Peasant Women' published in *New Time*. Writes 'The Grasshopper' and completes the one-act play *The Anniversary (Jubilee)*. Six-week tour of Western Europe with A.S. Suvorin. Helps with medical relief of famine victims in Central and South-East Russia.

1892–3   Twenty-one stories published, including 'Ward No. 6' (1892). Buys small estate, Melikhovo, fifty miles south of Moscow, and the family moves there in March 1892. Opens clinic and practises medicine for local peasants while continuing to write.

1893–4   Non-fictional work *The Island of Sakhalin* is completed and appears serially in *Russian Thought (Russkaya mysl)*, leading to some penal reform.

1894   Writes 'The Black Monk'. Publishes another collection of selected stories, *Stories and Tales*. Travels again to Western Europe.

1895   'Three Years' published, and appears in book form. Writes 'Ariadne', 'The Murder', 'Anna Round the Neck'. Begins writing *The Seagull* in the autumn. First meeting with Lev Nikolayevich Tolstoy.

1896   Revises *The Seagull* for première at the Imperial Alexandrinsky Theatre, St. Petersburg, 17 October. Extremely hostile reception devastates him.

1897   'Peasants' published. Publishes *Uncle Vanya* but refuses to allow performance until 1899. Undertakes work for national census. In March he has haemorrhage of the lungs and is diagnosed with tuberculosis. Visits Europe in August, for convalescence, and spends winter in southern France.

1898   'Ionytch', 'A Man in a Case', 'Concerning Love' and 'Gooseberries' published. Supports Zola over Dreyfus Case during the trial, resulting in near break with Suvorin. Nemirovich-Danchenko persuades a reluctant Chekhov to let him produce *The Seagull* at the new People's Art Theatre (later Moscow Art Theatre). Leaves France for Russia in early May. Attends Moscow Art Theatre rehearsals of *The Seagull*, September. Meets the actress Olga Knipper (later to be his wife), but leaves almost immediately for the Crimea before winter. Successful first performance of *The Seagull* by Moscow Art Theatre (MAT), 17 December, establishes Chekhov as a playwright. The fiasco of the first production (1896) had resulted in Chekhov's unwillingness to risk another public performance. Stanislavsky did not want to take the play but was persuaded by co-founder of MAT Nemirovich-Danchenko. In spite of some interpretative misunderstandings (which characterised all MAT productions of his plays) the production was a success. Meets Gorky in Yalta, where he buys land to build a house. Father, Pavel Yegorovich Chekhov, dies.

1899   'Lady with a Little Dog' and two short sketches, 'The New Villa' and 'On Official Business', are published. Begins writing *Three Sisters*. Completes contract with A. F. Marx, publisher, for *Complete Edition of Works*. Première of *Uncle Vanya* at MAT, 26 October, is moderate success. Chekhov confined to Yalta for health reasons and unable to attend. Olga Knipper visits Melikhovo, which he sells in June. Moves to Yalta with his mother and sister Masha.

1900 Completes 'In the Ravine'. First two volumes of the Marx Edition of *Chekhov's Works* appear. MAT Company visits Sevastopol and Yalta and he sees *Uncle Vanya* for first time. Reads first draft of *Three Sisters* to MAT in November. Begins courting Olga Knipper.

1901 Première of *Three Sisters*, MAT, 31 January, with Olga Knipper as Masha, has moderate success. Ten of the eleven volumes of Marx Edition published by the end of 1901. Chekhov marries Olga Knipper, 25 May, in quiet ceremony in Moscow.

1902 Completes 'The Bishop' and begins work on *The Cherry Orchard*. His strength noticeably declines in the winter.

1903 Completes 'The Bride' and works on final volume of Marx Edition. Finishes first draft of *The Cherry Orchard*, 26 September, but undertakes second and third drafts, both only completed by 12 October. Arrives Moscow in early December, for MAT rehearsals of *The Cherry Orchard*. Disagrees over the casting and interpretation, with Stanislavsky advocating its serious nature above its comic elements.

1904 Première of *The Cherry Orchard*, MAT, 17 January, proves a success. Chekhov attends during third act. Leaves for Badenweiler 'to take the waters' in the Black Forest with Olga Knipper, where he dies of tuberculosis on 15 July. After a drink, his last words to Knipper are: 'It's a long time since I drank champagne'. Confusion of funeral procession as his coffin is transported in a railway wagon labelled 'Fresh Oysters'. Buried beside his father in Moscow.

NOTE

1 Even in Chekhov's lifetime, Taganrog was beginning to be superseded as a trade centre by Rostov-on-Don, given the development of the railways in the 1870s (see chapter 10 in this volume). The growing port of Odessa, directly on the Black Sea, also superseded Taganrog's position as a trade centre.

EDITORIAL NOTES

Transliteration

The editors took the decision *not* to standardise the various systems of transliteration used by contributors from Russia, from the United States, France, the Irish Republic and the UK. In the case of this volume, where there are different scholarly approaches, varied angles, emphases and priorities, one contributor may need one of the four systems of transliteration (American Library of Congress, Systems, I, II, III, IV) while another may require either a different system – or none at all, as in the case of chapters 9 and 11, for instance. We have therefore left each contributor free to choose the transliteration system that suits him or her best, rather than enforce consistency of any one system.

Translation and titles

In many instances, Russian-speaking contributors have translated their own excerpts from the plays or stories. Where contributors have relied on English translations of Chekhov, *The Oxford Chekhov in 9 Volumes*, translated and edited by Ronald Hingley, Oxford, 1965–80 (vols. I–III the plays; vols IV–IX, selected stories of 1888–1904), is for general reference (quoted by permission of Oxford University Press). For that reason we have retained, for reference purposes, Hingley's translation of Chekhov's act and scene divisions which Chekhov discontinued for the last four major plays e.g. Act Four, Scene IV.

The four volumes of stories translated by Ronald Wilks for Penguin, have also been used (by permission of Penguin Books Ltd.). The titles of stories and plays in English are those used by Ronald Hingley in *The Oxford Chekhov*, and Ronald Wilks' Penguin editions of selected stories. (See Appendix 1.)

Russian-speaking contributors have used material from the following:

Collected Works, Letters, 1944–51, Chekhov, Anton, Polnoe sobranie sochinenii i pisem A.P. Chekhova, v 20i tomakh, edited S. D. Balukhaty and others, Moscow, 1944–51.
Collected Works, Letters 1960–64, Chekhov, Anton, Polnoe sobranie sochinenii i pisem v 12i tomakh, edited by V.V. Yermilov and others, Moscow, 1960–4.

Unless otherwise specified, the references to *Works and Letters* are from the most recent and comprehensive collection:

Chekhov, Anton, Polnoe sobranie sochinenii i pisem v 30i tomakh, 1974–83, (Chekhov, Anton, Collected Works and Letters in 30 volumes, Moscow 1974–83), edited by N. F. Belchikov and others, Moscow, 1974–83.
Chekhov v vospominaniyakh sovremennikov (Chekhov in the Memoirs of his Contemporaries), edited by N. I. Brodsky and others, Moscow, 1954.

For non-Russian readers, the editors would like to emphasise the centrality to English-language Chekhov studies of Ronald Hingley's *The Oxford Chekhov* (above), and *A New Life of Chekhov*, London, 1976.
For further source material see Selected bibliography.

Calendar dates

Dates before October 1917 conform to the old-style Julian calendar. Not all contributors, however, have followed this system of dating.

PREFACE

Editing a collection of essays on a writer as internationally renowned, complex and productive as Chekhov must, inevitably, result in some hard choices. We knew, however, that these choices would define themselves given three essential prerequisites with which we began. First, we wanted the book to include contributions from professional practitioners of Chekhov's work in the theatre, namely actors, directors, designers, writers and critics, since it is from practice that much of theory arises – or may be tested. Second, the momentous changes in Russia (and thus Eastern Europe) starting with the Gorbachev era have enabled us to take full advantage of contributions from some of Russia's leading Chekhov specialists, whether practitioners or academics (a 'division' not recognised by our Russian colleagues): the director, Leonid Heifetz; the literary manager of the Moscow Art Theatre, Anatoly Smeliansky; the leading critic, Tatiana Shakh-Azizova, and the theatre historians and Chekhov scholars, Alexander Chudakov and Emma Polotskaya. Each brings a particular perception to the subject at a time when history is being redefined and reevaluated, whether political, social or theatre history. Finally, we wanted the book to offer the reader as much insight as possible into other aspects of Chekhov's work, although the emphasis of the collection as a whole is on Chekhov and production. Thus the many screen versions of Chekhov's works – far more than of such contemporaries as Ibsen, Strindberg, Wilde or Shaw or, later, Brecht – are analysed by one of Britain's leading film critics: Philip French, who reviews films of the plays *and* also some of the stories. Equally, Chekhov's short stories, although *seemingly* confined to only one chapter by Donald Rayfield, are also discussed by several other contributors, particularly Alexander Chudakov, Emma Polotskaya and Cynthia Marsh, and are referred to by others where the dramatic and literary Chekhovian themes become inseparable in content, although not in medium or genre.

Writing about Chekhov with the historical perspectives of 1999 has cast an unusual light on the importance, treatment and approach to Chekhov throughout the twentieth century, so we would hope that the volume provides the student of Chekhov with different viewpoints from those of previous collections.

It is evident, too, from the work of all our contributors, of whatever nationality (Russian, American, British, Irish or French) that some chapters have the end of this century *and* the coming millennium as an implicit subtext, with a sense of time and movement which would obviously have been lacking either fifty years ago or, for different reasons, during the period of the Cold War. This collection is inevitably informed by the 'symbol' of 1989: the collapse of the Berlin Wall, and all that has subsequently followed over the last ten years.

However diverse the approaches, personalities and specialisms of our contributors, they all share an expertise in Chekhov's work – differences in interpretations arise not only through the normal variations of reading, but also through the diverse perspectives of their relationship to his work. Thus Ian McKellen brings to the subject the perspective of a great British actor who has played many Chekhovian roles; directors like Trevor Nunn and Leonid Heifetz approach the plays from another angle in which sometimes minute detail from a production alternates with broad brushstrokes. In his chapter on *The Seagull*, the writer Thomas Kilroy debates the relationship between the original play and his own version, set in Ireland, which raises many new and important issues. Likewise, the scenographer Arnold Aronson draws the reader in to the vital area of visual interpretation and the staging of many of the plays. No less significant are the chapters by the theatre scholars and historians, Laurence Senelick (author of a major study of the plays in performance), Edward Braun and Patrice Pavis. It is relevant to their perceptions that some have themselves created viable production texts: Edward Braun translated an innovatory version of *The Cherry Orchard* for the British director Peter Gill, while Patrice Pavis is both scholar and commentator of all Chekhov's major plays in French – an important aspect of Pavis' work which is not always generally known outside France, but the popular and accessible *Le Livre de Poche* editions of the plays are introduced by Pavis.

Further aspects are provided by the major academic critics and Slavists: Donald Rayfield writes directly about the short stories, yet brings them into a natural relationship with the dramatic works; while Cynthia Marsh, another Slavist scholar, explores what may be seen as a particular 'female' (as distinct from 'feminist') critique of Chekhov's work. Alexander Chuda-kov's biography of Chekhov provides some material either little known or previously under-emphasised outside Russia, while both Emma Polotskaya and Tatiana Shakh-Azizova offer the non-Russian reader or spectator significant new perspectives and insights. All of the contributors have in common their shared interest in, affection for, and specialist knowledge of Chekhov's work.

Emanating from this is a basic and essential humanism which is needed all the more given the vacuum of ideas or even ideals with which we face not only the end of a decade, and the end of a century – with reason described as 'the century of barbarism' – but also the new millennium. It is hard to imagine that Chekhov's literary and dramatic works would or could attract the interest and respect of those who do not place human needs and human rights as a central part of their individual priorities and beliefs – surely one explanation of the paucity of Chekhov productions during the Stalinist period. Shakh-Azizova quotes the Soviet novelist Vasily Grossman, in whose *Life and Fate* one of the characters says: 'Chekhov's way is the way of Russian freedom, the embodiment of the Russian democracy, true and humane, which never took shape.' And in their respective chapters, both Trevor Nunn and Ian McKellen emphasise the 'egalitarian' process of Chekhov in production: a collective and ensemble-forming process in which Chekhov is – in McKellen's words – 'a friend to the actor', requiring as much of a seemingly 'small' role, like Charlotta Ivanovna in *The Cherry Orchard* as of Ranevskaya or Lopakhin: 'Chekhov appeals to me [as an actor] because you cannot realise the play in production *unless* every part has been worked on fully'. In this way, Chekhov's philosophy, his dramatic form, and the *process* of production are all inextricably bound up with the egalitarian, the humane and the democratic. His plays simply could not flourish under *any* dictatorship – or political and social system in which ordinary people (the subjects of his stories as much as of his plays) are not perceived as important, and within whom some elements of potency potentially reside.

Thus even if a performer or a reader or spectator is more concerned with form, Chekhov's plays are almost inevitably going to invite the interest and concern of the humanist – of those attracted by his deep understanding of human beings and psychology; of our place in relation to a social and economic context, and the metaphysical determinants of life, death, nature, the seasons, the passage of time and our place in the written and as yet unwritten history of human kind. Chekhov was as much aware of the need to have financial sufficiency if one is not to be 'dispossessed' and so 'disempowered' as he was aware of the need to live usefully, to make a contribution to life – not a judgemental or loaded issue in the works, but an inherent value system which is often articulated by the characters. This is not to say, however, that Chekhov himself may be associated with any particular character – in fact, his objectivity and detachment provoked much criticism during his lifetime, and may still lead to interpretative misunderstandings. His objectivity, however, is not a denial of commitment. To this end, he avoids the sentimental or melodramatic *or* deliberately utilises them to deflate and expose. It is here that one finds the greatest controversy attached to his plays, depending on the epoch and 'culture' which 'reads' him: his work has been seen as tragic, gloomy, heavy or, to put it in the terms of one of the earliest books on him: as 'the voice of twilight Russia'. But with such an interpretation the director has to go against the *form* of his work – and ignore the vital role of the comedy which enables Chekhov's tone to remain non-judgemental, detached and reserved. The interpretation of a 'gloomy' Chekhov requires a slow pace of action, as in the Pitoëff Company's Paris production of *Uncle Vanya*, over thirty years ago, in which the first page of the script lasted nearly fifteen minutes. The yawns and silences of Astrov and Marina were echoed by the audience.

This is a central production question of all of Chekhov's plays, and similarly found in both Beckett's and some of Pinter's plays: how to illustrate the boredom or lethargy or aimlessness of the characters without sending the audience to sleep? The answer, of course, lies in the pace of the production – and full use of the comic devices which remained largely unacknowledged by Stanislavsky and certainly by many of Stanislavsky's followers, particularly filtered through Lee Strasberg's reinterpretations – based as they were on the wildly inaccurate English-language translations of Stanislavsky's writings. As several contributors point out, whether Shakh-Azizova, Smeliansky, Braun or Senelick, it has only been over the last twenty-five to thirty years that directors have risked innovatory Chekhov – directed by Heifetz and Nunn, and other radical directors such as Richard Eyre, Mike Alfreds, Anatoly Efros, Peter Gill, Otomer Krejča, Andrei Serban, Yannis Kokkos, Adolph Shapiro, Peter Stein, Giorgio Strehler, Yuri Lyubimov, Jean Vilar, Oleg Yefremov, and, of course, Peter Brook. This radicalism was also instigated and inspired by the varying visual interpretations of some of world theatre's leading designers such as Valery Levental, Josef Svoboda, David Borovsky, Barkhin, Sofiya Yunovich, Santo Loquasto, Kokkos, Motley, Ashley, Martin-Davies, Pamela Howard – amongst many scenographers whose visual interpretation has carried not only place, space and time, but also image, symbol and metaphor. And over the century there have been different approaches to acting Chekhov: the performances by Ian McKellen and many other actors have made it possible for the plays to be reconceived – and rediscovered. This has also happened through different versions of the plays – from Trevor Griffiths' version of

The Cherry Orchard, Thomas Kilroy's reconception of *The Seagull* which gave it a completely new dimension, the innovatory reinterpretation by Efros, or Peter Brook's interpretation of *The Cherry Orchard* as timeless.

The collection attempts to raise some of the central questions about Chekhov's work – although the emphasis is primarily on the plays. The book falls into three parts: 'Chekhov in context', 'Chekhov in production' and 'Chekhov the writer'. And given the diversity of contributors, we hope that a diversity of approaches is evident: whether the biographical; the historical, both social and theatrical; the 'woman's perspective', for want of a better description; the critical, and the production-based perceptions of different theatre specialists. Ian McKellen sums up many of the salient points about acting Chekhov: he is 'hard to pin down' given 'many, many different styles within his writing' and 'so many themes going on'. And also, a point made earlier, it is the group, or emerging ensemble, which *makes* the production since 'no one actor is allowed to run away with the play'.

Chekhov is frequently linked with Shakespeare, not only in Russia but internationally, a point made by Shakh-Azizova, Heifetz and Nunn – if this volume fails to justify this comparison in terms of importance, constant reinterpretation and frequency of performance, then it can only be through the failure of the editors, and not the contributors. Few editors could have met with such sustained courtesy, patience and expertise as from the contributors of this volume. Like others in the Cambridge Series, contributors have responded to faxes, phone calls, e-mails and ordinary letters: in spite of the difficulties of distance and time zones, responses have been unfailingly swift and generous, making the role of editor a delightful and enjoyable task.

It is, perhaps, unusual to mention the Chekhov specialists whose work could not be included in this volume solely given limitations of space, but it would be wrong to leave the important work of John Tulloch, for example, or Patrick Miles, Maria Shevtsova, Harvey Pitcher or Harai Golumb amongst others, simply to the bibliography. Their influence may be felt in different parts of the book. Equally, those whose help has had a direct bearing on the volume are justly mentioned in the acknowledgements, though none are responsible for any errors – those are entirely the responsibility of the editors.

June 2000

I
CHEKOV IN CONTEXT

I

ALEXANDER CHUDAKOV

Dr Chekhov: a biographical essay (29 January 1860–15 July 1904)

Chekhov was a first-generation intellectual: his grandfather was a former serf, his father a small shopkeeper. 'There is peasant blood in me', he wrote (*Letters*, vol. V, p. 283).[1] But in the history of Russian culture, the name of Chekhov has become synonymous with intelligence, good upbringing – and refinement. How did these qualities come to be acquired by a provincial boy who spent his crucial formative years up to the age of nineteen in a small Russian town? Taganrog, Chekhov's birthplace, was typical of Russian provincial towns of the time: taverns, little shops, 'not a single sign without a spelling mistake'; oil lamps, and wastelands thickly overgrown with weeds. Chekhov's memories, of his 'green' years growing up in Taganrog, are full of references to puddles and unpaved streets.

Taganrog was also a southern port. The second floor of the Chekhovs' house where Anton spent his early secondary school years overlooked the harbour crammed at the height of summer with steamers and sailing ships. One could walk several miles along the shore and not see a single Russian ship – instead, there were vessels from Turkey, the Greek Archipelago, Italy, Spain: the *San Antonio*; the *Sophia*, the *Ogios Gerasimos*, the *Movludi Bagri*. They brought wine from Madeira and Asia Minor, lemons, oranges, olive oil from Provence, and spices. Taganrog was the staging post for the supply of provisions to the whole Azov region. By the time Chekhov was born this trade had already passed its peak, but it remained extremely active throughout his schooldays. The streets were filled with the babble of foreign languages. Near the port was a street with coffee-shops, and when the weather was fine the tables were packed with Turks, Greeks, French and English. Pavel Yegorovich Chekhov's store was on the ground floor of a house, and for a time the first floor housed a casino. Nearby was the London Hotel, with a female band to entertain the sailors in the evenings. Taganrog was the Russian equivalent of the Mediterranean French ports.

Pavel Chekhov decided to give his elder sons a Greek education. There were six children: five boys and one girl, Maria Chekhova. Chekhov's younger brother, Michael, recalled: 'At that time rich Greeks were the cream of Taganrog society . . . and father was convinced his children should follow the Greek example, and perhaps even complete their education at Athens University.'[2] So Anton and his brothers were sent to the Greek school. Nothing came of this, though they spent one year studying under the terrifying headmaster, Nikolai Vuchina.[3] They spent the whole summer bathing in the sea, swimming long distances. When Chekhov, by then a well-known writer, was returning from Sakhalin via the Indian Ocean, he amused himself by diving from the bow of the ship while it was sailing at full speed, and catching a rope hanging from the stern. Once he saw a shark in the company of pilot-fish. This episode is described in his story, 'Gusev' (1890). The impressions of a winter sea with its terrible storms are reflected in Chekhov's story 'On Christmas Night' (1883).

Taganrog was a southern town, surrounded closely on all sides by the Steppe. Anton and his brothers spent their summer holidays in the village of Knyazhi with their grandfather, a steward on the estate of Countess Platova. The village was forty miles from the town and the journey in a bullock cart took more than a day. At night they camped out on the Steppe, under the stars. After six years at grammar school, Anton spent a summer on the estate of the parents of his private pupil, Petya Kravtsov. That summer, the Taganrog student and 'tutor' became a skilled shot and an excellent horseman. Many years later, in 1898, Chekhov wrote: 'I love the Don Steppe. At one time it was like home to me and I knew every little gully' (*Letters*, vol. VII, p. 322). The Steppe landscapes are described in his earliest stories ('29th June' and 'The Mistress' (1882)), and in his first major work, the story 'The Steppe' (1888). From childhood experience of the Steppe, nature became a part of his very being. During his trip to Siberia in 1890, he took delight in studying nature at close quarters, and in his letters he describes with rapture how for a whole month he watched the sunrise from beginning to end. He was acutely aware of his bond with nature; his moods reacted to the changes in the weather like a barometer. The influence that nature exerts on the human psyche is reflected in stories such as 'The Student' (1894) and 'The Murder' (1895). So trees, flowers, clouds, dogs and wolves feel and think like people, as demonstrated in 'Agafia', 'Rusty' ('Kashtanka'), 'Patch' ('Beloloby', 1895) and 'Terror' (1892). They grieve, rejoice, worry and feel sad. Many Russian writers have portrayed nature and animals. Perhaps the works of Sergei Aksakov or Mikhail Prishvin[4] will survive to become unique evidence of how our planet *used* to be, and what amazing creatures lived on it. But for the present, we are more concerned with the experience of Chekhov who wrote not about the solitary life of man at one with nature and the birds of the

air, but about the everyday encounters of modern civilised man pursuing an
urban existence, living in a flat or a suburban dacha. Both in his writing
and in his personal life, Chekhov offered us examples to follow in our
dealings with our fellow creatures.

The theatre in Taganrog was far from typical of the Russian provincial
stage. How many of the smaller theatres could be regularly visited by
touring Italian opera companies? Or by Sarasate,[5] or Liszt's pupil, Laura
Carer. Tommaso Salvini sang the title role in *Otello*. The repertoire featured
operettas by Suppé, Lehar, Lecocq and Offenbach. Perhaps these other
aspects of Taganrog served only to accentuate 'the lethargy and boredom'
of day-to-day reality.

On 23 August 1868 Anton Chekhov entered the preparatory class of the
grammar school, where he was to study for the next eleven years (he
repeated the third and fifth years). It was a classical grammar school and
special significance was ascribed to the study of classical languages. At the
graduation examinations, Chekhov got top grades in German and Scrip-
ture. In his earlier years the young Anton was hindered by having to help
his father in the shop after school, working there until late at night. But if
the work at the shop – under the sign 'Tea, Coffee and Other Groceries' –
did not help Chekhov make progress at school, it certainly helped him in
his creative writing. The shop sold a variety of goods, including oil, fish,
flour, tobacco, buttons, coffee, knives, confectionery, candles, spades, shoe
polish, and herrings. It provided not only an education in objects, but it
also served as an animated lexicon. A shop in the provinces was a kind of
club where people went not only to buy things, but also to drink a glass of
vodka or wine. It was frequented by cooks, shop assistants, the wives of
officials, policemen, cab-drivers, fishermen, teachers, school students, and
sailors. They all talked, so from his early childhood Anton listened to the
language of people of the most varied occupations. Later critics were to be
amazed by Chekhov's knowledge of nautical terms, the language of timber
merchants or of haberdashery assistants.

From early childhood Chekhov was kept busy with domestic chores: he
shopped, cleaned the flat, fetched water from the well and even did the
laundry. Household duties are exhausting in their monotony, in the meaningless repetition day after day of the same tasks, and such duties are
especially burdensome for a young person. And not only for a young person
– Chekhov would show later in his writing how anyone who lives only in the
material world and lacks the ability to resist it becomes completely stifled by
the everyday, and then the spiritual gives way completely to the material. In
describing this situation, Chekhov understood this not merely as a detached
observer but knew it from personal experience.

No less forcibly, Chekhov was exposed from early childhood to the full force of the Church Slavonic language through compulsory church attendance, singing in the church choir, religious rituals at home and studying the Bible. But all this 'brought A. P. into contact with the beautiful ancient language of Church Slavonic, never allowing him to forget it, as happened with the great majority of Russian intellectuals, and nurturing in him an acute feeling for the simple vernacular tongue'.[6] Thus this childhood, divided by the airless store and the open sea, the corridors of the grammar school and the endless Steppe, between the narrow milieu of the petty clerks and the free and easy natural life of the country people, offered a vivid contrast between nature and the material world which promised to foster an artist with a most unconventional aesthetic perception of life.

Chekhov's father went bankrupt and was facing prison, so he and the family moved to Moscow. Anton spent the period from 1876 to 1879 alone in Taganrog, making a living as a tutor whilst managing to send money to his parents. It was a time of solitude during which his character took shape.

In 1879, he joined the Faculty of Medicine at Moscow University, where his lecturers were such eminent medical scientists as Grigory Zakharyin, Aleksei Ostroumov and Nikolai Sklifasovsky. Early on, he became acquainted with the theories of Charles Darwin, which he continued to study after graduating: 'I'm reading Darwin. What a treat! I simply adore him' (Letters, vol. I, p. 213). Studying the natural sciences 'exerted a colossal influence on the whole framework of his thinking. For him, the truths of the natural sciences radiated a poetic light and it was such truths as these, rather than socio-political doctrines, which shaped his fundamental perception of life as it is, and as it *should* be, and of man's place.'[7] This is confirmed by Chekhov, who in 1899, wrote in his autobiography: 'There is no doubt that my study of medicine strongly affected my work in literature' (Works, vol. xvi, p. 271).

Even as a first-year student, Chekhov was already contributing short stories to comic magazines (his first story appeared in The Dragonfly in 1880, but his main publisher was the magazine Fragments). It was not untypical for writers to start their careers in popular publications: this was true of Nikolai Nekrasov, Leonid Andreyev, Mark Twain and Ernest Hemingway, to name but a few. But none of them published as many comic stories, sketches, spoof advertisements, scenes or anecdotes as did Chekhov. It is widely believed that this involvement with comic magazines distracted Chekhov from serious literary work. But it was not as simple as that. Comic magazines offered freedom of form: there were only two requirements – humour and conciseness. Nothing else, whether plot, composition, technique or style, was bound by any literary rules. None of these publications belonged to any 'established' literary school or style. The small press was by its very nature eclectic. Authors were free to write in any manner, invent new techniques, modify the old conventions and experiment with new forms.

Chekhov realised this very early on. Like any great talent, he knew how to turn any circumstances to his own advantage. He was forever experimenting with new styles, assuming new *noms de plumes*, exploring ever changing areas of life. If one looks at stories he wrote in the first five years of his career, it is difficult to discover a social stratum, profession or trade that is *not* represented amongst his characters. There are peasants and landowners, shop assistants and merchants, sextons and priests, policemen and tramps, detectives and thieves, schoolteachers and students, medical orderlies and doctors, civil servants of all ranks, soldiers and generals, coquettes and princesses, reporters and writers, conductors and singers, actors, prompters, impresarios, artists, cashiers, bankers, lawyers, hunters, tavern-keepers, street-cleaners. From the beginning, Chekhov was an innovator who limited himself to no one area of subject matter, a writer of universal social and stylistic range. Yet for the reader there exist two Chekhovs side by side: the one who wrote 'Fat and Thin' (1883), 'A Chameleon' (1884), 'A Horse's Name' (1885), 'The Complaints Book'; and the other famous for 'A Dreary Story' (1889), 'The Artist's Story' (Chekhov's title is 'The House with the Mezzanine' (1896)), and 'A Lady with a Little Dog' (1899). What could these 'two' authors possibly have in common? Certainly that was his contemporaries' view. In 1897, the prominent critic Nikolai Mikhailovsky wrote: 'It is difficult to see anything in common between 'Peasants' (1897) and 'Ivanov' (1887–89), between 'The Steppe', 'Ward Number 6' (1892), 'The Black Monk' (1894), and vaudevilles like *The Bear* (1888), or the numerous comic stories.'[8] But in reality they are closely linked: Chekhov's 'humorous' past had a significant bearing on the evolution of his innovative creative thought. His early works contain the first sketches, the silhouettes, of his future acclaimed characters: Bugrov in 'A Living Chattel' (1882) foreshadows Lopakhin in *The Cherry Orchard* (1904), while other characters prefigure those in the later works, such as Toporkov in 'Belated Blossom' (1882), 'Ionytch' (1898) (Hingley's title is 'Doctor Startsev'); the lathe operator Petrov in 'Sorrow' (1885) – and the coffin-maker Yakov in 'Rothschild's Violin' (1894), and many others.

Many of the artistic principles, explored by Chekhov in his first five years as a writer, remained constant for the rest of his career. There were preliminary expositions of the situation, no excursions into the characters' past, or similar introductions to the narrative – it always began instantly. It is the characters who create the action, and there is no explanation or, more accurately, *exposition*, as to the causes of these actions. As Chekhov wrote: 'Characters must be introduced in the middle of a conversation so that the reader has the impression they have been talking for some time' (*Works*, vol. IV, p. 359). The avoidance of extended authorial comment, as well as the famous Chekhovian evocation of landscape, are also traceable to his early work. Equally, many of the distinctive features of his dramatic works have the same 'humorous' genealogy, such as random or meaningless remarks through mutual misunderstandings, and so on. Thus, it is not a character's biography or some universal 'problem' that furnishes the basis of a comic story, but invariably some quite specific everyday disagreement or situation. For example, a character finds himself in the wrong place (the hen-house instead of the dacha), or is mistaken for somebody else (a swindler is taken for a doctor). Such mishaps occur all the time in everyday life and a comic story cannot exist in isolation from them. No matter how profound or sharply satirical the content may be (in, for example, 'Fat and Thin', 'The Death of a Clerk' (1883), 'A Chameleon' (1884), his comic stories are always developed out of an entirely concrete situation.

In his late prose, Chekhov focussed on more complex socio-psychological problems, but again they were never made explicit or central to the plot. The plot never revolved around such a problem, as is the case with Dostoyevsky. Or around a character's life-story as in Turgenev or Goncharov. As with the earlier works, the basis of the narrative is always furnished by some particular circumstances of everyday life. It could even be said that every problem is resolved against a particular background drawn from everyday life. But that is not quite accurate: everyday life is not the background, the backdrop to the scene; it lies at the very heart of the plot, is interwoven with it. The hero of a comic story is steeped in the material world. He cannot exist or be presented outside this world. In Chekhov's stories he is depicted in a bathhouse, a hospital, a railway carriage, a horse-drawn tram. He is depicted while fishing – or retrieving orange peel from a decanter.

Circumstantial detail permeates Chekhov's late prose as much as it does his comic stories. Characters meditate and philosophise while bathing, riding in a carriage or doing the rounds at a clinic, breaking off to deal with some mundane trifle or other.

Every character in the comic stories, whether a clerk, telegraphist, reporter, actor with a provincial company, or guest in some cheap hotel, invariably has some problem to deal with: how to get to a dacha, how to get to sleep when the next-door or upstairs neighbours are playing the piano or wailing about how to retrieve their own new boots in return for the worn-out ones that they took by mistake. Perhaps such characters help to reveal the tight bonds between people and the objects that surround them and so lead Chekhov to the conclusion that everyone is bound by his or her material environment and can never break free from it, and that this is the only way to portray people. Chekhov's comic sketches always take some fragment of life, with no beginning or end, and simply offer it for inspection. And don't his later works follow the same pattern, beginning 'in the middle' and ending 'with nothing'? The new artistic world that Chekhov created, the world of 'The Duel' (1891), 'The House with a Mezzanine', 'The Bishop' (1902), gives no indication of its humorous antecedents, but even so, the debt is considerable.

In Moscow the Chekhovs lived in poverty (sometimes with all six adults and children crammed into one room). For the summers they went to Voskresensk, outside Moscow (now called Istra), where Chekhov's brother Ivan was principal of a school and had a flat. For three summers (1885–87), Chekhov and the family stayed in the village of Babkino, not far from Voskresensk, where Chekhov worked in the local clinic. His impressions of life and nature in the countryside around Moscow are reflected in many of his short stories, such as 'The Conspirator', 'A Dead Body' (1885), 'Children' (1889), or 'The Kiss' (1887).

February 1886 was a landmark in Chekhov's literary career: his work began to be published in one of the most prestigious and popular Russian newspapers, *Novoye vremya* (*New Time*). The offer, unrestricted by volume and terms, came from the owner and managing editor, Alexey Suvorin. Within two months *Novoye vremya* had published 'Office for the Dead', 'The Enemies' (1887), 'Agafia', 'A Nightmare' (1886), 'Easter Eve' (1886) – all ranked amongst Chekhov's best short stories.[9] 'The five short stories, published in *Novoye vremya* caused a commotion in St. Petersburg' (*Works*, vol. I, p. 242). The eminent writer Dimitri Grigorovich wrote to congratulate him. There were material benefits too: the money for the first story from *Novoye vremya* was more money than he could earn in a month from the journal *Fragments*. 1886 was the year of Chekhov's greatest productivity: he wrote more than a hundred works, and his first collection, entitled *Motley Tales*, appeared in print. Prior to this, he had only one small collection of six stories published in 1884, which appeared under a pseudonym.[10] Then in 1887 Chekhov wrote his first play, *Ivanov*.

Chekhov's collaboration with *Novoye vremya* continued through the late 1880s to the early 1890s, strengthening his friendship with Suvorin,[11] whose aesthetic views he valued very highly. For his part, Suvorin loved Chekhov and always helped him in hard times. The 337 surviving letters Chekhov wrote to Suvorin over the period 1886–1903 are the most fascinating of all his epistolary writings. In 1891 and 1894 they travelled abroad together. Suvorin published the first short story collection, *At Dusk* (1887), and it was partly due to Suvorin's enthusiastic backing that the book was awarded the Pushkin Prize. It was also Suvorin who published *Short Stories* (1888), *Gloomy People* (1890), *Motley Tales* (1891) and *Plays* (1897), all of which were then reprinted several times. A rift in their relations occurred after the Dreyfus Case, on which Suvorin's paper took an extreme nationalist stand.[12]

The late 1880s and early 1890s saw a blossoming of Chekhov's talent. New collections of his stories appeared, and he was awarded the Pushkin Prize, as noted above. His vaudevilles *The Bear* (1888) and *The Proposal* (1888–9) were staged by both professional and amateur companies in, for example, Kazan, Kaluga, Kostroma, Novocherkassk, Simbirsk, Revel, Tiflis, Tomsk, Tula, Yaroslav. Chekhov's fame grew, and his first major story, 'The Steppe', was reviewed in dozens of papers across the country.

At the very height of his success as a short-story writer and dramatist, Chekhov made his journey to Sakhalin – 'it was a place of the most unbearable suffering that could ever befall a man, whether captive or free' (*Works*, vol. IV, p. 32).[13] For a time, Chekhov was spared the necessity of working on the verge of the impossible, such as completing, while sitting his medical exams, a hundred stories a year – a task he had set for himself. By 'reading, looking around and listening, there is much to learn and to discover . . . Besides, I believe this trip, six months of uninterrupted physical and intellectual labour, is absolutely necessary for me, because my Ukrainian laziness has started to show of late. It's high time for me to get back into training' (*Works*, vol. IV, p. 31). This 'training' continued throughout his life, and is the outstanding characteristic of this most accomplished self-taught writer.

The trip to Sakhalin was beset with the most enormous difficulties. Chekhov had to travel right across Siberia, including 4,000 kilometres in horse-drawn vehicles. Within three months of his arrival, working on his own, Chekhov had made a complete census of the Sakhalin population, filling in over 8,000 reference cards. He spoke literally to each one, in their homes or in their prison cells. In 1895 his book, *The Island of Sakhalin*, was published. Impressions of the trip were also incorporated in stories such as 'Gusev' (1890), 'Peasant Women' (1891), 'In Exile' (1894) and 'Murder' (1895). After Sakhalin, Chekhov began to write such philosophical stories as 'Duel' (1891) and 'Ward No.6' (1892), questioning the meaning of life, death and immortality. Throughout his life Chekhov engaged in matters that were not directly related to literature: he organised relief for the famine-stricken provinces, practised as a doctor and built schools. These activities increased notably after March 1892 when he bought the Melikhovo estate, not far from Moscow. In 1892 and 1893 he ran a free medical centre on the estate in response to a cholera epidemic. Where previously his medical practice had been occasional, now he treated more than 1,500 patients in two years. Thus he extended the range of his experience.

Living in the country, Chekhov not only practised medicine, but also personally financed the construction of three schools in the neighbourhood and served as a member of the examination board. He also participated in all local affairs, making no distinction between major or minor issues, whether fighting the cholera epidemic, digging wells, building roads – or opening a post office at the railway station. 'It would be great if each of us left behind a school, a well or something of that kind so that one's life wouldn't vanish into eternity without trace' (*Works*, vol. XVII, p. 70). His impressions of Melikhovo are reflected in such major works as 'Peasants' (1897), 'In the Cart' (1897), 'New Villa' (1899) and 'In the Ravine' (1900).

Chekhov entertained many guests at Melikhovo: the famous artist Isaak Levitan, the actor Pavel Svobodin; the writers Ignatiy Potapenko, Ivan Leontiev-Shcheglov and Vladimir Nemirovich-Danchenko (shortly to co-found the Moscow Art Theatre), and Alexey Suvorin. Among the guests there were always young ladies.

By nature Chekhov was very reticent, and so little is known about his relations with women. He had his first sexual experience at the age of fourteen with a Greek woman, and his affair with an Indian girl in Ceylon is known only because he wrote about it in one of his letters. His complicated relationship with Yevdokia Efros lasted for a year-and-a-half. Chekhov even referred to her as his fiancée and the episode is reflected in the relationship between Ivanov and Sarah in *Ivanov*. No less complicated an affair was the one Chekhov had with 'beautiful Lika', Lidia Mizinova, a friend of his sister, Maria Chekhova, and later of the whole Chekhov family (echoes of this affair are found in *The Seagull*). His affair with the actress Lydia Yavorskaya was turbulent, but brief. During Chekhov's trips from Melikhovo to Moscow he was often seen in the company of ladies from Moscow's 'bohemian' artistic circles.

Once Chekhov was established as a serious writer the main criticism levelled at him was his lack of a central idea, a clear-cut outlook, a unifying theme. This criticism was best expressed by Mikhailovsky, who wrote in 1890: 'Chekhov treats everything equally: a man and his shadow, a bluebell and a suicide . . . Here oxen are being driven and there the post is being delivered . . . here a man is strangled and there people are drinking champagne.'[14]

Beginning with the story, 'The Steppe', almost all of Chekhov's works were criticised for their lack of a clear-cut structure; for their excess of incidental and irrelevant detail that impeded the flow of the narrative. For many years, he continued to be criticised for his random sequence of episodes which made it impossible 'to grasp the overall picture'. Critics called into question his narrative patterns in the short stories, the absence of extended introductions, of definite conclusions, of the elaborately detailed pre-histories for his characters, or clear-cut motives for their actions. Particularly annoying was the total absence of an authorial view. Thus Chekhov's innovative descriptive style was considered a violation of traditional canons of fiction writing, and parallels were drawn between him and new European artists such as the Impressionists. But in general, from the early 1890s, both critics and readers began increasingly to single out Chekhov from the majority of his literary contemporaries. Only Vsevolod Garshin and Vladimir Korolenko and, amongst younger writers, Maxim Gorky, were ranked with him. More and more, critics ranked Chekhov on a level with the Russian classical writers – Nikolai Gogol, Ivan Turgenev and Lev Tolstoy.

Recognition of Chekhov's drama was equally belated. *The Seagull*, premièred on 17 October 1896 at the Alexandrinsky Theatre in St Petersburg, was a flop. The author was deeply upset by its failure and that night said to Suvorin: 'Even if I live for another 700 years, I'll still not offer a single play to the theatre . . . I'm a failure in this sphere.'[15] But the reason for its failure was Chekhov's innovative dramatic technique, which was not understood until 1898 when the 'theatre of the new century', the Moscow Art Theatre, staged its hugely successful productions of *The Seagull*, and subsequently all Chekhov's other plays.[16]

Following the MAT productions, Chekhov's fame entered a new phase. His plays were produced across the Russian Empire. Each successive new work was a literary and theatrical event. From 1899 onwards, articles and reviews of his works appeared in the Russian press almost every day (up to 300 articles a year). Books devoted to Chekhov began to be published both in Russia and abroad (about ten such books were published in Chekhov's lifetime). How did he react to his fame? He objected to the clamour and to the incessant demands that were made of him, but in private he had high self-esteem, he knew his worth and was fully aware of his position in Russian literature.

From 1897, Chekhov's health deteriorated rapidly as tuberculosis began to take hold. As a doctor, Chekhov knew that his way of life had to change, but he persisted in working himself into the ground. His doctors recommended that he move to Yalta, so he sold the Melikhovo estate and went to the Crimea, where he spent the last five years of his life. In those times he wrote such masterpieces as 'A Lady with a Little Dog', 'In the Ravine', *Three Sisters* (1900–1), 'The Bishop' (1902) and *The Cherry Orchard* (1903–4). But Chekhov did not like Yalta with its palm-trees and idle tourists. He loved the countryside of Central Russia, and he loved Moscow. Nevertheless, he bought a plot of land and built a lovely house. But the house had one serious defect, particularly for a sick man: in winter it was cold. The winter climate in Yalta is bad, with frequent cold winds. Chekhov had always felt an affinity with nature, a dependence on it with the seasons of the year marking important phases in his life. Rain, snow, any change in the weather was as equal in importance to him as his literary or public affairs. In his letters references to work are regularly interrupted by such observations as: 'it has started to snow' or, as he wrote to both his wife and his sister in Autumn 1902: 'big news – it rained at night'. (*Letters*, vol. XI, p. 41).

There was another reason why Chekhov disliked Yalta, and, indeed, why it seemed like a prison to him: he had become involved with the MAT actress, Olga Knipper, and in 1901 he married her. Knipper stayed in Moscow, performing at the MAT, while Chekhov could not visit there as often as he wished: 'It is neither my fault nor yours that we are separated, but the demons who planted the bacillus in me and the love of art in you' (*Works*, vol. IX, p. 124). Nevertheless, he missed her dreadfully and his letters are full of complaints and requests for her to come, which were echoed by his friends and acquaintances. Thus, the director and writer Leopold Sulerzhitsky wrote to Knipper: 'Anton Pavlovich needs you. He is suffocating within his four walls. You mustn't forget that he not only belongs to you, but he is also a great writer and you should come and visit him, for you are the one person who can cheer him up and help restore his health which is vital for everybody, for Russian literature, for Russia.'[17]

In Yalta Chekhov missed the literary milieu and his friends, although old and new acquaintances helped to relieve his isolation: writers such as Ivan Bunin, Maxim Gorky, Alexander Kuprin and Nikolai Teleshev; the opera singer Fyodor Chaliapin and the composer Sergei Rakhmaninov. In April 1900, the MAT made a special visit to Yalta to perform Chekhov's plays for him.

In spite of worsening health, Chekhov still engaged in public and charitable activities in Yalta, giving money to build schools and clinics, and writing an appeal for help for tubercular patients which was reprinted in many papers and magazines across Russia. In 1902 Chekhov and Korolenko gave up the title of Honorary Academician in protest at the Tsar's decision to reject the election of Gorky to the Academy, as inadmissable on political grounds.

On the occasion of the première of Chekhov's last play, *The Cherry Orchard* in January 1904, Moscow honoured its much-loved writer, but by that time he was so ill he could barely stand. The celebration seemed more like a farewell. By the summer Chekhov's health was even worse and he and his wife went to the spa of Badenweiler in Germany for the cure. He died there on 15 July. Right to the end, he remained courageously composed.

In enumerating Chekhov's achievements throughout his life, one might take him for a public figure. He practised medicine; organised aid for famine-stricken provinces; ran a medical station during the cholera epidemic; built schools and hospitals; donated to public libraries; made public appeals for aid, and personally helped hundreds of people in need and misfortune. He wrote articles on social and political subjects, and a book about the prison island of Sakhalin, to which he had undertaken an arduous journey right across Siberia. All of this was done by a man who was always plagued by ill-health. And at the same time he was engaged constantly in the most titanic literary labour, writing a new page in the artistic history of the world.

NOTES

Titles of the stories are generally from Ronald Hingley's *The Oxford Chekhov* or Ronald Wilks' Penguin editions in four volumes, to enable non-Russian speaking readers to find many of the stories in English. See Appendix I.

1 Unless otherwise specified, the references to *Works* and *Letters* are from N. F. Belchikov and others, eds., *Anton Chekhov, Polnoe sobranie sochinenii i pisem v 30i tomakh*, Moscow, 1974–83 (*Anton Chekhov, Collected Works and Letters in 30 Volumes*, Moscow, 1974–83).

2 M. P. Chekhov, *Around Chekhov*, in *Memoirs*, Moscow, 1981, p. 32.

3 Nikolai Vuchina, the eccentric headmaster of the Greek school, who seems to have taught largely through torture (such as a form of crucifixion, lashing boys to the window shutters), unlike more usual pedagogues. Certainly Anton and his elder brother Nicholas left after a year without learning any Greek, except for a few swear words.

4 Sergei Aksakov (1791–1859), member of the dynasty of a famous Slavophile Russian family. He came to writing late in life, and was renowned for the unique work *Notes on Fishing* (1847), and *Notes of a Hunter of Orenburg Province* (1852), both remarkable for their systematic description of every detail. He was also the author of the 'fictional' *Family Chronicle* (1856), based on his own despotic landowning family.

Mikhail Prishvin (1873–1954), prose writer, whose stories are like Aksakov's in their mix of science and poetry in describing nature. His works have been called 'verbal landscapes' and record meticulously the change of seasons, climate, and effect of time on nature, and the animals of Northern Russia. Courageously Prishvin used Peter the Great's order to carry overland his great fleet from the White Sea to the Baltic as a metaphor for Stalin's use of forced labour in building the Baltic–White Sea Canal in 1933. The human cost can never really be known.

Alexander Chudakov's point here relates to descriptions of nature which even now is changing and in some cases disappearing.

5 Pablo de Sarasate (y Navascuez), 1844–1908.

6 A. Ismailov, *Chekhov: 1860–1904. Life, Persona, Work*, Moscow, 1916, p. 62.

7 G. A. Byaly, *Late 19th Century Russian Realism*, Leningrad, 1973, p. 159.

8 N. Mikhailovsky, 'Literature and Life', Russkoe bogatstvo 6, 1897, p. 121.

9 For the original Russian titles of these and the other stories mentioned in this chapter, see the list of variations of English titles from the Russian (Appendix 1).

10 Chekhov's pen-names or pseudonyms ranged from 'My brother's brother' to 'A. Chekhonte' and other comic names.

11 Alexey Sergeyevich Suvorin, wealthy owner and publisher of *Noveye vremya* (*New Time*), and Chekhov's first *real* publisher, who also became a friend for many years. Their friendship survived Chekhov's move to the more progressive *Russkaya mysl* (*Russian Thought*), edited by Vukol Lavrov, and even survived their vehemently opposed views over the Dreyfus Affair. They disagreed also over the row created by the rejection of Gorky, on the orders of the Tsar, as a proposed Honorary Academician when the Academy refused him membership on political grounds – and both Chekhov and Korolenko resigned in protest. Suvorin took a characteristically reactionary approach to both these and other major political events and issues. Many of Chekhov's most important letters were written to Suvorin, for whom he felt personal loyalty even when politically opposed. Suvorin died in 1912.

12 The Dreyfus Case, in which Dreyfus, an innocent French Jewish army officer, was accused of treason, and the trial became a *cause célèbre* throughout Europe. Dreyfus was found guilty, sentenced to exile and penal servitude on Devil's Island, and would have died had it not been for the public support of Emile Zola, who accused the French army and government of anti-Semitism. Reactions to the case were sharply divided across Europe between the reactionaries who assumed Dreyfus' guilt, and the progressives who insisted on his innocence.

13 The island of Sakhalin was a Russian prison-island, near the coast of Japan, comparable in function and purpose to the French Devil's Island, to which Dreyfus was sent, and – more recently – South Africa's Robbin Island where Nelson Mandela and other political prisoners were held. Chekhov's journey, made at great personal risk given the subsequent effect on his health, produced a book which *did* influence and achieve some penal reform. The book, titled in the English edition, *The Island, A Journey to Sakhalin*, trans. Luba and Michael Terpak, London, 1987, appeared in Russian, German, French, but in English only in 1987. The edition above has an introduction by the major Russian poet, Irena Ratushinskaya, who puts the work in its humanist, pragmatic, but nonetheless historically limited, perspective. At the present time, the island of Sakhalin and other islands in that area are still a source of territorial dispute between Japan and what is now the recently formed and named Russian Federation.

14 *Literary Critique*, Moscow, 1957, p. 606.

15 M. Krichevsky, ed. and foreword, *A. S. Suvorin's Diary*, Moscow–Petrograd, 1923, p. 125.
16 See chapters 3 and 14 in this volume for detailed accounts of these productions. For an account of the negative aspects of Chekhov's plays in production at the MAT, see chapter 5, 'Stanislavsky and Chekhov', in Edward Braun, *The Director and the Stage*, London, 1982, pp. 59–76; and chapter 3, 'Moscow Nights', in Laurence Senelick, *The Chekhov Theatre – A Century of the Plays in Performance*, Cambridge, 1997.
17 Olga Leonardovna Knipper-Chekhova, *Correspondence: 1896–1959* (Part 2), Moscow, 1972, pp. 30–1.

2

EMMA POLOTSKAYA

Chekhov and his Russia

The geographical settings in Chekhov's literature are extensive: his characters are found in small villages; in provincial towns; on a nobleman's estate; in the two 'capitals' – Moscow and St. Petersburg; in the Caucasus and the Crimea, Siberia and Sakhalin. There are also endless roads and numerous encounters on country lanes, tracks on the steppe, and encounters in railway stations and on trains.

No less diverse is the social world populated by his characters: intellectuals, merchants, peasants, landlords, shepherds, fishermen, firemen, military of all ranks and civil servants of all grades,[1] policemen and thieves, actors and scholars, students, doctors, teachers, lawyers and clergymen – of different generations, ages, levels of education and culture.

But the geographical dimension, the social backgrounds and professions are not as important as Russia's inner state and the way this shapes people's individual destinies. The purpose of this chapter is precisely to explore this interdependence, while the subject may be defined as 'turn-of-the-century Russia' through Chekhov's eyes or – to put it another way – 'Chekhov's images of Russia'. This interdependence is explored from a variety of perspectives: the vastness of Russia's territory and the abundance of its nature as the Russians' existential context, and Russia in the contexts of the world, and of the universe. Chekhov's judgements are never categorical or blunt, just as the symbolic 'images' of Russia are never unequivocal, and reflect the complexities and controversies, the combination of light and darkness, good and evil, that typify the Russian way of life and Russian sensibilities at that time.

An example of Chekhov's complex perceptions of Russia are his feelings about the south of the country where he was born, combining deeply personal and emotional impressions with objective, unprejudiced observations. In 1887 Chekhov, already a popular author of short stories, revisited his home town of Taganrog. His impressions of local customs and manners, found in his letters, are full of irony. Having lived in Moscow for seven years, he found many of the local customs alien and even detestable: the lack of culture, the idle talk of the philistines who 'only eat, drink, breed and have no other interests' (*Letters*, vol. II, pp. 54–84).[2] But beneath this irony is a touching and uncynical admiration for the charming sounds, colours and smells of the Southern lifestyle: music in the city park and the smell of lilacs and acacias, but most of all the 'little hillocks, kites, larks and blue vistas' of the Don Steppe. A distinct memory of his childhood experiences is expressed in the story 'The Steppe' (1888)[3] as the image of a 'beautiful, stern motherland' (*Works*, vol. VII, p. 46).

In the 1880s the writer whose childhood was spent in this setting, was faced with quite a different reality – depressing and ominous. Having finished work on 'The Steppe', Chekhov wrote to Dmitri Grigorovich about his realisation of the fundamental hostility to man of Russia's vast expanses:

> On the one hand, there is physical weakness, nervousness, early sexual maturity, passionate desire to live and find the truth, dreams of work which, like the Steppe, have no boundaries; edgy analysis and lack of knowledge combined with the irrepressible flight of thought; and on the other hand – endlessly flat land, severe climate, a grey and severe nation with its hard and cold history, the Tatar yoke, bureaucracy, poverty, ignorance, rainy capitals, Slavic apathy, and so forth . . . Russian life beats the soul out of the Russian . . . In Western Europe people die because their space is cramped and suffocating. In Russia they die because the space is an endless expanse.
>
> (*Letters*, vol. II, p. 190)[4]

It seems this image of Russia is quite different from the *beautiful* motherland of 'The Steppe'. Chekhov had found a rationale which he expressed through artistic intuition in his short stories 'The Witch', and 'On the Way' ('Na puti', 1886), where frost and snowstorms become symbols of restless souls or the spirit. The only common thread in his letter to Grigorovich and these stories is the conflict between the 'passionate desire to live and find the truth' – and man's impotence in such a vast and cold space.[5] Although these words about the cold were written by a southerner, born near the warm sea, they echo the widespread European perception of Russia as a cold country. (Was this perhaps the reason why in the British première of *The Cherry Orchard*, the actors wore fur coats and fur caps?)

Chekhov himself nearly froze to death in Siberia in 1890, and in the Nizhni Novgorod province in 1892, so the motif of a cold climate destroying the human physique and psyche is not accidental in his works. 'In this climate one expects it to snow at any time, and now all this philosophising' (*Works*, vol. XIII, p. 178). These lines of Masha's in *Three Sisters* contain a subtext, suggesting the dreadful ambience in the house, dominated by the heartless rationalist, Natasha. This atmosphere is as unbearable as apprehension of the cold winter which will soon come in the Urals – as Chekhov wrote, the action of the play is set 'in a provincial town, like Perm' (*Letters*, vol. IX, p. 133).

Having moved to the south of the Crimea in the late 1890s, but still possessed by the memories of Melikhovo, the splendour of central Russian winters, the joy of sledging in the abundant and pure Russian snow, Chekhov returns to the problem of Russian destiny in the endless expanses of the country. In the short story, 'On Official Business' (1899), he portrays a low-grade country policeman, subserviently engaged in meaningless paperwork, against the backdrop of a snowstorm. As a member himself of the Serpukhov Sanitation (Health) Council, Chekhov knew such policemen who, for thirty years, had timidly endured the petty tyranny of local administrators. The protagonist in Chekhov's story, investigator Lyzhin, watches the snowstorm and thinks he sees the little policeman walking hand-in-hand with the dead insurance agent, whose failure to cope with the pressures of harsh reality had driven him to suicide. In Lyzhin's mind the old policeman, of peasant stock, and the bygone intellectual, are merged in the single image of a hardworking man, breaking his back under the burden which ought to be carried by society as a whole. And the protagonist has feelings of guilt about such vulnerable people.

References to the harsh image of the 'cold' motherland as an ideal milieu for the bureaucratic state are found in Chekhov's two aphorisms: 'Russia is a bureaucratic country' (*Works*, vol. XVII, p. 167), and 'Russia is a vast plain across which a dashing horseman recklessly rides' (*ibid*). The latter aphorism was echoed by the eminent statesman Konstantin Pobedonotsev[6], who also said that 'Russia is an icy desert across which a dashing horseman roams'.[7] It is not known who first used the epithet *'icy'* with reference to Russia, but it matches perfectly Chekhov's general image of his homeland.

The 'daring' of the Russian brings us back to the issue of unrealised individual aspirations. Where is the daring, dashing horseman riding so recklessly? This question also relates to Gogol's proverbial comparison of Russia as 'the troika swift as a bird', and to Gogol's rhetorical question: 'Russia, whither do you fly?'.[8] The concept of man's conflict with Russia's vast expanses is linked in Chekhov's mind with the problem of suicide which, by the end of the last century, had become almost commonplace, especially amongst the young. (Treplev's attempts and suicide in *The Seagull* are relevant here.)

Another scourge of society which concerned Chekhov was the psychological disease known as a 'persecution complex', which flourished in the fertile soil of Russian police terror and outrages, causing the people to live in constant fear of arrest, and of administrative or criminal punishment. Such a persecution complex damaged the mind of the refined intellectual, Ivan Gromov. Seeing shackled convicts in the street, escorted by guards, he convinces himself that this will happen to him, and he ends up in a lunatic asylum. The story 'Ward No.6' (1892) came as a real shock to the reading public. Chekhov's most terrifying 'experiment' in the aesthetic exploration of Russian society resulted in the exposure of yet another aspect of Russia: 'Ward No. 6' became a metaphor for the country as a whole. The paradoxical motif of the claustrophobia of Russia's vast expanse in Chekhov's letter to Grigorovich acquired *literal* meaning in 'Ward No. 6'. The action is set in an enclosed space, cut off from the rest of the world, and the ward in the clinic looks like a prison-cell. Dr Ragin identifies the clinic with the prison, which can be seen from the window, and comes to the conclusion: '*This* is reality' (*Works*, vol. VIII, p. 121). The only way to escape it is to die. So Ragin dies.

The sense of 'Ward No. 6' as the symbol of a feudal Russia which represses human freedom, was shared by the painter Ilya Repin, and the writer Nikolai Leskov: '"Ward No. 6" is everywhere . . . This is Russia' (*Works*, vol. VIII, p. 458). And Vladimir Lenin confessed that when he was young, he was terrified by the story, as though he himself was locked in the ward with madmen.

It was later that Chekhov became interested in man's reaction to such grim realities. And he discovered that horror at the prospect of being imprisoned often results in transference into the desire to see *others* jailed. This motif first appeared in the early short stories such as 'Cases of Mania Grandioza' (1883) or 'Sergeant Prishibeyev' (1885). The only way such people can cope with the fact that their reality *is* a prison is to adapt – and make others do the same. This method is used by the teacher of Greek, Belikov, in 'A Hard Case' (1898). He creates his own microcosm, and voluntarily imprisons himself in it: a bedroom that looks like a 'box'; window blinds permanently closed; the habit of sleeping with his head covered by a blanket; and a robe, a cap, things in cases, invariably galoshes and an umbrella. The wretched Belikov is terrified of any sign that others are unwilling to live according to the same rules, and when he dies they put him in his last case – a coffin. But Chekhov leaves his readers with no illusions: 'And how many more such men "in their cases" are still around, and how many more are yet to come . . .?' (*Works*, vol. X, p. 53). The symbol of the case, and the man who voluntarily locks himself in it, became Chekhov's wider metaphor for the grim social atmosphere of the 1880s.

Such dark images of Russia have an original source *and* a synonym: Sakhalin. At a time when his knowledge of penal servitude in Sakhalin was limited to sources from 'special' or restricted literature, Chekhov realised that 'this is a place of unbearable suffering' (*Letters*, vol. IV, p. 32). During his visit to Sakhalin Island in 1890, Chekhov was able to obtain proof of his assumptions. Crowds of convicts, many of them falsely condemned, suffered from a cold climate, of which Chekhov wrote: 'This is not a climate. It is the most foul weather . . . this island is the foulest place in Russia.' The only word Chekhov used to describe this dreadful climate, combined with hard labour, was 'hell'.

In his book, *The Island of Sakhalin* (1895), Chekhov expressed the hopelessness of the convicts' existence, doomed to endless physical and moral suffering. The worst-off were people like the fratricide Yakov Terekhov, described in 'Murder' (1895), who had not yet lost his irrepressible longing for freedom. He had tried to escape many times, was brutally punished, but his soul purified itself through suffering and he acquired faith in God which previously had been lacking for him. And peering into the distance towards the motherland with anguish and love, he dreams about sharing his cruel experiences, even if only with one other person who might therefore be saved. No matter who he is, man's soul is as multifarious as Russia itself.

In much of Chekhov's work, Sakhalin became the symbol of repression. He once observed that all his works of the 1890s are 'Sakhalinized throughout'.[9] Equally, the 'ravine' symbolises the abyss that has swallowed up not only the village of Ukleyevo but the whole of Russia. This image was born out of Chekhov's observations in Melikhovo (his estate outside Moscow), from his close contacts with peasants, merchants and the owners of the nearby factories, depicted in the story 'In the Ravine' (Hingley's 'In the Hollow', 1900). The ravine is a dark, unclean place: 'swampy mud, even in summer, foul-smelling river, polluted by factory wastes . . . shadows which the old willows cast on the house and on the courtyard. Darkness outside reflected darkness in the house and sin loomed like fog in the air' (*Works*, X, pp. 144, 146). And the only pure creature, Lipa, daughter of a poor widow, is kept by the rich family as if in a prison – gaining freedom cost too high a price: the loss of her little son, victim of a family row. The story ends with the fall of darkness as the village again sinks into the ravine. At the same time, however, the literal sense of 'ravine' remains part of nature. And thus this deep cavity with steep slopes performs another, psychological, function in accentuating the characters' experiences. The intelligent Vera Kardina in the story 'In the Home-Stead' (1897), is so horrified by the landlord's violent outburst at a peasant girl that she feels violently dragged back decades to the time before the abolition of serfdom, and she runs, away from herself, to the ravine where she finds peace of mind. She decides to change her life and 'become one with the luxuriant steppe', with its beauty and vistas. And although this offers her no personal happiness, the function of the ravine in Vera's imagination is parallel to the steppe in the 1888 story of that name: here too is the embodiment of Russia's endless expanses.

In the story 'Peasants' (1897), the cliff – like a ravine it too is associated with steep slopes – is related to the degradation of a Russian village which, however, is seen against the backdrop of the beauties of rural nature with sunset on the river, the church, the 'soft and indescribably clean air'. That is how the devout Olga, sitting with her sick husband on the edge of the cliff, sees the village on the day of their arrival. Her spirits are not yet darkened by poverty or their relatives' hostility towards them as self-invited guests. And at the end of the story, Olga is again sitting on the edge of the cliff. She has survived a severe and hungry winter, has lost her husband, but she admires the river and the church and dreams of how she will return to Moscow.

The contrast of darkness and light in the symbols of nature echoes the differences within the characters, such as the peasants. The derogatory nickname of 'lackey-land' given to the village of Zhukovo is not a general metaphor of the country, or the nation. After all, the peasants were not born lackeys, boors, thieves or drunks. They acquired these vices through living in unbearable conditions, hard labour, poverty and the injustice of local administrations. Such vices only disappear when 'humanitarianism' and faith in God take over. Like Dostoyevsky, Chekhov regarded the Russian soul, whether of a peasant or a landlord, an intellectual or a casual labourer, as the receptacle of both good and evil, strength and weakness, degradation and rebirth. As a psychologist, Chekhov particularly valued moments of insight, and of the sudden awareness of a wasted life. Likewise, the convicts Chekhov met and interviewed on Sakhalin provided no exception.

These negative symbols of a rich and multifarious country are juxtaposed with the images of a 'stern and beautiful motherland' in 'The Steppe', and Russia as 'our orchard' (Works, vol. XIII, p. 227) in Chekhov's last play, The Cherry Orchard. Amongst other symbols between these two works one must include the forest in Uncle Vanya (1896). It is as beautiful as the steppe or the orchard, and with the same inevitability, it is becoming scarce. The forest and the lives of the characters are vividly interwoven. The beauty of Sonya's feelings is futile, as are the feminine beauty of Yelena Andreyevna, Astrov's talents and his efforts to protect the forest, or Waffle's innocence and naivety. But the most dramatic is Voinitsky's (Vanya's) awareness of his wasted life, while only the nanny, Marina, with her quiet simplicity and faith in God, personifies the healthy spirit of the people.

In *The Seagull*, the lake – as the natural scenic setting for Treplev's play about the distant future of mankind – bears the authentic traits of Russian life: people fish in it, gulls fly over it and living on its banks is a girl (Nina), who dreams of getting out of the provinces to Moscow where the 'real stage' is. But all this could happen in any country: the national specifics carry universal meaning. The same applies to the seagull symbol in the play. It contains a variety of meanings, both explicit (references to Nina's ruined personal life) and implicit (when Treplev says that 'soon he will kill himself in the same way as the seagull') (*Letters*, vol. XIII, p. 27). The play contains allegorical references to art which triumphs over people's personal sufferings; in a sense this bird, killed in 'real life', but resurrected as the *symbol* of art and the beauty of life, echoes those symbols of the mother-land which has endured much suffering in the past, yet still remains a potent source of vitality.

Nina's longing for Moscow reveals one further aspect of Russia which the artist can see in his favourite city. First there is the Moscow–Petersburg *antonym* in Chekhov's works. Moscow is the symbol of Russian statehood, 'the widow in purple' as Pushkin described it in *The Bronze Horseman*, 'a widow' who stood aside, overshadowed by the new capital. But Moscow turned out to be the kind of 'widow' who has not lost interest in the world – or taste for the joys it offers. Deep in their hearts, the majority of Russians always preferred Moscow to St Petersburg. Hospitable, famous for the promenades along the Sadovoye and Boulevard Circles, with its cosy seven hills and numerous churches, Moscow appeared more homely to the ordinary Russian than St Petersburg with its European style and planned avenues. It was not by chance that the story 'Misery' (1886) of the old drayman and his tragic loneliness since he lost his son, is enacted against the backdrop of cold and indifferent St Petersburg crowds.

Chekhov's stories[10] of human drama are also set in Moscow: such as 'A Dreary Story' (1889), 'Three Years' (1894), or part of 'A Lady with a Little Dog' (1899). Moscow was more dear than St Petersburg to both Chekhov and his characters (such as Yartsev and Kochevoy in 'Three Years'). He even liked it for its coolness and 'grey misty days'.[11] In Chekhov's writing, departure to St Petersburg is usually related to the characters' hopes of changing the circumstances of their lives – for example, in 'Practical Jokes' (1886), or 'The Artist's Story' (also known as 'The House with a Mezzanine', 1896); or for careers – Doctor Blagovo in 'My Life' (1896); and the longing for Moscow arises from the desire 'to start life from scratch' – as in

'The Russian Master' (1894). But Chekhov always makes exceptions: in his last short story, 'The Marriageable Girl' (1903), Nadya Shumina, eager to start life from scratch, merely passes through Moscow on her way to St Petersburg where she is going to study. It may be that this was related to Chekhov's sympathy with the (radical) student movement which was very much alive in St Petersburg over the years 1899–1902.

Moscow as the symbol of a desirable new life became central to Chekhov himself throughout his 'exile' to Yalta, and in *Three Sisters* (1901), this is given the most powerful expression. It seems also symbolic, however, that the sisters' dream does not materialise. The very idea that a new life may start *just* by changing places is itself an illusion. And one of the sisters, Irina, who has the opportunity to change places, does not go to Moscow, but becomes a teacher and so will be faced with new and unpredictable realities.

Chekhov's perception of Moscow as the heart of Russia is also illustrated by the fact that in his creative or fictional meditations on the future of Russia he always thought of Moscow's historical past. The teacher, Yartsev, in 'Three Years', admires the up-and-coming new generation, believing that Russia is 'on the eve of a great triumph', but he also says that 'Moscow is the city that will have much to suffer' (*Works*, vol. IX, pp. 74, 75). Paradoxically, to prove these words he looks back to the past, to the times of raids by nomadic tribes on Russia at the end of the eleventh century when Moscow already existed. It is suggested to Yartsev that he write a play about those times for the young generation, of whom he has such great expectations. Drafting a play that will never be written, Yartsev imagines a scene with a captured Russian girl, tied to the saddle, who watches the dreadful conflict 'sadly and wisely' – sadness and wisdom symbolising the suffering of the nation, yet endowed with great patience and prepared for further ordeals. Thirteen years later, Alexander Blok also prophesied the return of violent times when Russia struggled against Tatar hordes: 'Yes, I *behold* you, the beginning /Of grand and stormy days' (my italics – E.P.).[12]

Chekhov, moreover, did not envisage the future of Russia as an ascent to 'glorious heights', although for many years Soviet Chekhov scholars tried to prove the opposite, referring to the memoirs of the writer's contemporaries, and the lines of some characters of his plays and later short stories. Amongst believers in a glorious future are Vershinin from *Three Sisters*, Sasha from the story 'The Marriageable Girl', and Trofimov from *The Cherry Orchard*. Chekhov's irony in relation to these characters was generally ignored, as were their evident limitations, predilection for high-flown rhetoric and ineffectual personalities.

Trofimov's aphorism 'All of Russia is our orchard' sounds like a call to work the soil for the future; and when he talks about the land which is 'vast and beautiful and with so many wonderful places in it', he means the Russian land. It is worth pointing out to non-Russian speakers that in Russian there is the same word for 'land' and for 'earth'. And when Chekhov dreamed about the 'flowering orchard' which will come in three or four hundred years,[13] he means the whole of the earth – the future of the motherland inseparable from the fortunes of all mankind.

With all the limitations of Trofimov's historical optimism, he is by no means a professional Russian revolutionary. As a participant in student protest marches (since Chekhov had to comply with the requirements of censorship, he could not make this explicit in the play – but he wrote about it in a letter to his wife), Trofimov did not call for the destruction of the old world, but for giving up the old mode of existence which allowed the few to live at the expense of others' labour.

Chekhov's characters dream of a 'glorious future' which is not connected with revolution (for this reason, in the 1920s many critics ranked Chekhov amongst those writers who opposed the proletarian revolution). On the other hand, up to the late 1960s, the myth about Chekhov's revolutionary views was carefully cultivated by official theatre historians who referred not only to Trofimov's tirades, but also to Tuzenbach's lines about the storm in *Three Sisters*, claiming that they echoed Gorky's call for the storm in *The Song of the Stormy-Petrel* ('Let it break in all its fury!'). But in contrast to Gorky's stormy-petrel, Tuzenbach does not expect the storm to be destructive. In fact *The Song of the Stormy-Petrel* was printed three months *after* the première of *Three Sisters*, and perhaps it was partly intended to continue a polemic with Chekhov's characters' idea of improving society. Tuzenbach dreamed of ridding society of 'idleness, indifference, prejudice against work, putrid tedium' (*Works*, vol. XIII, p. 123), and that was all.

Chekhov's memoirs testify that his vision of Russia's future was not as optimistic as we were taught to believe. He wrote about events that 'will turn everything upside down': 'Our time is much like that lived through by our fathers shortly before the Crimean campaign, except that we are in for a *greater ordeal*. I know this for sure' (my italics – E.P.).[14] That was written in 1903, and a month later the war with Japan broke out. At first Chekhov entertained some hopes about the outcome of that war ('We shall beat the Japs.') (*Letters*, vol. XII, p. 54), and even wanted to serve as a field doctor. After the defeat of the Russian army, analogies with the Crimean campaign became widespread.

Missing the Russian weather in the Crimea at the end of 1901, Chekhov wrote: 'An endless field and a lonely birch-tree. The name of the picture is "loneliness"' (*Works*, vol. XVII, p. 84). And he wrote this about Isaak Levitan's picture *Hay-Ricks*: 'A meadow, hay-cocks, forest at a distance, and reigning over them all is the moon' (*Letters*, vol. IX, p. 81). These sketches betray the melancholy, lyrical, or as Chekhov would say, 'Levitanian mood'. It is similar to the heroine's mood in 'Three Years' who looks at a landscape in an art gallery, and feels the air filled with loneliness, and silence.

Finally, there is one further point on this subject which Chekhov wrote in Yalta in 1899: 'A conversation about earth from another planet 1,000 years from now: do you remember that white (birch) tree . . .?' The image of Russia is placed in a global context. It is about the time when 'all lives have made their woeful circle and died out', but the earth and its satellites have not yet turned to ashes, as The World Soul prophesied in Treplev's play in *The Seagull*. In other words, this is post-apocalyptic. Hence the date: '1,000 years from now', according to the New Testament, meant the end of 'the earthly history', mentioned by the black monk in the story of the same name (1894).[15] And for Chekhov, by that time the former inhabitants of the earth will have moved to another planet and even forgotten the name of the birch-tree. The birch-tree, without which the Russian landscape is inconceivable, becomes the symbol of both Russia and the world.

But while Chekhov had a grim vision of the earth's future, abandoned by human species, he also had faith in the triumph of man in the context of earthly reality. He pins his hopes for a better future for Russia not on a social class, but on individuals: 'I have faith in individuals, I seek salvation in individual people, whether intellectuals or peasants. They are scattered all over Russia, they have power, although they are scarce' (*Letters*, vol. VIII, p. 101). And it was Chekhov's constant and firm position not to divide people into classes or social groups: 'No division is good, for *we are all* a nation and the best things we do are for the nation' (my italics – E.P.) (*Works*, vol. XVII, p. 9). In spite of all the human weaknesses and vices that he saw so clearly and exposed so ruthlessly, Chekhov had faith in individuals.

This faith was fed by the rise of 'social awareness' (*Letters*, vol. VIII, p. 101) in Russia, of the educational, cultural and ethical standards of the Russian intelligentsia,[16] as well as by the blossoming of Russian spiritual culture at the turn of the nineteenth (and twentieth) centuries. Chekhov's contemporaries and acquaintances were such outstanding personalities as Lev Tolstoy, Feodor Chaliapin, Peter Tchaikovsky, Isaak Levitan, Konstantin Korovin, Sergei Rakhmaninov (whose genius Chekhov was amongst the first to recognise), Vladimir Nemirovich-Danchenko and Konstantin Stanislavsky. The ideas of others of his contemporaries, such professional revolutionaries as Lenin, Plekhanov and others, were profoundly alien to Chekhov, although he could not help sympathising with political prisoners (many of whom he met on Sakhalin). But Chekhov's rejection of the class-oriented model of change, as well as of all forms of violence, made it impossible for him to accept the revolution which he felt was about to break out.

The premonition of calamity on the eve of the revolution, combined with strong faith in Russia, was shared by his successors in literature. In his article, entitled 'Timelessness' (1906), Alexander Blok wrote: 'Some devilish vitality helps us burn and never burn out.'[17] And as for the present when, as Tolstoy once put it, everything in Russia 'has gone head over heels and cannot get back on its feet',[18] we need only to repeat, after the philosopher Berdyaev, that our hope is in Russia's 'hidden resources'.[19]

In the story 'In the Ravine' the wise old man observes reassuringly: 'Life is long and there will be many good and bad happenings. Mother Russia is so vast' (*Works*, vol. x, p. 175). In this statement, different aspects of Russia merge into one. A Russia that is eternal.

NOTES

1 In pre-Revolutionary Russia there were fourteen grades of civil servants.
2 Unless otherwise specified, the references to *Works* and *Letters* are from N. F. Belchikov and others, eds., *Anton Chekhov, Polnoe sobranie sochinenii i pisem v 30i tomakh*, Moscow, 1974–83 (*Anton Chekhov, Collected Works and Letters in 30 Volumes*, Moscow, 1974–83).
3 The translation of the story titles is from Hingley, *The Oxford Chekhov*, vols III-IX. See Appendix 1.
4 Although in a different context, Chekhov's point is also quoted by Anatoly Smeliansky in his 'Chekhov at the Moscow Art Theatre', chapter 3 in this volume. The reiteration is significant for Europe both historically *and* as we approach the new millennium.
5 R.L. Jackson was the first to write about Chekhov's interpretation of Russia's endless expanses, in his chapter 'Times and Travellings: A Metaphor of All Times', in *Chekhoviana, Chekhov in 20th Century Culture*, Moscow, 1993, pp. 8–9.
6 For a version of this phrase, see V. V. Rozanov, ed., *Collected Works*, vol. VII, *The Legend of the Great Inquisitor*, by F. Dostoyevsky, Moscow 1966, p. 52: 'Deserted and dark fields with a dashing horseman riding across them'.
7 Cited by O. N. Mikhailov with reference to D. M. Merezhkovsky, but without source given. See *Literary Gazette*, 11 October 1989, p. 2.
8 N. V. Gogol, *Dead Souls*, in *Collected Works in 6 Volumes*, Moscow, 1949. vol. v, pp. 248–9.
9 See T. P. Krestinskaya, *Motifs of Sakhalin in Chekhov's Works*, Nizhni Novgorod Teacher's Training College, Nizhni Novgorod, 1967, vol. XX, p. 111.
10 See Appendix 1 for Russian titles and English variations.

11 An acquaintance of Chekhov's from Yalta recalls: 'Moscow for him was truly
    the holy land, the concentration of everything Chekhov loved in Russia . . . It
    was clear that the names of the streets, Samoteka or Pushchikha, the thawed
    street dirt in March, even the grey misty days were dear to him, and filled his
    heart with pleasant feelings.' S. Y. Yelpatyevsky and others, eds., *Chekhov v
    vospominaniyakh sovremennikov [Chekhov in the Memoirs of his Contempor-
    aries]*, Moscow, 1960, p. 570–1.

12 A. A. Blok, *Works in 2 volumes*, Moscow, 1955, vol. I, p. 288.

13 See A. I. Kuprin, *In Memory of Chekhov*, in *Chekhov in the Memoirs of his
    Contemporaries*, p. 541.

14 See A. Mamontov, *Two Meetings with Chekhov*, in *Russkoye slovo*, 2 July
    1909.

15 I. N. Sukhikh interpreted the black monk in Chekhov's story as a prophet of
    Doomsday. See I. N. Sukhikh in *Problems of Chekhov's Poetics*, Leningrad,
    1987, pp. 108–9.

16 See A. I. Kuprin, *In Memory of Chekhov*, pp. 542, 775.

17 See A. A. Blok, *Works in 2 Volumes*, vol. II, p. 31.

18 Quoted in L. N. Tolstoy's *Anna Karenina*, in *Collected Works in 14 Volumes*,
    vol. VIII, Moscow, 1952, p. 349.

19 See N. A. Berdyaev, *Spirits of the Russian Revolution (1918)*, in *Russkaya mysl*,
    May–June 1918, and in *Literaturnaya ucheba*, March–April 1990, p. 139.

3

ANATOLY SMELIANSKY

Chekhov at the Moscow Art Theatre

Chekhov's relationship with the Moscow Art Theatre is a story in itself, and quite a tangled one at that. It is the story of how Chekhov's theatre came into being and Stanislavsky and Nemirovich-Danchenko's struggle to master the poetics of his drama. It is the story of how even in the dramatist's lifetime the Chekhov canon evolved into a theatrical straitjacket from which it became necessary to break free. It is the story of the deep divisions between theatre and dramatist involving the most fundamental questions concerning the art of theatre: the precise genre of Chekhov's plays; his view of character and his attitude towards the whole historical development of Russia itself. In an attempt to console Stanislavsky after Chekhov's death, Nemirovich-Danchenko said: 'We had already lost Chekhov with *The Cherry Orchard*. He would never have written anything else.'[1] This merciless verdict expresses all the tension that existed between Chekhov and the Moscow Art Theatre.

After Chekhov's death, his plays began to be perceived in the light of new theatrical developments. The MAT's productions of Chekhov started to break free, not from Chekhov himself, but rather from the style of the 'theatre of mood' and from the detailed naturalism that had only recently brought fame and success to the young company. A few words should be said about this naturalism, which was to come under attack not only from Meyerhold but from Stanislavsky himself (which was how the two men came together and established the Studio on Povarskaya Street in 1905).

The techniques of the early MAT are well known. The audience of Treplev's play (in *The Seagull*) casually sitting with their backs to the audience; Astrov swatting mosquitoes in *Uncle Vanya*; the evening half-light in the house of the three sisters; the crackling of logs in the stove; the chirping of a cricket; a single candle-flame; the sounds of the fire; hushed, non-actorish voices, the child's abandoned chair on Ranevskaya's estate – all of this combined to create a powerful sense of the flow of life. Hence, the effect of the so-called 'fourth wall'.

The early MAT revitalised the art of acting, made a cult of the pause, the subtext and the constant interaction of characters. There emerged the concept of the ensemble and a psychological style of acting. The productions of Chekhov at the MAT gave birth to a new Russian audience, shaping its tastes and expectations. This is arguably one of the most important aspects of the theatrical reforms that were initiated by the company.

Chekhov changed the scale of what is called 'an event' in drama. He changed the very object of theatre: instead of 'the drama *in* life' 'the drama *of* life itself' became the focus of his compositions. He deliberately obscured plot, refused to express his own ideas through the dialogues and monologues and coldly distanced himself from his characters, not identifying with any of them. In the words of Pasternak, he inscribed his characters into a landscape and took their words, together with the air in which they were uttered – an impressionist technique. Chekhov gave up teaching and preaching – those main elements of Russian high classical literature. His narrative motifs contain not a single resolution or even a clear explanation. It is impossible to understand *why* the three sisters never got to Moscow or *why* Ranevskaya couldn't save her estate. The most that can be said is: life's like that. His characters arc defined by the 'out-of-joint' world that gave rise to new causes and effects in both life and in drama. Chekhov expressed this change of viewpoint in a brief note: 'Now they shoot themselves because they are sick of life, and so on. Previously, they did it because they had embezzled public money.'

Each of Chekhov's plays at the MAT had a different 'lifespan': the shortest was that of *The Seagull*, which survived for only 63 performances; *Uncle Vanya* was performed 316 times, and *Three Sisters* 229. The one which lived longest was *The Cherry Orchard*, which ran right up to the October Revolution and then was revived in 1928, resulting in a total run of 1,209 performances. The play and the production became a metaphor for 'moving house'. When Olga Knipper-Chekhova decided to leave Russia in autumn 1920, she wrote a letter to Stanislavsky in Moscow. Instead of going into long explanations, she used one of Ranevskaya's lines: 'Life in this house is over.'

The Revolution was to change the approach to Chekhov for many years. Furious attacks by the 'leftists' (in 1920, Mayakovsky wrote that 'Chekhov and Stanislavsky stink'), coincided with fundamental changes in the organisation of the Moscow Art Theatre. Talking to actors in 1919, Stanislavsky stressed the importance of rhythm in Chekhov: 'There was a time when our productions of Chekhov were appallingly bad. Incredibly long pauses, ponderous rhythm, dreary tempo. When we perform

Chekhov like that, we reduce him to the ordinary, to a Chekhov "generalisation".'[2]

But it was the rhythm of history, not of theatre, that had changed. When the Civil War ended in 1922, Stanislavsky and the MAT went on tour to Europe and America. Sitting in his hotel room in Berlin, Stanislavsky wrote back to Moscow saying how difficult it had become for him to play the old Chekhovian characters: 'Acting the scene where Vershinin says goodbye to Masha in *Three Sisters*, my mind is confused. After what we have been through, it is quite impossible to be moved because an officer has to leave and his lady has to stay behind. I am not enjoying Chekhov. On the contrary, I would prefer not to be acting in his plays.'[3] This letter was addressed to Nemirovich-Danchenko, who had stayed in Moscow, keeping an eye on events in the Revolution's new capital. Shortly before the company was due to return from America, Nemirovich-Danchenko sent them a series of warning letters – the main message, according to Nemirovich himself – being *memento mori*:

> I want to shout to them across the ocean: what repertoire?! *Uncle Vanya* is out of the question. *Three Sisters* should not even begin rehearsal, considering the content [in the context of the Civil War, the play was believed to sympathise with the 'officer class'] and the ages of the performers. *The Cherry Orchard* will not be allowed. I mean that they won't allow a play which is seen to lament the lost estates of the gentry. And it won't stand an updated ('welcome new life') treatment. *Ivanov* is completely out of tune with this positive, 'cheerful' epoch.[4]

Those were the specific circumstances which had to be taken into account. The archives contain Nemirovich-Danchenko's note, dated 1925, when, in an effort to respond to the challenge of the times, the MAT staged Trenyov's *The Pugachev's Revolt*. For Nemirovich, the production of this play signified the voluntary rejection of a quarter of a century's accumulated experience. The rejection was categorical: 'It is necessary to exclude from the MAT repertoire . . . works of literature that are unacceptable for the present day (for example, all of Chekhov's plays, at least in their old interpretations).'[5]

The Cherry Orchard was restored to the repertoire in 1928. Yury Sobolev wrote: 'Everything that could be done to somehow freshen up the play was done. This was especially true of the tempo of the first act where there is now much more laughter than before . . . The elegiac mood of the last act was somewhat toned down.'[6] Such 'revisionism' altered the essence of the MAT. Time itself had corrected 'the mood' of *The Cherry Orchard*. Other productions in the thirties (as distinct from the MAT's, of course), placed Lopakhin at the forefront, interpreting him as an entirely 'positive hero' who takes an axe to the cherry orchard. In the late thirties, Nemirovich-Danchenko, by this time without Stanislavsky who had died in 1938, presented a new version of *Three Sisters* which in many ways served as a polemic with the original turn-of-the-century production. In a letter to Maria Knebel,[7] Nemirovich formulated his directorial interpretation and ideas, aimed at dispelling the MAT's acting clichés. Amongst these was the 'exaggerated and distorted use of the device of "the objective" (the style of intensive interaction with a partner which Stanislavsky had invented at the beginning of the century, as a means of overcoming the practice of directly addressing the audience and ignoring one's on-stage partner, which was habitual in the Imperial theatres). Nemirovich went on to criticise 'a drawn-out tempo' (here, as we have seen, he was in agreement with Stanislavsky); 'talking inaudibly to oneself' (for the sake of poorly understood simplicity) and sentimentalism instead of lyricism. In opposition to such clichés, Nemirovich-Danchenko proposed new directorial techniques for Chekhov: a clearly defined 'core' for the production i.e. a new 'super-objective' with a fully understood and sustained subtext, 'robustness', poetry, simplicity and *genuine* theatricality.[8]

In achieving his ends, Nemirovich as director proved to be quite a virtuoso. A new poeticised Chekhov emerged, complete with an avenue of birch trees, and with 'the yearning for a better life' as the firm core of the production. But even this directorial masterpiece was subject to the limitations imposed by its time. Nemirovich ruthlessly cut a number of motifs from the play, the result being that its Chekhovian symphonic quality was lost. Thus, in the final scene he shortened the cynical yet infinitely meaningful line of Chebutykin that prefigured the Theatre of the Absurd: 'If only we knew', and Chebutykin's 'Tarara-boom-deay', lines *not* belonging to two different plays but to the one play by Chekhov with his acute perception of the meaning of life, his harshness and restraint – qualities that were to be in such demand after the Second World War and after the death of Stalin, when a new generation of directors would take over.

In the post-war years, the tradition of Chekhov at the MAT became shallow and meaningless. Michael Kedrov's 1947 production of *Uncle Vanya* (assisted by Litovtseva and Sudakov), was an attempt to interpret the play in the optimistic spirit of Socialist Realism. The only redeeming feature of this well-intentioned but wholly imitative production was the splendid performance of Boris Dobronravov in the title role. Devoid of any ensemble work, it was a mono-play, or solo performance, that threw the theatre back to pre-Chekhovian times.

The most popular of the MAT revivals was *The Seagull*. There was an attempt to make a jubilee production of the play to mark Chekhov's one hundredth birthday in 1960, directed by Stanitsyn and Rayevsky, but it did not stay long in the repertoire. Boris Livanov's 1968 production, on the other hand, ran for many years even though there were really no new ideas in it. Stanislavsky would have described its style as 'ordinary Chekhov'.

Partly as a riposte to Livanov's romantic and 'ordinary, generalised' Chekhov, *The Seagull* was produced in the late sixties at the Sovremennik (Contemporary) Theatre,[9] which had begun as the MAT studio-theatre, and which remained linked to its origins in a strained and fractious polemical relationship. The director was Oleg Yefremov who shortly afterwards became Artistic Director of the MAT, a post he has now occupied for thirty years. For this reason it is worth taking a closer look at his first serious encounter with Chekhov. In his work on *The Seagull*, Yefremov identified certain cunning qualities in this 'inspired and heretical play'. This play can start a theatre – but it can also finish it off. *The Seagull* marked the end of Yefremov's work with the Sovremennik.

The Seagull at the Sovremennik reflected the situation at the end of the sixties when 'The Thaw'[10] came to an end, and when Soviet tanks entered Prague. Chekhov's text, seemingly completely irrelevant to these events, nonetheless responded to them. The death of 'the common ideal' set the tone for the production. Chekhov's text was flooded with all the mutual recriminations, disappointments and hostilities that had accumulated over the previous years. Yefremov turned the author of *The Seagull* into a lampoonist, bored rigid by intellectual conversation and critical of writers and actors who talk a lot and do nothing. Yefremov imparted to *The Seagull* the ideological confusion and despair that typified the late sixties. People had stopped hearing or listening to each other. All they did was strike attitudes, make scenes and squabble. And dig for worms for fishing from the flower-bed that the designer, Sergei Barkhin, had installed in the middle of the stage.

At the MAT Yefremov avoided Chekhov for nearly seven years. Perhaps he was discouraged by the failure of his *Seagull* at the Sovremennik. He returned to him again in 1976 with *Ivanov*.

The play – about human decay – which had been so out of tune with the 'cheerful' epoch of the early twenties, now proved to be exceptionally appropriate to the 'stagnation' of the 1970s. In the MAT production, this stagnation was polarised by using two basic colours, black and white. Hovering in the 'background' are the uncouth and useless young guests in Act Four, called 'cavemen, troglodytes' by Lebedev, attacked by Sasha in Act Two and described by Lvov as: 'Those wretched people. Vultures, birds of prey. They only come to tear each other to bits.' These and the constant motif of the 'gooseberry jam', combined with Misha Borkin's bumptiousness (performed by Vyacheslav Nevinny) – were all meant to counterpoint the lofty confessional tone in which Innokenty Smoktunovsky[11] performed the title role. The situation, with Ivanov's *apparently* unmotivated depression, suddenly revealed its 'long-term' meaning. Such complete emptiness of the soul, the 'disease' which Chekhov rated worse than syphilis or sexual impotence, was presented by Smoktunovsky with frightening lyrical profundity.

This MAT production followed another *Ivanov*, directed by Mark Zakharov at the Lenkom Theatre, with Yevgeny Leonov in the title role. Instead of presenting a 'Russian Hamlet',[12] Leonov made him just an average intellectual, not *the* Ivanov – but *one* Ivanov, 'the million and first', as Alexander Kugel once described him. What was important was the typicality of this remarkable actor; Leonov's human dimension matched that of everyone in the audience. In contrast, Smoktunovsky performed precisely the 'Russian Hamlet', an extraordinary man, of undoubted strength, but sick from the common disease of the times. His Ivanov suffered and agonised, unable to define a place for himself either in life or in the space of the MAT stage. Significantly, it was the arrangement of the space, designed by David Borovsky, that physically conveyed the nature of the disease, the desperate but unsatisfied desire for fulfilment that Smoktunovsky tried to enact. The designer furnished the actor with a bare stage enclosed by the colonnaded facade of the manor-house, with the autumnal garden casting the sombre shadows of its leafless branches on the walls. Thus Ivanov acted in a space that looked devastated, as though pillaged, where he literally could find no place for himself, or even anything to lean on. At first the actor rejected this spatial solution, fearing that in this play about everyday life he would be left exposed, without support or cover. The director insisted and in the end the protagonist's anguish in the empty yet claustrophobic space powerfully conveyed Chekhov's perception of life, which caused him once to observe that in Western Europe, people die because their space is cramped and suffocating, while in Russia they die because the space is an endless expanse, in which a little man has no way of finding his bearings.[13] 'The land looks at me, like an orphan', Chekhov's character repeatedly says – and Smoktunovsky conveyed this feeling with exceptional inner strength.

In this *Ivanov*, his former fellow-student, Lebedev (performed by Andrei Popov) looked guiltily into his eyes, trying to comfort Ivanov and explain the nature of his malaise, mumbling something about the milieu 'eating you up', embarrassed by the banality of his own words and trying to dispel his unease with the inevitable shot of vodka, served unerringly on cue by his manservant. Smoktunovsky conveyed a distinctive spiritual paralysis, caused by a sense of meaninglessness, of eternal emptiness and stagnation.

Those, like Lebedev who can drink, get drunk. Those, like Borkin, who can get carried away by some idiotic project, get carried away. Those, like Count Shabelsky (splendidly performed by Mark Prudkin) who take pleasure in perpetrating some vileness or other, even at their own expense, do so. Ivanov can do none of these things. All he can do – is capitulate. So Ivanov accepts death as deliverance. The only time in the production that he smiled was when the emancipated girl, madly in love with him, attempted to awaken him to a new life by repeating silly words she had read in books. At that moment he somehow became fully aware of the shamefulness of his situation and took his own life. We did not hear the shot. Quite simply, the guests – the 'barbarians' in Lebedev's house, assembled for the wedding breakfast, drew back, and on the floor in the middle of the stage we saw the dead man.

In 1980, ten years after his Sovremennik *Seagull* and four years after *Ivanov*, Yefremov returned to *The Seagull*. As we have seen, in the Sovremennik production, the flower-bed with worms had boldly replaced Chekhov's 'enchanted lake', the trees and even the air that Chekhov's characters breathe. And now, ten years on in his life and in that of the MAT, Yefremov took a fresh look at the play. For the first time in his directorial career, he introduced the concept of transcendent nature which alters the scale of human conflicts. The intellectual debates no longer interested the director but gave way to the drama of life itself. In 1970, *The Seagull* was interpreted as a pamphlet; in 1980, the predominant motif was that of reconciliation, understanding and forgiveness.

The Seagull marked the beginning of Yefremov's long collaboration with the stage designer Valery Levental. He responded to the new attitudes towards life and towards the theatre, which for Yefremov were always indivisible. *The Seagull* was designed by him as a symphony of light, a dance of curtains in a flickering space. Chekhov's characters became part of the landscape, like trees or clouds; they lived amidst nature, dissolved in it and died amidst the beauty of its indifferent world. The main sound effect was the seagull's cry, but it was not so much poetic as oppressive, disturbing, expressing the theme of an endless circling in search of something that might comfort the soul.

For the first time since coming together ten years earlier, the MAT company performed as a perceptible ensemble: Lavrova as Arkadina, Vertinskaya as Nina, Smoktunovsky as Dorn, Andrei Popov as Sorin, Myagkov as Treplev, Nevinny as Shamraev, Kindinov as Medvedenko – these were actors capable of understanding the Chekhov that Yefremov was in the process of rediscovering for himself. There was no lack of opportunities to act. In contrast with the Sovremennik production, at the

MAT Yefremov wanted to make every character heard. He immersed the 'words, words, words' in the glittering foliage. True, these characters of Chekhov were garrulous, so garrulous that they did not even notice someone dying: in this production, Sorin (Andrei Popov). But despite all the disillusion and loss, the motif of faith amidst decay was gaining strength – the kind of faith that is fed not by love or hatred, but by an understanding of the basic reality of life as an insoluble drama.

The director and designer moved the pavilion-theatre downstage – making it a further animated 'character' in the play. This pavilion functioned with a rhythm of its own, at one moment advancing to the very front of the stage, and the next dissolving into the depths of the autumnal park. In this pavilion, the theatre of Kostya Treplev and Nina Zarechnaya came into being. By the end of the play it looked devastated, the wind blowing through the cracks in its walls and ruffling the tattered white curtains. Anastasia Vertinskaya as Nina Zarechnaya repeated Treplev's monologue but this time not as the empty phrases of an apprentice writer. Kostya Treplev's death brought out the *real* meaning of the abstruse lines about the world-soul, people, lions, eagles and partridges. And these lines were spoken not by a provincial girl, but by an 'actress' with a capital 'A' who had walked her path of suffering and reached the source of the symbolic visions. The idea of merging material matter with the spirit achieved a real human dimension. To carry one's cross *and* keep the faith – that was said not only of Nina Zarechnaya.

In an odd way, Chekhov at the Moscow Art Theatre accompanied not only the profound changes at the theatre itself but in Russia as a whole. *Uncle Vanya* was premièred in February 1985 and on 30 April it was seen by the newly elected General Secretary, Mikhail Gorbachev. He saw a Chekhov who, in his own way, summed up the consequences of a 'constrained' life. The motif of creative patience became central. Yefremov did not attempt to turn Uncle Vanya, with his complaint 'I haven't lived', into a hero. (How could he not have lived when by definition his life was in fact itself life?) As Astrov, Yefremov was embedded in the daily trivialities of existence – and struggled to break out. The MAT stage revolved, revealing the interiors of the house. Astrov took to drink and there was a brief respite when his soul became free – and everything around him was turned upside down. The undistinguished Herr Professor Serebryakov (played by Yevgeni Yevstigneyev) continued to tyrannise his wife and indulge his whims, and *then* the storm broke. And as a consequence the confessions came flooding out. One person was drinking, another was praying, rendered helpless by unrequited love, while yet another was suffering from lack of self-fulfilment. And together, they made up all human life. Levental had placed the house upstage against the background of an autumnal landscape in the style of Levitan.[14] When the stage was plunged into darkness, we suddenly noticed through the mist a faint light suspended above the dewy ground. It was a small window in a house on a distant hill. The light shone dimly in the darkness, but it shone invitingly, showing the way. Such was the end of the performance, premièred on the very eve of changes that were to transform not only Russia but the entire world.

On 7 May 1985, Gorbachev telephoned Yefremov to give his reactions to the production, saying that he had liked Astrov and that he had found Uncle Vanya simply heartrending. Then he said how much there was to do, that they should meet to discuss the problems of theatre, and that in general it was time 'to set the fly-wheel in motion'. Could he have imagined then where that fly-wheel would end up? I happened to be in Yefremov's office during this conversation, and Yefremov seemed to be speaking in his usual manner, making no attempt to flatter his caller. After hanging up, he suddenly wiped the sweat from his brow. Seeing my surprise, he smiled guiltily and paraphrasing Chekhov, said: 'You know, it's hard to squeeze the slave out of yourself.'

A later production of Chekhov at MAT was *Three Sisters*. It opened in February 1997 during the preparations for the MAT centennial. It bore all the signs of an attempt at 'summing up'. It was as though Yefremov was replaying all the main themes of his productions of Chekhov, beginning with the fate of 'home' – and ending with the theme of patience and submission to the merciless cycle of life. This time, Levental located the house of the Prozorov sisters in a kind of cosmic sphere which changed colour four times: from the white of spring on Irina's name-day to the sombre blue of winter; from the red suggesting the fire to the rusty colour of the autumnal final act. These symbolic changes of colour reflected the rhythm of life that carries the characters from hope to despair. The closing scene of the three sisters bidding farewell to the departing officers was tragically expressive, and choreographed almost like a ballet. The sisters' arms interwove as they tried to hold together in a circle, but some invisible force drove them apart and broke their embrace.

Yefremov learned Chekhov's most important lesson long ago, one that is now being experienced acutely by the whole of Russia. He grasped his objectivity, his detachment from any ideology, doctrine or political label. The age of ideologies that crushed human beings is receding. And Chekhov now stands revealed to us in all his strange, disquieting profundity.

In contrast with the 1940 production of *Three Sisters*, Yefremov's 1997 version lacks *any* optimism, any signs of poetic exaltation. The strains of

1   Moscow Art Theatre production of *The Three Sisters* at Brooklyn Academy of Music,
     January 1998. Sets and costume by Valery Levental, directed by Oleg Yefremov.

the march as the regiment leaves the town very quickly give way to
Chebutykin's nonsense song. But even his 'Tarara-boom-deay' doesn't
embrace the entire expanse of life. The full stop in this production is not 'If
only we knew', but the dancing image of the vanishing house. This house
that has so stubbornly resisted the change of seasons, retreats upstage,
dissolving in the darkening autumn landscape. The sombre, threatening
music of Scriabin develops and reinforces the mood of departure. It is as
though this play, born at the turn of the century has half anticipated the
latest turn of events. In the play Vershinin philosophises that 'in the past',
mankind was busy with wars, campaigns, raids and victories, 'but now' it
is all gone and there is nothing to fill this vast empty space . . .

   At the end of the twentieth century, Russia finds itself again in this 'vast
empty space'. We are trying to fill it. At this time of spiritual hiatus,
Chekhov is truly a 'constant companion'.

NOTES

1 Letter from V. I. Nemirovich-Danchenko to K. S. Stanislavsky, after 26 July
   1904, from V. I. Nemirovich-Danchenko, *Selected Letters of V. I. Nemirovich-
   Danchenko in Two Volumes*, Moscow, 1979, vol. II, p. 378.

2 K. S. Stanislavsky, *Collected Works of Stanislavsky in 8 Volumes*, Moscow, 1974–82, vol. V, p. 134.

3 Letter from K. S. Stanislavsky to V. I. Nemirovich-Danchenko, October 1923, Berlin, from *Collected Works of Stanislavsky*, vol. VIII, p. 29.

4 From a letter by V. I. Nemirovich-Danchenko to Olga Bokzhanskaya on 9 March 1924, from *Selected Letters of V. I. Nemirovich-Danchenko*, vol. II, p. 304.

5 MAT Museum, Archives of V. I. Nemirovich-Danchenko.

6 See *Chronicles of the Life and Works of Stanislavsky in 8 Volumes*, Izdatelstvo VTO, Moscow, 1973, vol. IV.

7 Maria Knebel (1898–1985), actress, director and teacher. Studied at the Studio of Michael Chekhov in 1918, and then at the Fourth Studio of the MAT. In 1924 she became a member of the MAT Company, with whom she played many roles, and worked on many different productions of the MAT, such as *Kremlin Chimes* and *Difficult Years*. In 1950 she left the MAT to work as director of the Central Children's Theatre. She also taught at GITIS (The Russian State Theatre School). See chapter 15 in this volume: Selected Glossary.

8 Letter from V. I. Nemirovich-Danchenko to Maria Knebel, April 1942. From *Selected Letters of Nemirovich-Danchenko*, vol. II, p. 536.

9 Yefremov worked at the Sovremennik Theatre from 1956 to 1970.

10 'The Thaw' is the term generally used to describe the end of Stalinist terror with Stalin's death in 1953, and the major speech at the 1956 Party Congress by Khrushchev in which he exposed and condemned many of the excesses of Stalinism, and the end of the long winter of Stalin's regime. With the destruction of 'The Prague Spring' in 1968, the period of 'The Thaw' came to an end. 'The Thaw' as a metaphor was first used by Ilya Ehrenburg in his story of that name, published in the magazine *Znamya* in 1954.

11 Innokenty Smoktunovsky is perhaps best known in Western Europe and America for his brilliant performance as Hamlet in Gregori Kozintsev's film of 1965.

12 The theme of 'Hamlet' runs throughout much of nineteenth-century Russian literature, drama and criticism. The use made of Hamlet was of a character incapable of taking any action about anything – whether his own life, or the needs of his society. For a detailed discussion of this major theme, see Ivan Turgenev's essay of 1858, 'Hamlet and Don Quixote'. For another example of Chekhov's (comic) use of the theme other than in *Ivanov*, see the short story 'In Moscow' (1891) or the dramatised version 'A Moscow Hamlet' in *A Chekhov Quartet*, trans. and ed. by Vera Gottlieb, Amsterdam, 1996. Ivanov has his own point to make about himself as 'Hamlet' in Act Two, Scene VI in *Ivanov* – and about himself as Don Quixote in Act Four, Scene IX.

13 See chapter 2, note 4 in this volume. This is an important reiteration of a major theme and perception of Russian life and Russian philosophy, as reflected in literature and drama. See chapter 2 for specific examples in literature.

14 Isaac Levitan (1861–1900), landscape painter and friend of Chekhov's artist brother Nikolai. They shared holidays at Babkino, the estate in the countryside of Moscow Province on which the Chekhovs bought a holiday cottage. Levitan's landscape paintings capture the essence of the Russian countryside, the seasons and country life. It was when out hunting with Levitan that Chekhov may well

have got the idea for *The Seagull*. As he wrote in a letter to his publisher Suvorin, on 8 April 1892 from his estate at Melikhovo: 'Last night we went out shooting. He shot a snipe and the bird, wounded in the wing, fell into a puddle. I picked it up: long beak, big black eyes, and beautiful plumage. It looked astonished. What should we do with it? Levitan frowned, closed his eyes, then begged me in a shaky voice, "My dear friend, hit his head against the gunstock . . ." I said, "I can't." He went on shaking, shrugging his shoulders, his head twitching, and begging me; and the snipe went on looking at us in astonishment. I had to agree with Levitan and kill it. One more beautiful delightful creature less, while two idiots went home and sat down to supper.'

2

CHEKHOV IN PRODUCTION

4

EDWARD BRAUN

From *Platonov* to *Piano*

Unlikely as it might seem today, the appearance in 1923 of a previously unpublished and untitled play by Chekhov seems to have aroused little interest in Russia outside literary circles. However, it is not surprising that it was ignored by the Soviet theatre of that time. Firstly, Chekhov was about the last dramatist likely to excite the new revolutionary avant-garde. Secondly, the Moscow Art Theatre was still in the grip of the artistic paralysis to which it had been reduced by the events of 1917, and seventeen more years were to elapse before it staged a new production of Chekhov. Finally, the prospect of a ramshackle text almost three times the length of any other Chekhov play would have deterred most theatres even at the best of times. In fact, it was not until 1957 that the work received its Russian première, though by that time it had been staged around the world in various versions and under a curious variety of titles.

In 1933 the text was included in the edition of Chekhov's works published by the Soviet State Publishing House for Literature, this time under the ponderous title *Fatherlessness (Bezotsovshchina)*. The evidence suggests that this play, which we now know as *Platonov*, is in large part the same as the one that Chekhov, still a schoolboy of eighteen in his home town of Taganrog, first drafted in 1878 and reworked extensively over the next three years, only to abandon it following its rejection by the Maly Theatre in Moscow.[1]

The action of *Platonov* takes place in early summer on a country estate 'in one of the Southern provinces' of Russia. Owned by Anna Petrovna, the beautiful young widow of General Voinitsev, the estate is the centre for every local intrigue, both romantic and financial. Irretrievably in debt to a string of local landowners and businessmen, Anna retains nothing but an inherited coal mine as security and the only solution to her predicament seems to be marriage to the wealthy but aging Porfiry Glagoliev or else becoming the kept woman of his odious son. However, confident that Glagoliev senior is certain to buy the estate and allow her to continue living there on credit, she renews her attempts to seduce Mikhail Platonov, an impoverished landowner and now at twenty-seven the village schoolmaster. Disgusted by her immorality, Glagoliev departs with his son for a life of debauchery in Paris, and in the final act it transpires that the estate has been bought at auction by the Jewish businessman Vengerovich, who plans to evict Anna Petrovna by Christmas, along with her idle stepson Sergei and his recently wedded wife Sofya. Earlier in the play, Platonov has first welcomed Anna's advances but then embarks on a passionate affair with Sofya, his sweetheart from their student days, and plans to run away with her, abandoning his young wife Sasha and their infant son. For her part, Anna Petrovna has in the past flirted briefly with Osip, 'horse-thief, parasite, murderer, burglar' (Hingley, *The Oxford Chekhov*, vol II, p. 41),[2] who now in a fit of jealousy makes a botched attempt at knifing Platonov. Prior to this, in the climax to Act Three Osip rescues Sasha from under the wheels of a train when she tries to commit suicide. In the final act we learn first that Osip himself has been lynched by a crowd of villagers, and then that Sasha has again narrowly failed to take her own life. Injured from Osip's assault and in a state of delirium from incessant drinking, Platonov is on the verge of shooting himself, but his courage fails him and instead he decides to seduce Maria Grekova, a serious-minded young chemistry student whom he has previously humiliated in public, thereby goading her to sue him for assault. Now, however, she confesses her love for him, whereupon Sofya enters, seizes his revolver and kills him.

Even allowing for Chekhov's numerous cuts, the original text would run for at least five hours and has twenty speaking parts, compared with fourteen in *Three Sisters* and only eight in *Uncle Vanya*. In *Platonov*, as in his next two full-length plays, *Ivanov* and *The Wood-Demon*, Chekhov follows the general nineteenth-century practice of subdividing acts into scenes to mark the characters' exits and entrances. But this is no mere matter of convention: the fact that the play contains no fewer than eighty-three scenes (hence eighty-three exits or entrances) is a measure of its frenetic tempo and incessant melodramatic confrontations – a far cry from the flow and texture of everyday life that Chekhov was to achieve to such unique effect in his later plays.[3]

Theatrical excess is least in evidence in the first act. As Anna Petrovna's guests gradually assemble for a lunch that signals the beginning of the summer's social round, Chekhov uses introductions and reunions with familiar deftness to acquaint his audience with the established pattern of relationships and to set up the conflicts that are to follow. Twice Platonov threatens the conviviality of the gathering, first by reducing the insecure young Maria to tears with his persistent teasing, and next by gratuitously trading insults with the rapacious Vengerovich, owner of sixty-three taverns. Both incidents abruptly raise the dramatic temperature, but neither seems dramatically contrived since they arise out of some obscure destructive urge within Platonov and clearly are only the latest in a series of incidents that he has provoked. Also, it is clear that by the time Platonov confronts Vengerovich he has been deeply disconcerted by his reunion with Sofya, the one true love of his life from the days when she saw him as 'a second Byron', before he dropped out of university and became 'a mere schoolmaster'. Twice in this act, and frequently through the rest of the play, Chekhov resorts to brief soliloquies, but this was a device that he continued to employ repeatedly, often at greater length, until *Three Sisters* when he finally eliminated it by using the old caretaker Ferapont as the deaf and uncomprehending audience for Andrei's bitter outpourings.

In Act Two, Part One, the same company is assembled in the garden for a nocturnal fireworks party. The unfolding intrigues are skilfully interwoven with the ebb and flow of guests, whilst the off-stage action is suggested by the noises of a game of skittles and piano and violin music. The whole scene is illuminated with festive lanterns and reaches its climax with the exploding of fireworks as Sofya resolves to yield to Platonov. By contrast, Part Two, which takes place some hours later by a railway line in the forest outside Platonov's schoolhouse, is a more obviously contrived sequence of dualogues, beginning with Osip telling Sasha about his passion for Anna Petrovna in what is virtually a self-contained short story, and culminating in a scene of pure melodrama when Osip pulls Sasha to safety as the train screeches past. In between, Chekhov resorts to a range of stock devices: concealments behind trees, eavesdropping, frantic soliloquies, comic drunken interludes – even the familiar letter of assignation, delivered by Sofya's maid.

Act Three, set in the schoolroom three weeks later, opens with Platonov drunk and dishevelled, having been abandoned by Sasha. The sequence of one-to-one confrontations resumes, but gains variety from a drinking bout between Platonov and Anna which Chekhov contrives to make both farcical and tender, and an hilarious rough and tumble from which Osip, the most deferential of assassins, readily desists as soon as Sasha returns. Osip's own dispatch the next day in Act Four is accomplished by the young Chekhov with insouciant brevity:

SCENE III

[ANNA *comes in and looks out of the window*]

SERGEI [*with a gesture of despair*]. This is the absolute end! [*Pause.*] What's going on out there?

ANNA   Osip's been lynched by the villagers.
SERGEI Already?
ANNA   Yes, near the well. Do you see? There he is.
SERGEI [*Looks out of the window*]. Well, it serves him right. [*Pause*.]
ANNA   Heard the news, dear? They say Platonov's made himself scarce . . .

(Hingley, p. 140)

Apart from one passing reference this is the last we hear of Osip, but the other tangles in the plot take rather more unravelling as the denouement gets further complicated, first by the news of Sasha's second suicide attempt (this time by swallowing matches), and then by Maria entering the competition for Platonov's favours. With Platonov increasingly delirious from alcohol abuse, seeing toy soldiers with pointed caps and a tiny piano crawling over Anna's breast, the mood of hysteria intensifies, reaching its climax of black farce in the final scene when Sofya rummages in a drawer to find a revolver, first fires at Platonov and misses, then evades Maria's attempts to shield him and shoots him point-blank in the chest. Amidst the grief and confusion it is Triletsky who pronounces Platonov's epitaph: 'Life's only worth a copeck. Goodbye, Michael, you've lost your copeck. What are you all goggling at? He shot himself. The party's over. [*Weeps*.] Who can I celebrate your funeral with? Fools! You couldn't look after Platonov.' (Hingley, p. 162)

Unsurprisingly, many critics have seen little more in *Platonov* than the adumbration of themes and characters that Chekhov was to return to in his mature plays and short stories. Not all have been as dismissive as F. L. Lucas who saw it as simply 'chaotic, unconvincing and tedious'[4] or Laurence Senelick, who called it a 'protracted piece of juvenilia'.[5] Michael Frayn, in a perceptive introduction to *Wild Honey*, his own reworking of the play, acknowledges all its obvious defects yet describes it as 'a remarkable and tantalising work' possessing 'precocious and inimitable virtues' (Frayn, p. viii). Kenneth Tynan was even more enthusiastic in his review of the London première in 1960: 'If anyone still lives who needs proof of Chekhov's genius, let him go and see *Platonov* . . . It makes a singular impression; as if a Russian novel of country life had been dramatized by Georges Feydeau and then handed over to Chekhov for total rewriting . . .'[6] In perhaps the most penetrating analysis of all, Mikhail Gromov writes: 'The play was put together with a profligacy that was inexcusable, and conceivable only in the writer's youth. At one and the same time it is a drama, a comedy and a vaudeville; or more accurately, it is not any one of these three. But that said, it is chaotic in a way that bore a remarkable resemblance to the reality of Russian life.'[7]

What Gromov identifies is the profound sense in which the mood of the play and, in particular, that of its central character, reflects the state of post-emancipation Russia in the 1880s. Glagoliev senior says as much to Anna Petrovna early in Act One:

> Well – I think Platonov's a superb example of modern vagueness. He's the hero of our best modern novel, one that hasn't yet been written, I'm sorry to say. [*Laughs.*] Vagueness seems to me typical of modern society, and your Russian novelist senses it. He's baffled and bewildered, he has nothing to hold on to, he doesn't understand . . . Everything's so vague and blurred – it's one great chaotic mess. And it's this vagueness which the sagacious Platonov typifies, I think. (Hingley, p. 21)

One major reason for this 'vagueness', this loss of direction, is suggested by the play's original title, *Fatherlessness*. With the sole exception of Isaac Vengerovich (a Jew, and hence an outsider), the entire younger generation treats the depravity and materialism of their elders with feelings that range from embarrassment to outrage. In the depths of drunken self-disgust, Platonov rails at his late parents: 'Depraved, drunken fools – always drunk, the mother a fool, the father a drunk. Father, mother -. Father -. Rot in your graves for the rotten mess you made of my poor life with your drunken folly' (Hingley, p. 105). What the play is trying to convey, though, is a picture of a whole way of life in terminal decline. As the Soviet critic Berkovsky has written, '*Platonov* depicts the collapse of the country estate, the decline of the gentry, overblown, extravagant, abundant in scandals and excess. And here, the end of the gentry is intertwined with the end of a whole age: *Platonov* is an attempt to write an extended epitaph to the nineteenth century in whose closing years it was written.'[8]

Berkovsky further observes that Platonov himself was an exceptional phenomenon: 'In everyday life, in the literature of the populists and their like-minded contemporaries, the village schoolmaster was regarded as an exemplary individual, the servant of what was good and true. In the schoolmaster Platonov there is nothing at all schoolmasterly. One doesn't really believe that he is capable of teaching anyone anything, be it handwriting or arithmetic.'[9] When he is not engaged in fits of self-loathing, the one thing that engages his still-sharp intellect is the denunciation of others, and what brings him to the point of suicide is the realisation that he is no better than they are. He is often described as a rural Don Juan, but this is to ignore the fact that it is the women who, one after another, throw themselves heedlessly at him. As Gromov points out, Chekhov never sought any explanation for love, but simply accepted its irrationality. In *Platonov* the fact that a drunken, boorish, inconstant nonentity is the object of four attractive women's desire is indicative both of the singular charmlessness of all other available partners and of the absurdity of the world they live in.

In 1928, five years after its publication, *Platonov* was given its world première in Gera, south-east Germany, in a version by René Fülop-Miller entitled *Der unnützige Mensch Platonoff* (*That Useless Person Platonov*). The following January this version was performed in Prague, first in German and then in Czech. Productions in Turin, Milan and Rome followed, then in 1940 the Provincetown Playhouse, Massachusetts, presented the first performance of the play in English, transmogrified into *Fireworks on the James*. It was first staged in French as *Ce fou de Platonov* on 17 May 1956 at the Bordeaux Festival, with Jean Vilar playing the title role in his own production with the Théâtre National Populaire. Finally, in 1957 the play was given its Russian première as *Platonov* at the Pushkin Theatre in Pskov. The critic of the Moscow journal *Teatr* was withering in her scorn for the production and could find no justification for staging the play at all. Nevertheless, it was revived in 1960 at the Vakhtangov Theatre in Moscow to mark the centenary of Chekhov's birth. Using an abridged version with the part of Maria Grekova cut completely, Alexandra Remizova's inventive production emphasised the play's comic aspects and was enthusiastically received by the public. Again, though, the critics were unconvinced that it was worth exhuming from the pre-history of Chekhovian drama: 'It's not even Antosha Chekhonte, let alone Chekhov', concluded Marianna Stroeva.[10]

Platonov was published in London in 1952 in an abridged version by Basil Ashmore called *Don Juan (in the Russian Manner)* in which, strangely, Anna Petrovna becomes a countess and Platonov is not shot but dies from his illness. It was this version that was used for the British première in 1959 at the Nottingham Playhouse, directed by Val May with Robert Lang as Platonov.[11] The play was first seen in London at the Royal Court Theatre on 13 October 1960, directed by George Devine and John Blatchley. For this production Dmitri Makaroff's translation was heavily cut to a running time of three hours, with Glagoliev junior discarded but a village priest added. With Rex Harrison as Platonov and Rachel Roberts as Anna Petrovna, the production was one of the hits of the season, playing to 91 per cent capacity for 44 performances. Unlike Kenneth Tynan, most critics were thrown into confusion by the production. Milton Shulman described it as 'an outrageous burlesque . . . with as much resemblance to Chekhov as *Sweeney Todd*', whilst others complained that it failed to guide the spectator into 'a stable emotional position'. In his biography of George Devine, Irving Wardle recalls: '*Platonov* was not the most polished of shows, but its supreme virtue was that it did avoid fixed emotional positions. In place of the expected journey through the flat Chekhovian landscape, it substituted an exhilarating switchback ride between the extremes of melodramatic hysteria and broad farce.'[12]

The next major British revival was in 1984 when the National Theatre staged Christopher Morahan's production of a new version by Michael Frayn entitled *Wild Honey* with a cast that included Ian McKellen as Platonov and Charlotte Cornwell as Anna Petrovna. Having rejected all the previous titles because of their suggestion that the action centres exclusively on the one character, Frayn explains his own choice:

> The best title to date seems to me Alex Szogyi's *A Country Scandal* [New York, 1960]. But Chekhov himself has provided an even better one in the text. The play covers the period of the Voynitzevs' honeymoon (and its catastrophic end). Anna Petrovna refers to it in a phrase that seems to include all the various sexual intrigues – 'a month of wild honey' (in the original 'a month smeared with wild honey'). This seems to me to evoke precisely both the wayward sweetness of forbidden sexual attraction, and the intense feeling of summer that pervades the play. (Frayn, p. xiv)

To Frayn, Anna Petrovna is a no less remarkable creation than Platonov:

> She is a most surprising character to find in a nineteenth-century play. There are plenty of heroines at the time who inspire erotic feelings in men (and who usually end up dead or disfigured for their pains) . . . But where else is there one who is permitted to express such shining physical desire, and to remain – though punished, it is true, by the loss of her estate – essentially unhumiliated? (Frayn, p. viii)

Whilst Anna Petrovna is without precedent, she initiates a sequence of self-assertive women in Chekhov's plays which includes Arkadina, Masha, Natasha and Lyubov Andreevna. However, none of these pursues the object of her desire with quite the same frank sexual intent or freedom from guilt, and none shares Anna's acute awareness of her plight as an educated woman with no occupation.

Starting from the assumption that Chekhov's text was a rough draft rather than a finished play, Frayn undertook a far more radical revision than any of his predecessors, preserving the main characters but giving the action a much more tightly focussed dramatic shape. Whole sub-plots are removed, the sequence of scenes is reorganised, and the number of characters is reduced from twenty to sixteen, with elements of Vengerovich senior, Bugrov and Shcherbuk incorporated in Glagoliev senior and Petrin. A frequent target for criticism in the original text have been the apparently uncontrolled lurches from one mood to another, and this is something that Frayn addresses, though without sacrificing the essential elements of farce.

In his introduction he writes 'I have tried to resolve the tone of the play by reducing the melodrama and the editorialising, and by moving from lighter comedy at the beginning, through farce, to the darker and more painful comedy of the final scenes.' (Frayn, p. xiv). Frayn's conclusion is set in the schoolhouse and is, if anything, even blacker farce than the original, with both Sofya and Anna vying to shoot Platonov as Maria shields him and Sasha begs them to kill her instead. He eludes them all by jumping through the window, but as they pursue him into the darkness:

> *He steps onto the railway line and runs in the opposite direction – downstage – glancing back over his shoulder at them like a fugitive. Then he stops, blinded by the brilliant headlight of the train approaching from behind the heads of the audience, its whistle screaming. He staggers back a step or two, trying to wave the train away like the flies. Then sudden blackness, and the great roar of the train, its note falling as it passes us. The red tail light of the train appears at the front of the stage and dwindles rapidly into the smoke left by the locomotive. There is a smell of sulphur in the air. Curtain.*

(Frayn, p. 104)

Thus, the fate from which the blameless Sasha has been snatched at the end of Act Two finally claims Platonov himself. The credit for its invention is entirely Frayn's, but mostly the work that he did involved cutting and reorganising the original material, creating a tightly structured text that stands comparison with *Ivanov* and *The Seagull*, if not with Chekhov's mature works. Writing in *The Guardian*, Michael Billington described it as 'a brilliant piece of theatre bearing the stigmata of genius', whilst in *The Observer* Michael Ratcliffe said: 'The effect is of an old clock completely taken apart and given a new movement. It is still Chekhov, but it is also Frayn.'[13] Opening on 19 July 1984, *Wild Honey* ran in the National Theatre's repertoire in the Lyttelton Theatre until 17 August the following year.

Since the early days of the silent cinema Chekhov has regularly attracted the attention of Russian film-makers, although it has been the short stories with their laconic narrative style and their arresting imagery that have yielded the most amenable material, the finest example being Joseph Heifetz's *The Lady with the Little Dog* (1959). However, as Mikhail Gromov suggests, if *Platonov* is widely known today it is thanks largely to the film version by Alexander Adabashian and Nikita Mikhalkov, directed by Mikhalkov and released by Mosfilm in 1976 as *An Unfinished Piece for Mechanical Piano*. Taking its title from a random idea in one of Chekhov's notebooks, the screenplay dispenses with all the melodramatic elements of the original to achieve a far more compressed narrative set entirely in the Voinitsev country house and its wooded surroundings, and running from afternoon to sunrise the next day. All the sub-plots are discarded: Maria Grekova, Osip and Vengerovich senior are cut; there are no suicide attempts by Sasha; Platonov's affair with Sofya is never consummated; and Petrin continues his benevolent underwriting of the estate, with no threat of eviction.

On the other hand, the late general's drinking partner, Shcherbuk, has two spinster daughters (restored from an early draft of the original text) and a young nephew, Petya. There is also a poignant scene in the middle of the dinner party when Gorokhov, a clerk from a nearby factory, appears and entreats the carousing Dr Triletsky to visit his sick wife, only to be fobbed off with a vague promise of 'tomorrow, or the day after without fail'. Though adapted from a scene in the original play when the drunken Triletsky refuses to tend Glagoliev, the episode could easily be one of Chekhov's short stories. Similarly, Platonov tells the assembled company a story that he says he 'read recently' but which is really a barely concealed account of his youthful love affair with Sofya. In fact, several of the actual stories furnish ideas and snatches of dialogue for the film scenario, notably 'The Russian Master', 'Three Years', 'My Life' and 'At a Country House', from which the character of the ultra-reactionary Shcherbuk is largely taken.

The overall result is a fluid narrative which captures the languorous passage of high summer, close in style to the late plays with their seamless interweaving of the inconsequential and the dramatic. As Alexander Svobodin observes, the action is punctuated with a number of 'refrains'.[14] There are repeated long-shots of the resentful manservant Yakov vainly trying to fish a chair out of a pond where some feckless master or mistress has dumped it. At intervals, the idle chatter of Anna Petrovna's guests is interrupted by the loud snoring of Triletsky senior. We see the small figure of Petya, in tranquil contrast to the posturing grown-ups, happily roaming the countryside and finally in carefree slumber. Thus, a sense of continuity, of life repeating itself, is established, retarding the film's tempo and ironically counterpointing the absurdity of the tragi-comic collisions.

The first half of the film reaches its climax when Anna Petrovna summons her guests to the terrace to marvel at the young peasant Zakhar effortlessly playing Chopin on a piano transported in for the occasion regardless of cost. As they gape in incredulity, she orders the young virtuoso to lift his hands from the keyboard, whereupon the piano is revealed as 'mechanical', a pianola which continues to play of its own accord. To Platonov's embarrassed scorn Sasha faints with shock, whilst Shcherbuk splutters with relief, confirmed in his assertion that no 'filthy peasant' could ever achieve such artistry – only to be coolly reminded by

Petrin that he, a mere filthy peasant, is underwriting the estate and all its guests' frivolities.

The closing sequence could not be further removed from the original text, but owes more than a little to the tragi-comic anti-climax of Act Three of *Uncle Vanya*, and even more to Sonya's radiant words of consolation to the unhappy Vanya at the play's conclusion. In despair and self-loathing Platonov attempts suicide by plunging headlong into the river below the house – only to find himself barely knee-deep in water and in the all-forgiving embrace of Sasha, who says: 'Mishenka, you're tired, you must rest and then we'll be happy again! And we shall live for a long, long time . . . and we shall be lucky . . . and we shall see a bright, new, pure life, and fine new people who will understand and forgive us. Only we must love, love, Mishenka! As long as we love, we shall live for a long, long time and be happy . . .'[15] As the remaining guests come down the hill and help Platonov and Sasha from the river we see the landscape still moist from yesterday's rain, glistening in the first rays of the sun, and hear a steamer hooting on the river, peasants singing in the fields on the far bank.

Admiring the teasingly open endings of Chekhov's short stories, Mikhalkov argues that in his very ordinariness Platonov does not merit a violently melodramatic death, whereas

> Sasha is the only one in our film who understands what her life is for and why she has to go on living . . . Of course, love is not the panacea for all suffering and misfortune. At this particular moment it acts as a stimulus. I don't know if it will be permanent, even if it will last for long . . . I wanted to end the picture on an upbeat, not because it's more comforting that way, but because it's something quite inherent in the nature and history of Russian art – faith, hope, love.[16]

Yet the closing shot of the film, of Petya in oblivious slumber, his slender back golden in the sun's rays, restores ironic perspective to the petty squabbling of the adult world, leaving the conclusion open to the viewer's interpretation.

In 1990 *Platonov* underwent yet another metamorphosis when Trevor Griffiths reworked Mikhalkov and Adabashian's screenplay as a 'theatrical mediation' entitled *Piano*, which was directed by Howard Davies and presented in the Royal National Theatre's Cottesloe auditorium on 8 August. In his preface to the published text Griffiths explains its relationship to the source material:

> The Russian film-makers, whether out of respect or simple unconcern, have allowed me to plunder their own piece in order to find my own; and I'm truly grateful for the generous space they've afforded me. If I call *Piano* a new play,

then it is in part because I have no right to saddle them (or indeed Chekhov) with the piece I've finally fashioned. For while in respect of character, relationship, incident and dramatic terrain, *Piano* draws heavily on these several ur-works, there is yet within it, at the level of tone, language, form, means and intentions something other than what they have sought to say, for which I must both claim and accept full responsibility.[17]

Amplifying this 'something other', he quotes Raymond Williams' definition of nineteenth-century realism from his *Modern Tragedy* (1966):

it was a way of seeing the world in which it was possible to experience the quality of a whole way of life through the qualities of individual men and women. Thus, a personal breakdown was a genuine social fact, and a social breakdown was lived and known in direct personal experience . . . Chekhov is the realist of breakdown, on a significantly total scale.[18]

This sense of breakdown, both personal and social, is conveyed in Chekhov's original text through the overall mood of moral disintegration and, most acutely, through the bitter inter-generational hostilities. Mikhalkov reinforces the impression of social breakdown by stripping away some of the distracting erotic entanglements, by introducing the Gorokhov episode, by stressing the banality of Sergei and Sofya's plans to 'improve' the lot of the peasantry, and by strengthening the Petrin–Shcherbuk antithesis. Griffiths retains these elements and follows the film's main story-line, whilst creating a *mise en scène* that translates the poetry and the incongruity of the original into vivid stage imagery. Thus, instead of vainly trying to fish a chair from a pond, Yasha rescues a mysteriously abandoned corset from a tree, carrying it indoors on the tip of a *'pole held like a lance'* (Griffiths, p. 8); as the fireworks display starts in Act Two, *'The first of a series of brilliant flare-like explosions convulsing their settled world order. Sophia moves quickly through empty space, a lamp in her hand, spectral in the weird off-white glow. Platonov appears in her wake: he wears a long off-white open burberry, mid-calf, like a Long Rider's coat'* (Griffiths, p. 45); when Glagoliev proposes to Anna, *'Another flare washes the terrace. Anna sits in a chair, legs crossed, foot swinging softly forward and back. Porfiry kneels on one knee before her, head slightly bowed, eyes fixed on the swinging ankle-boot, rabbit to snake'* (Griffiths, p. 47). Platonov's botched suicide attempt is sublime tragi-comedy:

He climbs out, ready to leap. Black. Light up. Sashenka appears on the bridge almost at once. A deep thudding splash below. She stares down in almost comical horror, fingers stuffed in her mouth. Rushes from the bridge. A slow salmony blush begins to colour the space. Silence. A figure slowly rises, down *below: Platonov, drenched to the skin, fetlock deep in shallow water. He stares hopelessly at the heavens.*

PLATONOV   You make it hard, Lord. Really.   (Griffiths, p. 54)

Elsewhere, there are significant changes to the screenplay. The date of the action is advanced to the early summer of 1904, capturing 'that eerie, humid moment which precedes the storm of disintegration and defeat'.[19] Petrin provides two coordinates for the date, in Act Two by reading from his newspaper a report of the strike of all two thousand workers at the Putilov plant in Moscow, then at the final curtain by reporting the death on 15 July of 'the playwright Anton Chekhov' at the Black Forest Spa of Badenweiler, quoting his last words: 'It's a long time since I drank champagne.'

Consistent with this historical repositioning is the far greater prominence given to the 'lower orders', correcting what Griffiths perceives as a surprising imbalance in the dramatic works: 'It's amazing how few peasants there are in Chekhov's plays when they bubble all through his stories.'[20] Like Mikhalkov, he rejects the maverick figure of the horse-thief Osip, but gives a crucial role to Radish, a character derived from the house painter of the same name in the story 'My Life' (1896).[21] Radish, 'gaunt and cropped', is first seen with the younger Zakhar in the opening scene, manoeuvring a massive wrapped object (later revealed as the pianola) across a narrow plank bridge. As they pause for breath Radish retells the story of his earlier life as a painter, a story of exploitation, physical abuse, wrongful arrest and ultimately four years' penal servitude, during which he learned reading, writing and 'thinking', which has to be learned 'Like making bombs. And laying them' (Griffiths, p. 3). The scene ends with Zakhar asking Radish what he believes in. He replies: 'Believe in, maybe not. But there are things I know . . . Grass dies. Iron rusts. Lies eat the soul. Everything's possible' (Griffiths, p. 4). At the play's conclusion Radish and Zakhar are seen once more on the bridge, 'looking down on the spectres below'. As Anna vainly reassures her guests that 'everything will be as it was', Radish echoes his words from the opening scene, ending with 'Everything's possible.' This time, however, Petya is with them on the bridge, a bright young hope for the future, more Gorky than Chekhov.

As well as positioning *Piano* at a specific historical conjuncture, Griffiths was equally concerned to give the play a contemporary resonance; referring to Williams' definition of Chekhov as 'the realist of breakdown' he writes: 'Should *Piano* prove to be about anything at all, I suspect it may prove, like its illustrious forebears, to be about just this felt sense of breakdown and deadlock; and thus perhaps, in a nicely perverse irony, about what it's like to be living in our own post-capitalist, post-socialist, post-realist, post-modern times.'[22] Rather as he had done previously in his version of *The Cherry Orchard*,[23] Griffiths employs judiciously planted neologisms in order 'to arch the play disconcertingly forward from time to time into the audience's lap'.[24]

Notwithstanding Irving Wardle's complaint that '[Griffiths] has transformed a tragi-comedy into a vindictive class-war fable',[25] the great majority of critics responded enthusiastically to the play and to Howard Davies' fluidly orchestrated production. The most penetrating of them, John Peter wrote:

> *Platonov* was a portrait of its own time, whereas, in *Piano*, Griffiths looks back on turn-of-the-century Russia from the vantage point of history. The difference is like that between a diagnosis and a case-history compiled after the patient's death . . . This play is much more than a pastiche: it is a homage to Chekhov and to Russia, and it is animated by the black, clownish humour of the transcendental, surrealist jokers who light up Russian literature from Gogol and Dostoyevsky to Chekhov and Nabokov.[26]

An Unfinished Piece for Mechanical Piano won the Golden Shell award for best film at the 1977 San Sebastian film festival; *Wild Honey* has been revived since 1984 in places as far apart as Israel, Belgium, Scandinavia, South Africa, Australia and New Zealand; there have been recent productions of *Piano* in Germany and Japan. In July 1997 the remarkable St Petersburg Maly Theatre under Lev Dodin presented a version of *Platonov* (called '*A Play without a Title*') in Weimar which left much of the original text intact and had a running time of four hours. Together, these productions reaffirm the continuing inspiration of Chekhov's original conception: its erratically grotesque dramaturgy, its psychological acuity and, above all, its prescient sensing of a crucial turning point in Russian history.

NOTES

1 See Mikhail Gromov, *Kniga o Chekhove*, Moscow, 1989, pp. 49–58; also Michael Frayn, *Wild Honey*, London and New York, 1985, pp. vii–xviii.
2 The play-texts from which page numbers are quoted in the text are: *Platonov* in Ronald Hingley, trans. and ed., *The Oxford Chekhov*, vol.ii, London, 1967; Michael Frayn, *Wild Honey*, 1985; Trevor Griffiths, *Piano*, London, 1990. Subsequently referred to as Hingley, Frayn and Griffiths.
3 It is true that not until *The Cherry Orchard* did Chekhov succeed finally in eliminating the gunshot from his plays (whilst parodying it with Yepikhodov's threat of suicide in Act Two), but in *Platonov* there are two murder attempts, the second successful, two failed suicides with a third contemplated, and a lynching (albeit offstage).

4 F. L. Lucas, *The Drama of Chekhov, Synge, Yeats and Pirandello*, London, 1963, p. 23.
5 Laurence Senelick, *Anton Chekhov*, Basingstoke and London, 1985, p. 30.
6 Kenneth Tynan, *Tynan Right and Left*, London, 1967, p. 39.
7 Mikhail Gromov, *Kniga o Chekhove*, p. 56.
8 N. Berkovskii, 'Chekhov. Ot rasskazov i povestei k dramaturgii (okonchanie)', *Russkaya literatura*, 1, 1966, p. 15.
9 *Ibid.*, p. 16.
10 Quoted in *Kniga o Chekhove*, pp. 58–59.
11 For a brief review see *Plays and Players*, May 1959, p. 32.
12 For an account of the production and its critical reception see Irving Wardle, *The Theatres of George Devine*, London, 1978, pp. 220–224.
13 Quoted in Frayn, p. i.
14 'Volny Chekhov', *Iskusstvo kino* 10, 1977, p. 125.
15 Unpublished screenplay '*Mekhanicheskoe pianino*', pp. 97–8.
16 Nikita Mikhalkov, 'Moy Chekhov' in *Mosfilm VIII: Razmyshleniya o filmakh*, Moscow, 1980, pp. 107, 132.
17 Author's Preface to *Piano*, London, 1990. Unnumbered.
18 Raymond Williams, *Modern Tragedy*, London, 1966, p. 139.
19 John Peter, 'Eavesdropping on a Doom-laden Past', in *The Sunday Times*, 12 August 1990.
20 Quoted in the National Theatre programme for *Piano*, p. 4.
21 'Red'ka' in the original. See Appendix 1.
22 Preface to *Piano*.
23 First performed at the Nottingham Playhouse, 10 March 1977, directed by Richard Eyre. See Appendix 2.
24 Letter to Edward Braun, 30 July 1990. Examples include: 'you miserable bag of snot, I'll smash your face in'; 'there's female liberation for you'; 'don't be so bourgeois'; 'spare me the bloody sermon'; 'I don't give a weasel's tosser what you think of me'.
25 'Chekhov Stolen from Himself', in *The Independent on Sunday*, 12 August 1990.
26 *The Sunday Times*, 12 August 1990.

5

VERA GOTTLIEB

Chekhov's one-act plays and the full-length plays

There is a paradox about Chekhov's one-act plays: although performed as frequently as Pinter's short plays, or Beckett's – and given the much longer period of time since their creation – much less has actually been written about them.

This may be due to Chekhov's own dismissive estimation of them as 'amusing trifles', and because critics have tended to concentrate on his major works. There is, however, a marked correlation between the one-act plays and the major plays (and equally some of the short stories). This relates to the use of comic techniques, to the inversion of 'stock' conventions, to his characterisation, and the extent to which action arises from character, rather than plot. It is in some of the short plays that one may see the *absence* of plot, and the developing use of action which, characteristically Chekhovian, is motivated by internal – and often subtextual – characterisation and dialogue. The short plays require redefinition within the context of the theatrical conventions of the time *and* as a major and serious part of Chekhov's achievement.

Chekhov does not make the case easy for anyone wishing to demonstrate that these plays *are* important, and more than merely 'amusing trifles'. Again and again he dismisses them, as in a letter of 22 February 1888 to the poet Yakov Polonsky: 'Having nothing better to do, I wrote a silly little French vaudeville under the title *The Bear*.'[1] Similarly, Nemirovich-Danchenko wrote that: 'Chekhov often advised me to write vaudevilles . . . because they were sure to bring me in a good income.'[2] It seemed that for Chekhov they were the theatrical equivalent of the comic short stories he dashed off for different papers and journals – and which did, in fact, bring in an income. In his lifetime, he earned more from the frequently performed short plays than the much misunderstood full-length plays, although this was partly because of the custom of 'benefit nights' – performances to aid particular actors (such as the one Svetlovidov has just completed when *Swan Song* begins). Chekhov in fact dedicated *The Bear* to the great

Russian comic actor, Solovtsov, and the play was often performed as a 'benefit play' or – like most of the others – a curtain-raiser.

The evidence demonstrates, however, that Chekhov disparaged the short plays no more than he did all of his work, and it is also significant that they were written over exactly the same period as the great plays – starting with *On the High Road* in 1885, and finishing with the last of *six* versions of *On the Harmfulness of Tobacco* (sometimes translated as *Smoking is Bad for You*) in the same year as *Three Sisters* – 1903. The fact that he *did* rewrite that play six times suggests a far more serious intention in using the vaudeville form, and with each version, the play becomes less exaggerated – and more serious. He makes the point himself in a letter to Suvorin after he had written all of the short plays with the exception of the final version of *On the Harmfulness of Tobacco*: 'It is much easier to write a play about Socrates than about a cook, which merely demonstrates that I do not regard the writing of vaudevilles as a frivolous occupation. Nor do you consider it as such, much as you may pretend that it is nothing but a lot of frivolous nonsense.'[3]

In common with the full-length plays, most of what Chekhov described as 'vaudevilles' have a subtitle. Just as *Uncle Vanya* is subtitled *Scenes from Country Life*, so *Swan Song* is called *A Dramatic Study in One Act*, as indeed is *Tatyana Repina* ('drama' meaning a play of a serious nature). As with all of Chekhov's plays, one ignores his subtitles at one's peril since they indicate not only the theatrical genre and *apparent* conventions which he was utilising in order to subvert those conventions, but also suggest intention, mood and atmosphere. Thus, *On the Harmfulness of Tobacco* is subtitled *A Monologue in One Act*, and *The Wedding*, *A Play in One Act*. Only four of his short plays are actually called 'farces' or 'vaudevilles': *The Bear*; *The Proposal*; *A Tragic Role* (sometimes translated, *à la* Molière, as *The Reluctant Tragedian*) and *Jubilee* (often translated as *The Anniversary*). *On the High Road* is the only one without a subtitle, although it is clearly 'a drama', dramatised by Chekhov from his own (very different) short story, 'In Autumn' (1883). It has two other aspects which are unique in Chekhov's dramaturgy, though not the short stories. First, it is the only play without any comedy in it; and second, it is his only 'lower depths' play, in which the characters are tramps, beggars, criminals and the dispossessed. Set in an inn at night, it partly concerns a gentleman who has 'gone to seed' after his wife's desertion on their wedding day. Written in 1885, it was neither performed nor published in Chekhov's lifetime, and its main interest lies in the extent to which he uses conventions *without* subverting them – so the result is a play which relies on an unlikely coincidence when the wife suddenly appears in the inn, and on melodrama in the murder attempt. The original story is evocative, an atmospheric sketch of a rainy autumn evening with characters more likely to be found in a play by Gorky than Chekhov.[4] Like *Platonov* which preceded it, the play is marred by melodrama, excess and over-seriousness, but *does* relate to the peasants and ordinary people described by Astrov in *Uncle Vanya* – and to the tramp whose sudden appearance significantly alters the mood and the action of Act Two of *The Cherry Orchard*.

Unlike *On the High Road*, the other short play which sits oddly in the genre is the unfinished and posthumously published *The Night before the Trial* (1890s). The play relies on a series of misunderstandings which arise from the ancient comic device of mistaken identity, and utilises other traditional comic devices like the cuckolded husband. It too was originally a story of the same title, written in 1886, and is Chekhov's most overt parody: stock situation, stereotypes, improbable plot or situation – and likely denouement. It is more closely related to *commedia dell'arte*, Plautus and Molière, than to Chekhov's other – later – dramatic works. But it is also worth comparing the treatment of the cuckolded husband with the very different treatment of Andrey in *Three Sisters*, whose wife Natasha is unfaithful to him – and everyone knows it, making him a tragi-comic character. Or to the characterisation of 'Waffles' – Telegin – in *Uncle Vanya* and, indeed, the very different treatment of Vanya's and Astrov's interest in Yeliena who, against all convention, remains faithful to her elderly and difficult husband, Serebriakov. This is not to suggest, however, that Chekhov does not make use of farce in *Uncle Vanya*, but he does so through the *reversal* of the convention.[5]

Chekhov does not make a clear distinction between 'farce' and 'vaude-ville', hence my own previous linkage of the two as 'farce-vaudevilles'.[6] His description of *The Bear*, in the same letter to Polonsky quoted earlier, reads in full:

> Just to while away the time, I wrote a trivial little vaudeville in the French manner, called *The Bear* . . . Alas! when they find out on *New Time* [the newspaper for which Chekhov wrote many stories, owned by Chekhov's publisher, Suvorin] that I write vaudevilles they will excommunicate me. What am I to do? I plan something worthwhile – and – it is all tra-la-la! In spite of all my attempts at being serious, the result is nothing; with me the serious always alternates with the trivial.[7]

This is *exactly* Chekhov's method: whether in his stories, his full-length plays or the short plays, he alternates 'the serious' with 'the trivial'. It is one of the most important characteristics of his style *and* intent: his concern, often expressed, was with the banalities and trivialities of everyday life –

and yet time passes, life slips by, opportunities are lost, and unhappiness and disappointment are poured out over a glass of tea. *The Proposal* is about everything except a proposal. Similarly, in *The Cherry Orchard*, Varya and Lopakhin seemingly lose the opportunity of being together because of a lost pair of galoshes – or in *Three Sisters*, Irina loses the chance of a little happiness or companionship or simply change when the Baron is killed in a ludicrous historical anachronism, a duel – while after the fatal shot (heard but unknown both to the on-stage characters and the audience) her brother-in-law disguises his own deep unhappiness at his wife's infidelity with Vershinin by fooling with a false beard confiscated from one of the boys he teaches at the local school. Equally, Vanya in *Uncle Vanya* – according to Chekhov's directions – just whistles. When people are really unhappy, Chekhov said, they just whistle. Space does not permit more examples, but this contrapuntal device emanates from characterisation and the cross-dialogue in which characters either cannot hear each other – or do not listen. This, of course, is an old comic device (found in Plautus or *commedia dell'arte*): the 'comedy of the deaf', but in Chekhov's works it becomes part of what he called 'the sad comicality of everyday life', which is subject, style and motivation. For Chekhov this is more than a device – it is a philosophy. Alexander Kuprin reported Chekhov as saying:

> In life there are no clear-cut consequences or reasons; in it everything is mixed up together; the important and the paltry, the great and the base, the tragic and the ridiculous. One is hypnotised and enslaved by routine and cannot manage to break away from it. What are needed are new forms, new ones.[8]

It is this alternation of the trivial with the significant, emanating not *conventionally* from situation, but from character, which demonstrates Chekhov's philosophy, his subversion of conventional techniques, and which provides the major clue to his structural devices, in whichever medium he was writing. And it also explains some Western European or American directors' over-used or misunderstood response to the stage direction: 'laughter through tears'. In essence, it is very simple and not some characteristically neurotic Russian feature: it *is* what happens in everyday life and conversation when people interact, yet follow their own train of thought; when 'the sad' is interrupted by 'the comic' – and tears and laughter come either one after the other, or simultaneously. This is the function of the contrapuntal: one train of thought followed, or interrupted *apparently* by accident, by another character's words. Or, particularly in the major plays, this structure may involve an off-stage sound which works as an effect in relation to what precedes or follows it, becoming a form of montage.

There are many examples of 'laughter through tears' in the one-act plays as well. In *The Wedding*, for example, the silly young show-off, Yat, the telegraph clerk, boasting about electric light, creates a row over the wedding dinner which changes the whole mood and prompts a furious response from the bride's mother, Mrs Zhigalov, who then continues 'tearfully'. And in the same short 'play',[9] the most respected and expected guest, General Revunov-Karaulov, virtually ruins the event by his literal deafness – the stock comic device, yet turned by Chekhov into something else: an exposé of the petty, the pretentious or hypocritical.

Such stock devices were well-known to Chekhov. Although writing about the requirements of the short story, he lists these in a letter to his brother Alexander on 17 April 1883:

1. The shorter the better.
2. A bit of ideology and being a bit up to date is most *à propos*.
3. Caricature is fine, but ignorance of civil service ranks and of the seasons is strictly prohibited . . .

But three years later, in another letter to Alexander on 10 May 1886, he is less facetious:

1. Absence of lengthy verbiage of political–social–economic nature.
2. Total objectivity.
3. Truthful descriptions of persons and objects.
4. Extreme brevity.
5. Audacity and originality: free the stereotype.
6. Compassion.

There is no contradiction here between 'total objectivity' – and 'compassion', and this too is a major feature of Chekhov's writing technique: the 'total objectivity' is what, mistakenly, prompted many to claim Chekhov as a 'naturalist', while the 'compassion' is one of several features which differentiate Chekhov's vaudevilles from the conventional – French – genre which he mentions in the letter quoted above in relation to *The Bear*. Equally, in his 'free the stereotype' he is referring to the conventional French models which flooded the Russian stage of the eighteenth and nineteenth centuries.

In 1880 Chekhov compiled a comprehensive list of *Things Most Frequently Encountered in Novels, Stories and Other Such Things*, which included many of the conventions he was later to subvert in both his one-act and full-length plays. The list included:

the impoverished nobleman, stupid footmen, nannies, governesses, people

*who are not beautiful, but pleasant and attractive, the height of the skies . . .
in a word: nature! . . .the aunt in Tambov, the doctor with a worried face . . .
and where there is a doctor . . . there is migraine, inflammation of the brain,
care of the wounded in a duel . . . the servant who has been in service with
the old masters, who is prepared to go through thick and thin for the master's
family, even go through fire . . . a dog who does everything except talk . . .
electricity – in the majority of cases, dragged in for no particular reason . . .
the gun that does not fire . . . incidental eavesdropping as the cause of great
discoveries . . . an endless number of interjections, and attempts to use an
appropriate technical term, subtle hints to rather weighty circumstances, very
often the absence of an ending, Seven Deadly Sins in the beginning and a
wedding at the end!*[10]

To give just a few examples of his use of these conventions, in *The
Wedding* the argument about electricity, 'dragged in for no particular
reason' by Yat, would be comic were it not for the fact that Chekhov's
subversion of the convention changes the mood of the festivities so that the
result is serious. It ceases to be comic because it is taken as a 'put down' by
Zhigalov *and* exposes the petty and narrow mentality of the characters.
Equally, 'the attempt to use . . . appropriate technical terms' is what
inflames Mrs Zhigalov about the 'important' guest, the deaf Revunov-
Karaulov, who keeps using naval terms.

In the full-length plays, 'the dog who does everything except talk' brings
to mind the governess, Charlotta Ivanovna, in *The Cherry Orchard*, whose
dog 'actually eats nuts' – yet this comic line is undercut by Charlotta's
unhappiness; or the 'servant who has been in service with the old masters'
could be Anfisa *or* Ferapont in *Three Sisters*, or Firs in *The Cherry
Orchard*; while 'the aunt in Tambov' becomes, in *The Cherry Orchard*, 'the
aunt in Yaroslavl', mentioned several times as a possible source of financial
salvation. As for the wedding at the end, Chekhov either does not provide
one – as in *The Cherry Orchard* with Lopakhin and Varya, and the
unhappy triangle between Yasha (the 'stock' figure of the 'inflated' servant),
Dunyasha and poor Yepikhodov – or offers a very unpromising one in the
case of Natasha and Lomov in *The Proposal*, or the unexpected future
marriage, as in the ending of *The Bear*. In both farces, the women are far
from conventional in their proactive and even manipulative roles – and
Chekhov sets up the future married life of both couples so we are left in no
doubt about their romantic or sentimental 'wedded bliss'.

In *The Seagull*, with the passage of time between Acts Three and Four,
we see the effect of a 'love' affair in the unhappy marriage between
Medvedenko and Masha. And there are the conventional love triangles on
which *The Seagull* is structured, which also form a major part of the action

(as distinct from plot). Similarly there is the love triangle in *Uncle Vanya* between Vanya and Astrov and the married Yeliena who – against all convention – insists on fidelity to her elderly, selfish husband. Or there is *The Bear*, in which the widowed Popova, with her dimpled cheeks, insists on grieving for her husband, which creates a love triangle in which Smirnov has to 'compete' with a dead husband. Subverting the convention again, and to different effect, are the love triangles in *Three Sisters* with two characters we never see: Vershinin's wife, and Natasha's very 'evident' lover, Protopopov. The result is either parody of what had become a stock plotting device – or the very credible and realistic, because painful, subversion of the device.

The most innovatory use of the stock situation is Chekhov's use of character *from which the action emanates*. Thus, instead of 'the stereotype' we are given three-dimensional character, and instead of 'plot' we are given action which comes only from character and the interaction between characters. Hosts and guests in *The Wedding* make it a dismal affair because of their pettiness, while with both *A Tragic Role* and *On the Harmfulness of Tobacco*, the monologue form allows the objective depiction of completely subjective and self-centred characters. In the first, the 'reluctant tragedian' Tolkachov brings it all on himself, whilst in the second, the monologue form is used in a highly complex way, and by an unhappy fellow called Nyukhin or 'Sniffler'![11]

The monologue form in *On the Harmfulness of Tobacco* is given an unusual twist in that the audience has a dual role: both as audience in the lecture room, addressed, cajoled and pleaded with by the 'lecturer' Nyukhin, and, of course, as audience at the play's performance. The roles shift with the change of focus, from close-up or empathy with Nyukhin, to long-shot, or objectivity about this little man, alternately cowering or strutting. And in a very real way the audience 'plays' a role as Nyukhin asks a question, addresses people directly with 'You, Sir' – or 'Madame' and then answers for them. A question to the audience is not simply rhetorical, but *seems* to carry the plausibility of an actual response or reaction. In *Swan Song*, there is a particular use of dramatic irony: we, the audience, have gone home. Yet we are audience to Svetlovidov's performance with Nikita.

The almost cinematic use of close-up followed by long-shot is a major technique used by Chekhov to alter our perspective on character. This, in turn, relates to the numerous occasions on which a character is simply talking to himself or herself – others may be present, may 'hear' – but do not 'listen'. This often creates the most revealing and touching three-dimensionality of character, as when Charlotta Ivanovna virtually has a 'monologue' at the beginning of Act Two of *The Cherry Orchard* – Dunyasha and Yasha are present but concentrating on each other, as Yepikhodov strums his guitar and watches Dunyasha, so it is only the audience who listen to Charlotta as she apparently talks to herself. A similar technique is used in *Three Sisters*, in Act Two, when Andrey unburdens himself *exactly* because Ferapont is literally too deaf to hear him. And lest we become too sympathetic to Andrey, Ferapont interrupts, altering mood, with completely irrelevant and nonsensical – comic – remarks about the rope stretched around Moscow, and the pancakes.

The subversion of the device is used differently again when a character such as Gayev in *The Cherry Orchard* begins his declamatory speech to the book case, and *is* heard by the others on stage, and his heightened reaction to events is deflated when the others laugh. And in a different mode, Astrov's impassioned speech in Act Three of *Uncle Vanya* about the forests and, in the broadest sense, about ecology, captures Yeliena's interest in the man – but not his 'cause'. Unlike Sonya, who listens to Astrov's ideals and aspirations, and which are a part of his attraction for her, Yeliena sees a man made attractive to her by passion, by style, not by content. There is a similar passion which motivates Masha's interest in Vershinin in *Three Sisters*, and in Irina's response to Tuzenbach's philosophy.

Perhaps the clearest example of this is demonstrated by the multifaceted reactions to Konstantin's play in Act One of *The Seagull*: each character responds *characteristically*. Thus Arkadina's inability to take it seriously is a rejection of Konstantin himself, and sets in motion the internal action of the relationship between mother and son, and the seeming inevitability of the ending of the play. Dr Dorn, however, does take the play within the play seriously, and provides not only a calming influence on the characters, but acts as a kind of conduit of objectivity for us as audience. Doctors appear on Chekhov's list of *Things Most Frequently Encountered* – and most of the major plays do have a doctor amongst the characters. It is only in the final act of the play, with Nina's secretive and disturbed return, that the true meaning of the 'desert' and 'wasteland' become apparent to Nina herself, to Konstantin – and to the audience. And there is the symbolism of the ripped curtain, flapping in the wind, still there in spite of the – two-year – passage of time.

This, in turn, relates to several features which are carried over from the one-act plays into the major ones: the absence of endings as such, and the shift of mood and atmosphere within seconds of stage or real time, which lift the plays onto another plane. As Nemirovich-Danchenko put it: 'Chekhov refined his realism to the point where it became symbolic.'[12] This is true of the time of day or night as, for example, in *Swan Song* when late at night Svetlovidov probably gives Nikita (and us) a better performance than anything either during or since his youth. Equally, the weather seems to work 'naturalistically' on the characters – too hot in Act One of *Uncle Vanya*; a heat-wave plaguing Tolkachov in *A Tragic Role*; stormy in *Uncle Vanya* and the last act of *The Seagull*; but simultaneously it has a meaning and effect greater than itself, and hence becomes 'symbolic'. In *The Bear* Popova's insistence on burying herself indoors for a year begins to change when Luka, her old manservant, first tells her what a beautiful day it is outside – and then ushers in 'the bear'- a large mammal, very much alive, breaking her seclusion from the outside world. Contrasting vividly with Popova's 'deep mourning' dress is the life-giving description of activities beyond the room in which she has shut herself away.

The absence of 'endings' is evident in the vaudevilles. At the end of *The Proposal* it becomes clear that the rows will continue even after marriage; at the end of *The Bear*, the change of both mood and mind by Popova is not going to result in tranquility; in *Swan Song*, Svetlovidov is led off by the old prompter, Nikita, to wake the next day no doubt with a hangover, and with his life unchanged by the flow of memory and even the resurgence of ideals which briefly illuminated his life the night before, and heightened the reality of his situation. And Nikita will continue to live in fear of the stage manager discovering that he sleeps each night in the theatre, having nowhere else to go. In *On the Harmfulness of Tobacco*, Nyukhin's miserable existence will continue as before since he lacks the courage to take control – and change it. He may tear off the 'image' of his life – his worn, shabby, ill-fitting tail-coat – but he will simply continue with what he knows only too well: 'this rotten, banal, tawdry life – this existence which has made me into a pathetic old fool – the life of an idiot'. At the end, his wife 'appears' in the wings. And he puts his coat back on, begging 'us' not to tell on him. It is only with Chekhov's last play, *The Cherry Orchard*, that there is a partial upbeat in the closure of the play: Anya and Trofimov leave the stage with the words: 'Good-bye, old life' – and – 'Hullo, new life!'. This is not to suggest any easy romanticism or sentimentality in their future life together, but a contrast with the bleak prospects that confront most of the other characters.[13]

In *A Tragic Role*, Tolkachov (whose name relates to 'pushed'), will continue to be 'pushed' by fulfilling everyone's demands, allowing himself to be treated like a cart-horse, while his friend Murashkin ('Shivers') – who has listened, or rather, *not* listened to this 'false' monologue (false because the presence of Murashkin theoretically justifies Tolkachov's tirade) – simply adds to his friend's burdens with his own requests. The comedy of Tolkachov's entrance (reminiscent of Lucky's in Beckett's

Waiting for Godot) is a rare example in Chekhov's works of comic physicality. Of all the one-act plays, only *The Bear, The Proposal, A Tragic Role* and *Jubilee* contain the physicality of action associated with farce – whether the best French examples of Labiche and Feydeau, or of the English variety like Pinero's *The Magistrate* or, more recently, some of the plays of Alan Ayckbourn or Michael Frayn.[14] *Jubilee* contains the physicality of farce in the creation of chaos; in the misunderstandings; in the exaggerated reactions of the characters (Meyerhold's 'Swoons');[15] in the 'demolition' of the respectable facade of a bank, and in the crazy 'tableau' ending.

Similarly, in the major plays, Vanya's murder attempt is both farcical – and tragic, but elsewhere only Yepikhodov in *The Cherry Orchard*, with his nickname of '22 misfortunes' (sometimes translated into English as 'Simple Simon'), suffers an endless series of farcical – physical – misfortunes, whether crushing a hat box, or tripping over objects. The difference, however, between Yepikhodov (or indeed Nyukhin in *On the Harmfulness of Tobacco*) and the conventional stereotype, is that each knows 'his fate'. Life is a series of conspiracies designed to torment, so that if something can go wrong, it will. That self-knowledge invests the character with the three-dimensionality of psychology, some dignity – *and* a way of life. And perhaps Medvedenko, the unfortunate schoolmaster who marries Masha in *The Seagull*, shares some of the misfortunes – and self-knowledge. A similar case may be made about Charlotta Ivanovna's tricks in *The Cherry Orchard*, or Pishchik's action in swallowing Ranevskaya's pills. But one of the most farcical moments in the play takes place *off-stage:* in Act Three, Trofimov's pompous reaction to Ranevskaya's teasing is to march off, offended – only to fall down the stairs. In a conventional farce, the audience would see that happen, but in a Chekhov play, the character might well be hurt. In the same act, Chekhov is careful to keep the balance of the 'sad comicality', so the fact that Varya hits Lopakhin over the head by mistake, an action taking place on stage, prepares us for the mistiming between the couple and deflates Lopakhin's entrance as the 'new owner' of the estate. And his head *does* hurt! Varya asks him: 'I didn't hurt you, did I?' – to which Lopakhin replies: 'No, it's all right. I'm going to have a wacking big bruise, though'. By contrast, the physicality in *The Bear* and *The Proposal* is to very different effect: there is no pain involved.

The best examples of Labiche or Feydeau (or Ayckbourn or Frayn) rely absolutely on the split-second timing of entrances and exits as the 'triangles' of husband, wife and either lover or mistress seek to avoid actual confrontation. Chekhov's use of the love triangle, whether in *The Bear* or *The Seagull*, is not based on such plotting devices, but on the psychology which creates the action: only in *Uncle Vanya* is there a moment which attunes with French farce, when Vanya enters with a bunch of flowers for Yeliena at the precise moment when Astrov and Yeliena make physical contact – a situation repeated in Act Four. The pain that this creates for all three removes it from the seemingly painless adulteries of French farce. It is partly the *accidental* coincidence of timing (as distinct from the conventionally contrived) which makes it more painful and awkward. The other moment of farce – defined also by its physicality – is when Vanya tries to shoot Serebriakov, an action which completely subverts the convention. First, Vanya misses – not once, but twice, and in a confined space; second, Vanya actually says: 'Bang!' which is a comic, if not 'stagey' line, often missed in the action; third, Yeliena tries to protect the Professor – as opposed to the convention which dictates that the man protects the woman;[16] then, the respectable, pompous and self-centred Professor is absolutely terrified; and last but not least, Vanya is driven by utter desperation caused by Serebriakov's insensitivity which negates everything that Vanya and Sonya had worked for, so it has much less to do with the love triangle than their whole way of life.

Finally, Vanya's pain is such that after failing twice in a murder attempt,[17] he is then driven to suicide – a suicide only just avoided by Astrov and Sonya in persuading Vanya to return the bottle he has stolen from Astrov's medical bag. This is a use of farce which becomes, in Chekhov's plays, a *philosophical* idea, and not merely a farcical action. Conventional farce of the French or British variety demonstrates a world out of the control of the characters; in Chekhov's farce, the characters *could* take control, but for often complex reasons, do not.[18]

It was not, however, the superbly crafted farces of Labiche or Feydeau on which Chekhov based his 'farce-vaudevilles', but the endless formulaic and often third-rate French imports which flooded the popular stages of Europe. And in which, no doubt, Svetlovidov in *Swan Song* regularly played – as would Nina, acting in provincial theatres, travelling second class from job to job, as she describes it in Act Four of *The Seagull*. Thus the chances are that when the audience or reader consider a Chekhov character 'melodramatic' or 'farcical', then that is exactly the reaction Chekhov intends: he uses melodrama to expose the melodramatic, and he uses farce to expose the farcical, as Beckett was subsequently to do in the twentieth century: as a – significantly different – philosophy of life. To put it another way: the spectator or reader should trust their own instinct and not inhibit such reactions with the thought that these are meant to be deeply serious 'Russian' (ie. 'heavy') plays. The danger, however, lies in playing them *slowly*, whether the one-act or full-length plays – an aspect about which Chekhov constantly complained.[19]

NOTES

1 Unless otherwise indicated, quotations from the letters are from N. F. Belchikov and others, eds., *Anton Chekhov, Polnoe sobranie sochinenii i pisem v 30i tomakh*, Moscow, 1974–83 (*Anton Chekhov, Collected Works and Letters in 30 volumes*, Moscow, 1974–83).

2 Quoted in David Magarshack, *Chekhov the Dramatist*, New York, 1960, p. 54.

3 Letter to A. S. Suvorin, 2 January 1894.

4 For a more detailed discussion of the play, see Vera Gottlieb, *Chekhov and the Vaudeville, A Study of Chekhov's One-Act Plays*, Cambridge, 1982, pp. 110–19.

5 *The Seagull* and *The Cherry Orchard* are both called comedies, while *Three Sisters* is subtitled *A Drama in Four Acts*. Not one of his plays, short or full-length, is called a 'tragedy', so even with Konstantin's suicide at the end of *The Seagull*, it remains a comedy, as does *The Cherry Orchard*.

6 Gottlieb, *Chekhov and the Vaudeville*, The short plays are analysed under genre: farce-vaudevilles, dramatic studies, a play in one act and a monologue in one act.

7 Letter to Yakov Polonsky, 22 February 1888.

8 Quoted in Sophie Laffitte, *Chekhov 1860–1904*, London, 1974, p. 16.

9 'Play' is used here as distinct from farces, such as *The Bear* and *The Proposal*, or a 'comedy' such as *The Cherry Orchard*, or a 'drama' such as *Three Sisters* or *Swan Song*.

10 A. P. Chekhov, *Things Most Frequently Encountered in Novels, Stories and Other Such Things* (1880–2), in vol. I of *Collected Works and Letters, Polnoe sobranie sochinenii i pisem*, vol. I, pp. 17–18. For the complete list in English, see Gottlieb, *Chekhov and the Vaudeville*, p. 17.

11 Every now and again Chekhov uses the stock device of 'meaningful names': in *The Cherry Orchard* the 'hanger-on' Pishchik is translatable as 'Squeaker'; in *Swan Song* Svetlovidov's name is associated with 'svet' or 'light' while in *The Wedding* Zhigalov relates to 'burning'; Revunov-Karaulov relates to 'howl-for-help'; the midwife, Mrs Zmeyukin, is 'snake'; and Mozgovoy is associated with 'brain'.

12 Quoted in Edward Braun, *The Director and the Stage*, London, 1982, p. 73.

13 See chapter 10 in this volume.

14 See discussion of Michael Frayn's use of farce in chapter 18.

15 For an analysis of Meyerhold's production *33 Swoons* see chapter 14. Also Edward Braun's *Meyerhold, a Revolution in Theatre*, London, 1995. And see Gottlieb, *Chekhov and the Vaudeville*. Parts of the last mentioned book have been reprinted in *Drama Criticism, Criticism of the Most Significant and Widely Studied Dramatic Works from All the World's Literature*, vol. IX, *A Special Volume Devoted to Anton Pavlovich Chekhov 1860–1904, One-Act Plays*, Detroit and London, 1999, pp. 162–94.

16 The conclusion of *Platonov* has a similar role-reversal with Sonya firing at

Platonov, Mariya trying to protect him, but Sonya does *not* miss and Platonov dies on stage (Act Four, Scenes XII and XIII). See chapter 4 in this volume.

17 See chapter 8 in this volume.
18 See chapter 18 in this volume.
19 'This really is dreadful! An act [*The Cherry Orchard*, Act Four] which ought to take a maximum of twelve minutes – you're dragging it out for forty minutes! All I can say is that Stanislavsky is ruining my play.' Letter to Olga Knipper-Chekhova, 29 March 1904.

6

PATRICE PAVIS

Ivanov: the invention of a negative dramaturgy

Ivanov (1887) occupies an unusual place in Chekhov's theatre because it is rarely staged. The four main plays, which are generally more enjoyable, are frequently performed – as indeed is *Platonov* (1882), in spite of being an early work, but in which every flaw may be excused as a sign of chaotic but promising genius. If, in fact, *Ivanov* is read as a play *either* from Chekhov's successful maturity *or* his impetuous youth, one will inevitably be surprised and even disappointed: the play is rather heavy and complicated; the characters are verbose and excessive, and the main springs of the action are both evident and predictable. But if one considers the play as an open-cast quarry from which all his dramatic works will be extracted, *or* as a school for experimental dramaturgy, one is amazed by the richness of this discovery: all the ingredients are offered up with complete openness, as if the writing process – erasing and burying more than creating – had not yet taken place. *Ivanov* should not be *under*estimated. It would even be better to *over*interpret it and imagine everything that has to be eliminated or covered up in order to find the tone, the concision and the economy of speech in the four major plays.

The year 1887 marks a precise turning point in European dramaturgy: Antoine founded the Théâtre-Libre, the birthplace of naturalism in the theatre, and Lugné-Poe opened his Cercle des Escholiers, which in turn led to the symbolist Théâtre de l'Oeuvre. Chekhov himself seemed to hesitate between naturalistic writing and symbolist vision, between realistic effects – and theatrical conventions. It might not have been apparent then that they are two sides of the same coin and that *Ivanov* is the 'negative' dramaturgy at the source of this revelation.

The invention of a new dramaturgy

To look first at a *negative* dramaturgy. *Ivanov* shows the transition from a classical (or neo-classical) dramaturgy to a new one, characterised by ellipsis, allusion and subtext. However, this process of erasing, of undermining and of 'burying' writing devices, is not an easy or painless one. The old dramaturgy of the well-made play, the heir of classical theatre, is still solid and visible: the story can be read easily, the numerous characters are psychologically and socially characterised and the conflicts are well defined. The dramatic action, which is still very externalised and taut, climaxes at the end of every act, with a crescendo within each act and from one act to the next, right up to the final conventional suicide. All actions and words are subordinate to the dramatic structure; they cannot detach themselves from it to become autonomous; they are constrained by the main dramaturgical pillars. All are centred around the main character, who talks a lot, giving away all kinds of details about his intentions and motivation. All characters express themselves more than is necessary, dotting the i's and crossing the t's, as if they were the mouthpieces of the author.

Have we then become prisoners of a problem dramaturgy? *Ivanov* looks very much like a 'problem play': the author uses the rather trivial story of an anti-hero in order to give a diagnosis of his time. He confronts a prematurely worn-out Russian society, an environment and a character who cannot resist weariness and degradation. The point seems obvious: the main character does not find the strength to fight back and causes his wife's death both by negligence and in the hope of a new life. Doctor Lvov, unable to cure Ivanov's wife, Anna, tries to protect her from her husband. He publicly accuses him of having premeditatedly killed his spouse in order to escape bankruptcy.

If Ivanov's motivation is supposedly clear – at least from the point of view of Lvov, his accuser – Lvov's own motivation is less obvious. And this is the main ambiguity of the play. The dialogue is indeed explicit, for no character fails to tell us what they think of Ivanov. Chekhov has not yet 'demotivated' his characters: he lets them pour out everything and nothing. He gives them hardly any *unspoken*, implicit, or indeterminate statements, whether in their words *or* in their situations. The reader's or spectator's reception is strictly guided and they reach conclusions with complete awareness.

Modern dramaturgy thus seems to hesitate on the brink of a complete void; it still clings to a thesis, a problem and an explanation, a key, even if these have become problematic in Szondi's sense,[1] since they seem out of touch with the new world-view. It depends on well-tried effects, on well-known conclusions, on credible explanations. It has not yet found an adequate form, particularly in relation to the dilution of content or statement within the whole textual network, or in relation to a polyphonic form instead of a univocal content. It still shows moments of concentrated, isolated meaning, where the individual word is weighed down by heavy explanations.

The various *coups de théâtre* in *Ivanov*, situated according to the neo-classical dramaturgical principle of effects at the end of each act, concentrate and resolve the tensions of every act and every situation in the manner of a coda for a musical piece in four movements. Only later, with *The Seagull*, will these hot spots disappear or be extended into the whole textual network, within an exchange of dialogue, or even within two successive lines. The actions are tightly linked; they are set up and performed without hesitation, according to the principle of maximum tension for each *coup de théâtre* which punctuates the end of each act. One dialogue leads to the next, instead of vanishing into the thin air of non-attentiveness. Whenever a character enters or exits, there is – in accordance with the rules of classical dramaturgy – a related change in the situation: any new incident increases the tension, particularly with the conventional triangle of Ivanov/Anna/Lvov as Lvov's persecutions become more and more insistent. Ivanov is increasingly caught in a trap, until he has no other choice but to destroy himself. The action remains essentially dramatic, according to what Bakhtin referred to as the dialectic of action/reaction or speech/action, visible in the characters' behaviour rather than in the textual network of discursive, rhythmical and dialogical counterpoints.[2]

The dramaturgy is indeed more positive than negative; it is very visible, linked to classical structures, and too solidly built to let the dialogues and discourses resonate together and provoke multiple and unexpected echo effects. It remains emotionally heightened and exaggerated (paroxysmic), albeit parodic, dramaturgy with an immoderate taste for obligatory scenes, teasing situations and calculated and predictable effects.

Later – whether in Chekhov's work to come or in rereading the play with the retrospective perspective proposed here in the light of Chekhov's classical work and his subsequent dramatic writing – this dramaturgy will become *negative*; it will become destructured, dematerialised, disorientated, and will let the textual networks gradually emerge. But in this neo-classical building, cracks are already visible, or rather audible. A form based on conflict, opposition, dualism and the contrasting qualities of good and evil is no longer adequate. It relies too much on the contradictions of *a priori* ideas (such as honest/dishonest; pure/criminal; normal/pathological). Even in 1887, and obviously more so today, one can no longer stick to a binary dramaturgy in a decentralised world, where oppositions cancel each other out and language games and polyphony disappear in a network of echoes. Thus the very summit of naturalism – the illusion that the world can be mimetically represented – leads exactly to its antithesis, to the questioning of a closed neo-classical dramaturgy and to the use of textual and discursive mechanisms. Thus dramaturgy and its rigid rules give way to internally motivated effects of language and textual mechanisms.

Within this strict framework we now find a wandering word, an unstable subject, a loose chain of ready-made motives and preconstructed themes, which will be taken up in the later plays. Words, subjects, and motives detach themselves slowly from the dramaturgical framework and its points of orientation, becoming free associations dependent on textual devices, which still have to be invented, or at least systematised.

Textual and discursive devices

The dramatic text can be analysed not only according to its macro-structure (its dramaturgy), but also to the textual devices which are much more tiny and subtle: language games, pragmatic use of language, stylistic effects. Given the visibility of the dramatic structure, one tends to see all textual and discursive devices as subordinate elements. Textual mechanisms/devices are under dramaturgical control; they are the emanations of the action and characters. This is why the dialogues often explain, in great detail, the characters' motivations. Their explanations never seem to end, even if only to repeat that they cannot find any explanation for their own behaviour. Each character has a very chatty and verbose way of speaking; a few language tics or mannerisms are enough for their characterisation. Everyone has his or her own thematic and linguistic obsessions: Ivanov performs his own existential auto-analysis; Lvov holds forth on the question of honesty; Shabyelsky makes cynical and tasteless jokes, or Kosykh talks only about cards.[3] All of them tend to *overexplain* their actions instead of performing them silently. Their words contain little subtext, very few silences, few points of suspension or unspoken elements, but instead a lot of *overtext*, loquacious and endless explanations.

This overtextual mode of speech uses fairly classical forms of discourse: conversations between two or three people; genre scenes where there is a group discussion, for instance in the drawing-room (Act Two); direct exchanges between two characters (Act Two, Scene XIII or Act Three, Scene IX, or Act Four, Scene VIII); long monologues (Act Three, Scene VI, Act Four, Scene I), and rapid and fast cuts (stichomythia, as in Act Three, Scene IV). These somewhat traditional dramaturgical forms, however, were already undermined and invaded by textual and discursive devices which only a few years later were to become the trademark of Chekhov's dramatic writing. These devices may not yet have reached their complete maturity, or had not always been activated, but they were already controlling the textual network. Briefly mentioned below is a selection of them, and these devices may only be understood within the dialectics of a negative dramaturgy.

(1) *The indirectness of lines* – the fact that the characters' lines do not go in one and the same direction, but are open to many possible paths – is not yet systematised in *Ivanov*: dialogues steer themselves towards a final resolution; connections are made without any ambiguity; the arguments are linear and unquestionable; the dramaturgical weaving follows a clear strategy. The smallest detail acquires a function within the story: for instance, it is not an insignificant detail that Lvov, who is blatantly against Ivanov, tells Anna that his 'father's dead, but [his] mother's still alive' (Act One, Scene VII).

(2) *Effects of announcement* prepare the reader for forthcoming actions in such a direct way that one wonders what else is left for the reader or spectator to still imagine. 'If he spent an evening at home he'd get bored, he'd blow his brains out' (Act One, Scene V), Lvov warns us, and Ivanov confesses to us that 'I just don't understand. I might as well shoot myself and be done with it' (Act Three, Scene VI).

(3) *Effects which play to the gallery*, beyond the personal opinion of the character, which impose on reader or spectator a given interpretation of the action, preventing them from judging for themselves. Thus: 'Once married, he won't pay what he owes her, and you can't very well take your son-in-law to court' (Act Four, Scene II), Kosykh tells the gallery. Here again, such an explanation must not be taken for granted, since it is also a signal for the spectator to remain critical, a decoy to conceal or forestall any untimely conclusions.

(4) *Explanatory chit-chat* which makes the characters' words so obvious that it seems, when judged by the standards of Chekhov's later plays, to be such a major dramaturgical flaw that it leads to the infantilisation of the reader/spectator. It is enough to refer back to the characters' obsessive tics in order to transform it into a deceptive and ambiguous device, precisely because it is so explicit.

(5) *Talking through their hats*, as most characters do, is also a way of discouraging reader or spectator from interpreting the characters' words literally. It is also a paradoxical way of allowing moments of absolute sincerity when a real emotion or authentic sentence suddenly breaks the stereotypic straitjacket – as when, for instance, Shabyelsky makes this unexpected and touching confession: 'I can't concede that a living person may suddenly drop dead for no reason' (Act Three, Scene II).

(6) *Swarming speech*, an uncontrolled outpouring, an infantile disease

from which all the characters in *Ivanov* suffer when they look for an answer to their crises in public confessions. Ironically, these crises stem precisely from their immoderate love of words and their refusal of any concrete *action*.

(7) *No collective discourse/dialogue* really counterbalances Ivanov's monologues. A remnant of the old dramaturgy produces conflict and debate between Ivanov and the others, between supporters and enemies. Only with *The Seagull* is the central figure 'extended' to all the characters, their discourse generalised and scattered within the dialogue of all the characters.

(8) *Changes of subject* frequently interrupt the flow of monologues, thus contradicting a conversation that was supposedly serious. Ivanov often skips from one subject to another, relativising his will to get to the bottom of things: 'I daresay I'm very much to blame. (*Listens*) I think they've brought the carriage round' (Act One, Scene v). Or 'when you start rescuing me and giving me good advice, a look of sheer innocence comes over you . . . Just a second, there's dust on your shoulder. (*Brushes the dust off her shoulder*)' (Act Three, Scene VII).

(9) *Prerecorded, preconstructed discourse* takes over in such instances, and sets the exchanges between characters on automatic pilot: there is no novelty, no authenticity in this exchange of quotes, phrases or obsessive remarks. All the songs, imitations of Yiddish pronunciation, technical terms from card games, aphorisms on Russian life, women or doctors, are only quotations and situations that are to be systematically recycled in the subsequent plays.

(10) *Thematic lines* connect different words which are taken up at regular intervals within a network of terms, whose emergence becomes meaningful as a kind of through-line, an *ideologem*, ie. a simultaneously thematic, narrative, discursive and ideological unit, which is also a key to the social relationships. For instance, the term *honest(y)*, which is applied positively and negatively to Lvov and Ivanov. This term becomes an empty element which demonstrates, somewhat ironically, the difficulty of judging the actions of human beings. It thus relativises any judgement and forces us to compare every context where the term is used.

(11) *Auto-textuality* (i.e. the reflection of the text upon itself, for instance, in the *mise en abîme*[4]) is not yet a discursive device which is extended to the whole play; it remains limited to a character's commentary on itself. Thus Ivanov sees himself as a provincial and a ridiculous 'Hamlet'-figure (Act Three, Scene VII), but the question of 'Hamletism' does not find any extension in the overall structure of the play. Later, as in *The Seagull* for example, auto-textuality is dissolved and generalised to the

whole texture, thus becoming one of the main keys to Chekhov's work, and obviously dependent on the old dramaturgy, which still imposes a certain reading of the conflicts and an evaluation of the characters. Chekhov certainly does not propose any solution – he rather suggests that the reader or spectator should decide, to the best of his/her knowledge and belief, and according to his/her own values, whether Ivanov is guilty or innocent. However, reception is greatly influenced by the idea that Lvov is more fanatical than honest, and that Ivanov is more a victim than guilty. Hence reception is in fact as open as it was to become in all the later plays.

All these textual mechanisms at work in the play, albeit in a limited fashion, do not yet prove that changing a few dramaturgical rules has already produced a new textuality. The mechanisms or devices still tend to cast themselves in constricting dramaturgical forms, not yet changing the nature of Chekhovian playwriting. Dramaturgical and textual innovation therefore remains very limited, even if one can anticipate all the possibilities of this negative and destructuring writing, which will untie not only dramaturgy and textuality, but also character and subject.

Ivanov's characters are somehow on the defensive. On the one hand they are drawn meticulously with all their contradictions of character, and on the other hand they already tend to erase themselves, for the benefit of a tapestry of discourse and language games.

Characters on the defensive

These characters exist, even before they open their mouths, since a naturalistic acting style gives them very precise characterisation. The tics in their behaviour, their ways of talking, the allusions to their time, are like Barthes' 'reality effects'[5] which give us the illusion that we are confronted by real people. And yet this does not make them understandable to us. In spite of all their auto-analyses, they – or at least the main characters – remain contradictory and unfathomable.

The fact is that the subject is in crisis: the very crisis of the years 1887–1900 which coincided with the discovery of psychoanalysis and *mise en scène*, two 'disciplines' in search of an unidentified object which has always, without knowing it, existed. In this evolving subject, the opposition between good and evil, guilt and innocence, vital desire and death-drive, no longer holds.

Chekhov invites us to find the key to his main character: like a Woyzeck of the Russian intelligentsia, Ivanov is 'as everyman, an abyss, which makes you dizzy when you lean over it', who is also beyond judgement for 'We all have too many wheels, screws, and valves to judge each other on first impression or on one or two pointers' (Büchner's *Woyzeck*, Act Three, Scene VI).[6] The self is made out of incomprehensible wheels. It is split, each half corresponding sometimes to different characters: for instance, the 'infernal couple' Ivanov–Lvov, where the latter is only the prefiguration of the former, ten years before. The dramatic wheel of the play is Lvov's hatred for Ivanov, in whom he sees a hated father-figure, an obstacle to Anna's recovery as well as to his own Oedipal desire for her. A divided self is even a scattered self, whose explosion we witness when Ivanov blows his brains out.

This crisis of the subject is at the same time the cause and the consequence of a deep crisis of language. This can be discovered in the terrible final confrontation between Ivanov and Anna. Anna accuses her husband not so much of betraying her with another woman but of lying to her from the beginning. She casts doubt on his word, and therefore, according to him, on his very existence; he only defends himself against the accusation of lying. Unable to silence her, he tells her that the doctor told him she would soon die. The word has become a desperate and fatal weapon: if the other no longer believes me, I have to kill him or her. Ivanov's anxiety grows not so much from not knowing any longer who he is and what he wants (Act Four, Scene x), but having no more words in the other's and in his own eyes, or only a word that kills.

The subject is whole and undivided; it is ready to die or to kill, only to prove its own existence. Whether for the character, the writing or the dramaturgy, the subject is made out of one piece, one solid block. One can still make distinctions between dramaturgy, textuality and characters as strong autonomous systems. The characters, and particularly the title character Ivanov, is the cement which still unites these systems and masks the cracks in the building. One can still look at his fate, his motivations and his psychology, which prevent us, inversely, from perceiving the play's textuality, its language games, and its dramaturgical forms. Chekhov desperately fills the gaps and cracks of the subject. He gives a very complete, dense, subjective representation of the hero and his surroundings, only to give the illusion of reality and to participate in its salvaging. However – and here comes the writing – the representation now needs, in order to appear more perfectly mimetic, to be meaningfully codified and structured. From now on, the representation of the real will not stop dematerialising, demotivating and destructuring itself into a more open text, where frontiers and differences between dramaturgy, writing and characters have become much more blurred, or even non-existent. For we are just about to move, even if the characters, so to speak, have not noticed it, to the level of metadiscourse – namely, the possibility of saying, of knowing whether one is speaking the truth, of remaining silent. These are metadiscursive techniques which take place not so much on the level of the characters' statements, as on the level of a discursive mechanism, of textual indecisiveness, of the continuum of character/dramaturgy/textuality.

Hence the slightly monomaniac monodrama unwinds and opens itself to multiple networks of allusions, echoes, subtexts, which are all the more complex as the motivations of the characters take flight and the readers or spectators erase, by themselves, the all-too-explicit information. This complexity and this indecisiveness are mythological, beyond *everyday* banality and triviality, *and* of the undecided unconscious beyond clear-cut statements: time inescapably devours its own children; the son curses the father before taking his place and falling into the same traps. The fault cannot be redeemed, even by violent death, because it is unnameable and daily. The high-flown questions – ('who am I, what am I living for, or what do I want?') (Act Four, Scene x) – do not receive any answers.

All this is in *Ivanov*, as always in a first play, but not all of this is Chekhovian. Chekhov will have to forget, to erase, to give up. A whole process of abstraction and stylisation will take place. To erase and to forget the purely mimetic representation/performance will lead to a greater theatricality, to a playful lightness in the dialogues and the gestures, to the double face of the Moscow Art Theatre, the naturalistic theatre and the theatre of mood. A double face that Meyerhold[7] had fully recognised and which is also *Ivanov*'s.

NOTES

1 See Peter Szondi's distinctions in *La Théorie du Drame Moderne*, trans. Patrice Pavis, *L'Age d'homme*, Lausanne, 1973. English translation, ed. Michael Hays, Minneapolis, 1987.

2 See Mikhail Bakhtin, *Le Principe Dialogique*, Paris, 1989. An English translation is *The Dialogic Imagination*, ed. Michael Holquist, trans. Caryl Emerson and Michael Holquist, Austin, Texas, 1981.

3 In chapter 3 of this volume Anatoly Smeliansky makes a related point, albeit within a different context.

4 An inner part which reflects the whole structure.

5 Roland Barthes calls 'reality effects' those details in the text which give the reader the impression of confronting the real world.

6 Georg Büchner (1813–37), a medical student and progressive political activist who wrote several subsequently renowned plays: *Danton's Death* (1835), *Leonce and Lena* (1836) and *Woyzeck*, unfinished by his early death in 1837 from typhus. Ahead of his contemporary theatre, Büchner's plays were only appreciated and subsequently performed at the end of the nineteenth century. His fragment, *Woyzeck*, prefigures much of modern drama in Büchner's determinism, his understanding of the fatalism of history and in his treatment of

an alienated, inarticulate ordinary soldier, Woyzeck, at the mercy of forces he cannot control or change.

7 Vsevolod Meyerhold, *Théâtre naturaliste et théâtre d'atmosphere*, in *Ecrits sur le théâtre*, *L'Age d'homme*, trans. Béatrice Piçon-Vallin, Lausanne, 1973, vol. 1, pp. 95–104.

7

THOMAS KILROY

The Seagull: an adaptation

Writers who are considered immortal or just plain good and who intoxicate us have one very important trait in common: they are going somewhere and call you with them . . . The best of them are realistic and paint life as it is, but because every line is saturated with juice, with the sense of life, you feel, in addition to life as it is, life as it should be . . .

Chekhov: letter to A.S. Suvorin, 25 November 1892.[1]

In 1981 I adapted *The Seagull*, resetting it on an Anglo-Irish estate in the West of Ireland, with the time of the action placed in the late nineteenth century.[2]

The first reason why I did this was, quite simply, because I was asked to do so by Max Stafford-Clark, then artistic director of the Royal Court Theatre. Max felt, and I agreed with him, that some English language productions of Chekhov tended towards a very English gentility where the socially specific Chekhov tended to be lost in polite vagueness. He believed that an Anglo-Irish setting would provide a specificity, at once removed from, and at the same time comprehensible to, an English audience. He also felt that an Irish setting would more easily allow the rawness of passion of the original to emerge, the kind of semi-farcical hysteria, which Chekhov uses in the scenes between Arkadina, Treplyov and Trigorin in Act Three, for example: a kind of rough theatricality somewhat removed from polite English comedy but common enough in the Irish comic tradition.

The second reason why I took the commission, an equally persuasive one, was that when I began to think about them, the parallels between Chekhov's Russia and nineteenth-century Anglo-Ireland became, for me, extraordinarily vivid and apt. The resonances of Chekhov's play became even more universalised while I was also able to articulate, in this borrowing from a great European playwright, certain perceptions that I have had about the history of my own country.

But who exactly were the Anglo-Irish gentry? In the definition of the historian F. S. L. Lyons, the Anglo-Irish were 'the descendants of English settlers in Ireland, to whom about the end of the nineteenth century the name Anglo-Irish was beginning to be attached. That name was not of their seeking, though it expresses very precisely the schizophrenia which was their natural condition.'[3]

Like Chekhov's gentry, the Anglo-Irish landowning class no longer exists, having been swept away in the foundation and later development of the new Irish state in the first decades of the twentieth century. In each culture, at the end of the nineteenth century, there was this pervasive sense of imminent, drastic change. It was very easy indeed to find an equivalent of the Chekhovian mood of approaching darkness in such an Anglo-Irish setting and as I went on, the common factors between Russian and Anglo-Irish gentry multiplied.

Both represented and enacted imperial authority over a much larger, subservient population. Both played significant roles in the Crown Civil Service and in military command which did so much to preserve that power in their respective countries. For both, the source and symbol of that power was the country estate with its dependent peasantry or serfs and the instability of this property in the latter half of the nineteenth century marks the first signs of the disintegration of the empires themselves. While this loss of power, for both Russian and Anglo-Irish gentry, came towards the end of the nineteenth century, both classes could look back with nostalgia to the preceding century as the period of their greatest flowering.

Here is how Lyons describes the cultural milieu of the Anglo-Irish and if one changes the actual references, one comes close to the Russian counterpart:

> At one level they gave a passable imitation of a governing class on the English model. They acted as deputy lieutenants of their counties, as high sheriffs or as justices of the peace, and they were prominent in local government until the end of the nineteenth century. Apart from visits to the Dublin Horse Show and to the winter season at the Viceregal Court, many of them resided all the year round in their Georgian houses – sometimes beautiful, sometimes ugly, but often dilapidated and generally uncomfortable – where they lived the sort of life that landlords lived everywhere. Shooting, fishing, and hunting, interspersed with hospitality more lavish than they could afford – this was the framework of their lives.[4]

There is, however, that all-important distinction of 'the English model', something which marks a crucial distinction between the Anglo-Irish and the Russian. The Anglo-Irish represented a foreign, English power in

Ireland. Chekhov's gentry at least shared a common Russian nationality with those around and beneath them.

The 'schizophrenia' of the Anglo-Irish that Lyons refers to is the classic condition of a pro-consular, governing class in a colonial situation 'torn between their country of origin and their country of settlement.'[5] Theirs was a see-saw condition, caught between two other, irreconcilable cultures, the English and what might be called, for want of a better term, the *native Irish*. For this reason, my adaptation of *The Seagull* is more overtly political in implication than the original. It brings to the surface the tensions between the Anglo-Irish and the much larger population of native Irish. It is also set against the Land War, which reached a climax in the 1870s, the radical campaign for tenants' rights which eventually destroyed land-lordism in rural Ireland and led to the establishment of modern Irish farming. In my version, the schoolteacher (Medvedenko in the original) is called James and he represents the native Irish people outside the estate walls, now stirring in the first movements towards successful revolution.

Having said all that, there was another common factor between the Russian and Anglo-Irish gentry which overrides the force of politics. This was the common fate of provincial isolation in a period before modern communications. Both worlds were at a remove from their metropolitan centres. These centres, London and Moscow, serve as the same focus for Anglo-Irish and Russian sensibilities, a focus of desire and ambition, of illusions and dreams, magnifying the pent-up emotions of those remote households and offering a prospect, a lure, too often unattainable by sensitive souls.

There is yet a further geographical detail of some importance to my adaptation. By resetting the play in the West of Ireland rather than elsewhere in the country I was able to find an equivalent for another, and charming, feature of the Chekhovian household – its promiscuous socia-bility, the way his houses fill up, not only with relatives but with a whole variety of hangers-on and the fact that this sociability crosses class lines.

We know from the novels of George Moore that the Anglo-Irish 'Big House' in the West of Ireland admitted and welcomed a great confusion of social intercourse, far more so than in other, more anglified, more socially stratified parts of the country. The political and social distinction between Protestant and Catholic, between landlord and professional or craft classes, between old money and new money, indeed, between landlord and tenant, seemed to dissolve or at least lose something of its rigid parameters west of the river Shannon.

One reason for this, also of immense importance in the major Chekhov plays, is that the Western Irish landlords tended to be more impoverished than elsewhere. They were not entirely insulated from their neighbours, their servants, through great wealth. Mutual poverty, relatively speaking, in reducing all, tended to efface the stiff-necked barriers created by politics and social snobbery. As in Chekhov, the constant topic of conversation in Anglo-Irish houses seemed to be about surviving financial collapse. This genteel poverty, familiar from the more recent novels of the late Molly Keane, was eventually to spread to the Anglo-Irish throughout Ireland. But in the late nineteenth century it was more common in the West of Ireland than elsewhere.

In my adaptation, Irina Nikolaevna Arkadina becomes Isobel Desmond, the Anglo-Irish actress of the London stage. Boris Alexeevich Tregorin becomes Mr Aston, a prolific but minor English novelist. Isobel is visiting the West of Ireland estate of her brother Peter, a former civil servant in Dublin Castle, the centre of British imperial power in Ireland prior to the foundation of the Irish Free State in 1922. Shamraev becomes a cousin, Gregory, and this extended family is a feature of the Anglo-Irish household. The running of the estate of an absentee landlord was often left in the hands of a poorer relation. The doctor, called Dr Hickey, and the teacher, James, in the play become Catholic outsiders, admitted into the Anglo-Irish circle but, particularly in the case of the teacher, significantly excluded as well. The two young people, Treplyov and Nina, become Constantine and Lily, and their passion for theatre becomes the most distinctive connection of all between the Anglo-Irish and Russian worlds.

The Anglo-Irish contribution to the English-speaking theatre has been immense. We tend to think of this exclusively, and understandably, in terms of individual playwrights: Farquhar, Sheridan, Goldsmith, Wilde, Shaw, Yeats, Synge, Beckett. But there were also figures like the actress Peg Woffington who, though of working-class background, rose through the stage to prominence in Anglo-Irish society in eighteenth-century Dublin; or Lady Gregory, herself a West of Ireland landlord, but also a playwright and theatre manager, who was highly influential in the foundation of the Abbey Theatre, Dublin, with Yeats and Synge.

In founding a new theatre for Ireland in the last decades of the century, Gregory, Yeats and Synge turned away, consciously, from the English model and drew their inspiration, instead, from Irish peasant culture and ancient Irish myths and legends (the translations of which, incidentally, had become available largely through the work of Anglo-Irish translators, scholars and antiquarians). The drama which they created had the same novelty and strangeness for its Anglo-Irish audiences as Symbolist drama would have had for the Russian audience represented by the household of *The Seagull*. So, in my adaptation, Treplyov's 'decadent' Symbolist play in

Act One becomes Constantine's 'Celtic' play based upon ancient Irish myth.

The presentation of this amateurish drama marks a significant divide between the generations, between the old and the new. Chekhov's target is not Symbolist drama as such but what the occasion reveals of the mother's attitude to the son. Constantine's play has exactly the same kind of effect on Isobel which Treplyov's has upon Arkadina. Both women are disturbed and strangely threatened by what they see and the ineptitude of the writing in each case allows them to fall back upon mockery. Arkadina's distress is related to the perceived threat to her kind of theatre represented by her son's play, a kind of ungainly, monstrous power threatening her out of the future. Isobel feels this, too, but in her case there is the added political threat in that Constantine's play comes out of the suppressed culture, which at all times was threatening rebellion against her class and the property of her family. We have an Anglo-Irish family divided: some still looking to England as its natural motherland, some looking to the native Irish tradition for its inspiration, and this division mirrors historical reality in the period. Like the poor imitators of voguish 'new' drama that Chekhov despised, there were many theatrically poor attempts at writing mythological drama in Ireland, side by side with the exquisite ones of Yeats and Synge. Constantine's is one of those.

The play-within-the-play in Act One of *The Seagull* is one of the passages singled out by Eugene K. Bristow in his Norton Critical Edition of the plays as presenting difficulties for the translator because of the precise, concrete cultural references used by Chekhov.[6] It is also the moment, as Bristow recognises, at which the central theme of art, and more specifically the art of theatre, is established by Chekhov. This runs like a spinal column through the whole play giving it its main structural cohesion. The kind of play, then, which Treplyov presents before his mother and the household and Chekhov's own attitude towards it, colours the whole subsequent dramatic meditation on art and and its relation to the lived life right up to the play's denouement.

This dramatic presentation of a cluster of ideas on art and the artist draws in each of the other characters. It is connected to the loyalty which both Sorin and Dorn display towards Treplyov's writing, one a simple loyalty, the other a more complex one. It is connected to Arkadina's much more complex attitude to the same subject. It touches Masha's pathetic appeal to the writer in Trigorin and her dreams of being in a book. Finally, it provides the nexus between Trigorin, Nina and Treplyov, a vocational base, as it were, against which is played out the fraught game of love and its loss, between the three. What it is to be an artist, what it is to be a writer, this preoccupation, this obsession, fuels the other feelings of affection, of love but also of hatred, of self-disgust in the play. In Chekhov, ideas are always enmeshed in passionate emotion.

I have tried to reproduce this network effect but using Irish references. Let me give some examples to show the changes which this produced in the text.

The most sustained, the most traumatic passage in the play in which an obsession with art is seen to affect feeling, with disastrous consequences, is that between Trigorin and Nina towards the end of Act Two. The scene is a remarkable demonstration of self-disgust as an instrument of seduction; Trigorin piles on the images of abject self-dismissal before this young girl who is so besotted by the notion of art that each disclaimer, each rejection of his own worth, simply makes her feel even more privileged, more privy to the inner secrets of the artist.

The first effect of my adaptation was radically to reduce the length of Trigorin's speeches. This was partly a matter of the taste of the production for which the adaptation was prepared. But it also had to do with my repossession of Trigorin in the shape of Mr Aston, the minor English novelist, who came to me without any of the flowering, Russian imagery; he became a dapper Victorian, parsimonious, edgy, neurotic and acutely aware of finding himself in foreign parts. The Chekhovian images of moon, relay horses, cloud, heliotrope, honey bees, gambler, fox hunt and missed trains became something less natural, more mechanical, more in tune with the vision of living death in Victorian England.

Here is the Bristow translation and my own adaptation:

There are some persistent notions that dominate a person's mind, for instance, when someone thinks constantly about the moon day and night. Well, I have my own kind of moon. Day and night one persistent thought obsesses me – I must write, I must write, I must . . . I no sooner finish one story than for some reason or other I must write the next, then a third, and after that a fourth . . . I write endlessly, exactly as relay horses run, and I can't do it differently. So I ask you, what's particularly beautiful or brilliant about that? Oh, what a senseless and remote way to live! Here I am with you, I'm overwrought . . .[7]

How curious. I've become quite excited, actually nervous, almost hysterical. Very well. Let us talk calmly, above all, accurately, about this beauty, this beautiful life, as you put it. To begin with, I'm obsessive. I have this obsession, you see, as many people do, by which I become a machine, an engine, utterly without will, feeling, without risk, cogs merely slipping into their places on the wheel. Click-click. Do you understand what I mean? Perhaps not. It is not important. In fact it is extremely monotonous. But of course you do understand. You are obviously an intelligent, sensitive young woman.[8]

Dorn's European trip is an ingenious device on Chekhov's part to allow a narrative summary at the beginning of Act Four, filling in the details for the audience of what has happened in the two-year interim. The doctor has to be told and in the telling we are brought up to date on the sorry condition of both Nina and Treplyov. But it is also a trigger to reintroduce that play-within-the play of Act One, rounding off the great meditation on art. In the original this is done by Dorn remembering the play's theme of a universal soul as he was buffeted by the warm turbulence of a crowd on the streets of Genoa. In my adaptation, the city becomes Paris and the experience is altogether more cultural. Here is Dr Hickey from the adaptation:

> Well, Paris is a different place to different people, I dare say. For me, it is the Salon and the Opera Comique. For others it may be the café life, the cuisine or the intellectual conversation. By the way, Constantine, did I tell you? There is great interest nowadays over there in the Celtic thing and all that. I believe Professor de Joubainville's lectures on the old Celtic mythology are highly regarded in the Collège de France. I thought of your play. Remember? *Moytura*. The one about the battle of the two giants, the Light and the Dark. The one which Lily acted for us, outside on the lawn. Was it two years ago? By the way, whatever has become of Lily?[9]

My use of Paris was to draw attention to the fact that the Anglo-Irish fascination with Celtic mythology and folklore was not confined to Ireland at that time. De Joubainville's lectures were attended by John M. Synge in 1898. This contact with ancient Irish lore in the lectures of a French scholar may at least have had as much effect as the famous injunction of Yeats to the younger playwright, two years earlier, that he return to the Aran Islands, off the West Coast of Ireland, and write about the people there, which Synge, of course did, with remarkable results.[10]

My use of Moytura as the myth of Constantine's play has another Anglo-Irish echo, one of some personal meaning to me. It was a myth which entranced Sir William Wilde, the surgeon-cum-folklorist father of Oscar Wilde to the extent that he named one of his summer homes by that name. The house was one of the few possessions left to the impoverished Oscar in his last years in Paris. Unfortunately, it was sold to pay creditors but it still stands just a few miles down the road from where I am now writing this chapter.

In *The Seagull*, as so often elsewhere, Chekhov is writing about the mysterious, contradictory effects of failure. The fact that he conducts this theatricalised discourse on art and its complex relationship to the life of the artistic practitioner, through the figures of a failed artist, a rather vulgar actress, a mediocre, self-hating writer and a young actress who may or may not succeed, accounts for the rich layering of ideas in the play. The fact that

Treplyov's play is a poor dramatic vehicle does not mean that Chekhov himself despised Symbolist drama or, indeed, new forms of theatre generally. It means that this is the way he sets Treplyov upon his journey through failure towards illumination and this illumination occurs moments before he shoots himself. To arrive at a conviction as to what is of value in life is not enough. If one gives all to being an artist and fails, there is no point in continuing and this is the bleak conclusion of this comedy. It is as if the struggle to be an artist has opened his own soul to Treplyov and what he has seen there is chaos.

Bristow identifies the moment of illumination in Treplyov as coming just before Nina raps upon the window in Act Four and is brought into the room. It is part of a monologue on style which engages the contrasting elements of exactitude, specificity, on the one hand and impressionistic lyricism on the other, precisely the elements crucial to Chekhov's own art. It is as if Chekhov is writing out of a ghostly version of his own youthful self, the one who might have failed. The great, but extremely difficult scene between the young couple that follows brings a final sundering and it is not merely one of emotion. In the steely accounting of this play she has drawn strength from failure, he has drawn despair, and thereby they are separated forever.

Here is that moment of Treplyov's illumination, firstly in Bristow's translation, then from my own adaptation:

> I've talked and talked a lot about new forms, yet I feel now that I too am slipping little by little into a conventional rut . . . Yes, I'm invariably coming more and more to the conviction that the issue is a question neither of old nor of new forms, but that a person simply writes, never thinking about the kind of forms, he writes because it pours freely out of his soul.[11]

> Useless, absolutely useless! 'We need new forms that will bring back the ancient wisdom of the people.' What does that mean? I have no contact with the people. Merely stories out of old books written in a strange, lost language . . . New forms! What does any of it matter so long as it is true to what one feels?[12]

Of course, I had another great writer in mind when constructing this Anglo-Irish Constantine, one, too, whose art moved between the concrete and the evanescent, the broken neck of a bottle and distant, tremulous music, the seen and the unseen. Yeats, too, like Chekhov, struggled to get that balance right. Like Constantine in my adaptation, he, too, was immensely aware of the obstacles in his attempts to write 'of the people'. He was a far more political creature than Chekhov and although he fought against extreme nationalism, his theatrical movement was but one of many movements towards national self-expression at the time, all of which came to a head in the country's War of Independence (1919–21). But Yeats would have immediately recognised the tragic perception in this young man's speech, that if the written word is not grounded in the deep personal feeling of the writer, it is nothing.

For a writer who is so dependent upon mood, tone, nuance, there is concrete material reality behind everything which Chekhov wrote. This hard, concrete specificity requires a similar exactitude in any adaptation and, indeed, in any production of the plays. Without it there is always the danger of a false Chekhovian style, a self-regarding surrender to that seductive mood of *ennui*. It was one of the extraordinary experiences of adapting *The Seagull* to find such specific details leaping out of the period of Irish history and from the English theatrical and literary background. But there was also the solid foundation for those more intimate, domestic details of Chekhov as well: the low wages of a schoolmaster hobnobbing with those of apparent wealth; the peculiar panic of the powerful when the power begins to ebb away; how aging changes the shape of thinking as well as the body.

The late Peggy Ramsay[13] was one of the great figures of post-war British theatre, a woman of immense influence far beyond that of a dramatist's agent. When I began work on *The Seagull* she said to me that translation or adaptation was 'a form of privileged conversation with an author' but that you would 'have to reach below superficial detail' before that privilege would be granted. It was some time before I understood what she had said and when I did, Russian and Anglo-Irish settings became irrelevant. What mattered was the amplitude of Chekhov's vision of human life.

In writing the plays he seemed to project himself into a future and from this mysterious point in time he looks back at the creatures of his imagination. In that sense, in writing the plays he was compiling a kind of history. Certainly, no other playwright has a more acute historical sensibility in the way the plays are authentic records of a time past but also by the way they are permeated by the ordeal of time passing and haunted by the glimmer of time to come. This sense of time and its effects is particularly underlined in *The Seagull* because of that two-year gap between Act Three and Act Four.

This almost Olympian perspective is the source or at least vehicle of his immense generosity as a writer, which somehow coexists with that implacable gaze. There are no heroes in Chekhov. Even the servants blossom into place because he understood how the process of time diminishes even the most Napoleonic of egos. When this process, as in *The Seagull*, is a demonstration of the awful persistence of failure and that the continuity of life depends upon moving through and beyond failure, then the drama becomes one of a moral testing.

Stars like to play minor characters in Chekhov, something which is not quite as true of Shakespeare. This distribution of attention by the writer to each character in the play is, at first sight, an immense technical achievement in play-making. But then you realise that it is essentially an acknowledgement of things as they are in the world – 'life as it is', a type of moral realism. This fierce grip on the present moment gives an almost unendurable pathos to those characters, like Nina/Lily, who reach out towards a future, to what might be, as if it were already in place, while we know that it may never actually materialise.

Certain voices, too, throughout the major plays (Tuzenbakh and Vershinin in *Three Sisters*, Astrov in *Uncle Vanya*, and Treplyov) allude to that future, often in words that recall Chekhov's own letters. The characters may be cynical, apocalyptic, absurd, romantic or astute, but what they add up to is a kind of negative self-portrait, an ironical subjection by Chekhov of his own, often passionately held, ideas to the levelling exposure of comedy. The self-effacement of Chekhov is but another way of describing a writer who accepted completely that he was himself subject to the same follies as his creations. At this late stage of the twentieth century, as we stagger about under the weight of its self-conciousness, this simple fact may appear exceptional, even radical.

The dynamic of *The Seagull*, then, exists well below its social detail in the humane but rigorous discriminations of Chekhov himself between the frailty of human behaviour and the absolute demands of love, between the generosity of love – and the imperiousness of art. The play is filled with those awkward, clumsy moments when people try to cope with daily living while at the same time in the grip of obsessions and aspirations, unable to see anything with clarity, unsure of putting one foot in front of the other. The condition is comic, of course, but a kind of comedy which invites many different responses from an audience. Here, too, is another version of time. For all their sense of imminence, of the moment about-to-be, all Chekhov's plays are rooted in an untidy present, full of inconsequentialities, of ordinary helplessness. *The Seagull*, like the other major plays, is placed in this curious shell of time, past–present–future, but each phrase, each gesture, is a grinding effort to deal with those immediate, troublesome moments of the here and now.

To those who are bothered about adaptations, seeing them as parasitic or even a violation of the original, there is simply only one answer. The history of theatre is a history of adaptation, beginning, and continuing, with the extraordinary variety of repossessions of the Greeks. There is no obvious explanation as to why this medium in particular (and also its offshoots in cinema and television) is so given to borrowing and recycling of material from within its own tradition. For some reason, theatre has always enjoyed this activity, has seen it as essentially theatrical and it has never felt that the integrity of the original has been damaged in any way. Quite the contrary. The good adaptation always sends one back to the original, afresh and with a new appreciation of its worth.

NOTES

Where the translations have not been made by the author himself, the English-language version used is that of Eugene K. Bristow (see note 6 below).

1 Quoted from Lillian Hellman, ed. and intro., *The Selected Letters of Anton Chekhov*, trans. Sidonie K. Lederer, London, 1984, p. 172

2 Thomas Kilroy, adapt., *The Seagull*, Loughcrew, Meath, Ireland, 1993. Premièred on 8 April 1981, Royal Court, London, dir. Max Stafford-Clark.

3 F.S.L. Lyons, *Culture and Anarchy in Ireland, 1890–1939*, Oxford, 1982, p. 18.

4 *Ibid.*, p. 19.

5 *Ibid.*

6 Eugene K. Bristow, ed. and trans., *Anton Chekhov's Plays*, New York, 1977, pp. xxiv–xxv.

7 *The Seagull*, Act Two, in *ibid.*, p. 25. Hingley, *Oxford Chekhov*, vol. II, Act Two, p. 255.

8 Kilroy, *The Seagull*, Act Two, pp. 48–9.

9 *Ibid.*, Act Four, p. 75.

10 This resulted in Synges' plays, *In the Shadow of the Glen (1903); Riders to the Sea* (1904); *The Well of the Saints* (1905); *Deirdre of the Sorrows* (1910); *The Tinker's Wedding* (1971, first production at the Abbey), and the famous *The Playboy of the Western World* (1907). The dates refer to the first productions at Dublin's Abbey Theatre.

11 *The Seagull*, Act Four, in Bristow, *Anton Chekhov's Plays*, p. 47. Hingley, *Oxford Chekhov*, vol. II, Act Four, p. 277.

12 Kilroy, *The Seagull*, pp. 81–2.

13 Margaret Ramsay (1908–91) whose agency, Margaret Ramsay Ltd., was one of the leading playwrights' agencies in the English-speaking theatre. After her death the agency continued as Casarotto Ramsay and Associates Limited. See Colin Chambers, *Peggy*, London, 1997.

8

LEONID HEIFETZ

Notes from a director: *Uncle Vanya*

In different periods of one's life as a director – as well as of a spectator or reader – one finds in Chekhov something which seems particularly significant at a specific moment in time. I have now done two productions of *Uncle Vanya*: the first, in 1969, at the Central Soviet Army Theatre (now the Russian Army Theatre) in Moscow; and then the second production in 1991, in Turkey at the Istanbul Municipal Theatre. Each done in different countries, *and* at different times.

In those intervening years, I have never been parted from Chekhov, whether in my thinking or in my practical work. I directed *Three Sisters* in Turkey (1988), and *The Cherry Orchard* as a television production (Moscow, 1976), as well as in the theatre in Kirgizia (1983), in Turkey (1986) and in Poland (1997). But my memories of those first encounters with *Uncle Vanya* remain uniquely precious. When I recall my memories, thoughts and experiences of that work, I always feel something had changed in that period of time, both in me and in my perception of the play. Yet at the same time, something has also always remained immutable.

An old entry from my diary reads: 'One evening I was rereading *Uncle Vanya*. Without any special purpose or reason. And suddenly I felt sad. This always happens when you read Chekhov. But towards the end of the play, I realised that something different had happened to me. And reading Sonya's final lines about stars, shining like diamonds, I felt not sadness, but fury. 'We shall rest!' These are not words of consolation, but of intransigence: we shall rest *irrespective* of anything or everyone. No matter how hard it is going to be: We shall rest. This is a challenge: Sonya's last outburst of fury and elevated courage became an internal imperative for remembering *Uncle Vanya* for ever and ever. . .'[1]

And I have always remembered. Nearly thirty years have passed since I made that entry. The century and the millennium are running out. The age has grown old, and so have we. And now I would find it difficult to ask the actress playing Sonya to express the feelings that overwhelmed us in the late 1960s: to do what young Natasha Vilkina managed to express with such tragic power. Perhaps today this challenge would sound inappropriate, even ludicrous. For now we know that we shall not see the stars, shining like diamonds, and that too many people would prefer to have diamonds not in the sky, but somewhere closer to hand. And these days I perceive Sonya's monologue as words of consolation. Now there is no fury, bitterness or challenge, but compassion and love. None of this, however, means that *Uncle Vanya* now seems to me a quiet and serene play. On the contrary, it is turbulent and passionate, but the sense of romantic protest has gone. The acuteness and scope of our present-day perceptions sharpen awareness of Uncle Vanya's agony. Not melancholy, but the specific agony of dying, and awareness that life has been a complete failure.

As a young director I did not realise the actuality of Uncle Vanya's talk of suicide as strongly as I do now. 'I'm forty-seven. Suppose I live till sixty. Thirteen years to go. A long time . . .'[2] Previously these words did not mean much to me but now, when I myself am long past forty-seven and have been through so much, the sinister actuality of the situation is disturbing. Suicide rates in the world have not declined and perhaps the next 'candidate' is here – in the audience . . . Why don't we try and save at least one life, keep him or her on this earth a little longer? How? By letting people feel they are not alone and are cared for, by trying to warm their hearts, by loving them more than we love ourselves. This will take an enormous spiritual effort, but today I can see no other meaning or purpose for staging *Uncle Vanya*.

Uncle Vanya's humiliation jarred on me when I was young. I couldn't understand how a man could be so crazy about a woman that he would give up all dignity, and beg her: 'I know my chances of any return are negligible. They are negligible. But I want nothing. Only let me look at you sometimes, hear your voice.' It would seem that then I was unaware of the magnetism of love, even though I was already a married man and had a daughter. Decades later, I became aware of this, but I'm still not sure if I can feel the entire measure of despair and exaltation which gives Uncle Vanya the right to speak those words.

It is, after all, a matter of sensibilities. They can evolve towards cruelty or the other way round. There was a time when classicism in the theatre gave way to romanticism which, in turn, was later 'dislodged' by naturalism. This evolution reflected changes in sensibilities, in the intensity of perception. Ostrovsky's plays were initially censored in Russia as too shocking and forthright. The emergence of the Moscow Art Theatre late last century was a reaction to the bombastic style of the Academic Imperial Theatres.[3] In the middle of *this* century, the Sovremennik (Contemporary)

Company was born – to speak the very truth which, under Stalin's totalitarian regime, was even more seductive than during the MAT's origin and development. The same has happened to our perceptions of Chekhov. The pensive lyricism of the MAT stagings gave way to the cruel style of the 1960s.

My 1969 production, condemned by critics for excessive cruelty, would today look slack and flabby, for our modern theatre is certainly more cruel. Even Peter Brook's acclaimed mid-1970s French production of *The Cherry Orchard* would seem serene and gentle compared to more recent stagings.

But to return to the play, *Uncle Vanya*. Let us read the very first scene, which I define as 'Astrov's grievance'. The grievance of the doctor called out to see a patient, risking a breakneck ride of thirty miles, only to find out that the patient is not at home and is apparently quite well. The nanny, Marina, loves Astrov and, knowing how he feels, she tries to put his mind at ease.

MARINA Have a bite, my dear fellow.
ASTROV Don't feel like it . . .
MARINA Have some vodka then?
ASTROV No. I don't drink vodka every day. Besides, it's hot. (A pause)

These first lines of the play, a superficially insignificant exchange, are absolutely remarkable for their intonation; for the music of the 'humanitarian' which sounds in both of them. The old nanny, or nurse, sees how bad the doctor feels, but how to convey his feelings?

In my production in 1969, Astrov was waiting for the supposedly 'sick' Professor Serebryakov, sitting on a chair and tapping with his stick, as though to emphasise the irony of the situation and to show that he doesn't take it seriously. But today I would suggest to the actors a quite different means of expressing Astrov's restlessness and grievance. The sensibilities of the mid-1990s call for a heightened level of tension. Astrov's ironic melancholy is insufficient and inadequate. The insult is gnawing at his guts. He is in the kind of mood when life seems especially meaningless and pointless. If the play opens with such a high pitch of emotions, it will achieve the driving force necessary to heighten dramatic tensions.

Now we have started the play. What I call 'Astrov's grievance' is the opening event. But in the Russian directorial tradition there is the notion of an 'initial event', a kind of point of departure which typifies Chekhov's drama. Out of necessity, at the first rehearsal I would talk with the actors about a typical Chekhovian situation: arrival – and departure. The whole story of *The Cherry Orchard* unfolds between two ordinary events: the arrival of Ranevskaya – and the departure of Ranevskaya. The story of

Three Sisters also has its boundaries: life in the town changes with the arrival of the artillery regiment – and returns to normal when the regiment leaves. In *Uncle Vanya* this situation is especially graphic: life on the estate was monotonous and peaceful until the arrival of the Serebryakovs, the Professor and his wife. With their arrival the pleasant dull rhythm of country life explodes, but again the story ends with a departure. (The story is the action, unfolding on stage in the eyes of the audience. But in the play, each character has a pre-history, something which has happened before the curtain rises, something unspoken and unperformed, but which can be guessed, deduced or imagined.)

Simultaneous with the 'initial event' which pushes the action, there is also the 'main event' – Uncle Vanya's violent revolt. One can imagine that after the Serebryakovs leave, the neighbourhood will gossip for a long time about something terrifying which happened at this house: the attempt to kill a man. One man fired two shots at the other. He missed, but this was a murder attempt, followed by a suicide attempt.

The audience sees Uncle Vanya fire at the Professor with his revolver, miss, collapse with despair and shame, and then try to kill himself with poison he has stolen from the doctor; and it takes considerable effort by his relatives to take this poison away from him. In contrast to my production of the late 1960s, today I would interpret the story of this rebellion with more emphasis on the cruelty. It *is* a scene of blood, even though blood wasn't spilt, and of two missed shots, fired one after another ('Bang! I missed? Missed again?!') – which can make the audience laugh. But it is both laughable and terrifying.

It is also necessary to talk to the actors about the accumulation of conflict. The social aspect of this conflict is only one of many, although Russian experience and mentality prohibit one from ignoring it completely. In my Turkish production of *Uncle Vanya*, the actor playing Voynitsky (Vanya) also threw his books and manuscripts at the Professor, and sheets of paper were flying all over the space. This scene, it seems, reflected some of my own personal experiences. It was *my* revolt, *my* protest against those vast volumes which until recently had filled our lives; against those idols we had worshipped and the false truths we had believed. I went through this personally – not that I threw books at anybody or burned them. My revolt was quiet: I walked away. Escaped. In this sense, Uncle Vanya is more straightforward and more honest. Illusions, causing us to make graven images, are an eternal problem for humankind. Illusions are perpetually created – and inevitably ruined. Our society is still buried under these ruins. Our way of life suddenly came tumbling down, exposing the previous lies, and throwing people into awareness of wasted lives – their own and those of others. In this sense, too, Chekhov's play has relevance and reference to the present day.

But the social aspect of the conflict is the director's concern. For the actors, it is important for them to know that at the core of *Uncle Vanya* are personal relationships. Vanya's disappointment in life essentially grows out of his unrequited feelings for Yelena Andreyevna. His mind is scorched by the thoughts of injustice when some people, like the Professor, have everything: no matter how old and grey, they are famous, loved by beautiful women and live in luxury, while others, like Uncle Vanya, have nothing. One has the feeling that in spite of all his pains and gout, the Professor will live for a hundred years, while Uncle Vanya will have expired much earlier.

The pattern of relationships in *Uncle Vanya* is so clear that one would have to work extremely hard to make this play incomprehensible – but this happens often enough, in both the Russian theatre *and* abroad. I have seen productions by directors who do not believe that love is always relevant to the present day – and who therefore look for something more topical or fashionable. But Chekhov's play rests entirely on love. The modern theatre seeks different approaches to Chekhov, but for me the only right direction is to dig deeper inside, because the depth of the soul, the depth of perception, the depth of pain, has no limits. But if there is no such searching deep inside, if social temperament or a predilection for 'effects' or new forms for their own sake impel directors to try and strike at the audience with some pioneering interpretation of Chekhov, then the audience does not usually respond.

My experiences abroad, beginning with the first production in the late 1970s, have helped me to realise the value of simple and eternal truths. Audiences respond when the director succeeds in conveying the essential affinity of human experiences. An Eskimo and an African go through basically the same experiences when they are born, live and die on this earth. This may be clichéd, but ignoring this makes it rather difficult for the director to convince and move the audience, especially a foreign one.

When I directed Chekhov's plays in Turkey, at first they seemed infinitely remote from that country's customs and traditions. But both *The Cherry Orchard* and *Uncle Vanya* played to packed houses for an unbroken five years. Why?

In the Turkish *Uncle Vanya* everything was focussed on love, something everyone understood. Here is a beautiful, charming woman, Yelena – [or in Hingley's version, Helen] – and three men around her. In the first rehearsal it was immediately possible to seat the woman in a chair, make the three men stand by the wall and explain to them their parts and the pattern of their relationships. One man loves and desires the woman and it looks as though she returns his feelings. The other also loves and desires her, but he doesn't have a chance. And the third man is simply her husband while the other two want to take her away from him. Inside such a 'triangle', tensions and struggles break out naturally. And at a certain distance from them, you place a girl with large eyes (Sonya) and tell her that the first man is your love and dream, and that you only feel alive when you see him. The other one, your uncle, is helpless and desperate. And the third man, your father, has become a terror in the home.

This is only a blueprint, an outline, but it makes everything become clear. It is clear what an elderly husband is. It is clear what it means to be a woman, living with an old man, when two other men in love with her are around. It may not be immediately clear how fallen idols break people's lives, but in the end this also may be understood. So working on *Uncle Vanya* in Istanbul, I had no problems with national specifics.

Another aspect is the degree of openness in expressing feelings. Turkey is an Islamic country with age-old household traditions and ethics, where expression is traditionally restrained, and a woman is certainly not the centre of the universe. And it took some effort to find the balance between the open expression of feelings which typifies modern life – and the Turkish theatrical tradition for performing love scenes. The power of feeling is the same, but different nations in different times express it differently. For instance, I don't know how, in the original Moscow Art Theatre production, Stanislavsky as Astrov declared love to Olga Knipper as Yelena Andreyevna: how he took her by the hand, and stole her kisses in that fleeting moment when Uncle Vanya was out picking flowers. In our modern theatre, I would recommend that the actor needs to be more energetic and aggressive. Today we can feel the powerful eroticism of Chekhov's play, we can talk about it and perform it. I believe there was a very strong masculine charge in Chekhov, and the tuberculosis, loneliness, anticipation and separation (from his wife, Olga Knipper) only activated it.

I am surprised to hear people arguing about whether Yelena *really* loves Astrov or at what moment they first notice each other. These two people are visibly burning with the desire to be close; they are on the verge of losing control of themselves – and not only in the 'interrogation scene' of the third act. It is difficult to explain the leave-taking scene at the end of the play logically, when everything is ready for departure, bags packed and loaded – the husband may enter at any moment, yet they still throw themselves at each other and Astrov again tries to persuade Yelena to stay and go with him out into the 'fresh air'. The stronger this desire for possession, the more the erotic charge is infused in the actors, and the more fascinating the performance will be.

I cannot say I fully managed to achieve this, either in the first, or in the second production. This can be done by actors, possessing some modern techniques, and having the courage and determination to perform *real* desire and carry it to the highest level. This is the source of many situations and conflicts in the play, but certainly not the only source. In Chekhov it is always important to maintain the balance and sum total of *all* the causes and components of the action: whether intimate and personal or social.

The objectivity and breadth of perception, the ability to see the underlying causes and to be fair, all typify Chekhov – and present major difficulties for us. Perhaps the best illustration of this is Chekhov's attitude towards his own characters. Separate moments and motifs of the play call for detailed discussion, but this is even more the case with the characterisation! It seems to me that characters in *Uncle Vanya*, as well as in the other plays, are very close to Chekhov. The only character in all of Chekhov's plays whom I really detest is Yasha in *The Cherry Orchard*, but working on that play, the actor and I tried to be objective and discover even this man's 'truth' too. As for *Uncle Vanya*, all the characters are close and clear to me, but this didn't happen immediately.

Another entry from my old diary: 'Sonya . . . It all started with her. Fascination with these unpretentious country-life scenes began with this twenty-year-old girl, the beauty and power of her soul, her unbending dignity, her love and despair. I even blamed myself for being unfair to other characters. But Sonya proved to be the clue to all the others. And if initially the play were to be retitled *Sonya*, then soon afterwards we would be rehearsing Astrov, Serebryakov, Waffles, Uncle Vanya and then again Sonya, Yelena Andreyevna, and so on.'

I am recalling the past only to stress that exploring Chekhov is *always* a process, a journey. It can start with any episode or any line, or with curiosity about one character or another: with Sonya, or Telegin (nicknamed 'Waffles'), or old Marya Vasilyevna (Maman), and each will lead you to the others – and, ultimately, to the whole play. Every one of Chekhov's characters has a faith, a truth, an individuality, and each one seems particularly close and important.[4]

I am trying to understand these people through myself, my age, my experiences and observations. Having lived for over sixty years, I have been through many of the situations and phases of life that are found in this play. The only character I have not been myself is probably Waffles, a lonely and good-hearted man who has become part of the family and the home. But even here there is a certain affinity: the loneliness following the loss of his wife. I too happen to have been left alone, like everyone on this earth.

I even try to put myself in Serebryakov's shoes. After all, it is unfair to think of Serebryakov as a monster, an evil creature and the *only* source of the conflict that strikes the family. Characters in Chekhov's plays do not lend themselves to division into the righteous and the guilty. They cannot be placed on two sides of the barricade. I would be bored to see a play in which the Professor is presented only as a talentless fraud. No doubt he has had command of his profession and has worked hard in the field of education. He has been loved by his students, *and* by two beautiful women: his first wife, Sonya's mother, and Yelena Andreyevna. Imagine yourself with a young and beautiful wife in the company of two men who are trying to take her away from you. Both are in love with Yelena and both quite openly despise the Professor. He sees it all, sees Astrov's attempts at wooing her, and this must be the reason why, from the outset, he abhors the doctor. It is not that he is right to insult Dr Astrov, but the point is that Serebryakov is unhappy in his own way, and has his own subjective truth.

Everything is important in Chekhov's characters: what makes them alike – and different; their past, and their destinies, and the subtlest nuances of feelings. The very title of the play, the notion of 'Uncle Vanya' is itself a nuance. This is very difficult to explain to a foreigner because Uncle Vanya embodies the national sensibilities of an average Russian intellectual: incapable of great deeds; the man who shoots twice – and misses, misses his revenge. But on the other hand, he is an extremely conscientious man, lonely, loving, lovable and dear, in a word – Uncle Vanya.

In spite of all the differences between Vanya and Astrov, they have common destinies and a common misfortune: that of failing to fulfil themselves, although one wouldn't say this when seeing Astrov for the first time. Failure in self-fulfilment or in realising aspirations, whether in private life or in a professional career, was as much a tragedy last century, in 1897, as it is now.[5] In the quarrel with the Professor and when he is at the height of his outburst, Vanya cries that he 'could become a Schopenhauer, a Dostoyevsky'. One knows that this is not true. He *could* have become someone else, but he didn't. He could have had a family, a loving wife, children but, like Astrov, he has not. Both have grim futures: it seems just as likely that Uncle Vanya will calm down as that Astrov will drink himself to death in the absence of love, in the hopeless humdrum dreariness of his existence.

In fact, everyone in this play is a loser. Not one has good luck in life. And the one thing such different women as Yelena, 'the splendid woman', and Sonya, 'the unattractive woman', have in common is bad luck. Unfortunate women, like Sonya, have always been abundant in Russia. In no other country is the loneliness of a woman expressed so painfully. Nowhere else does a woman have to 'be' everything in a large house, and in a ridiculous and disunited family have to be the mother and the sister, to exhaust herself by hard work because there are no prospects for love and personal fulfilment. It is all the more remarkable, therefore, that in her situation Sonya manages to preserve the purity and beauty of her soul.

As a character, Sonya has always been loved by actresses. There is a clarity about Sonya which is absent from the other characters, but there have been many failed performances in playing her part. With Yelena's character it is different: she is a mysterious woman, and much depends on the actress who plays this part. In her performance, she has to explain and justify the storm of passions which breaks out around her. If other characters' fascination with her has to be 'imitated', and if the men in the audience don't share these feelings, then the play will not work. The actress must not just be beautiful and feminine, but 'splendid'. She must arouse desire, turn heads.

But even this is insufficient. Every heroine in Chekhov's plays has some mystery. The mystery of Yelena is – she is profoundly unhappy. She is not what her admirers, worshippers, think she is when they are caught up in their frustration: she is not a *femme fatale*, or 'a mermaid'. She is alive and decent, and life is hard on her. It is hard to put up with the situation when she is with her husband and the men are struggling over her. It is hard to conceal her growing passion for Astrov, for whom, from the moment they meet, she has been burning with desire and love. But her breeding, strict morals, the presence of her husband, her own conscience and reticence, and that wretched Uncle Vanya who chases her everywhere, or Sonya who herself is in love with Astrov – all this keeps Astrov and Yelena apart, and their paths will never again cross . . .

Much more could be said about this play, about each of its characters and scenes. The longer one lives, the more there is to say. The play pulls you in irresistibly. And in spite of all the turbulence of the action, all the squabbles and rebellions, and the hopelessness of this dreary everyday life, there is cajoling poetry in this play. This is the poetry of feelings and words, of nature and lifestyle, which grows out of the simplest things.

Perhaps in no other play of Chekhov's have I heard such mournful and touching music of departure, expressed in just one word: 'Left'. (Or 'Gone'.)[6] The Serebryakovs will exit, the bells will jingle and Astrov will say: 'Left'. The nanny, Marina, will enter, followed by Sonya: 'Left'. And the old Maman will echo: 'Left'. This refrain alternates in perfect rhythm with simple actions and exchanges of neutral phrases. Then Astrov will leave ('Left', 'Left' . . .) – and these people will remain to live out their days.

The twentieth century is running out. The Russian poet Osip Mandelshtam called this century 'the wolf-hound'. And I would call it the age of Chekhov. Not of Hitler or Mussolini, of Stalin or Chairman Mao, of Churchill or of Roosevelt. It is more likely that this is the age of Charlie Chaplin and of Einstein, but most of all, of Chekhov. The age of his triumph, his bloodless victory. Very soon (with only an instant in eternity before the new millennium is upon us) we may be plunged into an abyss. This evil, blood-thirsty, disgusting century will lapse into the abyss, to the roar of missiles, the rattling of assault weapons and the groans of the victims of war. But it will go down in history as the age of Uncle Vanya's bitter revelation and great love, along with Chekhov's warning against making false, graven, images. Biblical truths transcend and triumph over centuries. And Chekhov has triumphed too.

I would be curious to know whether a young director in the next century, reading Sonya's monologue, will feel fury?

NOTES

1 Excerpts from this diary were published in *Teatr*, 3, 1978, pp. 85–94.
2 N. F. Belchikov and others, eds., *Anton Chekhov, Polnoe sobranie, sochinenii i pisem v 30i tomakh*, Moscow, 1974–83, (*Anton Chekhov, Collected Works and Letters in 30 volumes*, Moscow, 1974–83). From *Works*, vol. XIII, p. 107. All subsequent – Russian – quotations from Chekhov come from this edition of the *Collected Works and Letters*.
3 Heifetz is here referring to such Imperial Theatres as the Moscow Bolshoi Theatre or the Maly Theatre, in fact to all theatres which were not privately owned or/and private or subscription theatres like the MAT, or Korsh's Theatre where *The Bear* was premièred.
4 Stanislavksy's famous and much-quoted remark that 'there are no small parts, only small actors' seems relevant here.
5 1897 was the year of publication of *Uncle Vanya*.
6 Often translated into English as 'Gone'. There is ambivalence and duality in either word, whether in Russian or English, and different no matter whether it is 'Gone' or 'Left'. Yet each carries the same finality.

9

TREVOR NUNN

Notes from a director: *Three Sisters*

Anything that I have to say about Chekhov from a director's perspective amounts to a testament to his extraordinary durability, the sheer toughness of the material and how well made his plays are. In fact, the experiences I have to relate are full of compromise at every level and thus quite opposite to any idealistic or ideological approach. What shines through my memory of the experience is the play – the indestructibility of the play almost beyond ruination. The story I have to tell more or less proves this.

I wanted the Royal Shakespeare Company both for political reasons *and* reasons proceeding from my own social convictions, to mount a kind of small-scale touring operation, which would enable the company 'to reach the parts of the country that other beers could not reach'.[1] I wanted to go to places where there were no existing theatre buildings, or where there was an absence of a theatre-going habit or tradition. By definition, there-fore, places that would seem to have been 'written off' for theatre.

I wanted this because it was a time (1979) when I was trying to get the Arts Council to think *differently* about the RSC's approach to touring, and to persuade them to invest money in us taking the *entire* Stratford operation for an extended period to Newcastle. I wanted to replicate the approach of the Berliner Ensemble, which had taken every aspect of their repertoire operation to different areas in East Germany for a period of time – a residency, rather than our touring system of taking one production fleet-ingly to a venue for a week at a time. But I realised that if I won that argument with the Arts Council, I *had* to be able to offer a concomitant form of touring to create a balance.

That balance would best be achieved by creating a small-scale operation which by definition would present a kind of 'rough theatre':[2] we would be taking our own stage platform and lighting towers, and going to places such as social centres, community halls, church halls, town squares. I was open to any and every suggestion about *where* the company might go, but it was axiomatic that our presentations would be 'unsophisticated'.

Finally, the new endeavour was approved by the Arts Council. As a result I thought I would have to get somebody of a very high theatrical profile to be responsible for the tour, otherwise it would happen more or less anonymously and unnoticed. The person I turned to was the leading actor with whom I had been working for the previous two years, Ian McKellen. I suggested to Ian that he should use and adapt the principles of The Actors' Company,[3] with which he had been involved as a founder member, and build up a company of artists for whom he would be ultimately responsible. I asked him to be involved in play selection, choosing and planning the repertoire along with the tour manager, and advised him to think of this as a semi-autonomous operation. Ian agreed. Then, a couple of months later, he telephoned me to say, 'I've formed a group, and according to Actors' Company principles, we have debated who we most want to direct us and now, representing the Company, I am saying that we want you.' Now that was not quite the point – I mean the idea of Ian organising the tour was that *he* should take responsibility for it and I would not otherwise be involved.

Anyway, his phone calls persisted and Ian said that it would make all the difference if I would validate the project by agreeing to direct. I understood his thinking, much though I resisted him; by then it was established that he was going to present a production of *Twelfth Night*, and was urging me to do a production of *The Seagull*. From then on, this story is increasingly about managerial pragmatism. I thought about the actors Ian had assembled. I understood, of course, that he must have assembled them with some sense that *The Seagull* would be an appropriate play for them. But I believed that it did not provide a balance to the casting requirements of *Twelfth Night*. I could see that there was great value in doing a Chekhov; actors know that working on a Chekhov play is likely to be a democratic experience and that everybody is required to provide an equal amount of contribution and initiative. The Chekhov play becomes 'company-forming' material. But I assure you, and I must be honest about this, my choice of Chekhov was hard-nosed and practical. I could see the company value of doing a Chekhov play, but I concluded they were talking about the wrong one. I decided to study the acting company that had been put together, and see which Chekhov play offered better casting opportunities. The cart was most emphatically before the horse.

I had seen *Three Sisters* in a very highly regarded production directed by Dr Jonathan Miller.[4] I think I had also seen a television version which was not particularly distinguished and I had seen a production at the World Theatre Season that struck me as being over emphatic, heavy-handed and self-indulgently slow. I had few preconceptions about the play. I knew that what Jonathan had done, according to critical authority, had been to free the play of a number of preconceptions, but I can't say I knew what those preconceptions had been. I read the play in an immediately available translation by Richard Cottrell,[5] with whom I'd been at university. I found it a very accessible translation with very clear intentions, but to some extent it lacked anything very idiomatic. It was careful, clear, clean. More than a literal translation, it had insight but no great sense of place or the Russian idiom. It occurred to me that it would be very good to work with such a translation so that something more richly idiomatic could be found during the rehearsal process, rather than to work with something minutely instructed by the translator from the word go.

So, I put it to Ian that in fact we should think about *Three Sisters*. Ian was happy to give me free rein just so long as *I* did something; it was not a case that I had to argue in any great detail. So by chance, rather than by design, I found myself involved in a production of *Three Sisters* and found myself more or less inheriting a cast. I suspect that this is a far cry from the circumstances in which most directors would agree to proceed, whether Stanislavsky,[6] Tovstonogov[7] or Lyubimov,[8] or contemporary directors who have learned from the Russian tradition. Such a contemporary director, like Max Stafford-Clark,[9] would, I am sure, never contemplate proceeding in this way. I was fortunate that the group of people who had been assembled were all immensely intelligent, and brought with them no *amour propre*, or the kind of personality in constant need of being stroked. They were immediately and passionately interested and engaged with their characters. It was really only as a second wave of perception that I began to understand that I had presented myself with a very considerable conundrum.

The circumstance of our travelling theatre necessitated the audience being seated on three sides. For spaces where there was no existing auditorium or raked seating, we had to erect a platform stage. So I was reading a play that has the specific requirements of rooms, doors and elements of furniture that would seem to be integral and then, of course, I went through a period of panic.

I feared that either the tour had to be rescheduled so we would go only to existing theatres, *and* that a full-scale design for the play could be made, *or* that we would have to reconsider and plan a different play. But then I started to think of *Three Sisters* as a *poetic* play, as a play of heightened language and poetic ideas. In a sense, I started to think of it in Shakespearean terms. The seventeenth-century bare stage and back wall provided actors with the capability of entering and leaving an uncluttered environment, the specificity and detail of which could be created through language. I found that this notion entirely released me from the panic, and as all of the clutter and furniture and bric-à-brac of nineteenth-century social life disappeared out of my mind, so a lot of the accretions of that theatre tradition disappeared. I suppose in my own defence I should add that this was before Peter Brook's brave stage adaptation of *The Cherry Orchard* which I think of as the best, the most affecting production of a Chekhov play that I have seen.[10]

It was clear to me that because I was planning a mixture of a 'poor theatre'[11] and 'rough theatre' relationship between the play and the audience, it was vital that everything be *suggested* and that the demand should be made on the spectators' collective imagination to provide whatever scenically was missing. For example, I had no problem with the demand for there to be a large number of people at a lunch party, necessitating a huge table and the need to solve the method of its arrival, as well as any ensuing sightline restrictions. A 'table' could be made by a group of actors using only chairs, forks and napkins. What was important was that they should be able to crystallise minute behavioural details at this lunch party, so *everything* of their characters' physical lives could be selected to provide a recognisable and convincing clarity, and could be choreographed to make each textual and comedic focus. I discovered that the absence of the furniture also made the scene intensely comic; I enjoyed doing those very things that would have been impossible with the table. That is *not* the same as saying we were no longer in a naturalistic play, but that instead we were presenting a heightened poetical experience.

The music for the production provided a similar case in point. It would have been contradictory in this 'poor' theatre environment to employ a sound department with state-of-the-art electronic amplifiers reproducing large-scale instrumental music cues. It was extremely releasing to know that I had to find an actor who could play the piano, an actor who could play the guitar, an actor who could play the violin and that the all-important music of the production would come only from those sources. This decision provided the production with an unshakeable authenticity. The music, which became fundamentally important to the experience of Chekhov's play, was organic. There was no 'background' score, nothing was overlaid or forced; instead the actors contributed what they could, which resulted in something touching and irreducible.

I suppose how we approached the incident of the spinning top, the child's toy given to Irina at the lunch party, demonstrates my point better than anything. Once I had banished the tapedeck as the provider of music cues, it became imperative to banish it for everything. The real spinning top we used made a perfectly acceptable and perfectly audible whirring musical sound when it was pumped up. But it was not haunting; it was not memorable; it was not poetic; and so one day I experimented with a silent spinning top and asked the actors to provide the sound.

Something much more extraordinary and, I felt, more organic was expressed than by the real sound. In rehearsal, I developed the possibility by asking each character to make their wish – in the spirit of the question: 'What would *your* birthday wish be?'. Then I asked each of them to concentrate on that wish, and transform it into a single and sustained sound. When eventually we put all those single sounds together, we found that there was an inexplicable mysterious cadence composed of low notes and high notes, sighing notes, yearning notes, impatient and frustrated and discordant notes. So the spinning top, surrounded by everybody at the lunch party, made this unplaceable, indefinable haunting sound. So what *we* in the audience were hearing, was what the characters were hearing, their inner thoughts about their future – their imaginations captured at a moment in time.

I decided not to interrogate the actors about these particular inner thoughts but it is probable that the girls were communicating a yearning for Moscow in one way or another. However, the yearnings that each of the characters in that boisterous household has, proceeding from unhappiness, experience or discontent, are complex and intrinsically interrelated to the presence of the other characters, so the exercise (and the resultant expression of it in the production) provided them with a moment of fusion, a time of complete interconnection.

The fact that I had removed everything of the traditional staging tools revealed for us exciting answers, more poetic and more integral answers than might otherwise have been the case. At the very beginning of the play, I knew that it was necessary to have the real sound of a piano and that Tusenbach should actually play the piano; we should see him playing the piano; it was vital to indicate the Baron's breeding and sophistication, his certainty that indeed he could provide in that household, in that town, what nobody else there could provide. So the presence of a real piano (which of course provides the image of a locked piano) was very important. Additionally, I needed something in the bare white space which would say 'we are in a house, indoors'; so I chose one very large, very male, leather armchair. Quite simply we agreed, 'That is father's chair.'

This solitary armchair was often occupied by all three sisters together. They clustered round it; there was a sort of seniority about who was on the seat, who on the arm. Because it was the only furniture in the room and because the sisters knew its significance, its presence had nothing to do with answering the usual naturalistic question: 'how is the room furnished?'. Rather, it had the identity of another character, a permanent reminder of loss, of change, an anchor that restrained the sisters and which they could not drag in any direction. It is entirely possible that some people in the audience may have seen the whole range of significance in our single chair; many would not, but what would have been unmissable was the connection that each of the three sisters had to that inanimate object and its history.

Two kinds of rehearsal work kept pace with each other. I mentioned that we worked improvisationally, but not exclusively so. It was important that we studied the textual material, so we analysed together – collectively we took every utterance in the play apart, and as a group we identified all the possibilities of textual meaning at each interrelated moment. We broke the play down into units, in the conventional Stanislavskian way. The analytical process was very exhausting. I think we spent more than two weeks reading and talking, and very occasionally turning our insights into action. But then in the evenings – we did our situational and individual improvisation work.

I found it immensely helpful that the textual and improvisational disciplines more or less kept pace with each other, and once we felt we had enough to go on, the middle period of rehearsal was exhilarating. We were not decision-making; possibilities were offering themselves and being lived through. I was able to allow improvised scenes to run on for longer than I normally would because the company had so much background. I also gave the actors licence to play with the text when they felt something more idiomatic was necessary. We would then discuss those textual variants and decide which had been unhelpful, and which had worked.

This process led to a sense that we were not dealing with a learned or received text, a text to be recited; we were able to shed the literary constraints which traditionally attach to a play that has been 'previously written down'. Instead, there was a sense that the play was developing its own rhythms and movements, because to some extent it was being written as it was being created in the moment. I am in danger of exaggeration here. This 'creative' textual process didn't seek to change Chekhov's content, but to discover an idiom.

The actors reported that they were liberated by being in an empty space and involved in making their improvised choreography; but simultaneously working in the minutest analytical detail, both before and after the improvised event, led to unfettered moments of emotional exchange. So rehearsals reached a point of imaginative 'lift-off'.

As for my input as director, I wish I could say that I had 'conducted' the play but I think that would suggest a controlled overview. I was too concerned about how the smallest influence of thought or gesture could change meaning, and so change what we had arrived at through consensus. Therefore, I would say I thought of myself as receiving more than initiating what was happening in rehearsal. Well, let's say it was two-way traffic.

The band music at the end was of course taped. This was the only point in the production where something occurred on-stage that did not grow organically from the work or invention of the company. We talked at length about how we might be able to achieve the passing band by other impressionistic means, but no satisfactory solution emerged.

John Napier's[12] work was very important. I have talked about a 'rough' theatre production but actually the environment John gave us, a white expanse, was a purifying environment. It enabled an audience to really see in clear images, as it were against a photographer's cloth, to see the smallest details of behaviour. But it also created a discipline which exposed whatever was extraneous as well. Our white environment required unusual economy from the actors and a strict discipline, so the production went through a further stage of refining the poetic spareness when the set arrived. Above and behind the characters was a faded 'pentimento' icon, barely visible on the white wall, which came to have a different meaning for each of them: regret that tradition was fading; pleasure or conviction that it must continue to fade; certainty that the future would lie in something else. The faint external hint also gave us a sense of the sort of town that the Prozorovs lived in. It was not so much an icon as a *memory* of an icon.

Curiously, *Three Sisters* is not a play I would want to do again. I had an indelible experience, even though I feel so much could so easily have gone wrong in such unusual and primitive circumstances. So much to do with the theatre concerns elements of chemistry and good fortune; mystical and indefinable elements which are quite intangible can turn out, like 'the force',[13] to be with you. They were overwhelmingly with me in this case. I felt deeply grateful for the experience and I wouldn't have the hubris to say I might do better with the play in a different version, or at a second attempt.

I hope to do another Chekhov play one day soon. At present, I'm terribly disappointed because I have just been beaten to the punch: for a number of years I have been planning to do a production of *The Wood-Demon* – largely I suppose because I want to show that *The Wood-Demon* is *not* a failed attempt at *Uncle Vanya* – a well-worn critical misapprehension both of this play and, more fundamentally, of how writers write. It is so clear that with *The Wood-Demon* Chekhov was making a play that was fundamentally optimistic – a heavily challenged optimism – but a fundamentally forward-looking and positive account of an assortment of young lives. Extraordinarily youthful in tone, the play is about not succumbing to life, but about surviving crisis. It has a last act where the young people are in the grip of regret and guilt but they come through it in their separate ways and they go on. Some writers and reviewers with twenty-twenty hindsight have suggested that because Chekhov reused some of this narrative material to write a very different play at the end of his career, he had been struggling to write *Uncle Vanya* but was in some way too callow or inexperienced to get it right. This is nonsense.

My much admired colleague, Richard Nelson,[14] agreed to translate the play. He did a wonderfully idiomatic and speakable job on it, but we both remained worried about the structure of the narrative. Richard's response was to ask me what we would do if we were in the film business and had encountered such structural problems? 'Let me keep all Chekhov's material', he urged 'but let me write the film script.' Wonderful idea. Of course what Richard fashioned was a totally 'stageable' film script,[15] and since *The Wood-Demon* is almost never done, I thought there would not be too much critical distress and academic complaint if I presented Richard's 'version'. So I was planning to do this version here at the Cottesloe but I have just heard that a company unknown to me is preparing a production of *The Wood-Demon* over the river at the Playhouse Theatre.[16] The difficulty is that if they do it very well, then clearly it would be a bad idea for another production to come along in quick succession, precisely because it is such a rarity. But Catch 22, if they do not do it well, opinion will be influenced against another production of an unsuccessful apprentice piece.

We are doing a new production of *The Cherry Orchard* at the Royal National Theatre in September 2000, in the Lyttelton Theatre. After the millennium celebrations, I feel that I want to direct a small theatre production of *The Cherry Orchard*. Chekhov is 'the other great writer' – Shakespeare and Chekhov. And like Shakespeare, Chekhov changes in meaning and relevance from generation to generation. No production is ever definitive. These are plays that one could work on for the whole of one's life and never exhaust them.

NOTES

This chapter is taken from an interview with the editors at the Royal National Theatre, London, June 1997.

1 This is a colloquial reference to a very popular Heineken lager television advertisement from the late 1970s which sold Heineken as a beer that 'reaches the parts that other beers cannot reach'.

2 See chapter entitled 'The Rough Theatre' in Peter Brook, *The Empty Space*, Harmondsworth, England, 1984, pp. 73–100. (First published London, 1968.)

3 The Actors' Company was created in 1972 with the intention of giving back to actors some of the creative and artistic control they had lost to directors, by *inviting* directors to work with them (instead of vice versa), and also partly to try and compensate for the decline of the repertory system. See chapter 11 in this volume.

4 *Three Sisters* directed by Jonathan Miller at the Cambridge Theatre, London, 1976.

5 *Three Sisters* directed by Trevor Nunn opened at the RSC's The Other Place, Stratford-upon-Avon, on 29 September 1979, before touring. The company consisted of himself as director, Richard Cottrell as translator, John Napier as designer and a cast which included: Timothy Spall as Andrey; Susan Tracy as Natasha; Janet Dale as Olga; Suzanne Bertish as Masha; Emily Richard as Irina and Edward Petherbridge as Vershinin. See chapter 11 in this volume.

6 Konstantin Stanislavsky (1863–1938). Co-founder with Vladimir Nemirovich-Danchenko of the (private) Moscow Art Theatre. Stanislavsky was the first director (at the Moscow Art Theatre) of *Seagull*, *Uncle Vanya*, *Three Sisters*, *The Cherry Orchard* and *Ivanov*. He was also the first performer of the leading parts of Trigorin (*The Seagull*, 1896); Astrov (*Uncle Vanya*, 1899), Vershinin (*Three Sisters*, 1901); and Gayev (*The Cherry Orchard*, 1904). Stanislavsky's 'System' of acting techniques – first *mis*interpreted then *re*interpreted in America, as 'The Method' – formed both the first coherent analysis of acting techniques *and* (often mistakenly) the method of approaching 'naturalistic' plays. Nemirovich-Danchenko was a more accurate interpreter of Chekhov's plays, and Chekhov's unhappiness with Stanislavsky's interpretation of his plays is now legendary, and well documented in several collections of Chekhov's letters. See Bibliography and Jean Benedetti's *The Moscow Art Theatre Letters*, and specifically Edward Braun in chapter 5 of *The Director and the Stage*, London, 1982. See also chapters 3, 12, 14 and 15 in this volume.

7 Georgi Tovstonogov, 1915–89. Born in Tbilisi, capital of what was to become the Soviet Republic of Georgia, Tovstonogov graduated in 1938 from GITIS (The Soviet State Theatre School). He became Artistic Director of the Gorky Theatre, Leningrad. Amongst many other innovatory productions, his production of *Three Sisters* in 1965 coincided with the post-Stalinist 'Thaw'. His 'credo' may be summarised as 'the elimination of what is possible but not essential'. For further information, see also a French version of his autobiography, *Guéorgui Tovstonogov: Quarante ans de mise en scène*, Moscow, 1976; Vera Gottlieb, *Chekhov in Performance in Russia and Soviet Russia*, Cambridge, 1984; Laurence Senelick's *The Chekhov Theatre: A Century of the Plays in Performance*, Cambridge, 1997; and see in this volume, chapters 14 and 15.

8 Yuri Lyubimov (1917–) was Artistic Director of the radical and controversial Taganka Theatre, Moscow – 'the hub of artistic dissent'. Lyubimov's 'Brechtian' approach to Chekhov's plays, and in particular to his production of *Three Sisters*, 1981, has made him, with Tovstonogov, Efros and Heifetz, one of the most radical of Russian interpreters of Chekhov on the Russian stage. Described by some as 'the theatrical conscience of his nation', and by others viewed as a

'deserter', Lyubimov had his Soviet passport withdrawn while working in London in 1984 on his production of Dostoyevsky's *Crime and Punishment* at The Lyric, Hammersmith. Lyubimov's productions are notable for his use of non-naturalistic techniques. See chapters 14 and 15 in this volume.

9 Max Stafford-Clark (born 1941) was Artistic Director of the Royal Court Theatre, London, from 1979–93, and is currently Artistic Director of the company Out of Joint, which he founded in 1993. Renowned both for his productions of many new plays – by Caryl Churchill, Timberlake Wertenbaker, and others – he is also a major classical director. His most recent Chekhov production was his 1996 *Three Sisters* at the Lyric Theatre, Hammersmith, London.

10 *The Cherry Orchard*, or in Brook's French translation, *La Cérisaie*, opened at Les Bouffes du Nord, Brook's Paris theatre, in May 1981, designed by Chloe Obolensky. See chapters 12 and 14 in this volume.

11 'Poor theatre' was a term originally coined by the Polish director Jerzy Grotowski, in his book *Towards a Poor Theatre*, ed. Eugenio Barba, London, 1976, p. 19. (First published in Denmark, 1968.)

12 John Napier is a renowned scenographer who has worked with Trevor Nunn on several productions. His designs include *Nicholas Nickleby, Les Misérables, Miss Saigon, Cats* and *Starlight Express*.

13 'May the Force be with you' was said by the character Ben Obi-Wan Kenobi to Luke Skywalker in the feature film *Star Wars* (1977) directed by George Lucas, designating the transmission of supernatural powers.

14 The playwright, Richard Nelson, whose work includes *Sensibilities and Sense; Two Shakespearean Actors; Some Americans Abroad*, and *Misha's Party* with the Russian playwright Alexander Gelman for the Royal Shakespeare Theatre Company and The Moscow Art Theatre.

15 See chapters 4 and 13 in this volume.

16 Directed by Anthony Clark at The Playhouse Theatre in London's West End in June 1997.

10

EDWARD BRAUN

The Cherry Orchard

In 1963, the Marxist critic and philosopher Georg Lukács resumed his critique of Brecht's epic theatre, questioning its necessity in the depiction of social change:

> Even without alienation effects, writers have succeeded not just in surprising the audience, but in moving them profoundly by dramatizing the contradictions of a given social order . . . [Chekhov's] plays are built on the conflict between the subjective intentions of his characters and their objective tendencies and significance. This constantly creates a divided impression in the minds of the audience. On the one hand, they understand the characters' feelings and can even sympathize with them. At the same time, they are forced into an intense experience of the tragic, tragi-comic or comic conflict between these subjective feelings and the objective social reality.[1]

Whether the objective social reality is apparent as a determining factor in all of Chekhov's major plays is debatable. Certainly, in his early drama *Platonov* (as it is now known) the chaotic action serves to convey a picture of the Russian landowning gentry in terminal decline.[2] Similarly, in his next play the character of Ivanov embodies the sense of worthlessness and disillusionment that paralysed the educated classes when the high hopes of liberal reform and modernisation engendered by the emancipation of the serfs were extinguished by the accession in 1881 of the autocratic Tsar Alexander III after the assassination of his more progressive father Alexander II. However, by comparison with these early works relatively little indication of the broader social context is given in the three plays that followed. It is true that in *Uncle Vanya* Astrov's hopeless struggle against rural backwardness mirrors Chekhov's own experience as a landowner and unpaid country doctor at his Melikhovo estate, but in *The Seagull* the only agrarian problem seems to be the availability of carriage horses for a drive into town at harvest time. Similarly, in *Three Sisters*, the pervasive atmosphere is one of provincial stagnation with little prospect of change, though there is an element of class conflict implicit in the vulgar Natasha's ruthless appropriation of the house from her socially superior sisters-in-law and their demoralised brother. However, it is not until *The Cherry Orchard* that the process of social change becomes the central concern, resulting in a text that in originality of form and complexity of subject matter went far beyond his earlier plays.

The decline of the landed gentry was a crucial problem in nineteenth-century Russia. By 1859 one-third of the estates and two-thirds of the serfs belonging to landowners were mortgaged to the state or to private banks. The Emancipation Act of 1861 was designed to address this crisis through the redemption payments that the peasants were to make for the land that their former masters chose to transfer to them, but in consequence the landowners could no longer call on the free labour, tools and animals of their former serfs. In the 1870s the gentry still owned one-third of all arable land, but by 1905 its share had declined to 22 per cent, of which one-third was rented to the peasantry. Few landowners had any grasp of agriculture or accounting and many of them spent long periods away from their estates, leaving their affairs in the hands of corrupt or incompetent managers (in *The Cherry Orchard* the responsibility is shared between the twenty-four-year-old adopted daughter Varya and the accident-prone clerk Yepikhodov). As a consequence of such neglect numerous estates came under the hammer to meet long-accumulated debts, not excluding such time-honoured names as Dolgorukov, Golitsyn, Stroganov and Obolensky. During the reign of Alexander III emergency fiscal measures were taken to halt the erosion of this class on whom the entire economic and social stability of the empire depended, but they failed to prevent vast tracts of land passing into the hands of a small minority of entrepreneurs, many of them emancipated serfs and their sons, who made light of the unfavourable credit terms available from the newly established Peasants' Bank and readily took to money-making as a way of life.[3]

The theme of bankrupt estates and the rise of the new entrepreneurial class was common in post-emancipation literature and drama, though it inspired no works of lasting significance. In the case of Chekhov, it is easy to forget amidst the mayhem at the end of *Platonov* that the spendthrift widow Anna Petrovna and her idle stepson face eviction from their estate following its purchase at auction by the rapacious businessman Vengero-vich. It was a subject that he was to return to in a number of stories, notably 'Late Blossoms', 'An Unwanted Victory' (both 1882) and 'A Visit to Friends' (1898),[4] in which the plight of the Losev family closely resembles that of Ranevskaya and her brother in *The Cherry Orchard*.

Chekhov was well placed to observe the fecklessness and incompetence of landowners during the six years he spent running his own five-hundred-acre property at Melikhovo, south of Moscow, which he purchased in 1892. During that time he also witnessed the gradual decline of the Babkino estate, which belonged to his old friends Alexei and Maria Kiselev. In December 1897, Maria wrote to Chekhov: 'At Babkino many things are in a state of collapse, from the owners to the buildings . . . the master himself has become an old infant, amiable but rather demoralised.'[5] Three years later the estate was finally sold, its value greatly enhanced by the completion of a railway line from Moscow which made the land a desirable location for dachas for city-dwellers. Alexei Kiselev became a director of a bank in the neighbouring town – just like Gaev, and with the same handsome salary of six thousand roubles.

Both 'A Visit to Friends' and *The Cherry Orchard* owed a great deal to Chekhov's observation of the Kiselevs. In 'A Visit to Friends' a Moscow lawyer, Podgorin, visits his old friends, the dissolute Sergei Losev and his wife Tatyana, whose estate is shortly due to be auctioned to pay off their debts after years of neglect. Tatyana fondly imagines that if only Podgorin would marry her beautiful sister Nadezhda all would be well, but faced with this prospect he makes a hasty departure for Moscow and permanent bachelorhood, abandoning the Losevs to their fate.[6] Whilst the story anticipates *The Cherry Orchard* in a number of details, it remains an encounter that takes place in the course of a day and a night within the immediate family circle, stopping short of the sale of the estate and the dispersal of the household.

The Cherry Orchard was an undertaking on an altogether different scale. As the Russian director Nikolai Petrov has written, 'Chekhov called *The Cherry Orchard* a comedy, but in essence it is a novel, an engrossing novel that embraces the whole period from 1861 to 1905 and describes the life of people in Russia just before Tsarism began to collapse.'[7] Nicholas II was only twenty-six when he came to the throne in 1894 following his father's sudden death from kidney failure, and he possessed neither the will nor the intelligence to control his deeply reactionary ministers. As the vast semi-feudal empire struggled to catch up with Europe through headlong industrialisation, massive foreign investment and a drive for exports, the rural economy was crippled by heavy taxation, crop failures, cholera epidemics, rocketing land prices and a massive increase in population. In 1901 crop failures resulted in the worst outbreaks of violence since the 1860s, and over the next two years thousands of starving peasants invaded the estates of the gentry in the southern provinces of Poltava, Kharkov and Saratov.[8]

In *The Cherry Orchard* the servants' quarters have been occupied by vagrants who, it is rumoured, are being fed by Varya on dried peas while

Gaev takes his sister to town by train for an extravagant lunch and then proceeds to hold forth to the waiters on the Decadent movement (pp. 302, 308).[9] The reference to these interlopers is typical of the oblique manner in which the action's wider significance is conveyed. In the course of the play there are passing references to well over thirty characters who never appear on-stage, including Lopakhin's brutal peasant father, Anya's aristocratic great-aunt in Yaroslavl, the rich merchant Deriganov, Charlotte's fairground artiste parents, Ranevskaya's late lawyer husband, Trofimov's chemist father, and many others.[10]

Similarly, the brief intrusion of the Passer-by in Act Two is more than a mere pretext for demonstrating Ranevskaya's thoughtless extravagance; as Michael Frayn points out, at the turn of the century in Russia the word for passer-by ('prokhozhy') implied someone tramping the countryside to escape from prison or exile in Siberia, and the original verses by Nadson and Nekrasov from which he quotes half-remembered snatches have a rebellious ring to them that echo Trofimov's radical sentiments, and are unlikely to have been lost on an audience of poetry-loving Russians.[11] *The Scarlet Woman*, Alexei Tolstoy's highly popular poem which is declaimed by the station-master during the makeshift ball in Act Three has no such connotation, though it could be construed as an unwitting allusion to Ranevskaya's easy virtue. However, as Firs remarks, the station-master, the post-office clerk and the other reluctant down-at-heel guests who have been roped in with the servants to make up the numbers for this desperate last fling are no substitute for the generals, barons and admirals who used to come flocking in the old days. The sense of humiliating social decline was exactly conveyed in the original Moscow Art Theatre production; to quote Stanislavsky's prompt book:

> A completely abortive ball. Very few guests. Half of those dancing don't know the steps of the quadrille and even fewer in the *grand rond* . . . Silence prevails the whole evening so that you'd think they'd come along to a funeral. As soon as a dance ends they all come to a halt, then disperse to their seats along the wall. They sit and fan themselves. The moment someone breaks the silence by running through the room or starting to talk, everyone is embarrassed and the offender immediately feels guilty at causing the disturbance, then the room becomes even more silent and embarrassed.[12]

In *The Cherry Orchard* the settings too are more significant in their detail and more clearly synecdochic than in any of the earlier plays. This is seen most clearly in Act Two, for which Chekhov spelled out his requirements with a precision that was lost on Stanislavsky and his designer Simov. The line of telegraph poles in the distance and the large town barely visible thirteen miles away on the horizon, contrasting with the long-abandoned shrine and neglected tombstones, are clearly intended to signify the encroachment of the new industrial age, their meaning underlined by the references to the recently completed railway, conveniently close to bring the new breed of city-dwellers out to their dachas,[13] by the Englishmen's acquisition of the rights to the 'white clay' on Simeonov-Pishchik's land (at a knock-down price, one suspects), by the sound of a 'breaking string', which the ever-practical Lopakhin is alone in identifying correctly as a winding-cable snapping in a distant mine shaft,[14] and finally by the sound of the axe felling the commercially redundant orchard.

With some justification, critics have pointed out that an orchard of the size indicated by Lopakhin's calculations in Act One (1,000 desyatins, or about four square miles) could scarcely have existed in reality, even if, as Gaev haughtily reminds Lopakhin, it is so remarkable as to merit an entry in the 'Encyclopaedic Dictionary'. Donald Rayfield comments:

> To a less literal-minded and more receptive audience, the cherry orchard takes on from this point symbolic qualities: it represents an economic and social dinosaur approaching extinction. A cherry orchard that could glut the world with cherries and yet cannot earn its owners a living symbolizes a decrepit world, a decrepit Russia for which ordered destruction is the only alternative to disordered ruination.[15]

However, notwithstanding the espousal of the play by the Russian Symbolists[16] and Chekhov's own regard for the mystical allegories of Maurice Maeterlinck, there is nothing 'symbolic' about the cherry orchard (or the breaking string, for that matter) in the sense of the universal, the transcendental or the ineffable. As a signifier, it is polysemic yet quite specific. For Lopakhin, the orchard represents both an 'economic dinosaur' and an unmissable business opportunity, as well as embodying the oppression suffered by his father and earlier generations before the emancipation. Paradoxically, it is also for him 'the most beautiful place in the world' – a beauty that (like Ranevskaya's) he can only ever dream of possessing, and which through possessing he is bound to destroy. For Ranevskaya and Gaev, it has always served as the provider of their idly squandered wealth, yet they are oblivious to its economic significance and it evokes only fond memories of their mother, their youth and their happiness. For Firs, it recalls a lucrative rural economy based on skills long forgotten through careless neglect. For Trofimov, it is the embodiment of a corrupt social order in which Anya's forebears 'owned living souls', whose eyes can be seen staring in baleful accusation 'from every cherry in the orchard, from every leaf, from the trunk of every tree' (Frayn, p. 318).

In Chekhov's earlier plays it is possible to identify one character who is the agent of disruption. In *The Seagull*, it is Trigorin, with his casual seduction of Nina; in *Uncle Vanya*, it is Professor Serebryakov, with his breathtaking proposal to dispose of Sonya's inheritance; in *Three Sisters*, it is Natasha, with her remorseless annexation of the Prozorovs' house. But in *The Cherry Orchard* it becomes clear that everyone is at the mercy of a process of change beyond their control and comprehension. Lopakhin is no exception; at the end of Act Three he seems as bewildered as anyone by his own acquisition of the estate, and he only begins to grasp its full implications when the keys are hurled at his feet by Varya. As he picks them up he remarks, somewhat superfluously, 'She threw away the keys to show she's not in charge here now.' But in truth it is a gesture (or rather 'Gestus') as profound in its social and economic significance as anything that Brecht himself would ever conceive.

The development of Lopakhin's character cost Chekhov more effort than any other in the play. Originally, he intended the role for Stanislavsky in the hope that his poise and stage presence would work against the portrayal of Lopakhin as the familiar stereotype of the vulgar self-made man. However, apprehensive that the part was beyond him, Stanislavsky preferred to play the 'aristocrat' Gaev and entrusted Lopakhin to Leonidov who, he assured Chekhov, was 'mild and gentle by nature'.[17] In the course of rehearsals Chekhov made a number of changes to the text designed to bring out the sensitive aspect of Lopakhin's character. In particular, he gave further emphasis to his concern in helping Ranevskaya and Gaev save the estate, and deleted an exchange between them referring to a second mortgage of 40,000 roubles advanced by Lopakhin. Also, he made clear the depth of Lopakhin's true feelings for Ranevskaya by adding in Act One the words '. . . to see your amazing, heart-breaking eyes looking at me the way they used to', and 'I love you like my own flesh and blood . . . *more than my own flesh and blood*' (Frayn, p. 292).[18]

The fact that Lopakhin can venture even this tentative overture to the daughter of his father's master is indicative of the collapse of the old social barriers – just as her failure even to register it shows how rooted she still is within her own class. Whilst Ranevskaya is ready enough to marry off her adopted daughter Varya to Lopakhin, it is only because 'she comes from simple people' (Frayn, p. 311) – and she may possibly have in mind as well the financial salvation that could ensue, even at this eleventh hour. As for Lopakhin, though he commands the deference of Yepikhodov and Dunyasha, calls Gaev 'an old woman' to his face and treats Varya as an equal, he is still acutely aware of his peasant origins: self-conscious in his white waistcoat and yellow shoes, and deeply ashamed of his lack of education. He celebrates his triumph at the auction in a manner worthy of his brutish father, but when he becomes aware of Ranevskaya's grief he consoles her lovingly, gently reproaching her for not heeding his advice and wishing tearfully that they might change their 'miserable muddled life' (Frayn, p. 334). At this point in his prompt book Stanislavsky noted 'He weeps. The more sincerely and tenderly the better. So why doesn't Lopakhin, sensitive soul that he is, save Ranevskaya? Because he is a slave to commercial dogma, because he would be ridiculed by his fellow businessmen. *Les affaires sont les affaires.*'[19] A further indication of Chekhov's concern to convey this dualism in Lopakhin's character is his late addition in Act Four of Trofimov's lines: 'All the same, I can't help liking you. You've got fine, sensitive fingers like an artist's. You've got a fine, sensitive soul, too' (Frayn, p. 338).[20] To which Lopakhin, reverting to mercenary type, responds by offending Trofimov's dignity with the ill-judged offer of a loan from the 40,000 roubles that he has cleared with the poppy harvest.

These abrupt contradictions in Lopakhin's behaviour, which veers from the caring and the sensitive to the clumsy and the downright offensive, from the compassionate to the triumphalist, reflect a persona struggling to adapt to a radically changed role. By contrast, Ranevskaya and Gaev simply deny change, maintaining the manners and attitudes of a dying age, of which Firs in his ancient livery and white gloves is the living remnant. Ranevskaya sees her return from Paris as a return to her lost childhood, an age of innocence and eternal values, and it is fitting that the room she comes back to in Act One is the old nursery, which gives an illusory sense of life returning as day breaks, the spring approaches and the cherry trees come into blossom once more. Once the orchard is sold the future can no longer be denied, and the nursery from which they take their leave is stripped bare and 'cold as hell', a scene of life departed and a bleak resting place for the carelessly abandoned Firs.[21]

Scarcely anyone in the play escapes the impact of social change, as the closing diaspora makes clear. It is a measure of Ranevskaya's fecklessness that, whilst taking Yasha back with her to Paris to survive for a brief spell with the money from the great-aunt in Yaroslavl,[22] she leaves Varya to enter service as a housekeeper for the Ragulins, readily accepts Anya's assurance that Yasha has taken Firs to hospital, and gives no thought at all to Charlotta who, destitute and with no passport, is left dependent on Lopakhin's charity. In a moment of abrupt gestic clarity Charlotta drops her comic persona and casts her swaddled 'baby' to the floor, where it lies abandoned like herself (Frayn, p. 342). As for Gaev, with his own survival comfortably secured by his position as a 'financier' at the bank (provided he can get up in the morning and dress himself without Firs' assistance), all he can say is 'They're all leaving us. Varya's going away . . . Suddenly no one needs us anymore' (Frayn, p. 342).

Apart from Lopakhin, the character who caused Chekhov the greatest difficulty was the 'perpetual student' Trofimov. As Orlando Figes comments, 'The universities had been the organizational centre of opposition to the tsarist regime since the 1860s. In the Russian language the words "student" and "revolutionary" were almost synonymous.'[23] In January 1901, following a wave of demonstrations, the Minister of Education, Bogolepov, ordered the conscription into the army of over 200 student leaders, then a month later was assassinated by a Socialist Revolutionary student. Despite violent police reprisals, demonstrations continued on a massive scale and in April 1902 a twenty-year-old student, Balmashov, gained entry to the Mariinsky Palace in St Petersburg and shot the Minister of the Interior at point-blank range. After these events it is hardly surprising that Chekhov wrote to Olga Knipper in October 1903, 'The point is that Trofimov is always being exiled and thrown out of university, but how can you show things like that?'[24] We can but guess at what Chekhov felt constrained to exclude from his portrayal, but the only passages in the completed text to catch the censor's eye were in Trofimov's two long speeches in Act Two, the first describing the living conditions of the workers, the second denouncing the Gaev family to Anya for 'The possession of human souls . . . living on credit, at the expense of others' (Frayn, pp. 314, 318).

Of all the characters in the play, Trofimov is the one who remains unscathed by the dissolution of the estate; if anything, he emerges with his convictions reinforced and ready to resume the struggle back at university. Chekhov's portrayal of Trofimov is finely balanced; his trenchant diagnosis of the state of Russia is irrefutable and close to the dramatist's own frequently expressed views, yet the rhetoric is a shade too practised and, as John Tulloch has observed, by 1904 'Chekhov could have told Trofimov that change *had* taken place, that his own medical group was establishing children's crèches, that libraries were being established (Chekhov himself was supplying a new one at Taganrog with books).'[25] Trofimov's 'mangy' appearance, his premature loss of hair and beard that refuses to grow are at comical odds with his heroic utterances, and his priggish assertion that he is 'above love' is deservedly ridiculed by Ranevskaya; yet his assessment of Lopakhin is both affectionate and shrewd, so that we are inclined to agree with him that Lopakhin's grandiose plans for the estate's transformation are little more than 'arm-waving'.

As the text neared completion, Chekhov wrote to Olga Knipper: 'It seems to me that, however boring it might be, there is something new in my play. And incidentally, in the entire play there is not a single gunshot.'[26] The understatement is typical of him: not only is there no gunshot (its elimination emphasised by Yepikhodov's comic threat of suicide), but gone is the familiar family doctor, gone are the servants who know their place and offer comic relief or ancient wisdom (forgotten, like the recipe for dried cherries), and gone is the central love intrigue, now parodied in the below-stairs burlesque of Yasha, Dunyasha and Yepikhodov, Trofimov's high-minded friendship with Anya and Lopakhin's erratic courtship of Varya. When Ranevskaya finally persuades him to propose to Varya, there is a moment when comedic closure seems imminent, but as they flounder in a succession of evasions and *non sequiturs*, it becomes painfully clear that such a match has no place in this new drama of Chekhov, with objective necessity not subjective desire being the ultimate determinant in human relations.

The achievement of this unique play is to present these two imperatives in equal, teasing complexity – yet how often in productions is one stressed to the neglect of the other. What Trevor Griffiths wrote in 1977 in the introduction to his version of the text still holds good today:

> *The Cherry Orchard* has *always* seemed to me to be dealing not only with the subjective pain of property-loss but also and more importantly with its objective *necessity*. To present it as the first is to celebrate a pessimism; as to see it as both is to redress an important political balance potent in the text Chekhov wrote but in *practice* almost wholly ignored.[27]

NOTES

1 Author's translated extract published in *New Left Review*, 110, July-August 1978, p. 90.

2 See chapter 4 in this volume.

3 See Orlando Figes, *A People's Tragedy; The Russian Revolution 1891–1924*, London, 1996, chapter 2; see also Richard Charques, *The Twilight of Imperial Russia*, Oxford, 1958, pp. 19–26.

4 The author's translation of titles is used throughout this chapter. For alternative translations in Hingley or Wilks, see Appendix 1.

5 N. F. Belchikov and others, eds., *Anton Chekhov, Polnoe sobranie sochinenii i pisem v 30 tomakh*, Moscow, 1974–83 (*Anton Chekhov, Collected Works and Letters in 30 Volumes*, Moscow, 1974–83), vol. VII, p. 504 (subsequently referred to as *Works* or *Letters*).

6 For an English translation of 'A Visit to Friends' (as 'All Friends Together') see Ronald Hingley, trans. and ed., *The Oxford Chekhov*, vol. IX, Oxford, 1975, pp. 225–42.

7 Nikolai Petrov, *50 i 500 vserossiiskoe teatralnoe obschchestvo*, Moscow, 1960, p. 405.

8 Chekhov does not specify the exact location of the estate, though the nearest

major town is Kharkov. Stanislavsky placed it in either the Orel or the Kursk District, to the north of Kharkov (letter to Chekhov, 19 November 1903).

9 Page references to *The Cherry Orchard* are to Anton Chekhov, *Plays*, trans. and intro. Michael Frayn, London, 1988, cited as Frayn. In some instances I have used my own translations – EB.

10 This observation is made by Petrov, *50 i 500 vserossiiskoe teatralnoe ob-schchestvo*, pp. 415–24.

11 For a translation of the complete texts of the two poems, originally published in 1881 and 1858, see Frayn, pp. 368, 316.

12 Inna Solovieva, ed., *Rezhisserskie ekzemplyary K.S.Stanislavskogo*, vol. III, 1901–4, Moscow, 1983, pp. 374–5.

13 The significance of the railways in Russia's economic transformation can be gauged from the fact that between 1891 and 1905 nearly 20,000 miles of new track were built.

14 As Donald Rayfield points out, it is clear from both the Moscow Art Theatre's original 1904 prompt book and from similar sounds described in two of Chekhov's short stories ('Fortune' and 'Rolling Stone', both 1887) that Lopakhin's explanation is the correct one. *The Cherry Orchard: Catastrophe and Comedy*, New York, 1994, pp. 74, 107.

15 *Ibid.*, p. 58.

16 See Andrei Bely, 'The Cherry Orchard' in Laurence Senelick trans. and ed., *Russian Dramatic Theory from Pushkin to the Symbolists*, Austin, Texas, 1981, pp. 89–92; Vsevolod Meyerhold quoted in Edward Braun, *Meyerhold: A Revolution in Theatre*, London, 1995, pp. 22–3.

17 *Letters 11*, p. 606. Chekhov never became reconciled to Leonidov's portrayal of Lopakhin; on 24 March 1904 he wrote to Olga Knipper 'I am very glad to hear that Khalyutina is pregnant. What a pity this can't happen to some of the men in the·cast, for example Alexandrov and Leonidov.' *Letters*, vol. XII, p. 69.

18 See *Works*, vol. XIII, pp. 321–4.

19 Solovieva, ed., *Rezhisserskie ekzemplyary K.S.Stanislavskogo*, vol. III, p. 425.

20 See *Works*, vol. XIII, p. 333.

21 Some critics have observed that Firs will be rescued when Yepikhodov returns from the station, but as he lies motionless and we hear the thudding of the axe and the sound of the breaking string, 'dying away and sad', this is hardly likely to be the effect in the theatre.

22 Rayfield (*The Cherry Orchard: Catastrophe and Comedy*, pp. 85, 90) is wrong in calculating that Ranevskaya will return to Paris with the unspent money from the great-aunt in Yaroslavl *and* the proceeds of the sale, making a comfortable sum of 105,000 roubles. Lopakhin makes it clear in Act One that the estate is being sold to pay their debts (p.292) and in Act Four Ranevskaya refers only to the money from the great-aunt (p.342).

23 Figes, *A People's Tragedy*, p. 165.

24 *Letters*, vol. XI, p. 279.

25 John Tulloch, *Chekhov: A Structuralist Study*, New York, 1980, p. 9.

26 *Letters*, vol. XI, p. 256.

27 Anton Chekhov, *The Cherry Orchard*, a new English version by Trevor Griffiths, London, 1978, p. vi.

II

IAN McKELLEN

Acting Chekhov: 'a friend to the actor'

Ian McKellen has played more Chekhov roles than any other actor of his generation. These have included Konstantin in *The Seagull* in 1961–2 for The Belgrade Theatre, Coventry; Tusenbach for radio in a Caedmon production of *Three Sisters*, 1966; Konstantin in a BBC Radio production of *The Seagull* in 1967; a radio version of Chekhov's story 'A Provincial Life', dramatised by Peter Gill in 1970; Svetlovidov in *Swan Song* for the opening of the (then) new Crucible Theatre, Sheffield, November 1971; Khrushchev in *The Wood-Demon*, the Actors' Company in 1973, directed by David Giles, in Ronald Hingley's translation, Edinburgh Festival and then touring; Andrey (a part taken over by Timothy Spall for the Stratford run and televised production) in Trevor Nunn's Royal Shakespeare Company production of *Three Sisters* in the 1978 touring production (see chapter 9 in this volume); Lopakhin in a revival of *The Cherry Orchard*, directed and translated with Lilia Sokolova by Mike Alfreds at The National Theatre, designed by Paul Dart, opened December 1985 (first performed at the Crucible Theatre, Sheffield, September 1981, with Roger Sloman as Lopakhin); Platonov in Michael Frayn's version, *Wild Honey*, of Chekhov's unfinished play *Platonov*, directed by Christopher Morahan, The National Theatre, 1984–6; Vanya in Sean Mathias' production of *Uncle Vanya*, translated by Pam Gems, with Antony Sher as Astrov and Janet McTeer as Yelena, Royal National Theatre Studio production, then the Cottesloe, National Theatre, 1991. Most recently (October 1998) he has played Dr Dorn in Jude Kelly's production of *The Seagull* at the West Yorkshire Playhouse, designed by Robert Innes-Hopkins, in a translation/ version by Tom Stoppard.

VG   With the exception of Shakespearean parts, you seem to have played more Chekhov roles than those of any other playwright: (in *Swan Song; Seagull; Ivanov; Uncle Vanya*; Platonov in *Wild Honey*; *Three Sisters, The Cherry Orchard* and *The Wood-Demon*.) Do you have a favourite part?

IMc   I suppose Vanya was the most *attractive* because I liked the production very much. It does depend on who you're working with, and how the production goes.

VG   Have you approached the characters very differently – or is there a common approach or basis when you play a Chekhov role?

IMc   I don't see any connection between, for example, Lopakhin and Vanya, but it depends on how the director sets things up. The big problem with Chekhov is that we don't do *Chekhov* – we do *translations* of Chekhov. Very few translators – at least those I've worked with – work from the original. Instead they come from literal translations. It varies: Pam Gems doesn't know Russian while Michael Frayn and Richard Cottrell both do. Richard did *Three Sisters* in which I played Andrey.[1] That explains the scepticism about English or American or German actors talking about playing Chekhov. It's constantly frustrating not to know how close you are to his intentions. I think it is a crucial question, but I have *never* had a satisfactory reply to whether in *The Seagull* Konstantin *does* kill himself when he shoots himself. Do we know? All the translators I've asked about it say: 'It's just shot.' And when I ask whether 'shot' means 'killed', they answer that 'it could be'. Chekhov put it there in the original – but I shall never really *know* because I don't speak Russian.

VG   In the original Russian it *is* deliberately ambivalent, but implicit is the sense that Konstantin *succeeds* with his suicide. [See postscript.]

IMc   There you are! Likewise, everybody *talks* about Konstantin's suicide – but *is* it a successful one or is it another failure? And there are other suicide attempts as well. Or there is the reference in *Three Sisters* to Soliony filling the room with smoke. It is not clear whether that is *literal* smoke or whether it's just the general upset which he causes wherever he goes. Also you cannot be certain about the rhythm. So Pam Gems and a lot of other translators *adapt* Chekhov, cut him without you knowing. When you are doing a production you are very much in the hands of the translator as well as the director. So you cannot connect the plays in the way that you might connect Shakespeare's where the acting problems are common to all the works. I couldn't say that about Chekhov's plays because I've never read them! It is a major problem. To give one example: I never won, but I wanted to change *Uncle Vanya* to *Uncle Jack*, or *Uncle Johnny*, which seems to me a fair translation. There is only *one Uncle Vanya*, but everyone's got an Uncle Jack. That is surely the point: that it *is* just Uncle Jack. But with *Uncle Vanya* you're already off into the realms of high art and romance. I think the original is a very unhelpful title in English, but I couldn't persuade the translator.

VG   Is this problem alleviated if the translation is, in fact, overtly *a version*? Thomas Kilroy unequivocally did a *version* of *Seagull*, set in Ireland.[2] Is it more honest to do that?

IMc   Let me put it this way: I'm a great proponent of doing Shakespeare in 'modernish' dress.[3] But Chekhov is so close to us, and the circumstances of life in Russia one hundred years ago are so readily available through people's writings, paintings, photographs, that you don't have to go outside of that context in order to understand it. I wouldn't have thought it particularly helpful to set it in Ireland because the Irish are not the Russians. I could see some point in doing it – but it wouldn't be *Chekhov*. I've never done 'a version'. I've always done what the translators have claimed *was* Chekhov. It's in the details when rooting around the translations that you discover that they've made their own changes.

VG   Particularly Michael Frayn?

IMc   The only one of his I've done is the *Platonov* play – *Wild Honey*.[4]

VG   The way he put it together made it very much Frayn's play rather than Chekhov's. What did you feel about the ending with the train and so the potential for melodrama? My memory of Chekhov's original is that it doesn't read melodramatically and with the assumption that Platonov is going to throw himself under the train. The critics seemed to think it melodramatic.

IMc   Acting it certainly didn't feel melodramatic, but I don't know how it ends in *Chekhov's* play. I always thought that probably Platonov had jumped on to the back of a train – and was already in Moscow by the time the audience had left the theatre! He can't simply die. I think his *spirit* survives, but is that melodramatic? I don't know. It seemed very much in keeping with Frayn's play. I always thought of it as 'Frayn's play', but I haven't read any of his translations of the plays that I know better, where presumably he hasn't taken liberties.

VG   It's vital that you find it frustrating not being able to work from the originals. Did Mike Alfreds approach *The Cherry Orchard* and the whole question of translation very differently?

IMc He was credited with the translation, but I don't know on what he based it – certainly not a knowledge of Russian.[5] He would have looked at lots of different versions, and he would have used a literal one as well. But his technique of rehearsing a play – and that is not just particular to Chekhov's – answers a lot of major questions about what's wrong with the general way of rehearsing. Alfreds is the only director I know who has actually worked out a method of rehearsal – a method which is virtually foolproof in creating a company, an 'ensemble' – *and* in freeing the actor's imagination and *keeping* it free right through performances.

There's nothing fixed in the blocking as to where the actors may move. Obviously they have to enter from the same place and on cue – but what you do thereafter, how you play the scene in terms of emotion, all that comes out of the circumstances you discover when you arrive on stage, which can differ from night to night. There's no attempt to *repeat*. That's particularly helpful with Chekhov where the audience is likely to be picking up as much information from a character who is quietly listening – or not listening, or not speaking – as the character who *is* speaking. There's a whole range of people on stage and each one of them is telling the story. I remember Alfreds saying that each of the actors should think they are playing the leading part. That would be inappropriate for many plays, but for Chekhov it's very helpful. On the whole Alfreds doesn't tell you what *his* views are because he would much rather let things emerge. Yet he did believe there was something vaudevillean in the play, and that while the characters certainly *could* be played naturalistically, they were also very much 'types'. He was interested in an acting style which would draw the audience's attention to that. Certainly the design of the production – and the costumes – were rather formalised. We all wore roughly the same colours, but changed for each act in keeping with the seasons.

I remember speaking to the Russian director Efros.[6] He made the point that Chekhov is not exclusively a naturalistic playwright, and that there are many many styles within his writing. You'd be hard put to know that from reading translations! Once you realise that you may be killing the effect of a Chekhov play by resolutely playing it in only one style, *then* you've a chance of unlocking its richness. So if Michael Frayn makes Chekhov's play into an English comedy, perhaps he has that right given that *Platonov is* a rambling, unfinished, unperformed play in a first draft. But with the other Chekhov plays, looking around for the possibility of different styles of presentation can be very helpful.

So the Alfreds' method works very well because the actors are free – they're not just being told what to do. I wouldn't very much enjoy being in a Chekhov production – or indeed of any play – where I was told exactly what to do – or that some specific effect had to be made on a particular line. More than most playwrights, Chekhov is very hard to pin down. There is life happening on stage which is real life – but at the same time it's theatricalised.

PA   Do you think that Alfreds was pushing you to quite specifically represent 'Russian culture' – or did it just evolve?

IMc   We did a lot of research collectively, but I've done that with other productions of Chekhov as well. Actors are given tasks. For example, when you're doing *The Cherry Orchard* or *Three Sisters*, it's fundamental to consider the distances that these characters are from the places they talk about – and indeed, the places they go to. On this little island it's difficult for us to conceive, to feel, what those distances must be like. I remember trying to work out the size of the cherry orchard. In one bit of maths (which I suspect was faulty), we worked out that the cherry orchard was eight times as large as Hyde Park – absolutely massive.[7] We tend to think of it as a couple of acres at the bottom of a path, but this was a big industry. The possibility of Lopakhin destroying it and building his houses indicates an entire town – not just a row of cottages. How do you get that over to an audience? All that knowledge has somehow to get inside you.

And as for being Russian, Lila Kedrova – when playing Arkadina[8] – had a sentence which she began in floods of tears and ended laughing her head off. That's something we English don't have. There is that lack of restraint at times, and a desire to share feelings which are not peculiar to Russians, but which are certainly not natural to British actors. I would always try and establish a bit of the flavour of that, and the Alfreds' method helped.

VG   This fluidity between laughter and tears in Russia, and in the language, is absolutely natural but when played in *English* it can often come over as neurotic – which is an acting problem, isn't it? It doesn't necessarily mean that the character *is* neurotic. My reading of Lopakhin is that he is not neurotic – many things motivate him, but not neurosis. Or Chekhov himself said that Varia is 'a cry-baby'. When he wanted someone to be a cry-baby, he actually said so. Is this a cultural problem which affects the plays? Have you found yourself worried about appearing neurotic in any of the roles you've played?

IMc   No, but I'm aware that this is not an easy thing. It's a volatility and an openness which perhaps actors have more than non-actors. But it isn't an 'actorish' quality in Chekhov's characters, nor is it peculiar to Chekhov's plays. We meet this all the time. The acting problem is exactly the same when you play people in Italian plays. You've got to be alert to their openness, their manners, and a willingness to show emotion in a public place, all of which go against British training. Which is probably why the British like actors so much – because they rather envy what they think is their free spirit.

VG   When Vanya fires – and misses – would you see this perhaps on one level as farcical, but on another level, deeply tragic, as part of this duality? In life it's almost impossible to fire a gun and miss three times in such a small space.

IMc   Fortunately, that's not my responsibility as an actor. That's up to the audience. I don't think it would be possible for Vanya himself to be so objective that he would find what he was doing funny. As an outsider watching the play, yes, I think it *is* perfectly possible to find that moment funny *and* pathetic. The aftermath comes in the next act of *Uncle Vanya* as he reverts to his old life, having had a good sniff of how his life *might* have been different. I feel desperately sorry for him, but at the same time I think he needs a good shake and that he should grow up. You're not as trapped as you think you are! I don't really like productions of Chekhov in which the audience is told what to think and what to feel. It's very difficult not to be tempted to direct their feelings – but all you've got to do is direct their *attention* - to say 'look at this'. I think that's what audience participation is. They are the editors, they are the judges. It's not like a movie where everything is decided. The audience can look where they want. That is why it's important in a Chekhov play that *wherever* they look, there should be extremely detailed life.

VG   May I ask about your performance as Svetlovidov in *Swan Song*? The one-act plays are considered by many as mere trifles. And Chekhov deliberately tried to put people off the scent by calling them 'trifles', yet he worked and worked at them. Was your approach to Svetlovidov similar to the mechanics of approaching the part of Vanya? Or was there something about the one-act form which altered your approach?

IMc   Obviously the scale is smaller – just two people and their relationship. But I wouldn't think of it as a trifle because he took a very deep view of those old men and their relationship as it happens that particular night.

PA   As an actor, do you have a sense of your audience's assumptions, and do you try to second-guess them at all?

IMc   No, you can't guess what kind of reaction there might be. I mean, it's true that if you want the audience to feel that it is perfectly alright to laugh at the character, you might exaggerate some effects to indicate to them that humour is allowed. I guess that's what Mike Alfreds wanted with the vaudevillean characters.

VG   Is it the difference between laughing *at* someone – or laughing *with* them? My feeling with almost everything Chekhov wrote was that one laughs *with* the characters, and not *at* them. There isn't a cruel element.

IMc   I think that would depend on who you were. You might laugh *at* them.

VG   I suppose you would laugh at Pishchik in *The Cherry Orchard* when he takes Ranevskaya's pills.

IMc   Yes, indeed. When we did *Wild Honey* in the United States, it was not well received. One person who had seen it explained to me that it was impossible to do a play 'for laughs' in the United States – this was about six years ago – in which the leading character is an alcoholic. That man was ill. It couldn't be a farce.

VG   Is that why it didn't work?

IMc   That *was* one explanation. I would say that Platonov is a comic character, but there are other ways of looking at people who drink a great deal, whether you do them to be laughed at or to be cured. What I'm saying is that all we can do as a group is to play a piece as it seems to *us*. It's up to the audience to judge and enjoy it on whatever level they want.

VG   My memory of your performance of Vanya was that it differed fascinatingly each time I saw it, but one of the constants was his rage. *Is* this your reading of the character?

IMc   He *is* a deeply frustrated man in many ways, partly sexually. His lack of self-fulfilment in middle age has been tolerable because he has been managing the estate. He's found a role for himself, a job as a professional, and he gets on with it. But when all his work is rejected, when he's fallen head over heels for the visitor, Yelena, whose husband Serebryakov has let him down – then rage, disappointment and frustration reach the point where he wants them to stop so much that he is going to kill.

VG   But when Vanya says 'I might have been Schopenhauer, a Dostoyevsky', he gives himself a potential role and then measures his failure against it. Perhaps what he needs is to find happiness in more modest terms.

IMc   I don't like that judgement. All *I* have to do as an actor is believe in what I'm saying at the moment I say it. I have to make decisions. Am I pretending? Am I lying? Do I really believe it? Do I feel it? How important is it that I get the other person to understand what I'm saying? Are they likely to? All those things. It's not up to me whether the character would have been better off if he had or hadn't said that. It's not up to me to say: is he foolish to say that? He just *does* say it.

VG   Yet is it not part of your work as an actor to decide if he's playing a role, albeit sincerely, for himself or for other people? Like Soliony in *Three Sisters*?

IMc   I don't quite see it in those terms. Soliony, to outsiders, is an unpleasant annoying man, although doesn't the Baron say that if you get him on his own, he's alright? He's a show-off, and he exaggerates the situation. All you have to do as an actor is ask if that gives him pleasure? Has he said it many times before? Does he believe it? One must always try to do this without judging him. He's a man who feels very deeply. It's not up to me to judge whether he is constantly putting scent on his hands because he doesn't want to smell of death. That's for the audience. But he feels things so strongly because he's frustrated that he can't see any different way of how to deal with his feelings except by affecting other people. He's very nicely complex. I'm always trying not to take an attitude, but delve into all the details of what the man is, and what he says he is, *and* what other people say about him – and presenting *that* as clearly as possible. I suppose I have an actor's canniness that this line might strike some people in the audience as funny. But to go out and try to get a laugh from Chekhov *reduces* Chekhov.

VG   So complexity is the key dimension of the characters?

IMc   Yes. I would find it very hard to write about Chekhov, but I don't find it very difficult to act.

PA   Are there any other technical approaches in Alfreds' method which help bring a group together?

IMc   Many. He has very long rehearsal periods, usually weeks and weeks. Much of the early rehearsal is sitting around and dissecting the text for information about your own character, and other people's. Throwing out long lists of what the characters do, what they say about themselves and about each other and what their past was. *All* of this material is garnered from the text. Chekhov's work has much more detail about people's lives, past and present, than in most plays. With a play like *Closer*[9] we know very little about these people when they are not relating to each other – we have no idea where they come from. Chekhov provides much more satisfying characters to play because you have such details that you don't need to guess. I think his instruction to Stanislavsky was that you should *not* guess, because the material is all there. So a lot of rehearsal preparation is spent on the actors inhabiting the world and their characters so completely that they can go on being credible whether they are sitting down, standing up, with their back to the audience, shouting, laughing or crying. Whatever they're doing, they just go on 'being'. As we all do in our own lives – we go on being ourselves. That's how it is in a Mike Alfreds' production.

Or you might one day do the play with the whole point of concentration on money – so that as you are doing *The Cherry Orchard*, you would be alert to what is said about money: knowing how much money you earned; how much you're *likely* to earn, and how much you have in your pocket. You discover that *every* character has some problem with money. Whether they've got it or not, they all know a great deal about money and when you do it like that, the whole play seems to be about money! *Or* you can make the point of concentration the past – and you then discover that they all talk about the past non-stop. Equally, the emphasis can be *the future* – and they all talk about the future!

There are so many themes going on in Chekhov's plays, but in such a delicate way, always rooted and expressed in the text. Or another technique is that one day you do a run-through – and then your point of concentration is one particular character. If it was Trofimov, for example, then you would only do Trofimov's scenes, and in those scenes the thing uppermost in your mind as an actor was *that* character. You might find yourself *ignoring* him, but you would *know* you were ignoring him – and why. Once that has been done with all of the characters, right down to the postman, you then realise as an actor that you can go on being Lopakhin – who I was – whether you are saying your lines to Trofimov, or to Ranevskaya, or to Dunyasha. It doesn't matter – you go on being yourself. And there's no end to the ways in which you can tell the story. This wouldn't necessarily work in a large theatre where stage pictures are very important, but in a small theatre, where the audience can see everything at close quarters, then I think it works.

Chekhov appeals to me because you cannot realise the play in production *unless* every part has been worked on fully. That isn't true of most playwrights. But it also means that it is all the more intolerable in *Three Sisters* if you have a weak Soliony or a poor Andrey. Chekhov allows the actors full rein and yet doesn't allow any one actor to run away with the play. It reaffirms what I most enjoy about acting in the theatre, which is working in a group.

VG   So is it playing with it, playing 'off' other people? Is that why every performance is different?

IMc   Every performance has to be different because everybody's trying to put themselves into it. Today the weather is different from yesterday; the audience is different – and you are different. How can you possibly do it the same way? You can't breathe the same air. It's not the same words you're saying. Those words have gone. It's a nonsense to try and make it the same. It cannot be done.

PA   Some actors try to do that.

IMc   Most. In a musical these days, if a singer decides for some reason to sing louder or softer it will be adjusted by the sound technician at the back who is *desperately* trying to fix the sound as agreed during the technical rehearsal.
   But returning to Chekhov, another big error with many productions is that the characters are so often 'impersonated' by actors who are the wrong age. Recently, there was a very young Vanya.[10] That's a little perverse, I think, unless you're doing a play *about* Vanya as opposed to the play *called* Vanya. Trigorin is normally played far too old. Trigorin and Konstantin are the same generation and you can't really feel the sexual tension and jealousy there in *The Seagull*, professionally *and* personally, unless you see that they are envious of each other *because* they are close in age.

VG   Equally, Chekhov said that Ranevskaya is an old woman. He didn't want his wife Olga Knipper[11] to play her because he thought she was too young.

IMc   Ages aren't always mentioned but you can usually work them out.

VG   Have you seen a Russian production of any of the plays which clarified contextual elements which you hadn't thought of?

IMc   There was a production in Moscow of *The Cherry Orchard* at the

Taganka Theatre.[12] At the beginning of the play, Lopakhin came on and although Dunyasha was on stage, he spoke directly to the audience. There are many occasions in Chekhov when a character is left alone on stage and is speaking. I've tried in this country, but I've never succeeded in persuading other actors that it *is* appropriate for the actor to speak directly to the audience as Shakespeare's characters constantly do – break through the fourth wall. When Alfreds talks about vaudeville I think it's connected to that. The characters are so self-confident, so needy to be themselves that sometimes there is no-one else around for them to speak to *except* the audience. It doesn't mean you have to stop being your character or that you are no longer in Russia. It's just the magic of the theatre that you can be in Russia *and* the theatre at the same time. Andrey, for example, hardly ever gets to speak to anyone else. When he speaks in Act Two, his wife doesn't listen and the other person he speaks to – Ferapont – is deaf. In the third act he speaks to his sisters who are behind the screens. I tried to suggest that Andrey might talk to the audience, but Trevor Nunn wasn't interested. So it's something we don't often see in a British production. I've always tried to get people to see Mikhalkov's film version of *Platonov – An Unfinished Piece for Mechanical Piano*. Even with film where directors have the upper hand and its as much *their* story as the author's, Mikhalkov had licence to shape the material as he wanted yet time and again the camera in his film is way back – and we see *all* the characters simultaneously.[13]

PA   Is there any more Chekhov that you're burning to do?

IMc   I'd like to do Vanya again because we only did it for about three months. I'm going to do Dorn in *The Seagull* this autumn at the West Yorkshire Playhouse, with Jude Kelly directing. That play is so essentially about theatre people that a company of actors can bring an awful lot of their own lives to it, even though it was written a hundred years ago and in another country. We're going to set up a company of actors who can do three or four plays one after the other. As usual, in those circumstances, Chekhov immediately springs to mind as a very good way of binding a group. The major joy of Chekhov is the group that does it. Also, every detail of the relationships between the characters, whether they speak to each other much or not, is very clearly present in the text. It's very easy and quick to read what the situation is, which isn't true of Ibsen, for example.[14] Chekhov is a wonderful friend to the actor.

2 Ian McKellen (Dr Dorn) and Claudie Blakley (Nina) in *The Seagull* at the West Yorkshire
Playhouse presented by the West Yorkshire Playhouse Courtyard Company, Leeds, October
1998 directed by Jude Kelly, designed by Robert Innes-Hopkins.

NOTES

This interview with Ian McKellen and the editors took place at the Royal
National Theatre, London, in May 1998.

1 See chapter 9 in this volume.

2 See chapters 7 and 9 in this volume.

3 In 1995 Ian McKellen co-wrote and co-produced *Richard III*, directed by
Richard Loncraine, as an extremely successful feature film, and played the title
role in 1930s military uniform. The parallels with the rise of Fascism were
evident in the military dress, the colour symbolism and McKellen's brilliant
manipulation of 'the people', highly reminiscent, though not imitative, of Hitler.

4 *Wild Honey*, Michael Frayn's version of Chekhov's unfinished *Platonov* was
directed by Christopher Morahan, and designed by John Gunter. It opened at
the Lyttelton Theatre, National Theatre, in July 1984.

5 Alfreds worked on the translation with Lilia Sokolova, who provided the literal
Russian translation.

6 Anatoly Efros, one of the great iconoclastic directors of the post-Stalinist years,
was responsible for the radically innovative production of *The Cherry Orchard*
which set the play *non-naturalistically* in a graveyard/huge bed. For a detailed
description of that production in English, see chapters 3, 12, 14 and 15 in this
volume. See also *Theatre Quarterly*, 7, 1977, pp. 34–47: 'Anatolij Efros directs
Chekhov's *The Cherry Orchard* and Gogol's *The Marriage*', in an article by
M. Shevtsova. And see note 12 below.

7 See chapter 10 in this volume on the size of the orchard.

8 Lila Kedrova, a French-Russian actress, played Arkadina in the production of *Seagull* translated and directed by Richard Cottrell, first done at the Arts Theatre, Cambridge, July 1970.

9 The reference here is to the play, *Closer*, written and directed by Patrick Marber, first performed at the Royal National Theatre, May 1997.

10 This is a reference to Katie Mitchell's production of *Uncle Vanya*, translated by David Lan, with the forty-one-year-old Stephen Dillane as Vanya – a Young Vic/ RSC co-production, 1 April 1998.

11 Olga Leonardovna Knipper (1868–1959), the actress who married Chekhov in May 1901, three years before his death from tuberculosis, and when he was already 'exiled' to Yalta for the winter months because of his illness. Knipper was the original Arkadina in the MAT production of *The Seagull*; played Yelena (Helen) in *Uncle Vanya* (against Chekhov's wishes); played Masha in *Three Sisters* (a part he wrote for her) and was the original Ranevskaya in *The Cherry Orchard* – again, against Chekhov's wishes since he felt she was too young. She died at the age of ninety-one (although a mistake on her passport made her officially two years younger, born in 1870, so dying aged eighty-nine) after playing those and other parts in successive MAT productions, many of which remained more or less unaltered from the original productions.

12 *Vishnevyi sad (The Cherry Orchard)*, directed by the innovatory Anatoly Efros in 1975, designed by Valery Levental. See chapters 11, 14 and 15 in this volume, and note 6 above.

13 See chapters 4 and 13 in this volume.

14 At the time of this interview, Ian McKellen was playing Dr Stockmann in Ibsen's *An Enemy of the People*, directed by Trevor Nunn at the Royal National Theatre, London.

Postscript:
Ian McKellen was filming in New Zealand at the time of final proof-reading, a major factor which did not, however, stop him from generously telephoning his corrections/ suggestions. Concerning the *exact* words Chekhov gives Dr Dorn at the end of *The Seagull* about Konstantin's suicide (see p. 122 of this interview), Chekhov uses the word 'zastrelilsya' (the past perfective), which literally translates that last line as 'Konstantin Gavrilovich has shot himself dead.' Or more idiomatically, 'Konstantin . . . has killed himself.' With reference to the editorial point in the interview, therefore, it is quite clear that Konstantin *has* killed himself this time. Also, Dorn *is* a doctor.

The ambivalence in English translation is born out by the following examples. In Hingley, *The Oxford Chekhov*, vol. ii, Act Four, p. 281, Dorn says: 'The fact is, Constantine has shot himself'. In E.K. Bristow's version, *Anton Chekhov's Plays*, New York, 1977, p. 51, it reads: 'The fact is, Konstantin Gavrilovich has shot himself'; this translation is identical in Elisaveta Fen's *Chekhov Plays*, Penguin Classics, 1960 (reprint of 1951), p. 183, and is *again* identical in S.S. Koteliansky's translation in *Tchekhov – Plays and Stories*, London, New York, 1974, p. 101.

This raised a more contentious question than I had realised at the time, and before going back to the original, so this postscript is also a belated apology to Ian McKellen for a misleading response in the interview which, however, does prove his point. The ambivalence is in the English translation, not the Russian original. V.G.

12

ARNOLD ARONSON

The scenography of Chekhov

The stage demands a degree of artifice . . . you have no fourth wall. Besides, the stage is art, the stage reflects the quintessence of life and there is no need to introduce anything superfluous on to it.[1]

These were Chekhov's words to an actor during the rehearsals for the Moscow Art Theatre première of *The Seagull*, and it encapsulates the ongoing struggles Chekhov would have with Stanislavsky's productions. Chekhov was a Symbolist playwright trapped in a Naturalist theatre. In his texts the settings were described with a stark, yet poetic minimalism and could be seen as part of the Symbolist project to fuse interior and exterior states of mind. For Chekhov, as for Maeterlinck whom he greatly admired, the concrete elements of the external world were manifestations of emotional states of being; what Richard Wagner called 'soul states'. The settings are virtual roadmaps to the psyche, and so complete is the identification of the character with the décor that if the setting were taken away the character would cease to exist. 'I love this house,' says Madame Ranevsky in Act Three of *The Cherry Orchard*. 'Without the cherry orchard my life would lose its meaning, and if it must really be sold then go and sell me with the orchard.'[2]

Such unity of scenography and self is unique among the playwrights of the time. Nora, in Ibsen's *A Doll's House*, for example, must have a house to leave, of course, but for all the specificity of Ibsen's stage descriptions, no single item has the resonance or necessity of the bookcase in *Uncle Vanya*, the dining table in *Three Sisters* or the nursery in *The Cherry Orchard*. These are crucial emblematic and atmospheric elements, and set pieces even function as determinants of the rhythm of his plays, such as the chair over which Yepikhodov stumbles in *The Cherry Orchard*. Yet Chekhov was not so much interested in the details of real life as in the evocation of a state of mind, of the so-called *nastroenie*, and everything on the stage was subordinated to this end. Chekhov's scenography aims at an emotional sensibility, not a documentary recording of domestic décor.

And yet, the popular conception of a Chekhovian setting is not the spare and evocative one implied by the stage directions, but one that is rich and cluttered; it is an image of painstakingly detailed houses, rooms and old furniture, all imbued with the crushing weight of memories and unfulfilled desires as in Michael Blakemore's production of *Uncle Vanya* (London, 1988) which was described by one critic as 'choc-a-bloc with saplings, samovars, and duff furniture.'[3] Chekhov has become so closely identified with this imagery that he has joined that small fraternity of playwrights who have lent their very names to the language as adjectives. But whereas Sophoclean, Shakespearean, Brechtian or Pinteresque, for example, primarily tend to identify a style of writing, a point of view, a particular content, or, more ephemerally, a dramatic world, the term 'Chekhovian', more than any other, conjures up a landscape. It is, almost by definition, a visual style. It is so ingrained in our consciousness that when performance artist Stuart Sherman created his rarified deconstruction of Chekhov's texts entitled, simply, *Chekhov* (1985) – a twelve-minute abstraction of gestures and sounds – his stage directions called for 'a realistic Chekhovian drawing-room, with large Persian rug and dining-table (on which can be seen teacups, playing cards, an ashtray containing a half-smoked cigar, and candlesticks) . . . an armchair, a samovar, and a cabinet, which holds icons, books and family photographs'. Though Chekhov may never have described such a room, it was instantly recognisable to spectators as the quintessential Chekhovian landscape. (This 'room', which occupied half the stage, was peopled not with actors but with two-dimensional cutouts on which were printed fragments of Chekhov's texts.)

But if such particularised scenography is not explicitly demanded in the texts, then why do we retain this impression? While the symbiotic relationship of Chekhov and the Moscow Art Theatre, of course, proved beneficial for both of them, the Naturalistic approach of Stanislavsky and his designer, Viktor Simov,[4] had the unfortunate effect of encasing the plays in a highly detailed, representational, physical world that has imprinted itself on theatrical consciousness. The plays and the décor have become inextricably linked, not unlike the later designs of Caspar Neher for Bertolt Brecht, or Jo Mielziner for Tennessee Williams. From the 1950s onward, however, directors and designers have tried, with varying degrees of success, to break away from the Naturalistic framework and find something more in keeping with Chekhov's Symbolist tendencies.

Given the theatrical practices of the day, the Naturalistic approach to scenography was probably inevitable. Neither Stanislavsky nor Chekhov had the vocabulary for creating a new style. Moreover, Stanislavsky, for all his influence on twentieth-century theatre, was immersed in the late nineteenth-century aesthetic. His work was a culmination of over a century of developments toward psychological realism in acting and Romantic realism in design. Scenographically, this meant the illusionistic practices of fourth-wall Naturalism. Chekhov, for his part, despite some knowledge of Western European Symbolist playwrights, had not, of course, seen the productions of Paul Fort's Théâtre d'Art in Paris. Even if he had, a formal Symbolist scenography was never clearly articulated, although playwright Pierre Quillard set forth a Symbolist approach to design when he stated, 'Speech creates scenery like everything else.'[5] Chekhov was inexorably approaching the same aesthetic on his own, something that Maxim Gorky apparently recognised in Chekhov when he wrote, 'You are a man who can create a character with a mere word, and with a sentence tell a whole story.'[6] Quillard called for a *mise-en-scène* that would 'emphasize the infinite multiplicity of time and space'. By abolishing the accretions of the Naturalist stage, the Symbolists hoped to free theatre from its inevitably flawed attempts to reproduce reality and instead allow theatre to 'be what it should be: a pretext for a dream'. Though Simov and Stanislavsky neither attempted nor achieved such a visual world, Quillard's aesthetic anticipated the post-1960 approach to Chekhov.

Chekhov's minimalist set descriptions, in fact, are closest in spirit to the ideas of Appia[7] (though with no direct influence since most of Appia's writings came after Chekhov's death). The second act of *Uncle Vanya* for instance is described thus: 'The dining room in Serebryakov's house. Night. The watchman can be heard tapping in the garden. Serebryakov is sitting in an armchair in front of an open window, he is dozing.'[8] That is all – no description of furnishings or décor, although there are references throughout the act that indicate the need for a table, a window, a door, a sideboard, and a few chairs. Think of Chekhov's settings as Appia declares: 'We shall no longer try to give the illusion of a forest, but the illusion of a man in the atmosphere of a forest. Man is the reality, and nothing else counts . . . Scenic illusion is the presence of the living actor.'[9]

By the time of *The Cherry Orchard*, Chekhov seems clearly to be attempting a Symbolist-like fusion of interior and exterior states of mind, one in which the very walls of the house seem almost transparent. The setting for Act One of *The Cherry Orchard* is described as 'A room that still goes by the name of the nursery. One of the doors leads to Anya's room. It is dawn and the sun will soon come up. It is May. The cherry trees are in flower, but in the orchard it is cold, there is morning frost. The windows in the room are closed.'[10] The locale is identified and we are told that there is a door and, significantly, where that door leads. If this were Ibsen or Shaw there would be detailed descriptions of furniture, bric-à-brac, carpets, wall coverings and the like. But what is important in this description is the *exterior*; there is a continuity between the nursery and the world beyond, as if the nursery can be understood only in terms of the context or environment in which it sits. Exterior scenes, in turn, have a fluidity that takes them beyond the mere confines of the stage. Act Four of *Three Sisters*, for instance, unfolds in 'The old garden attached to the Prozorov house. A long avenue of fir trees at the end of which is seen the river. On the other side of the river – a forest. On the right is the terrace of the house.'[11] The house is almost an afterthought. What is clearly most significant for Chekhov is the vista stretching into the distance with its implication of continuity and the promised land that the sisters can never reach: a garden, a river, a forest – left unstated, of course, is Moscow, far beyond.

While the stage directions for *The Seagull* are the most detailed of the major plays, Chekhov already evinces an eye for the larger picture and the unseen world that surrounds his characters:

Part of the park on Sorin's estate. A broad avenue leads from the view of the audience into the depths of the park toward a lake. A platform stage – pieced together and hastily built for a home performance – has been placed across the avenue in such a way that the lake cannot be seen. To the left and right of the platform stage is shrubbery. There are a few chairs and a small table. The sun has just set . . .[12]

In *My Life in Art*, however, Stanislavsky describes the same setting with the pride of someone who has learned well from the Duke of Saxe-Meiningen and André Antoine.

On the very forestage, right near the footlights, in direct opposition to all the accepted laws and customs of the theatre of that time, almost all the persons in the play sat on a long swinging bench characteristic of Russian country estates, with their backs to the public. This bench, placed in a line with some tree stumps that remained from a destroyed forest, bordered an alley set with century-old trees that stood at a measured distance from each other. In the spaces between their trunks, which seemed mysterious in the darkness of night, there showed something in the form of a proscenium that was closed from sight by a large white sheet. This was the open-air theatre of the unsuccessful and unacknowledged Treplev.[13]

The problem was conflict of intentions. Chekhov, doctor that he was, observed the real world in careful detail, but then distilled it to poetic essences. Stanislavsky took the essences and fleshed them out again into three-dimensional illusions. In his correspondence with Stanislavsky regarding *The Cherry Orchard*, for example, Chekhov indicates a very specific inspiration for the environment. 'It's an old manor house,' he said of the Ranevsky estate. 'Some time ago the people who lived there did so on a very rich scale, and this must be felt in the setting. A feeling of richness and cosiness.'[14] A few weeks later he provided more details:

> The house is a large two-storied one . . . [It] has to be large and solid: made of wood or stone, it doesn't matter which. It is very old and of enormous size of a kind which holiday makers don't rent but pull down and use the materials to build summer cottages. The furniture is old-fashioned, stylish, and solid; their financial straits and debts haven't affected the furnishings.[15]

Yet Chekhov did not intend for Stanislavsky to build an actual house; after all, we never see the exterior. The point was to create the essence of such a house on the stage. Stanislavsky, nonetheless, moved toward greater and greater detail. Meyerhold described how the 1905 revival of *The Seagull*, for instance, became even more illusionistic:

> Every corner of the set was laid bare: there was a summer house with a real roof and real columns; there was a real ravine on stage . . . In the revival the windows in the improved set faced the spectator so that the landscape was visible. Your imagination was silenced, and whatever the characters said about the landscape, you disbelieved them because it could never be as they described it; it was painted and you could see it.[16]

While he may not have had a specific Symbolist vocabulary with which to describe his settings, Chekhov understood the contradiction of mingling the found objects of the real world with the careful artifice of the stage. 'There's a genre painting by Kramskoy,' he explained to an actor during the rehearsal of *The Seagull*, according to Meyerhold, 'in which the faces are portrayed superbly. What would happen if you cut the nose out of one of the paintings and substituted a real one? The nose would be "realistic" but the picture would be ruined.'[17] A few years later, shortly before his death, Chekhov would echo this sentiment when he wrote of *The Cherry Orchard*, 'Stanislavsky has ruined my play.'[18] By mixing two-dimensional painted scenery with real furniture, not to mention a very real crying baby, Stanislavsky had, in essence, put a real nose in the artistic framework of the play.

Chekhov went in and out of favour in Russia and the USSR over the following decades. Despite a move towards a more lyrical and Impressionist décor, especially in the designs of Vladimir Dmitriev in the 1940s, the scenography was still solidly in the tradition of Simov with one notable exception. In 1944–5, Alexander Tairov directed a theatricalist production of *The Seagull* at the Kamerny Theatre that was clearly intended as a rejection of the Naturalistic style of Stanislavsky's productions and especially those of the Socialist Realism dominant in the Soviet Union at the time. Perhaps inspired by the demand for new forms by the character of Treplev, and with a nod to Appia and Craig,[19] Tairov largely replaced illusionistic scenery with platforms and black velvet drapes and an almost exclusively black and white colour scheme that led some critics to describe it as funereal. In the waning days of World War II and in the wake of Stalin's purges, the starkness of the set must have been striking. By the 1950s, in both the Soviet Union and elsewhere, the conventional 'Chekhovian' set – more accurately, a 'Simovian' set – began to seem dated by modern standards. Moreover, the elements of Chekhov's settings which once served as a subtle and detailed semiotic guide to a complex psycho-social world became meaningless except as self-referents. Naturalistic settings whether for Chekhov, Hauptmann, or Strindberg became indistinguishable allusions to a previous century. And the specific props, costumes and set pieces now associated with Chekhov no longer signified aspects of Russian society at the turn of the century but came to stand for Chekhov's plays themselves. New approaches were needed.

Directors and designers working since the 1960s have attempted to rid the stage of lingering nineteenth-century sentimentality while emphasising the fluidity of inner and outer worlds. The pastiche approach typical of postmodernism was particularly well suited to Chekhov. Designers seemed to be following the advice of avant-garde composer and theoretician John Cage who, when asked about how to treat classics, suggested that rather than simply rejecting them, they should be 'quoted' in new productions. Fragments of traditional Chekhovian scenography placed and juxtaposed within a more abstract environment became increasingly common in productions from the 1970s onward.

The first step in breaking the realistic, sentimental grip was taken in a 1960 production of The Seagull directed by Otomar Krejča and designed by Josef Svoboda at the Tyl Theatre in Prague. (See Appendix 4.) Svoboda encased the stage in black drapes so that the actors were in a theatrical void. The park – indeed, the natural world – existed emblematically as leaf-filled branches hanging over the stage through all four acts. Interiors were suggested by furniture and fragmentary scenic units such as a window with drapes (but no surrounding walls). More important, the atmosphere of each scene was created through the use of changing 'light curtains', one of Svoboda's technological creations, that created a scrim-like effect. Thus, the entire play occurred in a fluidly changing, but essentially unified environment. Exteriors and interiors blended and the external world was always visibly present in the house.

The same year witnessed similar approaches for the first time in the Soviet Union. Nisson Shiffrin's décor for *The Seagull* (1960) at the Moscow Art Theatre included a surround that depicted trees and the horizon as well as the sky in both exterior and interior scenes; the interiors contained no ceilings and only partial walls. At the same time, tall window drapes, taller than the rooms, hung in the exterior as well as interior scenes, creating an ever-present sense of spatial memory or anticipation. For *The Seagull* at the Tsvilling Theatre in Chelyabinsk (1979), designer Daniil Lider used over-hanging branches, remarkably similar to Svoboda's, as well as a sort of curtain hung on a clothes line in his design. The motif of branches overhanging the stage through exterior and interior scenes proved popular in the USSR and could be found in Mikhail Kurilko's design for *Uncle Vanya* in 1966 at the Kupal Theatre in Minsk and in Enar Stenberg's 1969 production of *The Seagull* at the Moscow Art Theatre.[20]

By 1962, the attempt to visually fuse the interior and exterior scenes appeared in England at the newly opened Chichester Festival Theatre. Sean Kenny's design for Laurence Olivier's production of *Uncle Vanya* consisted of a simple wooden back wall with two windows and a door. With the windows blacked out in the first act it became the garden; with light coming through them the stage was transformed into the interiors of the last three acts. The great innovation, however, was the use, perhaps for the first time anywhere, of a thrust stage for Chekhov. Not only were the internal boundaries destroyed, but some of the separation between the stage and the audience seemed to disappear as well, leading a contemporary critic to note that '[Chekhov's] people had not been more closely allied to us'.[21]

Olivier continued the atmospheric, non-Naturalistic approach in his famous 1967 London production of *Three Sisters* at the National Theatre with designs by Svoboda. Here Svoboda's light curtains were replaced by a surround of stretched cords tied from floor to grid, while window-frames were placed between two layers of cords. Through the use of light, the cords could become 'solid walls, delicate bars, or shimmering depths without precise limit'.[22] The cords also served as a screen for Svoboda's trademark projections. Although minimal pieces of furniture were em-ployed, this was an essentially abstract setting creating a theatrical rather than illusionistic environment.

By eliminating naturalistic approaches to scenography, the associations that go with it are likewise eliminated and the stage reasserts itself. It is no longer an *illusion of* reality, but an *allusion to* reality. Walls, doors and especially windows become ephemeral, transformable elements which, as Svoboda noted, are at the heart of Chekhov:

Windows are very special things in Chekhov. The thoughts and desires of the characters fly out through the windows, but life and its realities fly in the other way. The windows must be created by means of light, like that of the French Impressionists – light dispersed in air . . . The windows lead us to all of Chekhov's atmosphere, the interiors are not bordered or limited, but diffused.[23]

Meanwhile, Soviet director Georgy Tovstonogov had expressed a similar point of view in his 1965 production of *Three Sisters* at the Bolshoi Dramatic Theatre (BDT) in Leningrad, designed by Sofia Yunovich.

In our production, the rooms in the Prozorov house were not delimited by walls, ceilings, windows or doors. Furniture . . . was distributed over all of our huge stage. A crystal chandelier hung over the table. Near the center of the stage stood a lonely Empire column, which supported nothing. Sunlight poured in through windows placed upstage behind a gauze which was hung along the circumference of the stage. The play of light and shadow on the column (caused by branches swaying behind the windows) and the soft twittering of birds created the atmosphere I wanted: spring, peace, and prosperity. A few minutes after the play had begun – more precisely, just before Vershinin's entrance – the light was cut on the windows behind the gauze, and they seemed to disappear. In the last three acts, in exactly the same way, there were illuminated windows in the Prozorov house, and an alley of birches (done three-dimensionally). And they disappeared in exactly the same way a few minutes after the act had begun. It seemed to me that these three-dimensional bits of scenery had served their purpose in indicating the place of action. All they could do further during the course of the play would be to distract the attention of the audience from the action itself.[24]

Tovstonogov also believed that the contemporary audience was more familiar with the experience of films than of the static theatre and that Chekhov would be more comprehensible if staged in a cinematic form. By using a revolve and mobile platforms that projected towards the audience he attempted to create the equivalent of close-ups, pan shots, reverse angles and the like – the vocabulary of the film which constantly alters the orientation of the spectators to the scene to enhance or replace the movement of actors.

Anatoly Efros' 1967 production of *Three Sisters* at the Malaya Bronnaya Theatre in Moscow went even further in fusing exterior and interior. The setting was reduced to nothing but a solitary, stylised tree with copper leaves which represented the avenue of birch trees and also served as a coat-rack. The influence of Samuel Beckett as the spiritual descendant of Chekhov was clearly making itself felt.

The conflation of inner and outer worlds has continued to be a strong motif in Soviet and Russian productions as seen in the designs of Valery Levental, Sergei Barkhin, David Borovsky, Mart Kitaev, Daniil Lider and Eduard Kochergin. Though each of these designers has a unique style, the productions are often typified by fragmentary set pieces or furniture sitting like icons or islands in the midst of an open stage; often nature is seen not only blending with the man-made world but seemingly overpowering it. The latter is evident in Vladimir Serebrovsky's *Ivanov* (1978) in Baku, in which the dining room was open to the garden and autumn leaves covered the floor, or David Borovsky's 1976 MAT production in which branches and vines overwhelmed the exterior of the house. (See Appendix 4.)

The most aggressive proponent of the fusion approach has been Romanian-born director Andrei Serban, who has worked since the early 1970s in the United States. In his 1977 *The Cherry Orchard* at the Lincoln Center, designed by Santa Loquasto, symbolic elements were isolated against a luminous background of barren trees, and the visual images were echoed by symbolic actions such as a plough dragged across a field by peasants. The ballroom was depicted as a structure that could be viewed as either a giant gazebo or as a cage. The white-on-white colour scheme suggested both a formality and isolation or barrenness. Despite a negative response this production received from the more conservative New York critics, it spawned a host of imitations. Serban did a *Seagull* in Japan in 1980, designed by Kaoru Kanamori, that took a more romantic turn but nonetheless carried on the motif of a continuous interior and exterior. The inside was suggested by a repetitive row of window-frames that, while reinforcing Svoboda's remark about the importance of windows in Chekhov, functioned almost as an abstract motif. A wood-planked stage floor unified the entire stage space.

Any hint of coldness gave way totally to the warm wood textures of Serban's 1983 *Uncle Vanya*, also designed by Loquasto. But just as the symmetrical row of windows of the Japan *Seagull* worked in opposition to the romanticism of the wood and trees, the romanticism of this *Vanya* was offset by the geometric pattern of the groundplan. The setting here consisted of platforms and steps with a few pieces of furniture – rooms and spatial divisions were defined by differing levels rather than actual walls. The idea for the set was generated by a reference in the play to the empty house being like a maze. The effect was, according to Loquasto, 'the sweep of a Beckett landscape, but one where you also had warm wood and familiar Chekhov textures . . . But by stretching the space, it took on the ascetic serenity of an Oriental walkway as well.'[25]

Yet another approach to the Chekhovian sense of fluidity has been to create a sense of endlessness through rooms and spaces that continue

3   *The Cherry Orchard*, Act One, Romanian National Theatre (1993), directed by Andrei
Serban, designed by Santa Loquasto, originally produced by the New York Shakespeare
Festival at the Vivian Beaumont Theatre in New York City.

4   *The Cherry Orchard*, Act One, Romanian National Theatre (1993), directed by Andrei
Serban, designed by Santa Loquasto, originally produced by the New York Shakespeare
Festival at the Vivian Beaumont Theatre in New York City.

beyond the spectator's view, thereby creating a tantalizing maze of off-stage spaces that remain frustratingly inaccessible to the audience. The intimation of such a world is already present in *Three Sisters* with the ballroom visible through columns behind the drawing room; in *The Cherry Orchard* where, again, the ballroom is visible beyond the archway behind the drawing room, or in the first act of *The Seagull* with the lake hidden behind the makeshift stage.

One of the earliest productions to approach the play in this way was the 1969 *Cherry Orchard* designed by Karl Ernst Hermann in Berlin. It employed a classic box set with faint echoes of the Teatro Olimpico. The two upstage doors that led to the drawing room were placed in the back wall in such a way that it was impossible for any one person in the audience to see the entirety of the inner room. Furthermore, these doors were echoed in the upstage wall of the inner room. There was an implication of infinity – if these doors were opened the spectators would see another room, and another and so on.

A 1970 production of the same play, designed by Jürgen Rose in Hamburg, also played with neo-classical perspective, but in a more blatant and unrelenting fashion. The eye was ineluctably drawn to a single vanishing point through a door in a stark box set. However, the neo-classicism was softened by the romanticism of flimsy gauze curtains and the warm tones of the walls.

John Conklin's design for Mark Lamos' production of *Three Sisters* for the Hartford Stage Company in 1984 continued the same basic idea – an upstage space visible beyond the main playing area – but Conklin opted for a colder formality. The upstage openings could be understood as pillars, doors or windows; the floor of the thrust stage had a polished surface, thus abjuring the warm textures associated with Chekhov. Beyond the openings was cold, unknown space, a void that could be anything.

The elements of formality, texture, isolated iconographic pieces and the implication of space beyond were epitomised, however, in a 1983 Cologne production of *The Cherry Orchard* designed by Rolf Glittenberg. This was almost a parody of a box set: towering walls seemingly inspired by Gordon Craig, though textured through the use of wood, dwarfed the performers and the few scenic elements which resembled the vestiges of some earlier Chekhovian set. But while suggesting a type of prison, the space was not impenetrable. The rear wall could split open, admitting bright light into this confined, barren world, and suggesting a paradisiacal world beyond. A thematically similar *Ivanov* was designed by Mark Thompson for Elijah Moshinsky's 1989 London production. A critic described the room as 'a bare and almost windowless cell, like some large prison space . . . The only relief from this stifling uniformity is a square hole, a glass-less window cut high in the back wall, through which can be seen a passing vista of blue and white clouds, and where Ivanov's watchful wife appears.'[26]

Chekhov's characters are often trapped in a life or philosophy that is represented by the concrete elements of a house. The freshness or freedom of the outside world is tantalisingly visible yet inaccessible. Chekhov creates an interior by describing the exterior. In the settings by Glittenberg or Thompson, however, a formidable barrier is created between the two worlds.

When Chekhov stated, in the quote that begins this chapter, that 'you have no fourth wall', he was expressing the need to acknowledge the theatricality of the event. But certain contemporary productions have attempted to take the breaching of the fourth wall more literally and incorporate the audience, to some degree or other, in the production or the world of the play. If this is done successfully, the spectator is implicated in the action and the play is transformed into an existential reflection of contemporary society. Needless to say, this is a risky strategy. Any production, whether Chekhov's or not, that incorporates or attempts to incorporate the audience and theatre into the staging, runs into the problem of the clashing worlds of audience and performance. The suspension of disbelief can extend only so far when we are surrounded and confronted with our fellow patrons and the accoutrements of the theatre. Nonetheless, the environmental theatre movement of the late 1960s and 1970s has inspired some attempts. Director André Gregory brought the audience into the setting for his 1974 production of *The Seagull* at New York's Public Theatre, in which the set consisted of furniture and shrubs, but no walls or even clearly demarcated boundaries, set in a bifurcated arena space. The audience sat around the outdoor setting for the first two acts, then moved to the other side of the stage for the indoor scenes of the last two acts. An alternative environmental approach was taken by iconoclastic Soviet director Yuri Lyubimov in *Three Sisters* at the Taganka (1975). The production began with the back wall of the theatre sliding open to reveal a military band on the street outside. The sheet metal wall then closed, reflecting the audience back on itself.

British director Peter Brook, as he has done so often, took a wide cross-section of all these trends and put them together in his acclaimed 1987 production of *The Cherry Orchard* at the Majestic Theatre in Brooklyn, New York.[27] The Majestic was an abandoned movie palace and vaudeville house that was only partially renovated as an annex for the Brooklyn Academy of Music. Fragments of plaster remained on exposed brick walls, the once gaudy paint of this theatre could be seen in faded patches on a decayed ceiling and the proscenium arch hinted at its former glory. The theatre became a perfect metaphor for the Ranevsky estate. In the rather cavernous space of the stage, made even larger by an extension over the former orchestra pit, Brook and designer Chloe Obolensky created dramatic locales through the use of a few well-chosen objects: an armchair, a bookcase, a screen, some Persian rugs and a few pillows. The performance extended into the decrepit stage boxes and used the proscenium doors to suggest entrances to other rooms in the house. It ranged from the back wall of the theatre to the very edge of the thrust. Brook and Obolensky had merged the fictional world of the characters with the very theatre itself.

The general trend of the late 1980s and 1990s has been a return to Romanticism – albeit tempered by the ironic eye of contemporary designers, as in the work of Greek-born French designer Yannis Kokkos, whose *Seagull* suggests a Simovian scenography filtered through an Expressionist aesthetic. (See Appendix 4.) But a decidedly anti-Romantic postmodernism has also arisen, nowhere more so than in the startling production of *Three Sisters* done by the Wooster Group in New York in 1991. Entitled *Brace Up!*, the piece was an adaptation/deconstruction by Paul Schmidt, directed by Elizabeth LeCompte, with sets by James Clayburgh and lights by Jennifer Tipton. Performed in a converted industrial space, the Performing Garage, the feeling inside the theatre was a strange mixture of stark high-tech and home-made shabbiness. The audience sat on steep tiered plank seating facing a simple platform stage framed by lighting towers on which were an assortment of industrial and film lighting equipment. An invented character, a master of ceremonies, addressed the audience, interviewed characters and called upon the translator (who also played Chebutykin) to provide dramaturgical commentary. Television monitors glided to and from the audience across the stage floor – not unlike Tovstonogov's platforms – on which could be seen live images of off-stage actor/characters who were captured on video as they spoke, on-stage characters creating a visual echo of the action and interpolations from popular movies. Like the Brook production, *Brace Up!* coalesced the fictional world with the physical theatre; the video fused on- and off-stage worlds as well as the world of contemporary culture with the historicity of the play. By apparently stripping away the frame of the stage, it created a new framework in which to house the play for the spectators and performers of a postmodern culture.

One hundred years after *Ivanov*, the adjective 'Chekhovian' still conjures a world of samovars, drawing rooms, old bookcases and beloved gardens. Yet the *nastroenie* or mood that Chekhov attempted to create through the implied transparency of walls, fluidity of space, juxtaposition of near and far and symbolic use of familiar items was a harbinger of Appia and Craig, the Surrealists and even, to a degree, Brecht, whose significantly charged props and set pieces sat in the midst of a stage void. It is tempting to contemplate what the landscape of twentieth-century Western theatre would have been had Chekhov lived and had Adolphe Appia turned his talents to Chekhov's drama as well as to Wagner's operas. The successes of the original Moscow Art Theatre productions are a testament to the fact that Chekhov's plays worked – in their time – in Simov's settings. But the Chekhovian landscape has not only adapted well to the qualities of modern and postmodern scenography but has thrived, almost as if it has found a more comfortable home. Chekhov's continued popularity on world stages suggests that not only the themes and characters remain relevant, but the visual landscape as well.

NOTES

Quotations from the plays come from *Anton Chekhov's Plays*, trans. and ed. Eugene K. Bristow, W. W. Norton & Company, Inc., New York, 1977. This is noted as B. followed by page number.

Given problems of availability of Bristow in the UK, the same quotations are referenced from *The Oxford Chekhov*, trans. and ed. Ronald Hingley, volume II: *Platonov, Ivanov, The Seagull*, London, 1967, and volume III: *Uncle Vanya, Three Sisters, The Cherry Orchard, The Wood-Demon*, London, 1964. This will be noted by H. followed by volume number and page number.

1 Anton Chekhov in rehearsal, quoted by Vsevolod Meyerhold in *Meyerhold on Theatre*, trans. and ed., Edward Braun, New York, 1969, p. 30.

2 *The Cherry Orchard*, Act Three, B. p. 195; H. vol. III, p. 179.

3 Steve Grant, '*Uncle Vanya*', *Plays and Players*, July 1988, p. 19.

4 Viktor Simov (1858–1935) – primary designer for the Moscow Art Theatre who designed the original productions of Chekhov's plays at the MAT.

5 Quoted in Frantisek Deak, *Symbolist Theatre*, Baltimore, 1993, p. 144.

6 Quoted in Siegfried Melchinger, *Anton Chekhov*, New York, 1972, p. 65.

7 Adolphe Appia (1862–1928) – Swiss theorist and designer whose ideas revolutionised theatre and opera design by replacing the Romantic Realism of the nineteenth century with suggestive, three-dimensional settings, often employing steps and platforms, and stages sculpted with light.

8 *Uncle Vanya*, B. pp. 64–5; H. vol. III, p. 30.

9 Adolphe Appia, 'Ideas on a Reform of Our *Mise en Scène*,' in Richard C. Beacham, ed., *Adolphe Appia: Essays, Scenarios, and Design*, trans., Walther R. Volbach, Ann Arbor, Mich., 1989, p. 106.

10 *The Cherry Orchard*, B. p. 165; H. vol. III, p. 145.

11 *The Three Sisters*, B. p. 144; H. vol. III, p. 124.

12 *The Seagull*, B. p. 5; H. vol. II, p. 233.

13 Constantin Stanislavsky, *My Life in Art*, New York, 1952, pp. 353–4.

14 Quoted in *Anton Chekhov's Plays*, trans. and ed., Bristow, p. 159.

15 Quoted in Nick Worrall, ed., *File on Chekhov*, London, 1986, p. 70.

16 Quoted in Braun, *Meyerhold on Theatre*, 1969, p. 26.

17 *Ibid.*, p. 30.

18 Quoted in Worrall, *File on Chekhov*, p. 71.

19 Edward Gordon Craig (1872–1966) – British theorist, director and designer best known for emblematic and symbolic settings that conveyed a sense of grandeur while stripping away the realism of nineteenth-century theatre.

20 See Viktor Berezkin, *Khudozhnik v teatre Chekhova*, Moscow, 1987, pp. 84–5.

21 J. C. Trewin, *Illustrated London News*, 28 July 1962, p. 154.

22 Jarka Burian, *The Scenography of Josef Svoboda*, Middletown, Conn., 1974, p. 49.

23 *Ibid.*, pp. 49–50.

24 Georgy Tovstonogov, 'Chekhov's *Three Sisters* at the Gorky Theatre', *The Drama Review* 13.2, 1968, p. 153. See chapter 15, and Glossary.

25 Quoted in Arnold Aronson, *American Set Design*, New York, 1985, pp. 113–14.

26 Nicholas de Jongh, '*Ivanov*', *The Guardian*, 4 April 1989.

27 Peter Brook's *Cherry Orchard* originated from work at his Paris theatre, Les Bouffes du Nord, in 1981. This derelict former operetta theatre serves as Brook's base for his 'Theatre of Nations'. The production toured to Moscow, as well as New York. See chapter 15, Glossary and Appendix 2.

13

PHILIP FRENCH

Chekhov on screen

Although Anton Chekhov was only thirty-six when the cinema was invented, serious film-making did not begin in Russia until a couple of years after his death. So, unlike his contemporaries Maxim Gorky (six years his junior) and George Bernard Shaw (four years his senior), who both took a passionate interest in the possibilities of the new medium, he did not live to see his work reach the screen. His niece however, Olga Chekhova, a sculptress who emigrated to Germany, appeared in F. W. Murnau's *Schloss Vogelöd* (1921) and René Clair's *Un Chapeau de paille d'Italie* (1927), and his nephew, Michael Chekhov, enjoyed considerable success in America as both teacher and actor, his most celebrated role being the psychotherapist to whom Ingrid Bergman takes Gregory Peck in Alfred Hitchcock's *Spellbound* (1945).

As early as 1911 there was a one-reel Russian comedy based on Chekhov's story 'Romance with Double Bass', directed by Kai Hansen. (The British comedian John Cleese directed and appeared in an amusing British version of this tale in 1974 with his then wife, Connie Booth.) In 1914 Boris Glagolin made movies of *Illegal* and *The Daughter of Albion*, and in 1917 Boris Sushkevich filmed *The Flowers Are Late*.[1] Meanwhile, in 1913, Vladimir Mayakovsky evoked the playwright's name in the magazine *Kine-Journal* in an article called 'Theatre, Cinema, Futurism': 'The theatre moves towards its own destruction, and hands over its heritage to the cinema. And the cinema industry, branching away from the naive realism and artifice of Chekhov and Gorky, opens the door to the cinema of the future – linked to the art of the actor.'[2]

Whether or not they took their cue from Mayakovksy, the movie makers of the Soviet cinema's Golden Age paid little attention to Chekhov. In 1926, while specialising in films for children, Olga Preobrazhenskaya directed *Kashtanka*, which won her the opportunity to make pictures for adults. But the first major Soviet production based on Chekhov was Yakov Protazanov's *Ranks and People* (1929), an adaptation of 'Anna on My

Neck', 'Death of a Petty Official' and 'Chameleon',[3] a pioneer example of the portmanteau movie or *film à sketch*, that was to become so popular in the 1940s and 1950s. A decade passed, however, before Chekhov movies began to flow from the Russian studios and, as the historian of Russian cinema Jay Leyda points out, flow from the film schools, where his stories became the favourite subjects for graduation films. There were numerous adaptations of the short comic plays known as vaudevilles and of the stories, the most celebrated being by Isidor Annensky, whose several Chekhov films include *The Man in the Case* (1939). The only major director to take an interest in Chekhov at this point was Sergei Gerasimov, though sadly his plans to make a biographical study of the writer ('I dream of showing in this film the meaning of modesty in combination with talent, of what results it gives in human life'[4]) did not come to fruition. In fact there was no truly important Soviet adaptation of Chekhov until 1960. Oddly enough, in the United States there was a major movie though it attracted little attention at the time.

In 1937, the Danish-born Detlef Sierck, a man of the political left with a Jewish wife, abandoned a promising career in the German cinema, emigrating to Hollywood via Switzerland, France and Holland. On arrival he changed his name to Douglas Sirk, and while he was to become one of the most commercially successful directors of his day, serious critical recognition in the English-speaking world did not come until the 1960s, by which time his Hollywood career was at an end and he had returned to work in the German theatre. Sirk's son by his first marriage, Claus Detlef Sierck, one of Germany's most handsome child stars, remained at home when his father emigrated. After appearing in six movies Claus died fighting with the Wehrmacht on the Eastern Front in March 1944, three weeks before his nineteenth birthday. This touching piece of biographical information is by no means incidental to Sirk's work, and especially his first two American projects, as his son's death preceded by three months the release of his Chekhov movie.

Sirk was a master of melodrama, a genre he employed to study character, expose hypocrisy and examine social and spiritual aspirations. After a couple of years in the States making documentaries and working on aborted projects, he got the chance to work with a team of fellow *émigrés* and refugees on two moderately priced independent productions. The first, shot in a week and then amplified with MGM money, was *Hitler's Madman* (1942), the story of the assassination of Heydrich and the destruction of Lidice. The second was *Summer Storm* (1944), a screen version of *The Shooting Party*, Chekhov's only novel, published in 1884, excluded from the 1899–1901 ten-volume edition of his works, and translated only once into English (in 1923 by A. E. Chamot and revised in 1986 by Julian Symons). This was not a standard Hollywood production. Sirk had initially developed it at the Ufa studio in Germany (where he had also done a screen treatment of William Faulkner's *Pylon*, which he finally filmed at Universal as *Tarnished Angels* in 1958).

In Chekhov's novel, a former provincial magistrate presents a manuscript to a Moscow magazine (edited by Chekhov himself) in 1880, agreeing to return three months later to receive the editor's verdict. It is the story of the cynical narrator's involvement with a dissolute Count, owner of a vast decaying estate, and how they both become the lovers of the beautiful, ambitious Olga, daughter of an insane woodcutter, after she has married the Count's middle-aged bailiff. During a shooting party Olga is murdered, the instrument used being a Caucasian knife given her by the Count. Her alcoholic husband comes on the scene with blood on his hands and a drunken, one-eyed peasant is discovered with blood on his tunic. The one-eyed peasant is murdered in the local jail (seemingly by Olga's husband) and, as a double-murderer, Olga's widower is sentenced to nineteen years' hard labour in Siberia and apparently expires on the outward journey. Early on in the narrative, the editor's footnotes (signed 'A.Ch.') question the text in a manner characteristic of eighteenth-century fiction, but now called Borgesian or postmodern. We are also in the presence of what Wayne Booth calls 'the unreliable narrator'.[5] Like Agatha Christie's *The Murder of Roger Ackroyd, The Shooting Party* is narrated by the killer himself. Chekhov's story contains both his confession and an arrogant defiance of society, for he believes only a few superior souls will be capable of recognising the clues that reveal his guilt. Thus he will go free, along with the weak-willed Count, who is sitting in a carriage outside, ready to share the money from the sale of the tale. The story does not quite add up, but Julian Symons in his introduction to the 1986 edition persuasively argues for it as 'a landmark in the history of the crime story'.

The modestly budgeted movie version of *Summer Storm* was made in that brief wartime period between 1942 and 1945 when America and the USSR were allies and Hollywood took a benign view of the Russian Revolution. The present time becomes 1919 and the story is told in an extended flashback to 1912. But as adapted by Sirk, it is the Count who brings the manuscript to the office of a newspaper in Kharkov, where the editor is not only a woman of the new Russia but also the fiancée whom the Judge had betrayed when he became infatuated with the peasant girl Olga. The Count, played by the prissy Edward Everett Horton, a specialist in camp valets and waiters, is comically conscious of being an outsider in the USSR and paying for his (and his class') past sins. The Judge is impersonated by the suave British actor, George Sanders, who was born in St Petersburg of British parents and spent the first ten years of his life in Tsarist Russia. During the movie he sings a song in fluent Russian. He brings a proper arrogance to the part and is able to suggest the Judge's inner conflicts. He also refers to the coming Revolution that will sweep them all away. As Olga, Linda Darnell, an actress best known for her sultry temptresses, is merely adequate, and as her deranged father, Sig Ruman reprises his comic commissar from Ernst Lubitsch's *Ninotchka*. But the movie is strong on mood (Sirk put aside his first script, written in collaboration with James M. Cain, because it had become too American-ised) and has dramatic power and moral ambiguity.

At the end of the film, when the Judge discovers that the Count has sold his manuscript, he hurries to the newspaper office to discover that his former fiancée has put it in an envelope addressed to the public prosecutor. But expecting him to come, she has not posted it, and she gives him the opportunity to do this himself. With a nice touch, that reveals the protagonist's divided character while also meeting the requirements of the Hollywood Production Code,[6] the Judge first posts the package, then attempts to retrieve it from the postman and is shot dead by the police after a chase through the streets. He dies on the floor of a café, referring in his last gasp to 'the heavenly electricity' (i.e. the lightning that had killed Olga's mother and by which she herself had expected to be killed). The final shot is of a wastepaper basket containing his fiancée's dance card which she threw away the night the Judge betrayed her and which he has carried ever since as a guilty memento.

Summer Storm, though a box-office success, was not well received at the time. The British Film Institute's *Monthly Film Bulletin* (1945, p. 131) concluded snootily: 'To blame Chekhov for any part of this cliché-ridden collection of the shallow and the commonplace is taking mean advantage of a dead author.' Although the Irish poet James Simmons was inspired in the 1970s to write a mocking comic poem about it ('Summer Lighting' in his *Poems 1956–1986*) posterity has been kinder to it and the movie is now widely regarded as a minor classic. In his *Biographical Dictionary of the Cinema* (1994) David Thomson acclaims '*Summer Storm*, a poignant dramatisation of Chekhov's *The Shooting Party* with George Sanders as one of Sirk's finest "weak interesting" men'.

The first truly outstanding Russian Chekhov film came in 1960 when the veteran Josef Heifetz, then in his mid-fifties, adapted 'The Lady With the Little Dog', a scrupulously faithful version of the tale of the love affair between two unhappily married middle-class people – a middle-aged government official (Alexei Batalov) and a young woman (Iya Savvina) –

who meet at a resort hotel beside the Black Sea. Shot in elegant black-and-white, the film recreates the late nineteenth-century world with immense subtlety, contrasting the summery Yalta with the wintry Moscow where the lovers have a reunion. The sadness, yearning, repression and brief liberation are captured in the landscape and architecture; the eroticism is implied with the camera turning away at the bedroom door. Heifetz demonstrated that the leisurely expansion of a short story was a better way to make a feature film than the contraction of a long novel, and his movie was universally acclaimed as the screen's best adaptation of Chekhov up to that point. Three years later he filmed another Chekhov story, 'In the Town of S', about the frustrations of a doctor in a torpid provincial town, which attracted favourable reviews but was regarded as less satisfying than the earlier film. Unlike *The Lady With the Little Dog*, it did not become a permanent addition to the art-house canon.

It was probably the success of Heifetz' movies that finally persuaded Soviet directors to turn their attention to the great Chekhov full-length plays, beginning in 1964 when Samson Samsonov, who had won a Silver Prize in Venice for his version of Chekhov's 'The Grasshopper', made a film of *Three Sisters*, with Lev Ivanov as Vershinin, Konstantin Sorokin as Dr Chebutikin, and Lyubov Sokolova, Margarita Volodina and Tatyana Malchenko as Olga, Masha and Irina. The play was opened out for the screen, and the text was severely cut (the philosophical speeches disappearing almost entirely) rather than rewritten. It was not highly regarded and did not find a distributor in the West, and in fact there were two British adaptations before the next Soviet ones.

In 1968 the American director Sidney Lumet, who had made an admirable job of filming Eugene O'Neill's *A Long Day's Journey Into Night* (1962), turned his attention to *The Seagull*, working with a largely British cast and crew in Sweden. As Arkadina, Simone Signoret is a trifle uncomfortable, but on the principle that it takes a star to play a star she brings conviction to the role, and James Mason (Trigorin), David Warner (Konstantin) and Vanessa Redgrave (Nina) are excellent. The movie opens with the disconcertingly bold touch of showing Trigorin sharing Arkadina's bed, but is otherwise a faithful transcription of the play (Moura Budberg is credited as translator and adaptor) until the final scene where Lumet makes a major change. Dr Dorn's speech, in which he conceals Konstantin's suicide from Arkadina, is dropped, and the film ends with the assembled company all aware of the appalling event that has just taken place in the room next door.

Lumet's *The Seagull* did not open in Britain until early in 1970, a few months before Laurence Olivier's film of *Three Sisters*, also using a translation by Moura Budberg which retains far more of the original text than the Samsonov film. This was substantially a screen version of the memorable 1967 National Theatre production with a modified form of Josef Svoboda's stage sets and lasting 165 minutes. Olivier himself plays Dr Chebutikin, Alan Bates (replacing Robert Stephens) is Vershinin, with Joan Plowright, Jeanne Watts and Louise Purnell as Masha, Olga and Irina. On only two occasions does Olivier depart significantly from the stage version. First, for a rather flat fantasy sequence before Act Four when Irina (Louise Purnell) dreams of a beautiful future in Moscow; second, when a flash forward to the fatal duel is cut into the final dialogue between Irina and the Baron. In the final moments, as the sisters stand together with Chebutikin reading nearby, a few bars of the *Internationale* can be heard from the distance, a hint of things to come. The best that can be said for the film is that it preserves (in a ponderous, slightly misleading form) a classic stage production.

In the Soviet Union in 1971 Yuli Karasik filmed *The Seagull*, which eventually reached the West but made no great impression. Though often pictorially striking (especially in the staging of Konstantin's awful play in Act One where the curtain parts across the widescreen to reveal the lake beyond), the film is heavy without being weighty, a lugubrious, low-key movie that misses the original's irony and wit. Rather better is Andrei Konchalovsky's *Uncle Vanya*, also made in 1971, with a formidable cast led by Innokenty Smoktunovsky as Vanya and Sergei Bondarchuk as Dr Astrov. But even with a much cut text it moves with a ponderousness quite absent from London productions of the time seen at the National Theatre and the Royal Court, and for no apparent reason the movie alternates between an attractive sepia tone and a fuzzy, often ill-lit colour. Indicative of the change of emphasis is the substitution of a handful of snapshots of the neglected poor for the elaborate ecological charts that Astrov shows to Yelena. We first see some of these pictures in a scene-setting montage evoking the privileged pleasures and general misery of pre-revolutionary Russia.

Significantly, Konchalovsky left Russia in the 1980s for Hollywood (he was the first Soviet director to find success there), and it was his younger brother, the actor-director Nikita Mikhalkov, who became, after Heifetz, the Soviet cinema's principal director of Chekhov. Mikhalkov's most popular movie in the West has been the Russo-Italian co-production, *Dark Eyes* (1987), based on several Chekhov stories, but mainly 'The Lady With the Little Dog', which won for Marcello Mastroianni the Best Actor Award at Cannes. If Konchalovsky's pictures are like recklessly heated pressure cookers on the point of blowing their tops, his brother's are closely watched pots that steadily simmer. *Dark Eyes* unfolds as the romantic reminiscences of the middle-class, middle-aged Italian Romano, once a prosperous man of leisure, now a waiter on a ferry boat in the Adriatic shortly before World War One. Romano meets an elderly Russian honeymooner and proceeds to regale him with his life and loves. As a young man he had ambitions to transform the world as an architect. Instead he marries a Roman heiress and becomes a pathetic, philandering playboy. But at an Italian spa he falls in love with a beautiful, unhappily married Russian and when she suddenly departs he pursues her to her remote provincial town under the pretext of setting up a glass factory there.

The film is visually ravishing in a sub-Visconti fashion with a lilting Francis Lai score. The pace is funereal, the humour leaden and the poetic evocation of Mother Russia a series of soft-focus clichés for the export market. Mastroianni, who in addition to the Award at Cannes got an Oscar nomination, does a near-parodic variation of his self-pitying passive amorist, but Silvana Mangano is superb as his chilly patrician wife.

Far more interesting than *Dark Eyes* is Mikhalkov's earlier film, *An Unfinished Piece for Mechanical Piano* (1976).[7] Subtitled 'Themes from the works of Anton Chekhov', the source is almost entirely Chekhov's first, unnamed play, discovered in 1920, published in 1923 and usually known in English as *Platonov*.[8] This vast, rambling text, written around 1881, contains the principal themes, situations and characters of his later plays and would take over six hours to perform uncut. Mikhalkov has shaped it into a 100-minute film that takes place on a single summer day on the estate of Anna Petrovna, a general's youngish widow, who is being visited by her weak stepson and his wife, the actress Sofya (Elena Solovei). Her guests, in addition to a couple of local landowners, are the drunken retired Colonel Triletzky, his doctor son and his simple daughter Sasha, who is accompanied by her husband, the thirty-five-year-old Mikhail Platonov (Alexander Kalyagin), a village schoolteacher. As a student, Platonov had had a passionate summer affair with Sofya, but seeing him after an absence of seven years she fails to recognise this overweight, disappointed man who had once been spoken of as a future minister of state or the second Lord Byron.

With great humour and sadness, the film charts the relationships between this large cast over the course of a day and night as they reflect on the past and contemplate the future. The old love between Sofya and Platonov is rekindled, threatening two marriages and leading to a suicide attempt, but ending in a stoic acceptance of things as they are. Clever emblematic use is made of the player-piano that gives the movie its title, a machine that performs Liszt unaccompanied, and sounds exactly the same whoever –

whether poet or peasant – plays upon it. Among the numerous ways in which Mikhalkov's screenplay differs from the 1984 version of *Platonov* that Michael Frayn made for the National Theatre as *Wild Honey* is the substantial role that Frayn accords to Anna Petrovna.

The success of Mikhalkov's film bears out some remarks made in my original review of Olivier's *Three Sisters* for *The Times* (30 October 1970):

> Frankly the picture – for all its manifest respectability and understandable reverence for the text – strikes me as a misguided enterprise, confirming the belief that Chekhov's full-length plays (unlike his fiction) are unfilmable. This has something to do with their perfection as theatre. Of course, a bold cinematic genius might be prepared to throw away the text entirely and attempt to re-create a Chekhov play from scratch as a movie.

An Unfinished Piece for Mechanical Piano goes some way towards that, and a similar kind of boldness informs the most interesting Chekhov pictures of the past decade or so.

There are first those movies that we might describe as Chekhovian – works that, by design or chance, resemble Chekhov in mood, theme and dramatis personae. Satyajit Ray's *Days and Nights in the Forest* (1969), the story of four young middle-class men spending the summer at a bungalow in the Bengali countryside and coming into contact with a wealthy local family, reminds most audiences of Chekhov. Interestingly, Andrew Robinson in his critical biography *Satyajit Ray: The Inner Eye* (1989) remarks of Ray's transposition to Bengal of *An Enemy of the People:* 'The introduction of the temple into the story is Ray's masterstroke: It enabled him to turn Ibsen into Ray – via Chekhov.'

Much more specifically Chekhovian is Louis Malle's *Milou en Mai* (1989), the elegiac story of the final gathering of a French family on a decaying estate in south-west France as *les événements* of 1968 sweep through the country. The declining vineyard evokes *The Cherry Orchard*; the eponymous middle-aged Milou (Michel Piccoli), who has thanklessly devoted his life to keeping the estate going, is a Vanya figure, and virtually all the characters have Chekhovian counterparts. In Nikita Mikhalkov's *Burnt by the Sun* (1994), one of the finest Russian movies of the 1990s and winner of an Oscar as Best Foreign Language film, the director himself plays a middle-aged ex-colonel, a hero of the Russian Revolution who is living in a rural community outside Moscow in 1936. It is as if Lopakhin, the self-made businessman in *The Cherry Orchard*, had married into Ranyevskaya's household and they were living idyllically on the old estate. In fact there are specific references to show that the characters themselves recognised the parallels with Chekhov. But this is the time of Stalin's purges and when the secret police arrive to escort the Colonel to the Lubianka and a show trial, *Uncle Vanya* turns into *Darkness at Noon*. In America, the Swedish actress Viveca Lindfors made her final appearance in Henry Jaglom's *Last Summer in the Hamptons* (1995), a charming and deeply moving film about a New York theatrical family that gathers every August with their friends at a big house on Long Island to mount a play in the gardens. This is to be the last production before the house is sold, the piece chosen is *The Seagull* and the director is played by André Gregory. All involved identify themselves with Chekhov's characters, their behaviour echoes the play and the film concludes with a fraught but successful production.

Secondly, there are the films that rework the text of the plays. In the early 1990s, two central European directors made new versions of *Three Sisters*. Margarethe von Trotta, who in such films as *The German Sisters* and *Rosa Luxemburg* has pursued feminist themes more thoughtfully than anyone in mainstream cinema, transposed *Three Sisters* to the entrancing northern Italian town of Pavia in the early 1980s. Her Olga, Masha and Irina are the stunningly beautiful daughters of the local university's late rector – Velia (Fanny Ardant), a liberal professor of literature; Maria (Greta Scacchi), wife of a popular TV comedian; and Sandra (Valeria Golino), a medical student. Their Vershinin is Massimo, a handsome astrophysicist, recently returned from a decade teaching in the United States. The twists are minor, but ingenious – Massimo is Velia's lover before switching to the sad, married Maria; his neglected wife becomes a friend, a feminist sister indeed, of Velia and Sandra. Odd details are amusing – the bored Maria, for instance, watches the soulful *Now Voyager* instead of her husband's tedious TV show. Elegant tracking shots follow the tastefully dressed ladies around the city and the autumnal countryside and no one could wish to leave this idyllic place for Rome or Milan. Chekhov's play is a tragicomedy or comic tragedy, while von Trotta's emotionally shallow, ideologically trendy movie is merely designer-angst.

Potentially a far better adaptation is the young Hungarian film-maker Andor Lukats' *Three Sisters* (1992) which transposes the play to a Russian barracks in a remote corner of Hungary in the late 1980s and concludes with the final withdrawal of Soviet forces in 1991. The text is pared down and does not seem to have been fully thought through in terms of the new situation, but an important change, of considerable significance to local audiences, is that Masha's pathetic schoolteacher husband is now a Hungarian, which in itself makes him an inferior being in the eyes of his wife and her sisters. Stylistically far removed from von Trotta's version, Lukats' film has a deliberately bleak, sickly look and the hand-held camera is constantly on the move around the claustrophobic barracks, using a wide-angle lens to distort perspectives so that walls and corners loom up at us menacingly. The movie is an oppressive, wearing experience, but I would not wish to make a definitive judgement after having seen it only once with a somewhat inadequate ear-phone commentary. (The same, incidentally, is true of the 1978 version of *The Shooting Party* directed by Emi Lotianou, of which I saw one exciting un-subtitled reel during a display of the director's work in Moscow.)

The most distinguished films of the plays have been the versions of *Uncle Vanya* recreated in different settings. In *Country Life* (1995), Michael Blakemore, one of the British theatre's finest exponents of Chekhov, transposes *Vanya* to a decaying estate in remote New South Wales and himself takes the role of Alexandre Serebryakov, who has become Alexander Voysey (a part intended for Nigel Hawthorne), a middle-aged Australian writer returning home (rejected as it transpires) after twenty-two years as a drama critic in London. The year is 1919, Australian troops are coming back from the European War and Alexander's family suffers from that famous 'cultural cringe' before all things English, with London as their equivalent of Moscow. His young English bride, Deborah (Greta Scacchi, who acted in Blakemore's London stage version of *Vanya* and von Trotta's film of *Three Sisters*), turns the head of Uncle Jack (John Hargreaves), who has sacrificed himself to running the estate, and attracts the local general practitioner Dr Askey (Sam Neill). Chekhov's sad, plain Sonya becomes Sally (Kerry Fox), hopelessly in love with Askey, protective of Uncle Jack, and the embodiment of selfless decency.

Blakemore has fashioned the play to highlight Australian themes while retaining a Chekhovian tone and ironic humour. Thus Dr Askey/Astrov's concern for ecology extends to allowing Aborigines to squat on his land, and his belief in the shaping of a local identity has led him to oppose Australian participation in the Great War. In a key sequence, angry ex-soldiers wreck the church hall where Askey is giving a lantern lecture on the environment. In the farewell scene between Astrov and Yelena in *Vanya* she takes a pencil as a souvenir; in *Country Life* Dr Askey and Deborah sneak a final kiss in the house's fancy lavatory (claimed by Jack as the first flush toilet in this part of the country), and when he accidentally tears off the chain-handle he presents it to her as a memento. This is both a wonderfully Australian gesture and a marvellously Chekhovian under-mining of sentimentality. The film's ensemble acting is impeccable.

August (1995) is a transposition of *Uncle Vanya* to the culturally isolated North Wales of the 1890s where gradations of class are registered by accent, ranging from the strong Welsh dialect of the workers to the received pronunciation of the English visitors. The screenplay is by Julian Mitchell, and the film is directed by Anthony Hopkins, who himself plays the middle-aged failure, Uncle Leuan. The frustrated conservationist and GP, Dr Lloyd (Gawn Grainger), tends to the poverty-stricken workers from the local slate quarries, and he is worshipped by Sian (Rhian Morgan), who helps Uncle Leuan run the family estate. The intruders from the distant metropolis who disrupt the household become the selfish, self-centred Professor Blathwaite (Leslie Phillips), a loathsome Englishman from London, and his second wife, Helen (Kate Burton), an American from Philadelphia who looks as if she might have been painted by John Singer Sargent.

Hopkins plays Leuan not as a sad, burnt-out man of mature years but as an angry, aged adolescent who has resisted growing up and is forever larking around and pulling faces behind people's backs. In a heavily cut text, he ends up dominating the play in a way that the Vanya in Blakemore's film doesn't. Consequently, the movie never quite achieves that ensemble effect by which one judges a perfectly realised Chekhov production. But at the end, in a self-abnegatory gesture, Hopkins almost withdraws from the scene, his head buried in his hands, leaving the stage to his niece. As Sian/Sonya, Rhian Morgan gives a poignant performance. Most Sonyas are so attractive that you wonder how Dr Astrov could have failed to notice them, and as if in awareness of this the actresses emphasise the character's rural gaucheness. Morgan, on the other hand, is neatly self-contained and has a plainness that makes the doctor's indifference credible. But in close-up her eyes express a buried passion and a deep spirituality.

Far more remarkable than either, however, and arguably the greatest screen Chekhov is *Vanya on 42nd Street* (1994), the final film of Louis Malle, who died the following year. For nearly forty years, Malle fruitfully combined complementary careers as a documentarist and a director of feature films. In 1981, he brought the two sides together in *My Dinner With André*, an artful movie purporting to be a dialogue in a New York restaurant between the avant-garde theatre director André Gregory and the actor Wallace Shawn. It was in fact carefully scripted and made with immense care in an improvised studio in Washington DC. Gregory and Shawn are also involved in *Vanya on 42nd Street*, which presents itself as a discreetly observed documentary record of a run-through of *Uncle Vanya* (in a fluent American version by David Mamet) at the cavernous, disused New Amsterdam Theatre, built at the turn-of-the-century and once one of Broadway's finest houses. Starting in 1990, André Gregory and his actors intermittently rehearsed this production for several years but never presented it to the public. Only at the end do we ponder precisely what we have seen. Is this *Vanya* a work-in-progress? Is it the definitive account of something that never found a final form? Or is it a fresh creation for the cinema, something existing in a ghostly limbo between stage and screen?

We first see the cast making their way through the raffish sidewalk crowd on 42nd Street. They are accompanied on the soundtrack by a cool jazz quartet, a kind of music associated with Malle ever since he persuaded Miles Davis to improvise a score for his first feature, *Lift to the Scaffold* (1957). Approaching the theatre, Gregory meets Wallace Shawn, who is to play the title role, and takes a piece of the hamburger he's eating. Shawn introduces him to a Mrs Chao (the Indian actress and cook, Madhur Jaffrey), daughter of Chekhov's Bengali translator. Mrs Chao is, in effect, the film's only fictional character, and it is to her that Gregory explains the play during the brief intervals. As the stage of the Amsterdam is too dangerous to be performed on, the actors work in the theatre's gutted stalls, wearing their street clothes and using a table, a bench and a few chairs. They are like Pirandellian ghosts, arising to bring an old play back to life.

Phoebe Brand (as the old Nanny) and Larry Pine (Dr Astrov) chat informally at a table about their current work and we scarcely notice the precise moment when they switch from theatrical small-talk to Chekhov's opening lines, from playing themselves, as it were, to playing Chekhov's characters. Malle works close in to the actors, more often cutting than panning. The lighting is harsh, but not grainy in a self-conscious documentary manner. While the play is in progress, Malle never cuts to the small audience, who only appear between acts.

There is nothing obviously or obtrusively avant-garde about Gregory's production or Malle's film. But the result is highly innovative. They succeed in making us experience in a new way Chekhov's great story of unrequited love, shattered dreams, lies and truth-telling, selflessness and stoicism. Rarely have Brechtian alienation techniques been used to greater effect.[9]

While constantly being kept aware of seeing a company of New York actors at work in the 1990s, we become painfully engaged in the problems and aspirations of the late nineteenth-century Russian characters they are playing. Without transposing *Uncle Vanya* to the United States or wrenching it from its historical context, Malle gives us, in effect, a modern-dress, demotic, American Chekhov. Yet no cheaply ironic parallels are drawn between the actors and their stage roles, and Malle and Gregory resist the temptation to modulate (like Olivier's *Henry* V) into a full-scale production with authentic décor on rural locations.

The cast is flawless. Julianne Moore is a strong, tragic Yelena. Her scenes with Sonya (the heartbreaking Brooke Smith) have a rare intimacy. George Gaynes, hitherto best known as the dithering commissioner in the *Police*

Academy series and the aging matinée idol smitten by Dustin Hoffman in *Tootsie*, brings a revealingly light touch to Professor Serebryakov. Larry Pine's Astrov recalls Jason Robards Jr. at his best, and Wallace Shawn is a magnificently unsentimental, bitterly comic Vanya. At the end we feel we have watched, become closely involved in, what is at once an astonishing piece of theatre and an authentic cinematic experience.

NOTES

1   See 'Variations of English titles', Appendix 1.
2   Jay Leyda, *Kino – A History of the Russian and Soviet Film*, London (first published 1960), 1982, p. 413.
3   See Appendix 1.
4   Leyda, *Kino*, p. 395.
5   Wayne C. Booth, *The Rhetoric of Fiction*, Chicago and London, 1961, p. 274.
6   The Hollywood Production Code (known informally as the Hays Office Code), adopted in 1930 and enforced from 1934 to the mid-1960s, stated as the first of its general principles: 'No picture be produced which will lower the moral standards of those who see it. Hence the sympathy of the audience shall never be thrown to the side of crime, wrong-doing, evil or sin.' As a consequence it was necessary that malefactors must always be seen to pay for their misdeeds.
7   See chapter 4 in this volume.
8   Also known as *Fatherlessness*. See chapter 4 in this volume and Appendix 1.
9   See *Brecht on Theatre: The Development of an Aesthetic*, translated by John Willett, London, 1964, pp. 94–6, 143–5, 191–5.

14

TATIANA SHAKH-AZIZOVA

Chekhov on the Russian stage

Chekhov is often internationally considered 'the Shakespeare of the twentieth century'. In his homeland, his plays have become part and parcel not only of the Russian theatre but also of the national lifestyle or psyche, an inexhaustible source of spiritual endurance. We take this so much for granted that we assume that it has always been so, but this is not an accurate view: Chekhov's climb to the stature of the author of *The Seagull* and *The Cherry Orchard* was long and difficult, while the process of creating Chekhov's theatre was even more laborious and painful.

In literal terms, the history of Chekhov in the Russian theatre dates back to autumn 1887, when his comedy, *Ivanov*, was premièred at the Korsh Theatre, a private theatre in Moscow. In the following decade, theatres in Moscow, St Petersburg and in the provinces produced almost everything the young Chekhov was energetically writing for the stage. Although this may seem a good beginning, this period in Chekhov's career as a playwright should more appropriately be seen as a *prologue*.

Both Chekhov's full-length plays and the 'miniatures' or short plays were produced with varying degrees of success. He described the one-act plays as 'jokes' or 'little scenes' and in letters referred to them as 'vaudevilles' which were initially and subsequently widely performed – and with invariable success. The secret of their success was clearly evident: Chekhov introduced many changes to the conventional vaudeville: omitting the traditional couplets, adding 'true-to-life' features, and ridiculing the traditional plots, often to the point of absurdity, while basically observing the rules of the genre (*Letters*, vol. II, p. 148).[1] Actors and audiences alike were fascinated by the sharply delineated characterisation, fast dialogue and irresistible comicality of these plays. After the première of *The Boor* [more usually translated in English as *The Bear*] at the Korsh Theatre, Chekhov commented: 'The audience was laughing nonstop and the performance was interrupted by bursts of applause . . .' But at the same time he assessed the acting as 'clumsy', 'non-artistic' and 'lacking subtlety'. (*Letters*, vol. III,

p. 50), while the performers at the Alexandrinsky Theatre's production of *The Bear* led Chekhov to observe that: 'Actors never seem to watch ordinary people . . .' (*Letters*, vol. III, p. 291), a serious criticism.

Chekhov's critique reflected an essential disagreement between his theatrical aesthetics and the prevailing stage customs, which accepted artificial and careless performance, while Chekhov presumably expected much greater precision and finesse. Another illustration of this disparity was in the reaction to Chekhov's full-length plays. The earliest of them was untitled (later appearing in repertoires under the title *Platonov*, or *Fatherlessness*), unpublished and unperformed in Chekhov's lifetime. The young writer brought the play to the Maly Theatre and was turned down, apparently in unpleasant terms. The Maly Theatre's justification for this depended not only on mistakes resulting from his inexperience, but mainly on the unusual length of the play, *and* its explicit and quite unprecedented outspokenness in exposing public behaviour. Also unique was the combination of scepticism and cynicism in the central character, the village schoolteacher Platonov, with his powerful quest for justice. *Platonov* was rejected by the theatre, and instead Platonov's place was taken by Ivanov, another complex man, both in himself and in relation to others.

Ivanov had more luck than its predecessor, not only because of Chekhov's developing professionalism and dramatic skills, but mainly because of the brilliant performance of Vladimir Davydov as the title character. He portrayed Ivanov as an average Russian intellectual: benign, soft-hearted and weak-willed. The production's very success, however, virtually resulted in scandal: the sharp and grim plot, the central questions – deliberately left unanswered by the author (questions such as who *is* Ivanov or who is responsible for his misfortunes?) were found fascinating by some – and seemingly revolted others. As for Chekhov's own view of the production, he criticised it for its lack of precision and for directorial mistakes. The subsequent history of Chekhov's plays in performance demonstrated the validity of these criticisms.

After the Moscow première, Chekhov rewrote the play, classified it as 'a drama', sharpened the conflict and the characters and provided tragic dimensions to the character or 'image' of Ivanov – for which reason he changed the final scene. In the meantime, and contrary to his usual approach, he explained at great length, and persistently, the meaning of the play in his letters (*Letters*, vol. III, pp. 109–16), something which he never did before or subsequently, and clear evidence of his need to be understood. The new version, produced at the Alexandrinsky Theatre, was more successful and had a better audience response. Nonetheless, Chekhov's complex and contradictory characterisation of Ivanov, a man lacking 'the energy of life', remained for many years one of the modern theatre's greatest enigmas. And for years after the play was first staged, *Ivanov* was repeatedly criticised for being unstageable, and its author accused of amateurism.

Such accusations became more persistent when the Abramov Theatre in Moscow (another private theatre) produced Chekhov's comedy *The Wood-Goblin* (usually translated as *The Wood-Demon*) in 1889. The production had little, if any, success in its very short run, while even the author himself disliked his play. It had two features which were quite uncharacteristic of Chekhov's plays and never recurred in any of his other dramatic works: romantic rhetoric – and a happy ending. The difficulty of combining drama and prose *with* an epic quality in the scenic elements (in his letters, Chekhov significantly referred to *The Wood-Goblin* as a 'comedy-novel') made the play too heavy. The prose, and the over-abundance of characters, details and situations, took the play over. However, the experience of *The Wood-Goblin* was not wasted and became the source of a new play – *Uncle Vanya* (1896). But before that, in 1895, there was *The Seagull*.

The 1890s were extremely eventful for Chekhov. His talents as a dramatist became much more mature, he gained more freedom and courage, and he eagerly imbibed new trends in the arts. Chekhov created *The Seagull* – the play later to become the symbol *and* the mirror of twentieth-century theatre. But that was yet to happen. Until then, and sharing the fate of many innovative artists, Chekhov had to endure the shattering fiasco of *The Seagull's* première at the Alexandrinsky Theatre in Autumn 1896.

Chekhov's dramatic innovation in *The Seagull* was daring. He wrote the play 'against all the rules of dramatic art' (*Letters*, vol. VI, p. 100), and yet strongly hoped for success. He especially counted on the actress who was cast to play Nina Zarechnaya and who rehearsed her part with awe and enormous poetic power – Vera Komissarzhevskaya. She would later be named 'the Seagull of the Russian stage', given the resemblances between the personalities and fortunes of the actress and her character, and their combined fate.[2] But even Komissarzhevskaya could not prevent the première from being a disaster (*Letters*, vol. VI, p. 231). The failure of the production seemed to be the result of a mistake and muddle: the première had been scheduled on the same day as a benefit performance for a particular comic actress, and the audience was therefore expecting to have fun and mock *The Seagull*. But that in fact could not have been the real cause. *The Seagull* was doomed to fail. The old conservative, traditional stage failed to pass the test set by the new drama. The play required careful direction, innovative preparation and special performance techniques.

In one of his letters Chekhov wrote: 'I didn't do the casting. No new sets were made. There had been only two rehearsals and the actors kept forgetting their lines. The result was general panic and total depression. Even Komissarzhevskaya was not half as splendid as she had been in one of the rehearsals . . .' (*Letters*, vol. VI, p. 211). The powerful mood of disaster and the reaction of both audience and critics were such that Chekhov vowed: '*Never* again shall I write or direct plays' (*Letters*, vol. VI, p. 197). He did not believe he had a chance of success and he was right: success could come only with the *new* theatre.

An encounter with such a theatre – the Moscow Art Theatre – was soon to come.[3] With the MAT, Chekhov at last discovered a community of spirit, met understanding and regained the opportunity to restore his reputation as a dramatic writer. It was for the MAT that he broke his vow and wrote two new plays: *Three Sisters* (1900) and *The Cherry Orchard* (1903).

This alliance created prerequisites for the emergence of *directors'* theatre, which affirmed the importance of everything that happens on stage, whether 'internal' or 'external' truth, where actors performed as an ensemble and where characterisation was expected to match the complex and integral image of reality, of the world outside the theatre. This was the period of perfect harmony between actors and characters, stage and auditorium. Chekhov's plays were staged, performed and attended by those who were themselves 'Chekhovians'. Life depicted in these plays was familiar to them, for it was *their* life and they were able to articulate it confidingly, simply, with genuine pain and concern. These productions owed their charm to a distinctive lyricism, and an inspired mood or atmosphere. It might appear, therefore, that in this way and *only* in this way could Chekhov's plays be staged and his characters performed. But this has not been the case.

Chekhov's plays have already had a long life, responding and adapting to the dramatic changes of their context, whether theatrical or social. They contain 'messages' to be discovered and meanings to be expressed by other generations. This '*otherness*' – the alternative to the established MAT style – was for a long time only theoretical, and not put into practice. Until the middle of this century, Chekhov's plays were viewed exclusively in the context of the MAT productions while the MAT remained the main Chekhovian theatre. But this reputation had to be re-examined and reaffirmed, which the company has only recently done.

In Chekhov's lifetime, and in the first decades of the twentieth century his plays were widely staged across the country by both metropolitan and provincial companies. But troubled times were fast approaching. In the

Soviet Russia of the 1920s and 1930s Chekhov's plays did not fit with the predominant ideology of social optimism. The public felt increasingly alienated from Chekhov's drama and productions of his plays became rare: *The Seagull* was produced only once, *Ivanov* and *Three Sisters* each twice, while *Uncle Vanya* was not staged at all (except for the reconstruction of the old MAT production).[4] *The Cherry Orchard* was played more often, but mainly because it proved more easily adaptable to predominant social tastes.

History repeated itself: Chekhov's vaudevilles were swiftly gaining in popularity, largely as a result of the efforts of such MAT 'offshoots' as Yevgeny Vakhtangov and Vsevolod Meyerhold. In the early 1920s, Vakhtangov dreamed about giving grotesque shape to the tragic and comic elements. He wrote: 'I want to do *The Seagull*. Theatrically. As it was conceived by Chekhov . . . Chekhov is not a lyricist, he is a tragedian.'[5] Vakhtangov did not stage *The Seagull*, but at his studio, which later became known as the Third Studio of the MAT, he twice produced *The Wedding*. The staging was sharp, vigorous, eccentric and at the same time filled not so much with mockery as with bitter compassion. Meyerhold's 1935 production of *33 Fainting-Fits* (sometimes translated as *33 Swoons*) at the theatre bearing his name, clearly lacked that sharp contrast of bitterness and satire. In Chekhov's three short plays, *Jubilee* (sometimes translated as *The Anniversary*), *The Bear* and *The Proposal*, Meyerhold counted 'thirty-three fainting-fits' by the characters. Under this title, rather than interpreting an existing script as a director, he created his own composition with fainting as the key 'gag'. And the performance became overloaded with comic effects.

There had been a time when Meyerhold performed Treplev in the MAT production of *The Seagull* and he clearly felt some inner affinity with this character. Meyerhold's directorial career began with a provincial production of *Three Sisters* in 1902. But thirty years later he maintained that 'Chekhov, with his *The Cherry Orchard* or *Three Sisters*, is remote from us today.'[6] Soviet class theory, applied to the arts and literature, aroused suspicion about the very nature of Chekhov's characters with their predilection for meditation, reluctance to act and inability to struggle.

But then times changed again. Discarded values were 'rehabilitated' or came back into fashion, and with it the rediscovery of Chekhov was in sight. This happened in the same place and in the same way as before: in 1940, the MAT staged *Three Sisters* and reaffirmed the immortality of Chekhov's characters and the author's reputation as a writer for all times. In the troubled pre-war and war years, renewed productions of *Three Sisters* became symbolic of the nation's spiritual resistance to the ruthless and evil external powers. And the challenges of time and fate became more intense. The 1940 production of *Three Sisters* lacked the tragic anguish that would be discovered later in Chekhov's plays. That 'other' Chekhov, with tints and colours that were absent from the lyrical staging of the MAT, was about to arrive. This 'otherness' was created by Alexander Tairov's 1944 production of *The Seagull* at the Kamerny Theatre, which was remarkable for its highly stylised staging, and the unforgettable performance of Alisa Koonen, who made her Nina Zarechnaya a profoundly tragic character, waging a hopeless struggle in life and art.[7]

This tragic element was also strongly present in Boris Dobronravov's performance in the title role of *Uncle Vanya* in the 1947 MAT production, as well as in Boris Smirnov's performance in the title role of *Ivanov* in Maria Knebel's 1955 production at Moscow's Pushkin Theatre.

Throughout the 1950s, the MAT style was waning: the internal resources for self-renewal were exhausted, and it gradually lost its powerful grip on the interpretation and production style of many plays, including Chekhov's. Timed for Chekhov's centennial (1960), the MAT's production of *The Seagull* was heavy and cold, demonstrating indifference and routine. But at the same time the Moscow Maly Theatre, which had not previously done any of Chekhov's major plays, opened with an energetic, passionate and innovative production of *Ivanov*, directed by Boris Babochkin, who also appeared in the title role. Babochkin's production continued once again the tradition of stripping the play of the romantic colouring that went back to the productions of Dobronravov and Smirnov. It seemed Babochkin felt no sympathy for his character, although the scale of Ivanov's personality was given full range and recognition. 'Throughout the play Ivanov is falling into an abyss and there is no way of saving him.'[8]

Austerity, vigour and strong tragic elements were the defining characteristics of the production interpretations of Chekhov's plays in the 1960s. This was how his works were seen by directors of different schools and different generations, using the 'mirrors' of the different plays. The old masters were the first to go: Babochkin was followed by Georgi Tovstonogov. In his 1965 production of *Three Sisters*, at Leningrad's Bolshoi Drama Theatre, the sisters were presented as tragic characters, gripped by a paralysis of the will. This tragic element was compellingly conveyed by the actors, and Tovstonogov as director pushed them 'to sharpen all the conflicts that advance the action'.[9] It is interesting that the audiences of the mid-1960s could not grasp what Chekhov's contemporaries identified with instantaneously: why can't the sisters go to Moscow? By the mid-1960s, such questions had to be explained and *performed* – in this way the underlying or subtextual idea of the play had to be emphasised and expressed. The Prozorovs' world, light and clear in the beginning, became cold and grim by the end, as though all life had drained out of it.

Symbol and imagery became central to the new Chekhov theatre. In Maria Knebel's 1965 production of *The Cherry Orchard* at the Central Soviet Army Theatre, Moscow, the design no longer represented a real house or orchard. Only the white curtains, fluttering lightly like the characters' memories or dreams, were used to *suggest* the orchard. In this period of 'angry Chekhov', this production seemed unusually soft and restrained, but reference to the present day was contained in the characters' quiet and melancholic escape from day-to-day realities. The characters aroused interest not because of their social status, or class as merchants or aristocrats, but by their human characteristics: they were quite simply fascinating people.

The reaction of the cultural authorities – traditionally suspicious (and not altogether without grounds) of innovative interpretations of the classics as manifestations of dangerous free thinking – was by this time virtually absent. The main reason was that these innovative versions were the work of *recognised* grand masters whose challenge to tradition was not particularly daring. What they offered was an innovative view of the past - and of people in that past. But 'next in line' were the younger artists who needed Chekhov's drama to speak for themselves about *their* time.

Thus Anatoly Efros'[10] extensive Chekhovian cycle opened with the 1966 production of *The Seagull* at the Lenkom Theatre in Moscow. The focus and emphasis was on the sharp conflicts in that play on such contemporary problems as alienation, the disconnection of human relationships and loneliness. The loneliness of the artist was a personal motif for Efros, and the protagonist in his production was Treplev: young, defenceless and betrayed by all, even by Nina Zarechnaya, and whose tragic ending seemed inevitable. The reaction to *The Seagull* was nothing compared to the stormy response to Efros' 1967 production of *Three Sisters* at Moscow's Malaya Bronnaya Theatre. The production was compellingly expressive of painful foreboding, of anguish, young hopes and bitter disappointments. Characters and spectators were the same people – sharing the same time and space, the same aspirations and the same disappointments. Their homes had long ceased to be fortresses, were long lost in the void, surrounded by the withered orchard. These people lived on an island, with cold winds blowing through it, waiting for their fate and, in the director's concept, the fate of people in exile. It was 'the exile of beautiful, intelligent people'.[11] Such was Efros' thinking and interpretation, reading the play and perceiving the world around him, debarred from culture and aesthetic expression and deprived of normal life.

The production expressed the spirit of the time. The post-war 'thaw' in Russia[12] was coming to an end and the hopes it had aroused proved to be delusions. The old values could only be talked about with irony – and in Efros' production there was much irony and anguish. Its message was perceived by those in the audience who shared the director's thoughts, *and* by those who, at that time, ran the theatres. Chekhov was becoming dangerous, but the classics cannot really be accountable, so the blame was placed on the director who had allegedly distorted a classical masterpiece. Efros' production had a very short run, and was then censored, but its message has continued up to the present day.

The next generation to come to Chekhov's theatre shared the sentiments of Efros and his audience. Leonid Heifetz's 1969 production of *Uncle Vanya* at the Central Soviet Army Theatre was permeated with sad irony.[13] The narrow opening of the stage was the realm or area of 'unfreedom' or a 'prison', where people were crammed, gasping for fresh air. This lack of freedom had sucked dry the soul of Uncle Vanya, and aroused young Sonya to protest, and in those two characters of different generations the young spectators recognised their fathers and themselves.

Thus with the beginning of the 1960s, the Chekhov theatre underwent truly revolutionary changes, however bizarre this may sound in relation to this seemingly most peaceful of Russian playwrights. But this playwright became a real 'trouble-maker', provoking upheavals in consciousness in particular, and in the arts in general. The old norms and dogmas came tumbling down, and there was an intensive search for new forms. The time chose Chekhov to express itself. And it is this, in part, which makes the analogy between Shakespeare and Chekhov.

In a Soviet writer's novel one of the characters says: 'Chekhov's way is the way of Russian freedom, the embodiment of the Russian democracy, true and humane, which never took shape.'[14] This refers to Chekhov as a person and writer, but it may also be fully applied to his theatre. In Russia's distinctive context, theatre has always longed and struggled, spontaneously and persistently, for the freedom of the individual and freedom of expression. This tendency started during 'The Thaw' and continued in the following decades up to the present. Democracy called for equality, and so the MAT was bound to lose its monopoly, but not just to another 'monopolist'. Henceforth, no *one* theatre had the privilege to monopolise Chekhov. Chekhov offered equality of rights and opportunities to all theatres, regardless of rank or artistic style. The MAT also had the right to partake in this opportunity, and when the time came, it exercised this right.

Thus in the mid-1970s, Oleg Yefremov managed to re-energise the MAT and restore its reputation, thereby creating precedents for the realisation of

Chekhovian projects. Yefremov's intention was to bring Chekhov back to his native stage, but to do so in the spirit of the new times and on the basis of new knowledge, combined with what, in the MAT, is called the 'grain' of tradition.

Another aspect of democracy is the balance between the capital and the provinces in staging Chekhov's theatre. For some time Chekhov was essentially a metropolitan author, but little by little the provinces – where in fact all of Chekhov's plays are set – gained more rights and more recognition. There are Chekhov Festivals held regularly in the writer's birthplace, Taganrog, and in the 1980s these Festivals demonstrated that innovative and unexpected visions could come from Siberia, from the modest republic of Kalmykia[15] or from the industrial centre of Lipetsk. Such diversity, inherent in Chekhov's plays, is the main source of freedom in his theatre. This portrait changes with the times: lyrical and melancholy Chekhov, sarcastic Chekhov, wise Chekhov, cruel Chekhov . . . all these features are present in the writer, and time chooses the one that suits it best. But the image becomes complete only when the span is the whole century.

Chekhov's plays take turns to become *symbols of the time*. In the mid-1970s it was the turn of *Ivanov*, in Mark Zakharov's Lenkom Theatre production, which combined grotesque representation of the social milieu with a serious treatment of the main characters. Yevgeny Leonov played Ivanov as quite an ordinary man, 'not renowned for extravagance', soft-hearted, honest and ashamed of living without belief or purpose. Oleg Yefremov's Chekhovian cycle at the MAT also began with *Ivanov* in 1976. As director and actor, Innokenty Smoktunovsky[16] discerned in this play the drama of consciousness and the tragedy of a remarkable man, 'the Russian Hamlet', doomed to loneliness and misunderstanding.[17] These two productions raised an important problem of that time: the problem or question of belief, of the 'general idea' that the best people, whether outstanding or quite ordinary, cannot find – and without which they cannot live.

Another motif that permeated stagings of *The Cherry Orchard* in the 1970s was that of eternal values, whether beauty, oppressed by pragmatism, or such notions as home, family, traditions or the past. In Anatoly Efros' 1975 production of *The Cherry Orchard* at the Moscow Taganka Theatre, the past was symbolised by the white branch hanging over the stage; by the family portraits, and by the cross on the family graveyard. The style of the production was energetic, rapidly paced, with an abundance of farcical effects, in the centre of which were two tragic figures. For the elegant and ironic Ranevskaya, represented by Alla Demidova in the style of Art Nouveau and the aesthetics of Russian Decadence, the ruin of the cherry orchard *was* the collapse of the (her) world. And next to her was the man who had unwittingly betrayed her, who belonged neither to the old nor the new times, and who was tormented by inner conflicts. Lopakhin was performed by Vladimir Vysotsky[18] with almost Shakespearean power. Here the cherry orchard ceased to be merely a natural phenomenon but became symbolic of essentials, of the elements. It no longer had to be literally represented on stage, for its meaning and its fate were written on the faces of people.

Valentin Pluchek, at the (Moscow) Satire Theatre, directed *The Cherry Orchard* in the style of a chamber performance, just indicating the orchard by light-and-shadow play and concentrating on 'the inner orchards' of the characters, first and foremost Lopakhin, sadly and ironically represented by the actor Andrey Mironov as a wise, loving, understanding man without the power to change anything.

In the 1980s, it was the turn of *Three Sisters*. Yury Lyubimov's[19] 1981 production at the (Moscow) Taganka Theatre was sharp and sometimes clumsy, and did not entirely break away from tradition. The past was created by the image of old Moscow outside the theatre, expressed in the recorded voices of actors from productions of the Moscow Art Theatre and the Bolshoi Drama Theatre (in Leningrad, now St Petersburg). But now everything was quite different: the audience had changed and so had the actors. The large mirror downstage, placed at an angle to the auditorium, reflected both performers and spectators, showing how similar they were and how different from those who came before them: another epoch, another atmosphere, other values and morals. Thus the seeming romance of the military, quartered in a provincial town, gave way to the grim image of barracks existence: the resonance of the rough and appalling reality of the Afghanistan war.

In 1982, *Three Sisters* was produced by both Efros at the Malaya Bronnaya Theatre and by Galina Volchek at Moscow's Sovremennik (Contemporary) Theatre. Both had personal reasons for their choice. Efros' memories of his old censored production still rankled and he wanted to recreate the story of the sisters with young actors. Volchek was preoccupied with the problem of the fate and situation of women, a *female* interpretation but not a 'feminist' one.

In this way each of Chekhov's plays has taken its turn at becoming symbolic of the time, except for *The Seagull* which has weaved its way through the entire century, reflecting the stamp of the times, trends in theatre and the individual experiences of the artists. It is, in itself, virtually about the sources of conflict, struggle and progress in the theatre world.

The conflict surrounding *The Seagull* originally started in the late 1960s. Boris Livanov's romantic and elevated version, emphatically detached from the 'boredom of everyday life' as presented at the MAT in 1968, was clearly a reaction to Efros' 'rough' interpretation. Then Oleg Yefremov responded with the intentionally down-to-earth rendering of the play at the Sovremennik in 1970, as an unseemly story of the struggle of petty ambitions – and the egos of small-minded selfish people. And the response to *that* version was to come later, initiated by Yefremov himself.

By the mid-1970s, Russian and also international theatre were swept by a wave of productions of *The Seagull*, reflecting the repentance of yesterday's Treplevs – the former avant-garde artistic rebels who then gave up their protest to favour the establishment and the mainstream – and became sterile. Alexander Vilkin's 1978 production at the Mayakovsky Theatre in Moscow became a bitter and acid commentary on this issue. In contrast, Oleg Yefremov's 1980 production at the MAT was an attempt to reconstruct the play's poetry. After his first experience, the director now journeyed through the play, soaked in its poetry, and time, no doubt, had also made him wiser. He brought back to the stage the beautiful and enigmatic world of nature and looked at the people in it with compassion, understanding and confidence. At the Lenkom Theatre in Leningrad, Gennadi Oporkov had also begun by presenting *The Seagull* as the cold, grim and lifeless world of 1973, but by 1982 he changed this world into a poetic and mysterious environment, created on a small stage which was shared by both audience and performers.

So for a quarter of our century, beginning in the 1960s, developments in Chekhov production gathered momentum, irrelevant to 'external' factors, whether anniversaries or social changes. The sources for scenic interpretations were found in Chekhov's plays, his prose and letters. Chekhov was a writer for theatre *and* film, for drama *and* music. Almost all Russian directors went through his 'school of theatre'. While scenic artists created the rich and fantastic visual worlds of the plays, the actors found in the characters the opportunity for self-expression, and anticipated the compassionate response of the audience. And then, suddenly, everything stopped. Froze.

Perestroika, which had begun in the mid-1980s, stimulated interest in other writers, and other literary and dramatic genres. Everyone was fascinated by literature which had been censored and was now available. New classics, like the work of Andrei Platonov or Mikhail Bulgakov, pushed Chekhov and other 'old-timers' into the background. As in the 1920s and 1930s, there was the sense that Chekhov was not a relevant or useful writer. This impression, however, was a delusion – and short-lived. What had seemed a complete break turned out to be only a natural pause. When it was over, the theatre began its slow but steady return to Chekhov.

The first evidence came at the beginning of the nineties and was related to the search for social resonances. Yury Yeremin, having long worked with Chekhov's prose, staged a dramatisation of Chekhov's story 'Ward No. 6' at the Central Soviet Army Theatre. The message was absolutely unambiguous: only the day before, the world itself had been a grim prison.

Then new young directors came to Chekhov's theatre. Their productions, as those of others before them, also sometimes reflected political tendencies, but the conflict was much broader. These 'perestroika' people felt the need to make their own connection with Chekhov. Thus Leonid Trushkin, for instance, began his theatrical career in Moscow with an eccentric production of *The Cherry Orchard* in 1990. And the Pokrovka Theatre in Moscow opened in 1992 with Sergei Artsybashev's chamber production of *Three Sisters*: actors and audience unified into a distinctive Chekhovian 'family'. A year later, Alexander Kalyagin's Et Cetera Theatre opened with *Uncle Vanya*. A series of Chekhov festivals swept across Russia. These were democratic or, in other words, initiated from 'below', not imposed from above. So, for instance, in the spring of 1992, a group of young actors and directors organised the 'Back to Chekhov' Festival in St Petersburg. In the autumn of 1992, Yekaterinburg was the venue for a children and youth theatre festival, called 'Between Shakespeare and Chekhov'. Later in the same year something quite unprecedented happened in Moscow: the repertoire of the First International Chekhov Theatre Festival opened in Moscow – and did not feature a single Russian production of Chekhov. So theatre practitioners got together to hold an *alternative* festival, called 'Playing Chekhov'.

This continued to expand and develop, recapturing the original scale and complexity of the previous quarter of a century. Various kinds of production, from different parts of the country, were involved in this process of expansion and reinterpretation, and these so-called 'plays of our time' were gradually performed at various theatres. *Uncle Vanya* was one of these plays, with six premières in 1993 in Moscow alone, and it was as if these productions were intended to heal or answer some shared social 'wound': namely, the position of a man who found the truth only when it was too late, turned his back on his old life but failed to find the way towards a new one. In this period of Russia's radical reassessment of values, this was truly a sore subject and it received a particularly powerful expression in Mark Rozovsky's production at the Nikitsky Gates Theatre.

The same theme was presented in an unusual and original *devised* production by Genrietta (Henrietta) Yanovskaya, at the Moscow Youth Theatre, under the renamed title of *Ivanov and Others*. Yanovskaya brought in motifs, characters and characteristic lines from Chekhov's other plays. While the result was the creation of a complex and bizarre world, nonetheless Chekhov's theme of a man who has lost the meaning of life remained both intact and prevalent.

Three Sisters, written in the first year of the twentieth century, has remained with us throughout the century, and is now staged more frequently than before. The play meditates on what has happened to people, to Russia and to the world as a whole over virtually the last hundred years – and it was with this play that Oleg Yefremov completed his Chekhov cycle at the MAT in 1997. *The Seagull* continued its flight over Russia in impatient and disturbing anticipation of its centennial anniversary. It has become common for many directors to regard *The Seagull* as a comedy, but a very special one in which the key 'comedian' is fate – and the audience is allowed to laugh at the characters, but only until the last act. In this final act everything is changed, the games, jovial or cruel, come to an end and for the denouement the comedy is transformed into drama.

Mark Zakharov's 1994 Lenkom production of *The Seagull* featured a wide variety of performance styles, ranging from vaudeville to tragedy. In theatres across Russia, whether Vologda in the north or Magnitogorsk in the Urals, productions of *The Seagull* are also done in many different styles, ranging from dark grotesque comedy to light and lyrical declarations of love for theatre, its world and its people. The 1996 Maly Theatre production of *The Seagull* evolved from fun to deep melancholy. And *The Seagull* has also returned to St Petersburg, where the centennial anniversary of the play's première was marked by a festival and conference called 'The Flight of the Seagull'. This flight still continues and there is no telling what distinctive features of *our* time may be reflected in it.

The twentieth century is at an end, and we can now sum up the development of Chekhov's theatre. The repertoire of the Second International Chekhov Theatre Festival (1996) included all Chekhov's full-length plays produced in Russia and elsewhere. At the Third Festival (1998), Chekhov's drama was seen in the widest possible context, as if the world theatre, on the eve of the third millennium, was reviewing the principal stages of its own development: classical (antique) drama – Shakespeare – and Chekhov.

NOTES

1 All quotations from Chekhov's works indicated in brackets are taken from N. F. Belchikov and others, eds., *Polnoe sobranie sochinenii i pisem v 30 tomakh*, Moscow, 1974–83 (*Anton Chekhov, Collected Works and Letters in 30 Volumes*, Moscow, 1974–83). Quotations are from the *Letters*.

2 Vera Komissarzhevskaya (1864–1910) – one of the most renowned actresses

of the late nineteenth century, playing both in the provinces and at the Alexandrinsky Theatre. She also opened her own experimental theatre in St Petersburg. See chapter 15 in this volume and Selected Glossary.

3 See chapter 3 in this volume.

4 'On the Soviet Stage', *Teatr* 1, 1960, pp. 163–4.

5 Yevgeny Vakhtangov, *Materials and Articles*, Moscow, 1951, p. 182.

6 Vsevolod Meyerhold, *Articles, Letters, Speeches, Talks*, in two volumes. Vol. 11, 1917–39, Moscow, 1968, p. 310.

7 Alexander Tairov (1885–1950), director, and his wife, the actress Alisa Koonen (1889–1974) jointly founded the Moscow Kamerny (Chamber) Theatre. See Nick Worrall, *Modernism to Realism on the Soviet Stage*, Cambridge, 1989. For a detailed description of Tairov's production of *The Seagull* in 1944–5, see Vera Gottlieb, *Chekhov in Performance in Russia and Soviet Russia, Theatre in Focus Series*, Cambridge, 1984.

8 Boris Babochkin, *In Theatre and Film*, Moscow, 1968, p. 200.

9 Georgi Tovstonogov, *The Range of Thoughts*, Leningrad, 1972, p. 220. For more on Tovstonogov see chapter 9 in this volume, note 7 and chapter 15, Selected Glossary.

10 For more on Efros see chapter 11 in this volume, note 6 and chapter 15.

11 Anatoly Efros, *Rehearsal, My Love*, Moscow, 1975, p. 64.

12 For more on the description 'The Thaw' see chapter 3 in this volume, note 10.

13 See chapter 8 in this volume.

14 Vasily Grossman, *Life and Fate*, Moscow, 1988, pp. 264–5.

15 Kalmykia, former Central Asian Republic of the Soviet Union, neighbouring Kazakhstan, the capital of which is Elista.

16 Innokenty Smoktunovsky is best known outside Russia for his performance of Hamlet in Kozintsev's award-winning film of 1964–5. See chapter 3 in this volume, note 11.

17 See chapter 3 in this volume, note 12.

18 Vladimir Vysotsky (1938–80) was a charismatic and famous Russian actor, poet and singer.

19 Yuri Lyubimov, see chapter 9 in this volume, note 8 and chapter 15, Selected Glossary.

15

LAURENCE SENELICK

Directors' Chekhov

A Selected Glossary giving details of directors/actors mentioned can be found at the end of this chapter.

Shortly before his death, when asked to name the actors he considered the best interpreters of his plays, Chekhov cited three members of the St Petersburg Imperial Theatre who had appeared in the first productions of *Ivanov* and *The Seagull*.[1] His slighting omission of actors of the Moscow Art Theatre reflected the nineteenth-century attitude that a player was supposed to enhance a playwright's words through virtuosity and instinctive affinity. However gifted the Art Theatre actors may have been, Chekhov regretted that their individual talents were subject to the overriding concept of a director.

The irony is that Chekhov's own plays had themselves evolved from vehicles for histrionic display into ensemble pieces, best implemented by a masterful director. His playwriting career culminated at a time when the director was emerging as prime mover in the modernist theatre. In common with the Wagnerian notion of *Gesamtkunstwerk*, the stagecraft promoted by Appia, Craig, Stanislavsky and Reinhardt required every component in the *mise-en-scène* to be integrated and controlled by a single vision. Chekhov's drama benefited from this development: actors might give outstanding performances of specific roles, but his plays rarely caught on with audiences unless packaged by a director into a comprehensible and congruent format. A comparison of, say, the romantic Hamlets of Kean, Devrient and Mochalov makes sense; but to compare the Ranevskayas of Valentina Cortese, Alla Demidova and Jutta Lampe to any advantage one must set them in the contexts created by Giorgio Strehler, Anatoly Efros and Peter Stein.[2]

The identification of Chekhov's plays with the original Art Theatre *mises-en-scène* was unavoidable. In pre-Revolutionary Russia, provincial entrepreneurs, innovators at the State Alexandra Theatre, and young directors such as Meyerhold, Rostovstev and Gaideburov all sedulously copied Stanislavsky when staging Chekhov: this entailed close attention to surface realism with an emphasis on atmospherics and sound effects. Between 1905 and 1937, the MAT displayed its masterpieces throughout Europe and the United States, while the Prague Group of Art Theatre defectors propagated their own versions of these productions. The residual impression left by these effective and well-acted stagings was that Chekhov was idiosyncratically Russian and best left to Russians; if non-Russians were to stage him, imitating the Art Theatre as slavishly as possible would produce the best results. Directors who had fallen under the Art Theatre spell, such as Eino Kalima in Finland and Eva Le Gallienne in the US, did their best to transmit its allure by reproducing its externals.

Chekhov was also transported in the baggage of post-Revolutionary *émigrés*, who validated their artistic passports by claiming to be kindred spirits. In this diaspora, Russian theatre practitioners advertised a link with the Art Theatre that was often factitious or tenuous, but plausible. Some directors, among them Peter Sharoff, Richard Boleslavski and Leo Bulgakov, were authentic products of the MAT studios, who had been exposed to Stanislavsky at different phases of his unceasing experimentation. Whatever the case, *émigré* and *ersatz*-Art Theatre Chekhov tended to be retrospective and elegiac in tone, hearkening back to a paradise lost.

Even those refugees who rejected the Art Theatre approach or never practised it carried on under its banner. In England of the 1920s and 1930s Theodor Komisarjevsky was regarded as the leading Chekhovian, although he had twice failed to be admitted to the MAT and Stanislavsky loathed the book Komisarjevsky had written about his system. 'Komis', as he was familiarly known, brought a whiff of modernist stagecraft to the commercial English theatre he despised. His Chekhov was shrewdly calculated to appeal to the taste of the average matinée-goer: by cutting eccentricities and long speeches, historicising the action and emphasising the love interest, and casting attractive young stars on the ascendant, he lent Chekhov the appeal of romantic melodrama. The stage was drenched in moonlight and music laid on to underscore an ambience of wistful lyricism. Komis' conversion of Chekhov into prestigious consumer goods elegantly displayed would be perpetuated in post-war Italy in the lush and decorative productions of Luchino Visconti.

Georgian-born Georges Pitoëff introduced an equally idiosyncratic Chekhov to the French, although his asceticism rarely attracted matinée audiences. Influenced as much by economic constraints as by the 'Itinerant Theatre' of his mentor Pavel Gaideburov, Pitoëff repudiated the cluttered naturalism of the MAT and situated his Chekhov amid black draperies and two-dimensional tree-trunks. Stripping down a play to a conflict between the sensitive artist and society, he imbued his *mises-en-scène* with melancholy and tragic foreboding. Although he rewrote and abridged to suit French conventions, Parisians preferred to regard these delicately wrought *études* as exotic effusions of a 'Slavic soul'.

The years between the World Wars might be called the sentimental period of Chekhovian production. For Western spectators, Chekhov was a man of sorrows and acquainted with grief; whenever a director attempted to bring out the comic strain, critics and audience became confused. Would-be clones of the MAT stagings cultivated protracted pauses, turgid rhythms and tears, and were titivated with stars in the leading roles. Informed by the well-entrenched notion that Chekhov was a psychological naturalist of the so-called Ibsen school, the *mises-en-scène* were confined to box-sets and the reproduction of 'everyday' details, including the obligatory samovar.

So long as these views prevailed, Chekhov's works held little appeal for the foremost directors of the time. In Bolshevik Russia, where Chekhov was dismissed as an outmoded chronicler of a feckless intelligentsia, Vakhtangov's tragic-grotesque staging of *The Wedding* (1921) failed to influence treatment of the major plays. Meyerhold took on Chekhov only near the end of his long career, with a mechanically slapstick rendition of three vaudevilles.[3] In Germany Max Reinhardt, possibly cowed by the aura of definitiveness about the Art Theatre productions, never got around to Chekhov, and directors who did appreciate him, such as Jürgen Fehling and Heinz Hilpert, failed to infect audiences with their enthusiasm. Stanislavsky's leading admirer in the US, the Group Theatre under Harold Clurman, abandoned a projected *Three Sisters* for its lack of social relevance and box-office drawing power.

To rid itself of the clichés of gloom and doom, Chekhovian staging needed a divorce both from the historical circumstances reflected in the plays and from the obsolescent techniques of the Art Theatre. Nemirovich-Danchenko realised this when he mounted an optimistic *Three Sisters* in 1940. In Russia a generation later, the popular theme of an idealist in a world of cynical compromise, found in the plays of Arbuzov, Rozov and Volodin,[4] was read into Chekhov's drama. *Ivanov* in particular was revived on a regular basis. Anti-domesticity was proclaimed by scenery that lacked walls and doors; ruined manor-houses were made to look like skeletal prisons, overgrown by a Sleeping Beauty's garden of lianas and brambles. This became a cliché of its own. (See Appendix 4.)

Unfortunately, after the Second World War Chekhov suffered in Central and Eastern Europe from being imposed as part of the Soviet cultural hegemony: he and Stanislavsky, now heavily alloyed with Socialist Realism, were thrust down the throats of the Czech, Polish, East German, Romanian and Hungarian theatres. Little wonder if, left to their own devices, they sought to discredit and supersede the MAT legacy. At the same time, Samuel Beckett and the Theatre of the Absurd offered models for bringing out the symbolist and alogical elements in Chekhov, and a spate of 'metaphoric' stagings and ruthlessly anti-sentimental, even caricatural inter-pretations mushroomed all over Europe. This Chekhov revival was chiefly due to Otomar Krejča and Giorgio Strehler, both leftists but of quite different stripe.

At the Divadlo za Branou (Theatre Behind the Gates) in Prague, Krejča worked closely with his actors to explore what Gorky had called the cold and cruel Chekhov, an impassive creator who flung his characters into a meaningless world. Without being a doctrinaire existentialist, Krejča channelled his own experience as a victim of Soviet domination into a version of Chekhov that administered the shock of recognition to his audiences. Mounting five Chekhov plays seventeen times throughout Europe in an increasingly unconventional manner, he became respected as the director most closely acquainted with the subtleties of the text.

Strehler's earliest Chekhov productions at the Piccolo Teatro di Milano had been political and satirical in bent; his finest achievement, *The Cherry Orchard* (1974), abstracted the nostalgia of Komisarjevsky and Pitoëff by enlarging it beyond the private sphere. Strehlerian epigones became most common in Western Europe and the English-speaking world, whereas in Central and Eastern Europe, Krejča's model of the cruel grotesque domi-nated, particularly in the work of Peter Zadek, Roberto Ciulli and Matthias Langhoff. The Romanian director, Andrei Serban, staging Chekhov in New York, Massachusetts and Japan as well as in his homeland, often seemed to shuttle uncomfortably between these two polarities. (See p. 143.)

Until recently, the English-speaking world has been largely impervious to innovations and radical reforms in Chekhovian staging. Psychological realism remains the preferred model, and the Chekhovian estate has been familiarised as the old homestead or the decayed manor-house. Firmly situated at the *fin de siècle*, he is a safe choice for repertory seasons, offering plum roles for actors and comforting the spectators with the dramatic equivalent of valerian drops. This may account for the large number of American plays about Chekhov's own life, in which he turns into, in Neil Simon's words, 'The Good Doctor'; or why British dramatists, such as Trevor Griffiths and Howard Barker, feel the need to rewrite his plays in a brutal and unambivalent style, in rebellion against genteel traditions of playing Chekhov's own words.

Under the pressure of postmodernist intellectual trends, Chekhov's status as a readily recognisable cultural totem makes him vulnerable to all sorts of co-optation. Directors bored with common-or-garden-variety Chekhov feel free to shuffle the dramatic structure to provide a metatextual gloss. Krejča experimented by playing Act Four of *The Seagull* with interpolations from earlier acts to comprise a montage of commentary (Divadlo za Branou, Theatre Behind the Gates, 1972). In Moscow, Yury Pogrebnichko reduced the same work to an anthology of Chekhovian allusions (Teatr na Krasnoy Presne, Theatre of the Red Army, 1989, 1992). An even more playful intertextualism was practised in Genrietta (Henrietta) Yanovskaya's *Ivanov and the Others* (Moscow Youth Theatre, 1993), filled with homunculi and in-jokes from the whole Chekhov canon. As the millennium approaches, Russian spectators, facing an uncertain future, appreciate these winks and nudges at a shared cultural experience. Elsewhere, the dichotomy still exists between productions which seek only to 'tell the story' to their public and an 'avant-garde' which tries to appropriate Chekhov and assumptions about him as media for its own messages.

The Seagull

With its awkward vestiges of nineteenth-century stagecraft and its inter-weaving of artistic debates with love affairs, *The Seagull* needs careful balance and an almost musical rendition to avoid coming off as melodrama or soap opera. Confessing that he had no idea of what the play meant, Stanislavsky used it as an exercise in *nastroenie* (atmosphere, mood); he recreated the facture and texture of everyday life through lighting, sound and behavioural traits. However, since the Art Theatre never toured the play and soon dropped it from its repertory, it had less impact than later MAT stagings.

The standard approach taken to *The Seagull* focusses on the conflict between a younger generation of idealists and an older generation of hacks. How directors deal with Treplev's Symbolist play in Act One usually indicates how seriously the audience is to take his pretensions to literary talent or, indeed, whether art or love is to be pre-eminent. The consensus shares Stanislavsky's opinion that Treplev was a mute, inglorious Pushkin kept down by the vile seducer Trigorin and Nina an inspired talent forged by suffering. Komisarjevsky's moon-struck London production (New Theatre, 1936) played up the theme of young love thwarted. Pitoëff's two Parisian productions (Théâtre des Champs-Elysées, 1922; Théâtre des Mathurins, 1939) were threnodies, with Treplev a type of martyred artist and Nina an ethereal muse; the later staging finally made

Chekhov popular in Paris, suiting the mood of anxious yearning on the eve of war.

The Seagull could be slanted to protest state-imposed uniformity in the arts. Aleksandr Tairov reopened his Kamerny Theatre in Moscow in 1944 with a *Seagull* distilled into a Platonic dialogue on art's eternal verities. Set against black drapes and a white piano, its lines pruned to keep the focus on aesthetic debate and Nina played by the middle-aged Alisa Koonen, the production was appreciated by the *cognoscenti*. Given Tairov's low prestige within the Soviet theatrical hierarchy, it was mainly ignored, however. In his first *Seagull* (Narodni Divadlo, Prague, 1960), Krejča tried to make Nina's gospel of vocation the play's message, a didacticism he forswore in his later work. Here too, realism was subjugated to the play's symbolist elements: Josef Svoboda replaced a constructed environment with pools of light and leaf-patterns.

In the post-Thaw[5] era, the fashionable Soviet literary contrast of adolescent ideals with middle-aged compromise maintained the earlier valency, favouring Treplev's transcendental efforts over Trigorin's workmanlike professionalism. When Anatoly Efros directed *The Seagull* in 1966 (Lenin-Komsomol Theatre, Moscow), the childish rebel Treplev stood adrift amid a host of nasty, strident elders, with even Nina played as a single-minded careerist. Boris Livanov's restaging for the Art Theatre (1968) pointed up the parallels with *Hamlet*, apotheosising the melancholy Treplev;[6] whereas Oleg Efremov's *Seagull* (Moscow, 1970), intended as a polemic against Livanov and reflecting the squabbling in his own Sovremennik Theatre, isolated each character in his self-involvement. After Efremov came to head the Art Theatre, he metamorphosed from Treplev to Trigorin: his *Seagull* there in 1980 was less judgemental, suggesting that, even *in extremis*, one could go on living.

Leaders of the American 'avant-garde', such as André Gregory and Joseph Chaikin, saw in the play the origins of their own creative striving, and there were five major restagings in New York in 1975 alone; Gregory's was the most daring, paraphrasing the lines and effacing the border between past and present. The play's subtitle 'A Comedy' was exploited by Lindsay Anderson, Jonathan Miller and Ellis Rabb, who relished the farce of Arkadina's histrionic behaviour but could not encompass the whole work within a comic vision. As usual, it was European directors who reformulated the play most drastically. Peter Zadek (Bochum, 1973) and Antoine Vitez (Paris, 1984) placed Treplev's platform on the apron, so that the audience on stage mirrored that in the house; the interlocking love affairs and their attendant frustrations were given bloated prominence. Liviu Ciulei, a Romanian director working in the US, initiated a much-imitated practice of beginning the play with Treplev's suicide, and then flashing back to Act One. Roberto Ciulli (Mülheim, 1984) reduced the play to a series of startling, evocative images: a blind Sorin feeling his way through velvet curtains, Nina dressed as Pierrot tied to a stake, the lotto game played against a mountain of suitcases around an empty bedstead.

The 'spell-binding' lake has also been made a central image, particularly in Japan. Andrei Serban (Shiki Theatre Company of Tokyo, 1980) and Hirowatari Tsanetoshi (Tokyo Engeki, 1993) both situated Treplev's platform at the centre of a pool. There, in Serban's staging, he 'drowned his book' and committed *hara-kiri*, falling face forward in the water. In Tsanetoshi's version, Nina attempted suicide in a moat of pellucid water that purled and babbled throughout the play as a symbol of eternity. More like Vincent Crummles' (the itinerant theatre manager in Dickens' *Nicholas Nickleby*) 'practicable pump' was the liquid element of Sergey Solyvov's expensive *Seagull* (Taganka, 1994), an 'against interpretation' counterblast to the deconstructions of Pogrebnichko. In the on-stage lake, naked workmen swam, a half-naked Trigorin fished, and Treplev shot himself in a boat. This return to naturalism drew less from Stanislavsky than from Hollywood.

Uncle Vanya

With its small cast, bound by what Osip Mandelshtam called 'propinquity,'[7] and its sharply focussed conflicts, *Uncle Vanya* has commonly been presented as a domestic tragedy or a *passage d'armes* between two strong actors. How the play works has had more to do with the casting of Voinitsky and Astrov than with any overarching directorial concept. Stanislavsky romanticised the country doctor, and his contemporaries took the play to be a mirror of the plight of the provincial intelligentsia. After the Revolution, despite official condemnation of the subject matter, a new proletarian audience continued to weep over the sufferings of Vanya and Sonya. The elements of despair made it a difficult work to incorporate into Socialist Realism.

The play's meaning became deracinated when it left Russian soil: early productions in Germany, England, Ireland and France were condemned as collocations of cranks. The first *Vanya* to win success with a popular audience was staged in 1930 by the Broadway producer Jed Harris, who shrewdly realised that, if properly rewritten and stellarly cast, Chekhov had box-office appeal. The script provided by Rose Caylor eliminated ambiguities and introduced sentimentalities; the company headed by Lillian Gish made Russians seem familiar. It inaugurated American all-star Chekhov, which was to culminate in the artistic débâcle of Mike Nichols' Broadway *Vanya* of 1973 (Circle-in-the-Square, NY). Pairing Nicol Williamson and George C. Scott, it proved definitively that a mere assemblage of celebrities, without strong directorial exegesis, could provide only an incoherent and cliché-ridden Chekhov.

Williamson's revival the next year at the Other Place, Stratford-upon-Avon, did demonstrate that an intimate spatial relation between actors and audience aided the play, allowing a microscopic examination of motives and reactions. Still, *Vanya*'s success in England is invariably tied to its leading actors, a pattern set by Laurence Olivier and Ralph Richardson at the New Theatre in 1945, and confirmed by Olivier and Michael Redgrave at the Chichester Festival production of 1962. Despite occasional interpretations that advance the themes of environmentalism or Christian fortitude, *Vanya* has remained an actors' showcase, which has enjoyed a remarkable lease of life over the past decade in films relocating the characters' isolation to the New Zealand outback or the Welsh downs. André Gregory's production of an American version by David Mamet (Victory Theatre, New York, 1991) received a wide audience when filmed by Louis Malle as *Vanya on 42nd Street*. Presented as a rehearsal in progress, unenhanced by period costumes or elaborate settings, the characters' raw emotions came across clearly. Mamet's English versions in which ambiguities turn into strongly worded assertions brought Chekhov closer to contemporary Americans who, like the director Nikos Psacharopoulos at the Williamstown (Mass.) Theatre, prefer their Chekhov red-blooded and tempestuous.

Others broke the naturalistic mould more aggressively. *The Uncle Vanya Show* of New York's Irondale Ensemble Project in collaboration with the St Petersburg Salon Theatre (1985–90) dismantled the play into a demented collage of vaudeville bits concerning a Michigan radio host who thinks he is Chekhov's hero. This work-in-progress was a deliberate grafting of pop on to what was perceived as high culture. More overtly political in its use of farce was the *Vanya* of Eimuntas Nekrosius (State Youth Theatre of Lithuania, Vilnius, 1986). Meant as an attack on Russian cultural hegemony, it reduced the characters to a set of antic monomaniacs; their actions were undercut by a chorus of floor-polishers whose earthy horseplay sardonically commented on the absurd aspirations of their betters. The Polish director Jerzy Grzegorzewski (Warsaw Studio Theatre, 1993) used repetition, cramped spatial dimensions and an arrest of time's passage to objectify the characters' predicaments: eternal recurrence was the point, and nothing ever came to a definite conclusion.

Three Sisters

Chekhov's first play written specifically for the Moscow Art Theatre, *Three Sisters*, is more ambitious than its immediate predecessors. The large and varied cast and the temporal span of seasons and years give it the sweep of a novel. A play more suitable for a permanent repertory company than a fit-up troupe, it can satisfy a director's ambition to create a microcosm and orchestrate a fugue of moods and genre-pieces. It was the most impressive of the MAT's Chekhovian stagings and the one most closely copied by Russian regional and foreign directors. Indeed, the director of the first *Three Sisters* at the Prague National Theatre wrote to Stanislavsky requesting detailed information on the music and uniforms he had used.[8]

Pre-revolutionary Russian audiences referred to attending the Art Theatre production as 'calling on the Prozorovs', and accompanied the performances with floods of tears and cries of 'Oh!' at the sisters' dismal fate. This attitude was in essence transferred to all its successors: the *donnée* was that the sisters were admirable heroines, downed by provincial philistinism and the ambitions of that petty-bourgeois bitch Natasha. Stanislavsky's and Kachalov's ennobling of Vershinin and Tusenbach made sure that no irony was heard in the oratory about hard work and the future. Predictably, Komisarjevsky overdid the glamour, setting the action in the 1870s, turning Tusenbach into a handsome juvenile lead and the whole play into a Pre-Raphaelite tale of blighted loves (Barnes Theatre, London, 1926; revived 1929). Pitoëff, after excising all the long speeches, made the play a plaint for an irrecoverable past, indulging his own sense of loss (Théâtre des Arts, Paris, 1929). A French director working in London, Michel Saint-Denis took a more objective view of the drama and, rehearsing a strong ensemble for an unprecedented eight weeks, was delivered of a well-balanced *Three Sisters* as strong on comedy as it was on pathos (Queen's Theatre, London, 1938).

Nemirovich-Danchenko, eager to reclaim Chekhov as a Soviet author, refurbished *Three Sisters* (1940) to make a positive statement: costumes were spanking clean, vocal delivery clarion clear, the settings suffused with light. Like those who regret the cleaning of the Sistine Chapel ceiling, Westerners deplored the over-painting of a subtle *grisaille* with the primary colours of propaganda. Within Russia itself, however, this *Three Sisters* recalled a pre-Stalinist world of decency and honour; it gave licence to seek inspiration in Chekhov, rather than dismissing him as an outdated chronicler of defeatism. The only true successor to Nemirovich in the post-war USSR, Georgy Tovstonogov of Leningrad's Bolshoy Dramatic Theatre, stripped down Art Theatre illusionism even further, enlarging the play into an epic which stranded the characters in space, while still endorsing faith in human potential (1965).

News of the renovation of Stanislavsky was slow in seeping into the American consciousness. The long-awaited Actors Studio *Three Sisters* directed by Lee Strasberg (NY, 1963) was supposed to vindicate his brand of 'Method acting', itself rooted in Russian *émigré* teachings of the 1920s. The narcissism and raw emotion it generated reduced the play to a set of acting exercises, an unfocussed display of individuals indulging in incoherent mannerisms. The production revealed not only the bankruptcy of a misunderstood Art Theatre model, but also the need for long-established ensembles, rather than hastily thrown-together casts of disparate background, to do Chekhov justice.

The first 'cruel' approach to *Three Sisters* came from Otomar Krejča. His production at the Divadlo za Branou (1965) was superficially recognisable – *fin-de-siècle* costumes, military uniforms, whiskers galore; but Svoboda's scenography reduced the setting to a few dominant symbolic elements. Instead of being understated, the acting was hysterical and violent. At the final curtain, discarding the typical statuesque tableau, the sisters whirled around the stage like blinded birds, as Dr Chebutykin (played by Krejča himself) soared over the first rows of the audience on a swing, crowing 'It doesn't matter! It doesn't matter!'

Post-Krejča European productions adopted his critical attitude to the sisters, re-examining their claims to moral or intellectual superiority over their surroundings. Masha's adultery, Olga's squeamish gentility and Irina's indifference to her suitors were seen to put them more on a par with Natasha. Lucian Pintilie's Paris production of 1978 turned them into facets of a single archetypal woman, erotic and repressed. A younger generation of Russians attacked the *idée recue* of *Three Sisters* as figurative of everything stagnant in establishment culture. Efros staged a scandalous *Sisters* (Moscow, 1967) that provoked angry letters to editors and was ultimately banned. His Prozorovs and their circle were deluded idealists, so cocksure of their own virtues that they were oblivious to their gradual absorption by evil. It was a strong message to Soviet intelligentsia that they had let their birthright be stolen. Yury Lyubimov's *Three Sisters* (Moscow Drama Theatre, Malaya Bronnaya), 1981), set in an inhospitable barracks *cum* lecture-hall, offered another sardonic comment on Soviet life. As if in response to the recurrent call 'To Moscow! To Moscow,' he opened a wall of the Taganka Theatre, letting in cold night air and a view of the contemporary capital. 'You yearn for Moscow?' he seemed to be saying. 'Well there it is, in all its noise and squalor. You aspire to a glorious future? Is this what you had in mind?' Sixty years of false aspiration were debunked in one moment. In the Gorbachev era, Pogrebnichko (Teatr na Krasnoy Presne, Moscow, 1990) turned *Three Sisters* into a museum exhibit set behind velvet ropes in a mass of antique detritus, prompting post-Soviet spectators to come to grips with a past that has left them washed up on the shoals of the present.

Regrettably, these innovations remained overlooked or ineffectual in the English-speaking world, even though Krejča's *Three Sisters* visited the World Theatre Season in London in 1969. A number of British productions, especially those of Jonathan Miller (Cambridge Theatre, 1976), Trevor Nunn (RSC, Warehouse, 1979),[9] and Mike Alfreds' Shared Experience Co. (1986),[10] tried to take a more jaundiced view of the characters' aspirations and self-justifications. The problem is that British and American audiences want to identify with the Prozorovs and are loath to accept productions which do not favour them. The outraged reaction to the *Three Sisters* staged by the great Georgian director Robert Sturua (Queen's Theatre, London, 1990) demonstrated this: his anti-sentimental and exuberantly physical approach evoked shudders of disgust from the critical and academic establishments. Yet this very approach, carried to an extreme more recently by Eimuntas Nekrosius, is a valuable corrective, the allegedly inadmissible inventiveness provoking fresh discoveries in an overly familiar text.

A wedding of Stanislavskian stagecraft to an 'objective' attitude occurred in Peter Stein's production at the Berlin Schaubühne in 1981. In taking psychological and environmental naturalism to their logical extremes, he burst through reality to reach another dimension. When the cast suddenly froze in Act One, hearkening to the hum of the spinning top, it was as if the music of the spheres had penetrated the Prozorov drawing room. At the same time, Stein's unflinching exposure of the neuroses of the well-bred sisters was meant to reflect on his own complacent bourgeois audience.

Of all Chekhov's plays, *Three Sisters* has undergone the greatest number of cultural transferences, reset in the Caribbean, Chinatown and a Pennsylvania coal-mining centre. The influence of Beckett was easy to trace in Squat Theatre's intentionally boring thirty-minute version in which three male actors stammered out the sisters' lines (New York, 1980); in Tadashi Suzuki's reduction of the play to an hour's worth of antiphony among three men and five women, some of them pent up in baskets (SCOT Company, 1984); and, most blatantly, in Hartmut Wickert's *Kommen und Gehen* (Tübingen, 1988), contrasting the 'dangerous zones' of silence with the cover-up of incessant chatter. Given the centrality of the sororal trio, the play also has a special appeal to lesbian and feminist groups, which stress the growing interdependency of the sisters, from distance and alienation at the start to solidarity by the finale. One of the most notorious deconstructions has been the Wooster Group's *Brace Up!*, directed by Elizabeth LeCompte (New York, 1990). To address and criticise the postmodern sensibility, sequential narrative was made impossible by omnipresent noise, video screens, rapid alternation and juxtaposition of images and time frames.

The Cherry Orchard

Chekhov's last play is his most complex. For all its grounding in reality, it pierces, in Andrey Bely's words, 'an aperture to eternity'.[11] The audiences of the original Moscow Art Theatre production were most taken by the sedulous reproduction of a life they knew, but even then there were dissenters, among them Bely, Meyerhold, and the Ukrainian art critic Nikolaev, who complained that the plethora of surface detail occluded the play's symbolic aspects. It was also clear, as Chekhov himself pointed out, that Stanislavsky's casting had unbalanced the play: the author had intended a comedy with Lopakhin and Charlotta Ivanovna occupying central positions. Instead, Stanislavsky as Gaev and Knipper as Ranevskaya, both prone to idealising their roles, directed the audience's sympathies to the displaced gentry. *Emigré* nostalgia intensified this imbalance after the Revolution.

Within Bolshevik Russia, *The Cherry Orchard* was the only major Chekhov play to be revived with any frequency because Lopkahin and Treplev could be made heralds of a brave new world. The most memorable revision was that of Andrey Lobanov (Simonov Studio, Moscow, 1934): the Gaev family and their dependants were shown to be despicable parasites and debauchees, and Trofimov's second-act harangues were delivered in a bathhouse to a crowd of avid secondary-school students.

Abroad, *The Cherry Orchard* invariably aped the Art Theatre, both in its look and in its values. Nemirovich-Danchenko attempted to set this right in 1933, when he directed it for Tatiana Pavlowa's company in Milan to bring out more of Ranevskaya's stylish egoism and Trofimov's ineptitude. Tyrone Guthrie's Old Vic production of 1933 also played up the comedy, due to his own penchant for irreverence and a cast containing such talents as Athene Seyler, Charles Laughton and Elsa Lanchester. The comedy tended to bewilder Western critics, used to a slow-paced and reverent treatment of Chekhov.

No serious rethinking of *The Cherry Orchard* took place until after the war, when Giorgio Strehler approached it as a timeless masterpiece on a par with *The Tempest*, *Faust* and *The Magic Flute*, sharing with them an ability to speak on a great many levels to a great many issues (Piccolo Teatro di Milano, 1974). Whereas Krejča believed that every directorial decision inevitably led down a path compromising the author's intentions, Strehler sought to conflate all the levels of meaning in the play: the narrative, the socio-historical and the universal metaphoric. The toys in the nursery, for instance, went beyond veristic props to become emblems of the characters' lost innocence and the arrested development of their world. Strehler's production, particularly his white-on-white décor with its over-head membrane of petals in a diaphanous veil, breathing with the actors and audience, had an indelible effect on most *Cherry Orchards* thereafter. All over the world achromatic costuming and scenery, a diaphanous sky-cloth or groundcloth and a toy train became indispensable accoutrements. Even Krejča's Düsseldorf *Orchard* of 1976 engulfed the characters in a forest of furniture under a luminous white dustcover. Andrei Serban's derivative staging in New York in 1977 (Vivian Beaumont Theatre) first made the US take notice that an alternative approach to the Art Theatre was valid; although most critics were ignorant of the European antecedents of Serban's *mise-en-scène*, they welcomed a break with the traditional *verismo*. In fact, Serban's directing lacked Strehler's intellectual coherence: his dream-like imagery here and in later restagings – a little girl laying a flower at a factory door, industrial workers silhouetted against the cyclorama – hinted at a political message, but, except for Trofimov's messianic fervour being played straight, it remained inchoate. (See p. 143.)

The avoidance of a political aspect to Chekhov's works has been common everywhere but in the Soviet bloc, where external circumstances filled even anodyne productions with *sous-entendus*. A striking exception to this neglect was *The Cherry Orchard* rewritten by Trevor Griffiths and directed by Richard Eyre (Nottingham Playhouse, 1977): a Marxist coarsening of the text enabled Trofimov and Lopakhin to become the *raisonneurs* for a playwright who distrusted *raisonneurs*.[12] Less solemnly, two East German Brechtians working in West Germany, Manfred Karge and Matthias Langhoff, combined politics with caricature to produce a George Grosz-like *Orchard*, a violent farce peopled with selfish vulgar-ians, analogues of the smug burghers of the Federal Republic (Bochum, 1981).

Peter Brook's *Orchard* (Bouffes du Nord, Paris, 1981) preferred simpli-city: with no more elaborate scenography than the ramshackle theatre itself and blue Oriental carpets, rolled up to represent trees, spread out as grounding for story-telling. The swift pace allowed no time for 'psycholo-gical' moments, pregnant pauses or maudlin bathos. The fortuitousness of the characters' fates was suggested by blocking that seemed haphazard but was in fact carefully arranged. When it toured to Moscow, this *Orchard* was welcomed as an epiphany. It offered liberation from both Stanislavsky's literalism and the 'Aesopic' metaphors of such as Efros, whose Taganka *Cherry Orchard* of 1975 had been set in a graveyard filled with family portraits. Admiring the productions of Strehler and Brook, in which human relations continued to count when all else was devalued, the Russians recognised that Western European Chekhov had a different genetic code from their own.

This lesson was driven home at the first Chekhov Festival in Moscow in 1991 which saw three new *Cherry Orchards*.[13] Peter Stein sought to make 'indifferent nature' itself a character, at odds with human passions; his staging was so illusionistic that it brought back the real hay of Stanislavsky's second act and so symphonic that it let events unfold in real time. Serban recreated his New York staging with a Romanian cast, pushing the political symbolism in the direction of anti-Communist rhetoric. Krejča seemed to be played out, his latest *Orchard* devoid of lyricism, colour or specificity. In the wake of these examples, recent Russian *Orchards*, such as that of Adolph Shapiro (St Petersburg BDT, 1992), are made object lessons for a society in disarray, whose Lopakhins are exemplary businessmen for the era of free markets and privatisation.

When Mariya Knebel, Stanislavsky's last pupil, came to the Abbey Theatre in 1968 to direct *The Cherry Orchard*, the Dublin actors were surprised that she didn't require a samovar on stage.[14] The samovar had always been the indispensable token of Chekhov's foreignness. In the last decades, however, in production after production, the samovar has been supplanted as emblematic prop by an old Victrola with a morning-glory horn. Chekhov is still associated with the past, but not a specifically Russian or historic past. Whatever reality the estates and garrison towns of Chekhov's plays held for its first audiences, they have now taken on a polysemic existence. They transcend their origins to become what David Cole calls *illud tempus*, a theatrical moment in which the event does not need to be recreated because it is always happening.[15] The world evoked in a Chekhov play by inventive modern directors confronts the past with the present – sometimes by painstakingly reproducing a bygone age, as in Stein's recent *Uncle Vanya*, sometimes by transferring it to analogous locales, as in *Seagulls* set in Martha's Vineyard or Celtic Twilight Ireland, sometimes by shattering the play into artifacts of a cultural legacy, as in *Brace Up!*. Interrupted meaning and faulty recollection rend the seamless web of the Stanislavskian simulacrum so that Chekhov our contemporary turns out to have more in common with Proust and Beckett than with Gorky.

NOTES

1 A. Ya. Altshuller, 'Chekhov i Aleksandrinsky teatr ego vremeni,' *Russkaya literatura* 3, 1968, p. 169. The actors named were Davydov as Ivanov, Sazonov as Prince Shabelsky and Vera Komissarzhevskaya as Nina.

2 The exception is *Ivanov*, whose meaning changes depending on whether the leading actor portrays the protagonist as a disillusioned idealist (Vasily Kachalov, John Gielgud, Innokenty Smoktunovsky), a manic clown (John Wood) or a perfectly ordinary person (Evgeny Leonov). See Selected Glossary.

3 See chapter 5 in this volume.

4 Aleksey Arbuzov (1908–86), Russian playwright. From his first success *Tanya* (1939), his bittersweet comedies, balancing the needs of the individuals against those of society, had great appeal for Soviet audiences. In the 1960s his plays used nostalgic theatrical effects to get beyond realism, and in the 1970s he opened a studio for young writers which fostered a whole generation of new dramatists. Viktor Rozov (b. 1913), Russian playwright. His play about a young man in wartime, *Forever Alive* (1956) became world famous as the film *The Cranes are Flying*. His greatest successes in the Communist world came in the 1960s and 1970s with plays about generational conflict, the elders compromised and the youth idealistic. Aleksandr Volodin (Aleksandr Lifshits, b. 1919), Russian playwright. Trained as a screen-writer, he used cinematic devices in his plays. He expanded the routine Socialist-Realistic agenda by exploring the personal aspirations of his characters, and moved away from uncritical optimism to a tragi-comic vision inspired by Cervantes and Shakespeare.

5 See chapter 3 in this volume, note 10.

6 The *Hamlet* analogy was taken to its logical extension by Ron Daniels at the American Repertory Theatre, Cambridge, Mass., 1989, when he directed both plays back-to-back with the same cast.

7 Osip Mandelshtam, *O pese A. Chekhova 'Dyadya Vanya'* (1936), *Sobranie sochineny*, Paris, 1981, vol. IV, pp. 107–9. Osip Emilievich Mandelshtam (1891–1938), Russian poet and essayist, whose fugitive remarks on Chekhov are particularly insightful.

8 Sh. Sh. Bogatyrev, 'Chekhov v Chekhovslovakii,' *Literaturnoe Nasledstvo* 68, 1960, pp. 760–2.

9 See chapter 9 in this volume.

10 See chapter 11 in this volume.

11 Andrey Bely, *'The Cherry Orchard'*, in Laurence Senelick, ed., *Russian Dramatic Theory from Pushkin to the Symbolists*, Austin, Tex., 1981.

12 See chapter 10 in this volume.

13 See chapter 14 in this volume.

14 Mariya Knebel, "Vishnevy sad' v Irlandii,' *Teatr* 5, 1969, pp. 158–66.

15 David Cole, *The Theatrical Event: a Mythos, a Vocabulary, a Perspective*, Middletown, Conn., 1975, p. 8.

SELECTED GLOSSARY

MIKE ALFREDS, English director who founded the Shared Experience Company of Oxford in 1975; his speciality is turning panoramic literary works into dramatic experiments in acting style. He has directed *The Seagull*, Crucible Theatre, Sheffield 1981; *The Cherry Orchard*, Roundhouse, London, 1982 and at The National Theatre 1985; *Three Sisters*, Bloomsbury Theatre, London, 1986; and *The Seagull*, Lillian Bayliss Theatre, London, 1991. See Appendix 2.

LINDSAY ANDERSON (1923–94), English director and critic, associated with the Royal Court Theatre, London (1957–72), where, with a minimum of décor, he created the first productions of many 'Angry Young Writers'. Influenced by Brecht and the American musical, he gravitated to film, where his absurdist panoramas of British life continue to confound reviewers. He directed *The Seagull*, Lyric Theatre, London in 1975 and *The Cherry Orchard*, Theatre Royal Haymarket, London in 1983.

HOWARD BARKER (b. 1946), English playwright, widely produced on the Fringe; an exponent of catastrophic theatre, confrontational, accusatory and theatrically eloquent. Without a specific political affiliation, his satire attacks all aspects of capitalist society and its marginalisation of human beings. He wrote a version of *Uncle Vanya* entitled *(Uncle) Vanya* for the Wrestling School in 1996. See Appendix 2.

ANDREY BELY (Boris Bugaev, 1880–1934), Russian poet and critic. Although Bely wrote only two plays, the mysteries *He That Is Come* (1902) and *The Jaws of Night* (1903), he was a leading theorist of drama, now supporting the Symbolist cause, now attacking it for its lack of pragmatism. He worked closely with Meyerhold and later with Michael Chekhov.

RICHARD BOLESLAVSKI (Bolesław Ryszard Szredniecki, 1887–1937), Polish actor and director, a charter member of the Moscow Art Theatre First Studio. He settled in New York in 1922 and through lectures and writings introduced Stanislavsky's early ideas to American actors. With Maria Ouspenskaya he founded the American Laboratory Theatre (1923–30), which taught their particular brand of the System; he later moved to Hollywood, where he directed fifteen films.

PETER BROOK (b. 1925), English director. After a distinguished career at the Royal Shakespeare Company, Covent Garden and in the commercial theatre, Brook began to explore the avant-garde, first with his Theatre of Cruelty season resulting in his *Marat/Sade* (1964), and then with *Orghast at Persepolis* (1971). In search of a universal language of theatre, he moved to Paris and with an international company has continued to experiment with the underlying myths of mankind. He directed *La Cérisaie (The Cherry Orchard)* at Les Bouffes du Nord, 1981, which subsequently toured to Moscow. See Appendix 2.

LEO (LEV) BULGAKOV (1888–1948). A member of the Moscow Art Theatre when it visited the USA in 1922–4, he remained in New York with his wife, Barbara. For the rest of his life, like so many *émigrés*, he capitalised on his past in the

Russian theatre to eke out an existence as actor (Provincetown Playhouse, Grand St Theatre), director (Yiddish Art Theatre) and teacher (Bulgakov School of Stage Art).

ROSE CAYLOR, wife of the American writer Ben Hecht, abridged and rewrote *Uncle Vanya* to make Chekhov more presentable to matinée goers. In her version, nothing goes unsaid.

LIVIU CIULEI (b. 1923), Rumanian director, designer and actor, who after running the Bulandra Theatre in Bucharest (1963–72), worked all over the world, running the Guthrie Theatre in Minneapolis (1980–6) and teaching at New York University. He returned to Rumania in 1990. A believer in retheatricalising the theatre, he promoted a syncretic style of staging, with the director as the *auteur*, melding all elements to create an eclectic realism.

ROBERTO CIULLI (b. 1934), Italian director, working chiefly in Germany. He founded the Theater an der Ruhr in Mülheim (1982) as a subsidised but free and socially engaged ensemble, dedicated to presenting the contemporary relevance of plays. He promotes the primacy of the actor over the dramatist, even though he chooses to stage highly literary drama.

HAROLD CLURMAN (1901–82), American director. After studying with Copeau in Paris, he co-founded the Group Theatre in New York (1931– 41), devoted to social progress and a Stanislavskian approach to ensemble acting. In 1966 he was appointed Director at the Lincoln Center Repertory Theatre. An admirer of French and Russian culture, Clurman was able to adapt his principles to the uses of the commercial Broadway stage.

ALLA DEMIDOVA (b. 1936), Russian actress, who trained with Lyubimov and was recruited by him into the Taganka. There she played leading parts in most of his productions: Elmire in *Tartuffe*, Gertrude in *Hamlet* and the title role in Tsvetaeva's *Phaedra*. She has an electrifying stage presence, exuding nervous energy. See Appendix 2.

OLEG EFREMOV/YEFREMOV (b. 1927), Russian actor and director. As co-founder of the Sovremennik (Contemporary) Theatre in Moscow in 1958, he was on the cutting edge of youthful idealism and a call for simplicity in acting. In 1970 he took over the moribund Moscow Art Theatre, where he tried to invigorate its traditions with greater contemporaneity. On his initiative, the Art Theatre was divided into two separate institutions (1987). Amongst many other productions of Chekhov's work, he directed *Uncle Vanya* for the MAT which visited the National Theatre, London, in September 1989. See Appendix 2.

ANATOLY EFROS (1925–87), Russian director, student of Maria Knebel. His productions of Radzinsky and Chekhov at the Lenkom Theatre, Moscow (1963–7) created a scandal; at the Malaya Bronnaya (1973–83) his inventive, improvisational treatment of classics and moderns were accepted more for their own values. He replaced Lyubimov at the Taganka (1984–7), a hopeless situation which led to a fatal heart attack. Amongst many other productions of Chekhov's work, he directed *The Seagull* at Lenin Komsomol Theatre,

Moscow, in 1966, and *The Cherry Orchard* at the Taganka Theatre, Moscow in 1975. See Appendix 2.

RICHARD EYRE (b. 1943), English director, whose work in Edinburgh and Nottingham won him a reputation as a champion of controversial new plays. For the National Theatre he developed successful musicals, and, on Peter Hall's retirement in 1986, he was appointed Artistic Director there. His regime led to the development of smaller units, often headed by adventurous younger talents, and to a more American flavour in the choice of repertoire. He directed *The Cherry Orchard* in a version by Trevor Griffiths at Nottingham Playhouse in 1977. See Appendix 2.

PAVEL GAIDEBUROV (1877–1960), Russian actor and director, a law student who went into the theatre to bring culture to the people. In 1905 he and his wife, the actress Skarskaya, founded the First Itinerant Dramatic Theatre, which took the best of the modern repertoire, including avant-garde Symbolist pieces, to the farthest reaches of the Empire. He was one of the first to eschew figurative scenery for simple draperies. After the Revolution, he continued his activities, organising kolkhoz theatres and other travelling troupes.

ANDRÉ GREGORY (b. *c.* 1930), a prime mover in the American theatrical avant-garde of the 1960s and early 1970s. His six-actor company, The Manhattan Project, offered psychedelic, cartoon-like, highly energised versions of Lewis Carroll, Beckett and Chekhov, praised for ingenuity and damned for infantilism. After many years as an actor, Gregory returned to directing with a deliberately unpolished *Uncle Vanya* which then became Louis Malle's film *Vanya on 42nd Street*. See Appendix 3.

TREVOR GRIFFITHS (b. 1935), English playwright, politically committed to a Gramsci-inspired socialist agenda, who admits to preferring television to theatre as a means of communicating with the working classes. His best play is probably *Comedians* (1975), which uses a group of stand-up comics as emblems of political action and inaction. He wrote a version of *The Cherry Orchard*, directed by Richard Eyre, at Nottingham Playhouse in 1977. See chapters 9, 10, 15 and Appendix 2.

JERZY GRZEGORZEWSKI (b. 1939), Polish director and scenographer, who worked at many important theatres, eventually running the Studio Theatre and Gallery in Warsaw. He has staged most of the great Polish playwrights, as well as works by Genet, Chekhov and Shakespeare. He is considered a 'Poet of the Stage' by his colleagues, creating images which compete with original text. He directed *The Seagull* at Warsaw Studio Theatre in 1993.

TYRONE GUTHRIE (1900–71), English director, whose wit, taste for action and manipulation of crowds breathed new life into Elizabethan drama at the Old Vic, Sadlers Wells and many other traditional houses. He pioneered the thrust stage at the Stratford Shakespeare Festival, Ontario (1953–7) and the Minneapolis Theatre (1963), inspiring the North American regional theatre movement. He directed Charles Laughton in *The Cherry Orchard* in 1933. See Appendix 2.

JED HARRIS (1900–79), American producer, notorious for his abuse of actors and his flair for commercial success. In the 1920s he made his fortune backing sharp-edged comic melodramas, *Broadway* (1926), *The Royal Family* (1927) and *The Front Page* (1928). Then, to confute his critics, he turned highbrow, producing *Uncle Vanya* (1930), *Our Town* (1938) and *The Heiress* (1947).

VASILY KACHALOV (Shverubovich, 1875–1948), Russian actor, who joined the Moscow Art Theatre in 1899. Although he began in such character roles as Julius Caesar and Baron Tusenbach in *Three Sisters*, his good looks and velvety voice turned him into a kind of matinée idol and attracted female fan clubs. He was the natural choice to play Hamlet, Brand and Chatsky in *Woe from Wit*. Later in life, he was popular as a platform reader. See Appendix 2.

EINO KALIMA (1882–1972), Finnish director, who became familiar with Stanislavski's work while a student in St Petersburg (1904–8). Directing in Swedish, Norwegian and Finnish with a prolific repertoire, he was instrumental in introducing Chekhov and psychological realism to the Scandinavian stage.

MANFRED KARGE (b. 1938). Beginning as an East German actor and playwright, he gained international fame as a director in collaboration (1963–83) with Matthias Langhoff. They ruthlessly modernised classics and reversed their value systems, their deliberate perversity sometimes reaching mythical proportions.

MARIYA/MARIA KNEBEL (1898–1985), Russian actress and inspiring teacher, trained at the Moscow Art Theatre Second Studio (1921). She began directing at the Art Theatre in 1935, becoming chief director at the Central Children's Theatre, Moscow, 1955–60. It is believed that Knebel preserved many of Stanislavsky's later ideas in a form unrevised by Soviet ideologues.

OLGA KNIPPER (1868–1959), Russian actress, who created the leading female roles in the Moscow Art Theatre productions of Chekhov's plays; she married Chekhov in 1901 and as his widow gained iconic status in the Soviet theatre. Praised for her delicacy and charm, she was eventually discounted by Stanislavsky, who disliked her resistance to his System and her tendency to oversweeten her roles. See Appendix 2.

THEODORE KOMISARJEVSKY/FYODOR KOMISSARZHEVSKY (1882–1954), Russian director and writer who promoted the idea of a synthetic theatre that would seek the appropriate style for each playwright. After emigrating to England in 1919, he naturalised many Modernist European theatrical innovations, even at the Shakespeare Memorial Theatre, Stratford, and popularised Chekhov by adapting him to the romantic taste of the average playgoer. He was both 'teacher' and husband to Peggy Ashcroft (1931–5) and directed her in *The Seagull* in which she played Nina, May 1936. See Appendix 2.

OTOMAR KREJČA (b. 1921), Czech director and actor. Prominent in the National Theatre, Prague, he began to experiment with his own ensemble and the scenographer Josef Svoboda at the Divadlo za Branou (Theatre Beyond the Gates, 1965–72). Out of favour with the Czech authorities, he worked throughout Europe, disseminating a cruel, unsentimental Chekhov. His favourite techniques involved making a collage of classic texts and keeping the whole company on stage during the performance. He returned to Prague in 1990. See Appendix 2.

JUTTA LAMPE (b. 1943), German actress, long associated with Peter Stein and the Berlin Schaubühne as his leading lady. Always a dynamic and versatile performer in such roles as Rosalind, Solveig and especially Titania in Botho Strauss' *The Park* (1984), she matured into a remarkably affecting Ranevskaya, Alcmene and Virginia Woolf's Orlando.

CHARLES LAUGHTON (1899–1962), English actor and director. After a distinguished career as a character actor on the West End stage, at the Old Vic and the Comédie Française, Laughton became a Hollywood star. This was insufficient to feed his considerable intellect, and he worked with Brecht on the world première of *Galileo* (1947), eventually returning to the stage to play Undershaft, Lear and Bottom. He played Lopakhin in Tyrone Guthrie's 1933 production of *The Cherry Orchard*, Old Vic, London. See Appendix 2.

ELIZABETH LECOMPTE (b. 1944), artistic director from 1979 of the American experimental collective The Wooster Group, housed in New York's Performing Garage. In collaboration, she and the members of the company compose plays heavily dependent on video technology and the wilful collision of various media. Texts are fragmented to create a theatre reality restructuring the relation between performer and audience.

EVA LE GALLIENNE (1899–1991), American actress and director. An admirer of Bernhardt, Duse and Komissarzhevskaya, she tried to introduce a serious literary theatre to the USA, founding the Civic Repertory in 1926. Against great economic odds, she managed to attract audiences to respectable if unimaginative stagings of Chekhov, Molnar, Ibsen, Hauptmann and Schiller, but failed to create a permanent company. See Appendix 2.

BORIS LIVANOV (1904–72), Russian actor and director, a gifted leading man at the Moscow Art Theatre, with a penchant for comic character roles; in Nemirovich-Danchenko's *Three Sisters* (1940) his interpretation of Solyony as a flamboyant figure of doom became the standard reading. He was one of the first Soviet directors to try and stage Dostoevsky's novels. See Appendix 2.

ANDREY LOBANOV (1900–59), Soviet director, whose earliest work, staged at Simonov's Theatre Studio in Moscow, displayed a coarse application of Marxism to the classics. Later, he became a straightforward reliable exponent of Socialist Realism, directing the first production of Arbuzov's *Tanya* (1939).

YURY LYUBIMOV/LIUBIMOV (b. 1917), Russian actor and director, the guiding genius of the Taganka Theatre in Moscow. Something of a licensed rebel, he galvanised audiences in the 1970s with productions usually based on non-dramatic material and featuring stunning visual metaphors: *Ten Days That Shook the World*, *Hamlet* with the chansonnier Vysotsky in the lead, and *The Master and Margarita*. Forced into exile, he repeated many of his successes in European and American cities, but after his return to Russia in 1992 he seemed out of touch with a post-glasnost world.

LOUIS MALLE (b. 1932), French film-maker. First associated with the New Wave of the 1960s, his films were distinguished by fantasy, breathless comedy (*Zazie dans le Metro*, 1960: *Viva Maria*, 1965) and an interest in juvenile sexuality (*Le Souffle au Coeur*, 1970; *Pretty Baby*, 1978). His experiments with André Gregory, the two-handed *My Dinner with André* and *Vanya on 42nd Street*, make a virtue of restrained simplicity. See chapter 13 and Appendix 3.

DAVID MAMET (b. 1947), American playwright and director, co-founder of the St Nicholas Theatre, Chicago, where he began his career. *American Buffalo* (1975) propelled him to the first rank of dramatists, and his subsequent work has been characterised by staccato, jargon-filled dialogue, psychological violence, power games and an obsession with macho one-up-manship. He adapted *Uncle Vanya* for film in 1990, directed by Gregory Mosher. See chapter 13 and Appendix 3.

VSEVOLOD MEYERHOLD (1874–1940), Russian director and actor. Apprenticed at the Moscow Art Theatre, before the Revolution Meyerhold was known for his experiments in hieratic Symbolist staging and *commedia dell'arte* techniques as well as sumptuous mountings of classical drama and opera. After the Revolution, he promoted a proletarian theatre, with constructivist, functional scenery, acting based on biomechanics, and texts fragmented into abstractions. He created 33 *Swoons* in 1935 consisting of *The Proposal, The Bear* and *Jubilee (The Anniversary)*. See Appendix 2.

JONATHAN MILLER (b. 1934), English director and physician who came to prominence as a member of the satirical revue *Beyond the Fringe*. Working usually with subsidised companies, both dramatic and operatic, he prefers unconventional readings and sharply detailed characterisations. Director of the Old Vic from 1987–9, his ambitious programme failed commercially, and he has freelanced ever since. He directed *The Seagull* at Nottingham Playhouse in 1968, and Chichester Festival Theatre in 1973; *Three Sisters*, Yvonne Arnaud Theatre, Guildford, 1976, and *The Cherry Orchard*. See Appendix 2.

PAVEL MOCHALOV (1800–45), Russian actor, known as the Russian Kean, because of his erratically impassioned performances. As leading man of the Moscow Maly (Little) Theatre, he was worshipped by the merchant class, but sniffed at by the cognoscenti for his lack of physical and emotional control.

EIMUNTAS NEKROSIUS (b. 1952), founder of the Lithuanian Youth Dramatic Theatre (1985), noted for his rock musicals. He became acclaimed when his work was seen throughout the USSR in the 1980s, and the world tour of his *Uncle Vanya* was a triumph. His untrammelled imagination and the visual polyphony of his stage metaphors contribute to the exhilaration of his productions.

VLADIMIR NEMIROVICH-DANCHENKO (1850–1943), Russian director and playwright. Co-founder of the Moscow Art Theatre (1896), he was more politically engaged and artistically advanced than his partner Stanislavsky. He introduced Chekhov to the Art Theatre, created a brilliantly simple staging for a two-part

Brothers Karamazov (1910), and cannily navigated the theatre through the shoals of Soviet bureaucracy. See Appendix 2.

LAURENCE OLIVIER (1907–89), English actor and director, long considered the paragon of Shakespearean players, the Hamlet of the 1940s, but also the definitive Macbeth, Coriolanus, Oedipus, Titus Andronicus and Archie Rice in *The Entertainer*. Director of the Chichester Festival (1962–5) and of the National Theatre, London (1962–5), Olivier endowed his characterisations with polished technique, physical agility and sardonic humour. He played Vanya in W. G. Fay's 1927 production, Birmingham Repertory Production; he directed *The Proposal* at the Old Vic, London, 1949; in 1963 he directed *Uncle Vanya*, Chichester, 1962, and then at the National Theatre, 1968, where he played Astrov to Michael Redgrave's Vanya. He directed *Three Sisters* at the National Theatre in 1967, designed by Svoboda. See Appendices 2 and 3.

TATIANA PAVLOWA (1893–1975), Russian actress and director, who had studied with Stanislavsky, but during the Russian Civil War emigrated to Italy, where in 1921 she began her own troupe. Engaging such compatriots as Nikolai Evreinov and Peter Sharoff, she introduced Italians to Ostrovsky (her favourite), Chekhov, Gorky and Tolstoy.

GEORGES PITOËFF (Georgy Pitoev, 1884–1939). Georgian-born director, expatriated to Paris in 1922, where he and his wife Ludmilla expanded the French repertory with minimalist productions of Chekhov, Pirandello, Shakespeare and Shaw. Believing in the artist as visionary, Pitoëff, whom Cocteau called a saint of the theatre, imbued his performances with a luminous mysticism. See Appendix 2.

NIKOS PSACHAROPOULOS (1928–89), Greek-born American director. A drama professor at Yale University, he founded the Williamstown (Mass.) Theatre in 1955, as a place where established actors could perform the classics during the summer season. The annual recurrence enabled Psacharopoulos, whose style ran to the emotional, to stage more Chekhov productions than any other North American director.

RALPH RICHARDSON (1902–83), English actor, who won fame as the bewildered protagonist of J. B. Priestley's enigmatic dramas. With Olivier, he co-managed the Old Vic, London (1944–7), when he was seen as the superb exponent of Cyrano, Falstaff and Peer Gynt. He played Vershinin in *Three Sisters* in 1951, Aldwych Theatre, London, directed by Peter Ashmore. He ripened into an exceptionally mellow performer of Pinter, Osborne and Storey. See Appendix 2.

IVAN ROSTOVSTEV/ROSTOVSKY (1873–1947), Russian director widely experienced on provincial stages. After the Revolution, he organised the first Moscow Workers' Theatre and similar enterprises throughout the USSR, settling eventually in Yaroslavl. One of the most important Soviet directors outside the big cities, he was distinguished for his productions of Ostrovsky, Chekhov and Gorky, which sedulously reproduced life before the Revolution.

MICHEL SAINT-DENIS (1897–1971), French actor, director and pedagogue. First working for his uncle Jacques Copeau, he founded the Compagnie des Quinze

(1930–1), then moved to England, where he ran the Theatre School at the Old Vic (1946–52). His teaching became widely disseminated when he directed the Centre National Dramatique de L'Est Strasbourg and then the Juilliard School in New York. Saint-Denis' main concerns were with the actor's virtuosity and the discovery of style, the appropriate conduit for the play's form and content. He directed Peggy Ashcroft as Irina in a 1938 production of *Three Sisters* and as Ranevskaya in *The Cherry Orchard* in 1961. See Appendix 2.

ANDREI SERBAN (Andrej Serban, b. 1943), Rumanian director, a student of Ciulei and an assistant of Brook, he made his name in the Off-Broadway theatre of New York (1969–89), before returning to Rumania in 1990. His syncretic approach downplayed the lexical meaning of the dialogue in an attempt to transform the spoken word into emotional music. Consequently, his most recent work has been in opera. See Appendix 2 and p. 143.

ATHENE SEYLER (1899–1990), English actress, witty and sprightly, a specialist in high comedy. Over the course of a long career (1909–66) she played most of the leading roles in Shakespearean, Restoration and eighteenth-century comedy, finishing up with *Arsenic and Old Lace*. Her handbook, *The Craft of Comedy* (1944), is still a useful guide to actors. She played Ranevskaya in Tyrone Guthrie's *The Cherry Orchard* at the Old Vic, London, 1933 and again in 1941. See Appendix 2.

ADOLF SHAPIRO (b. 1939), Ukrainian-Jewish director. Taking over the artistic management of the State Youth Theatre of Riga in 1964, he became the youngest chief director in the Soviet Union. Strongly influenced by Vakhtangov and Italian Neo-Realist films, the teachings of Maria Knebel and Michael Chekhov, he tried to provide 'complicated theatre for the young', expressing life's contradictions and a complex inner life. He also introduced Brecht to the Latvian stage. He directed *The Cherry Orchard* at the Bolshoy Dramatic Theatre, St Petersburg in 1992.

PETER SHAROFF (Pyotr Sharov, 1886–1969), Russian *émigré* director. After working as an actor with Stanislavsky and Meyerhold, he became a member of the expatriate Prague Group of the Moscow Art Theatre. His productions of Chekhov, Gogol and Ostrovsky perpetuated Art Theatre traditions of discipline and ensemble in Italy (where he became a citizen), West Germany, Austria and Holland.

SERGEY SOLYVOV, a former colleague of Yury Lyubimov, who wrested the Taganka Theatre away from him in the period following the collapse of the Soviet Union. For *nouveau riche* audiences, he staged grossly luxurious productions, claiming he was humanising Chekhov.

KONSTANTIN STANISLAVSKY (Alekseyev, 1863–1938), Russian actor and director, co-founder of the Moscow Art Theatre (1896). As a director, he stressed subtext, ensemble playing and the creation of atmosphere; this approach has proved successful in staging Chekhov, but not Shakespeare and Molière. Seeking a source of inspiration for the actor that would prevent tension and lead to enhanced creativity, he was constantly formulating a System, which at first relied on emotional memory, but later emphasised physical action. See Appendix 2.

PETER STEIN (b. 1937), German director, co-founder of the collective Schaubühne am Halleschen Ufer in East Berlin (1970), which became one of the great theatres of Europe. Stein insisted on his company researching the socio-historical milieu of every play, but in time moved away from political activism towards a more aesthetic historicised style. His justification to his critic is that remembering is a political act. He directed *Three Sisters* at Berlin Schaubühne in 1984 and *The Cherry Orchard*, which played at the International Chekhov Festival, Moscow, in 1992. See Appendix 2.

LEE STRASBERG (1901–82), Galician-born American director and actor, leading apostle of Stanislavsky in the US. After studying with Boleslavski, he co-founded the idealistic Group Theatre (1931) and in 1949 began to teach at the Actors Studio, New York. More important as a pedagogue than as a director, he inspired several generations of actors with his highly individualized version of the Method, exhorting them to find their personal instrument. See Appendix 2.

GIORGIO STREHLER (1921–97), Italian director, co-founder of the Piccolo Teatro di Milano (1947) and artistic director of the Théâtre d'Europe, Paris (1982–9). A socially committed Brechtian, he was undogmatic in style, expert at finding exquisite visual metaphors in his productions of Goldoni, Shakespeare and Chekhov. A strain of melancholy ran through his best work, deriving from frustration at the inability to express all of life's multiplicity. See Appendix 2.

ROBERT STURUA (b. 1938), Georgian director, who infused world classics with the temperament and colour of Caucasian folklore. The underlying principle of his productions is rhythm, and the staging is almost choreographed to a musical soundtrack. He is best known in the West for his terrifyingly totalitarian *Richard III* (1979). See Appendix 2.

TADASHI SUZUKI (b. 1939), Japanese director, noted for his intercultural amalgams of play and production style. Working with texts by Shakespeare, Chekhov and Greek tragic poets, he borrows devices from Noh and Kabuki and themes from pop and classical music to provoke dissonance in reception. In 1982 he founded the Toga Festival to showcase his new work and advance his actor-training method. He directed both *The Cherry Orchard* and *Three Sisters* in Toga in 1986.

JOSEF SVOBODA (b. 1920), Czech scenographer, long associated with Otomar Krejča at the Prague National Theatre and the Divadlo za Branou, though from 1963 he worked outside Czechoslovakia. Considering scenography as both a participant in and a function of the dramatic action, he prefers architectonic spaces, complicated lighting and unusual building materials to express the play and implement the actors' movement. He designed Olivier's *Three Sisters* at the National Theatre, London, in 1967. See Appendices 2 and 4, and chapter 12.

ALEKSANDER TAIROV (Kornblit, 1885–1950), Russian director. Leader of the Kamerny (Chamber) Theatre, Moscow (1914–49), he insisted on the primacy of the actor's physicality and musical principles in staging. His repertoire was eclectic, preferring non-Russian authors: Kalidasa, Wilde, Scribe, Racine, Claudel, O'Neill, Shaw; his highly stylised productions usually featured his wife, Alisa Koonen. He directed *The Seagull* at the Kamerny Theatre, Moscow, 1944–5. See Appendix 2.

GEORGY (GEORGI) TOVSTONOGOV (1913–89), Russian director, the imposing head of the Bolshoi Dramatic Theatre (BDT), Leningrad from 1956. Without abandoning realism, he found a way to synthesise Stanislavsky, Meyerhold and Brecht, imbuing the classics with a lush lyricism and ensemble playing. Adept at both the tragic and grotesque, he rediscovered Dostoevsky, Gorky and Chekhov for post-war Soviet audiences. See Appendix 2.

HIROWATARI TSANETOSHI, Japanese director, whose Tokyo Engeki ensemble toured a curiously hybrid *Seagull* to Russia in 1993. It respectfully sought to engraft deeply rooted national images on to a venerated foreign author.

EVGENY/YEVGENY VAKHTANGOV (1883–1923), Russian actor and director; studied with Stanislavsky but preferred fantastic realism, a sharply etched grotesquerie grounded in genuine emotion. His masterpieces were Strindberg's *Erik XIV* with Michael Chekhov (1921), Anski's *The Dybbuk* staged in Hebrew with the Habima Theatre, and Gozzi's *Princess Turandot*, a triumph of modernised *commedia dell'arte* (both 1922). He directed Chekhov's *The Wedding* in 1921. See Appendix 2.

ANTOINE VITEZ (1930–90), French director, acting teacher, poet, a student of Russian capable of making his own translations. He began as a Brechtian apostle of people's theatre but, as director of the Théâtre National de Chaillot (1981–8) and the Comédie Française (1988–90), developed a more elitist idea of mystical artificiality. Inspired by postmodern notions of disruption and montage, he often encouraged actors to play against the text, and offered interpretations of coruscating if opaque intellectuality. He directed *The Seagull* at the Théâtre National de Chaillot in 1984. See Appendix 2.

GENRIETTA (HENRIETTA) YANOVSKAYA (b. 1941), Russian director, who works in close collaboration with her husband Kama Ginkas. A student of Tovstonogov, she is housed in the Moscow Art Theatre of the Young Spectator, where her stylised approach satirised traditional Soviet attitudes. An Absurdist adaptation (1987) of Bulgakov's *Heart of a Dog* (1925) best displayed her penchant for mordant and expressive stage pictures.

PETER ZADEK (b. 1926), German director educated in England. Considered an *enfant terrible*, Zadek shocked audiences at the many West German state theatres he ran with his unconventional, provocative stagings. Telling the story is his motto, but in the process he tends to displace the emphasis. He directed *The Cherry Orchard* at Stuttgart Staatstheater in 1968 and *The Seagull* in Bochum in 1973. His 1996 Vienna *Cherry Orchard* became a play about four women in pursuit of happiness.

3

CHEKHOV THE WRITER

16

DONALD RAYFIELD

Chekhov's stories and the plays

Even to those who loathed Chekhov's plays, his unorthodox drama was marked by the techniques of a short-story writer who refused to limit his imagination to the confines of the stage or meet its demands for intrigue, denouement, climax, let alone recognise its genres of comedy and tragedy. An all-controlling author-narrator refused to get off the stage. In November 1889 the actor-manager Lensky told Chekhov after the rejection of *The Wood Demon* by the Imperial Theatre Committee not to write plays: 'I'll say one thing: write long stories. Your attitude to the stage and to dramatic form is too contemptuous, you respect them too little to write a drama. This form is more difficult than narrative form, but you, forgive me, have been too spoiled by success to study dramatic form properly . . . or to come to love it.'[1]

The history of Russian drama is made, however, of fools who rushed in where angels feared to tread and forced actors and audience to take from the stage what was previously found in lyrics or in novels. Chekhov was at times actively hostile to the theatre (which he had described as a beer-garden and its denizens as 'Machiavellis in skirts'). Only when Nemirovich-Danchenko and Stanislavsky formed the Moscow Art Theatre, and showed the same desire to repress actors' egoism and clichés and the same refusal to let existing stagecraft confine drama, could Chekhov use on drama the techniques with which he had revolutionised short stories. Understatement, ambiguity, inconsequentiality make the Chekhovian short story: it points to, but refuses to open the cupboard where the skeleton is concealed; it peters out.

Many scenes typical of the Chekhovian short story are fundamental to his plays: for instance, the non-proposal, when a couple are left alone in a garden or a room and fail to agree, is typical: we find it in Act Two of *Uncle Vania* and Act Four of *The Cherry Orchard* in a form recognisable from 'Verochka' of 1887 to 'Ionych' of 1899. The structure of his prose, from hopeful spring to despairing autumn, is applied to drama. Off-stage noises – the night-watchman banging a rail – that punctuate *Uncle Vania* are found in stories such as 'My Life'. The smell of fish wafts across the stage at the end of Act Three in *The Cherry Orchard* just as it punctuates the conversation of the hero of 'The Lady with the Little Dog'. Moonlight changes the mood of *The Cherry Orchard* as it does that of 'Ionych' or 'The Bishop'.

There are also differences so regular between the plays and the stories that they imply a deliberate link. For instance the doctor, with the exception of the eponymous hero in 'Ionych', is a martyred hero in Chekhov's prose. In each successive play (excepting *The Wood Demon*), however, the doctor becomes more clownish, more uncaring. In both narrative prose and drama the doctor is god, but the divinity of the Professor of Medicine in 'A Dreary Story' belongs to a different pantheon than the god represented by Doctor Chebutykin. They are united only in their inability to help.

There are, however, concessions to the stage in Chekhov's transition from prose to drama. In all the plays but *The Cherry Orchard* (although it sports both rifle and revolver) a gunshot is a crucial event. Guns rarely fire in Chekhov's prose, and death comes more insidiously; for the plays the instrument of death (even if it misses its target) is dramatically graphic. Likewise, a main motor of action in comedy, the servants who exceed their role, is rarely found in Chekhov's prose, but is the key to the comedy of even serious drama, like *Three Sisters*.

Nevertheless, Chekhov's plays can best be understood through the short stories whose characters, situations, techniques and even phrases they recycle. This association appears in the first of Chekhov's major plays to be staged, *Ivanov*, a play written to a challenge from a theatre director, rather than nurtured by Chekhov's own work.

Our understanding of *Ivanov* gains from placing it with Chekhov's 'Jewish' stories of the mid-1880s, from 'The Slough' (where a Jewish moneylender swindles and seduces her Russian creditors) to 'Tumbleweed' (1887) where the Jewish hero, converted to Christianity, is a crippled wanderer. In the late 1880s, when pogroms first shook Russia and measures to enforce the 'pale of settlement' in Moscow were underway, *Ivanov* was, like several Chekhov stories, a counter-attack on antisemitism. Like 'Tumbleweed', it deals with the baptised Jew: Sarra-Anna, like the wandering Aleksandr in that story, is, as a baptised Jew, in the same gulf as the 'doctored horse and pardoned thief',[2] cut off from her family, and infected with tuberculosis. The play's sympathy for the Jewish victim is a counterblast to the anti-Semitic letters Chekhov was then receiving from Suvorin's son Alexey Alexeyevich, who saw Jews in Russia as 'five million barrels of dynamite under the Kremlin',[3] as a sexual and financial threat to the nation. If such stories as 'The Slough' contributed to that view of the Jew, then *Ivanov* was an act of contrition, for the Jew is seen as victim, not oppressor. The sensitivities of Russian audiences show in the reactions reported from performances in the provinces, where spectators yelled out, 'Jew girl, get what's coming to you.'[4]

Unlike *Ivanov*, *The Wood Demon* was not commissioned by a theatre, and its material, as well as the circumstances of its composition, show Chekhov vacillating between novel and drama. Initially a collaboration with Alexey Suvorin, Chekhov's friend and publisher, it is laden with biographical material (from the Suvorin family and from the Lintvariovs, with whom the Chekhovs were spending the summer of 1888). Common biographical sources link this play to stories written at that period (notably 'A Dreary Story'), just as common sources link *The Seagull* to the story 'Ariadna'.

The Wood Demon is organically linked with stories, already written or being composed, that stem from Chekhov's journey in 1887 to Kharkov and Taganrog. Two groups of story relate to *The Wood Demon*. Firstly, stories that Chekhov wrote after his first return to the steppes and woods of his childhood – 'Panpipes', 'Fortune', and 'Steppe' – are a valedictory celebration of nature, irreversibly destroyed by human myopia and greed. The 'wood demon', a man who frantically saves forests and repairs the ecology, both natural and human, reflects the author dismayed by the disappearance of a childhood idyll. The wood demon's speeches reflect the authorial persona of the stories of 1887 and 1888. The other stories relevant to *The Wood Demon* are stories of alienation: notably 'A Dreary Story'. Chekhov worked on 'A Dreary Story' at the same time as *The Wood Demon*. The tragic first-person story and the melodramatic, idyllic comedy share, despite divergent genres and moods, both protagonist, an elderly professor tormenting himself and his family, and many scenes and images.

The cult of nature in *The Wood Demon* was original in drama: it is the world's first 'green' play. Chekhov raised his conservationist's message from his stories where the narrator cites the laments of simple countrymen and here, in the play, made it the arguments of educated men. In 'Panpipes' the hero complains, 'They are cutting the forests, and they are burning and drying up and nothing new grows. Whatever does grow is cut down straight away; it sprouts today and tomorrow before you can blink people have felled it.'[5] This is lifted into the Wood Demon's plea to Serebriakov: 'Don't do it . . . To fell a thousand trees, to destroy them for the sake of two or three thousand roubles . . . so that posterity will curse our barbarity!'[6] The play takes up themes from Russia's agricultural and horticultural journals, the threat of deforestation and consequent degeneration in human life. The message of *The Wood Demon*, however clumsy, is that the destruction of the environment and of people's lives by selfishness are closely linked processes.

When in autumn 1896 Chekhov, by miraculous surgery, extracted *Uncle Vania* from the debris of *The Wood Demon* he reinforced the play's links with the earlier stories. We have the motif of greyness standing for stifling provinciality that we are to find in stories of the 1890s. In Act Three of the play Elena bursts out: 'instead of human beings grey spots wander about, you hear only trivialities, when they only know that they eat, drink, sleep'. The colour grey typifies the closed world of the Chekhovian heroine: Elena's complaint anticipates the despair of the Lady with the Little Dog in the story of that name, and explains (as in the story) her susceptibility to the cynical enchanter.

For Astrov's conservation speech Chekhov strengthened the motifs of the Wood Demon (then called Dr Khrushchiov) and returned to his stories of late 1887. Specific phrases are to be found in 'Panpipes'. The narrative in this story begins with the Wood Demon's motif of the young birch tree; then the ranch-manager Meliton complains that over forty years the birds have been dying out, that once they had been more than the eye could take in (*vidimo-nevidimo*) – exactly the same flocks of birds *vidimo-nevidimo* that Astrov cites. Meliton ends with the same message lamenting destruction: compare his 'Whatever grows, they hack it down, so without end until nothing more is left' to Astrov's 'A frozen hungry sick human being . . . destroys everything, not thinking of the morrow. Almost everything is now destroyed.'

In recycling earlier story material, Chekhov raises dialogue from narrative to drama, and language from peasant to intellectual register: he talks of 'degeneration', of 'struggle for existence', a neo-Darwinian vocabulary with which Chekhov had endowed his Darwinist von Koren in 'The Duel' (1891). The battle between activist Astrov and quietist Uncle Vania has many phases that stem from the conflict, also between the outlooks of science and of art, between von Koren and Laevsky in that story. Another new factor in *Uncle Vania* is that we now have a geographical co-ordinate: the Serebriakovs have decided to flee to Kharkov, a town which also figures at the end of 'A Dreary Story' where it typifies the squalor in which the disillusioned professor faces up to his imminent death.

The Seagull, however, though written before the making of *Uncle Vania*, is the first completely Chekhovian play: it owes nothing to the influence of others – of Korsh or Suvorin – nor to considerations of performance. In the making of *The Seagull* none of Chekhov's actor or theatre-director friends had even the limited say which Davydov had in the shaping of *Ivanov* or

Svobodin in the birth pangs of *The Wood Demon*. The making of *The Seagull* shows a story writer reckless of the demands of another medium, confronting the incomprehension of actor and audience.

The Seagull is even more intimate than many stories of the first half of the 1890s, for it not only reproduces phrases, situations and characters of Chekhov's friends and associates, but, uniquely in the author's work, satirises himself. Even more than the stories 'The Grasshopper' or 'Ariadna', *The Seagull* incorporates, recognisably for those who were involved and for their intimates, many persons and situations in Chekhov's own private life. Despite the warning Chekhov had received from Lika Mizinova after publishing 'The Grasshopper', that he did not appreciate what pain he caused by transposing past relationships into art, Chekhov went further. His intense love life of the winter of 1893–4, the sufferings of Lika Mizinova, pregnant in exile, the relationship with Potapenko, his fellow writer (and lover of Mizinova), the attentions of other women, notably Lidia Avilova, even the past of the Suvorin household (where a son committed suicide in circumstances like Treplev's) were publicly exhibited. Not only in the writing, but in the production, *The Seagull* was an instrument for distancing others, as had 'Ariadna' in the previous year. As a letter to friends, *The Seagull* differs from the intimate stories only in that those who provided the material for fiction were to be confronted with that fiction not individually and in private, in their homes, but in public, together, in the auditorium. The difference between drama and narrative prose is in both text and reception.

The parallels which the text of *The Seagull* offers with Chekhov's own writing are well known. Treplev in an envious monologue complains that Trigorin has a set of tricks which make his writing easy: 'He has the neck of a broken bottle shining on a weir and the dark shadow of a mill-wheel – and there you have a moonlit night' – a passage from Chekhov's 'Wolf' of 1886. In January 1896, Lidia Avilova gave Chekhov a medal inscribed with page and line numbers from his last book: Chekhov consulted the book and found the lines in his 'Neighbours' of 1891, 'If you should need my life, come and take it.' He gave that line to Trigorin's book, *Days and Nights*, to which Nina refers on a medallion, giving page and line numbers. Chekhov lent Avilova's medal to the actress Komissarzhevskaia for the Petersburg production. There are parallels too with Chekhov's own letters: Trigorin's complaint to Nina about his life being a compulsive process, 'I must write, I must write, I must write', repeats word-for-word phrases of a letter from Chekhov to Mizinova in 1894.

It is not just auto-reference that links *The Seagull* to Chekhov's prose. Its philosophical ventures echo Chekhov the narrator. The passing of human life over future eras into a lonely battle between good and evil, the development of Treplev's play-within-a-play from a catalogue of creatures to a cosmic vision of death reminds us of passages in 'Panpipes' of 1887 or Ragin's musings in 'Ward No. 6'. It will develop into the satanic noises and lights of the story 'An Incident in Practice'. The effects of Konstantin's play, the horn, the sulphur and the glowing red eyes, are effects from Chekhov's prose. They recall the panpipes of 1887 and anticipate the devil's eyes in 'An Incident in Practice'.

In literary allusion, too, *The Seagull* is strikingly intertextual. Most prominent of all is Maupassant. Maupassant's stories are reflected throughout Chekhov's development. The put-upon prostitute of 'Boule de Suif' is found in early pieces such as 'The Chorus Girl' or 'A Man Friend'; Maupassant the ardent fisherman is reflected in Chekhov's stories (e.g. 'The Burbot'); Maupassant's melodramatic story of the destructive supernatural force 'Le Horla' echoed in 'The Black Monk'. Maupassant is singled out for praise anonymously in 'A Dreary Story', where the Professor of Medicine prefers 'French writers' to inhibited Russian contemporaries. In 'A Woman's Kingdom' Maupassant is praised with extravagance that verges on satire as a 'locomotive that runs you over'. The very opening lines of *The Seagull* continue this tribute, for the exchange, 'Why do you wear black' – 'I'm in mourning for my life', is distilled Maupassant's *Bel-Ami*. In Act One Treplev compares his horror of vulgarity with Maupassant's panic attack at the sight of the Eiffel Tower. Act Two quotes Maupassant's travel writings *Sur l'eau*, while the plot line of a young woman seduced and abandoned by an older man, recaptured by an older woman, follows a Maupassant pattern. *The Seagull*, more than reflecting Chekhov's prose, has a common source with it.

Similarly, Shakespeare's *Hamlet* saturates Chekhov's prose as much as it does *The Seagull*. Most of Chekhov's prose up to 1895 quotes and ponders *Hamlet*. Chekhov uses Hamlet's line of bewilderment, when faced with an actor merging with his role, 'What's Hecuba to him and he to Hecuba?' It is not just the Hamlet role of the Russian intellectual, torn between the state he hates and the people he stands above; it is Hamlet, bemused by art, tormented by sexuality, the lover of the sea, who is so close to Chekhov. The hero of 'Tumbleweed' and Laevsky in 'The Duel' are Hamlets. *Hamlet* is not quite purged in *The Seagull*; Lopakhin parodies it in *The Cherry Orchard*, but after *The Seagull* it disappears from Chekhov's late prose.

While the writer's predicament is not discussed anywhere in Chekhov's published work, apart from *The Seagull*, his prose reverts several times to the miseries of a provincial actor. The early work, such as 'A Means of Sobering Up' or 'The Wallet', treats the predicament grotesquely or farcically. In 'A Dreary Story', however, it is serious. Katia, the professor's ward, like Nina in *The Seagull*, returns, changed beyond recognition to meet again the man who is most fond of her. Her private life and her illusions about stardom are destroyed. Nina in *The Seagull* is less wrecked than Katia. Full of stamina, intoxicated by the joy of acting, as she travels from one provincial backwater to another, she is nevertheless as much a victim of the theatre as Katia in 'A Dreary Story'. The later prose also sees the provincial theatre as hell – whether the foyer of the opera in 'The Lady with the Little Dog' or the debut of Kleopatra, dumbstruck and pregnant, in 'My Life'.

In *The Seagull* Chekhov concludes a theme he had repeatedly turned to: the suicide, or suicidal protest, of the adolescent intellectual. It was broached as a possible continuation to the story of a boy, 'The Steppe'; it was first realised in 'Volodia', where Chekhov's final version adds a fatal revolver shot to the adolescent's initial protest against his mother's love life – a story which distressed Suvorin, whose son Volodia had committed suicide (following his mother's example), after his father had ignored the comedy he had just written. Konstantin Treplev's suicide was sufficiently like that of the real and fictional Volodia to upset Suvorin after watching the play's first performance. Suicide in *The Seagull* is a device to end a play, or at least a third act, as in *Platonov, Ivanov* or *The Wood Demon*. It is perhaps significant that after *The Seagull* Chekhov never uses suicide in the plots of his plays and in only one later story, 'On Official Business' does it even have secondary meaning.

The Seagull on 17 October 1896 flopped: Chekhov wrote no new play for nearly five years. Only after two triumphs at the Moscow Art Theatre, in 1898 and 1899, was Chekhov's confidence restored and the Moscow Art Theatre's pressure for a new play sufficiently strong. *Three Sisters* was composed in a different atmosphere: Chekhov no longer needed to take theatrical conventions by the horns. Nor does he use biographical material directly: if anything, *Three Sisters* anticipates, rather than reflects, Chekhov's own marriage and family conflicts. More important was the fact that his creative energy was now spent not in writing new work, but in selecting and revising all the former work that could be retrieved from periodicals to be republished, under a very stringent contract, by Adolf Marx in Petersburg. The positive effect was that Chekhov reviewed and recycled earlier themes, and *Three Sisters* shows the influence of prose excavated from the past, as well as anticipation of the few stories Chekhov was to write.

English elements construct *Three Sisters*. A biography of the Brontës which Chekhov had read in 1895 is one; so is *The Geisha*, an operetta by

Sidney Jones. The third English (or American element) was the music-hall song 'Tarara-boom-deay', which spread from America in 1891 to all Europe in countless variations. In English (and in French) its verses were sung by a louche schoolgirl ('Not too shy and not too bold, Just the sort for sport I'm told') while an enthusiastic male chorus sings 'Tarara-boom-deay'. In Chekhov's work the refrain became a euphemism for sexual intercourse: in Russian versions the text was sadder. The main verse might be the story of a man fallen into depravity and the chorus a bitter lament. The phrase 'Tarara-boom-deay' had already served Chekhov as a leitmotif in the story of 1893 'Big Volodia and Little Volodia', where little Volodia seduces the heroine (who is married to a Colonel) to this motif. Later the song was orchestrated as an artillery regimental march. Already, in Chekhov's mind it was associated with a military setting (which he had first used in 'The Kiss' of 1887) and with seduction. Undoubtedly, the officers of Chekhov's fictional battery in *Three Sisters*, as they leave the northern town where they have enchanted, and disenchanted, the three Prozorov sisters, march out to the tune of 'Tarara-boom-deay', the very song that Dr Chebutykin sings (as all Chekhovian males sing) to heighten the distress of the heroine to whose sexual liaison it alludes.

The only Chekhov play set in a town, *Three Sisters* uses Chekhov's provincial-town material. Kulygin, the Latin teacher, in his sycophancy, 'in case anything might happen', transposes Belikov in 'The Man in a Case'. The contrast between Natasha and the three sisters is the contrast between predator and prey that recurs in Chekhov's late prose, and continues on a more genteel level the rivalry of sisters-in-law so deadly in 'In the Ravine' of 1899. Even Natasha's green belt links her with the imagery of green that connotes death – the green dress and eyes of the killer Aksinia in 'In the Ravine', features which make her seem like a wolf in a sheep-fold. Natasha breeds her sisters-in-law room by room from the house; Aksinia does the same thing, despite her sterility, by scalding her sister-in-law's baby to death. Both Natasha and Aksinia destroy the household into which marriage has brought them, and leave the males on which the household once relied as helpless degenerates. Old Tsybukin and Chebutykin share more than the last syllables of their surnames: they end the story or the play in useless senility. Similarly, the son of the household, the policeman Anisim in 'In the Ravine', like Andrei the would-be professor in *Three Sisters*, is disgraced and sidelined. Like Startsev in 'Ionych', Andrei degenerates scene by scene, fatter and more ill-tempered as the bourgeoisie envelops him; like Chekhov's late heroines, the three sisters lose their accomplishments: Masha stops playing the piano, Irina forgets her Italian: school-teaching or marriage degrades the heroine.

Nature too is doomed in *Three Sisters* as in all Chekhov's late work. The avenue of firs and the maple, doomed in Act Four of *Three Sisters*, like the birches in Act One, give way to Natasha's flower-beds. This contrast of noble trees and ignoble flower-beds is found in 'The House with the Mezzanine' and the unfinished 'Disturbing the Balance'.

The ideological structure of *Three Sisters* reverts to stories from 'The Duel' to 'My Life'. The philosophising of Vershinin and Tuzenbakh takes over the arguments of N. and Lida in 'The House with the Mezzanine' and of Misail and Blagovo in 'My Life'. The same discussion between 'activist' and 'quietist', whether activity is needed to bring about the millennium, or whether some great possibility in the future will lead us there, makes the conversation of Vershinin and Tuzenbakh in front of the sisters a futile mating display just as the artist and Lida Volchaninova argue their politics only to possess the soul of the nubile, vulnerable Misius. The dichotomy of 'My Life' is strongly re-enacted in *Three Sisters*. Tuzenbakh's thirst for manual work, his 'dropping-out' from his barony and his army career, his slow-witted goodness repeat, tragically and absurdly, the process by which Misail seeks moral peace; Vershinin's affair with Masha and his desertion of her, his indifference to the present and speculations about the future are Blagovo's.

Much of *Three Sisters* was recycled into prose. Chekhov's last story, 'The Bride' (or, more accurately, 'The Fiancée') is set in the same northern town. It too has three women, though arranged vertically as grandmother, mother and daughter (not horizontally as three sisters), of which one tries to escape from a strangling relationship to the metropolis. Here too an unviable male called Andrei plays the violin as a hobby. Here too, the girl's mentor entreats her to run away 'without looking round' (*bez ogliadki*), using the same phrase and tone that Chebutykin gives, too late, to the trapped Andrei in *Three Sisters*.

'The Bride' is a bridge between Chekhov's last two plays. It gives to *The Cherry Orchard* as much as it takes from *Three Sisters*. The malleable heroine, Nadia, has the temperament of Masha in *Three Sisters* and the vulnerability of Ania in *The Cherry Orchard*. Her ragged-trousered philanthropist-mentor, Sasha, gives the same advice, spouts the same anarchism and is as pathetically dependent as Trofimov in *The Cherry Orchard*. Much *Cherry Orchard* material comes from 'The Bride': the escape from a family heritage, from a neurotic mother and a ruined garden; the heroine who listens to a tubercular intellectual denouncing 'stench, bedbugs, cockroaches? Just like twenty years ago, no change.' 'The Bride' ends ambiguously, not showing us any final scattering to the winds, but the vision of the future which enchants the heroine incorporates the same utopianism as Trofimov's.

This last play summarises all that Chekhov ever wrote. Cherry orchards go back to childhood memories of southern Russia before the deforestation of the 1880s. In 'The Steppe' (1888) the boy's first sights on leaving town prefigure two elements in *The Cherry Orchard*, the graveyard and the cherry trees:

> the cosy, green cemetery, walled in by cobblestones; you could see cheerful white crosses and headstones over the wall, they were hidden in the greenery of the cherry trees and in the distance they seemed like white spots. Egorushka recalled that when the cherries flowered, these spots of white merged with the cherry blossom and became a sea of white; and when the cherries ripened, the white headstones and crosses would be spattered with spots as scarlet as blood. All day and all night Egorushka's father and grandmother slept under those cherry trees behind the cemetery wall.[7]

The most famous effect of the play, the breaking string, has a history. The image occurs in the epilogue of Tolstoy's *War and Peace*, warning of revolt to come. Chekhov refers to it in his first play, and then in stories of the steppe. In Act Two of *The Cherry Orchard*, when Gaev is silenced by younger listeners, we hear the famous 'noise of the breaking string'. 'Suddenly there is a distant sound, as if from the sky: the sound of a breaking string – dying away, sad' (Act Two, *The Cherry Orchard*). This sound comes from Chekhov's stories of the steppe undermined by mine shafts and hidden cables. Gaev and Trofimov lose credibility, attributing the noise to a heron or an eagle-owl: Lopakhin shows his solidarity with the author by identifying the noise: 'Somewhere a long way off, in the mines, a winding cable has parted.'

'Fortune' has an old shepherd, like Firs, who remembers ominous noises, and the 'broken string' of *The Cherry Orchard*:

> In the quiet air, scattering over the steppe, a sound passed. Something in the distance groaned dreadfully, struck a stone and ran over the steppe, going 'Takh, takh, takh.' When the sound died away, the old man looked inquiringly at Pantelei, who was standing unmoved, motionless. 'It's a bucket that's broken away in the mine shafts,' said the younger man.[8]

'Tumbleweed' expands the significance of the broken cable.

> You've seen people being lowered into the seam itself. You remember, when the horse is got going and the wheel made to turn, then one bucket goes over the pulley into the seam and the other comes up? Well, I got into a bucket, I begin to go down and you can imagine, suddenly I hear 'trrr'. The chain has broken and I flew hell bound.[9]

The prose of 1887–8 is sometimes closer than the earlier plays to *The Cherry Orchard*. The theme of the nunnery for which Varia longs recalls the poetry of the monastery of Sviatye Gory of those earlier stories, just as Lopakhin's teasing her, as Hamlet teases Ophelia, is a device used in earlier works.

The primary source in Chekhov's prose for *The Cherry Orchard* is 'A Visit to Friends', which Chekhov wrote in Nice. Perhaps because he wrote it in France and had considerable annoyance over the proofs, Chekhov took a dislike to this piece, the only late story that he excluded from his *Collected Works*. Possibly, he was embarrassed by parallels between the characters and the Kiseliov family, now facing ruin, of Babkino; certainly, he re-used fundamental elements of the plot, speeches and settings in *The Cherry Orchard* five years later.

Readers have no grounds for regarding 'A Visit to Friends' as inferior work. The story takes up the theme of 'Verochka' of 1887. A loving, beautiful girl attracts the hero, yet he cannot find in him the response that the girl and the scene ought to arouse, and he flees. This theme is elaborated in 'Ionych' at the end of the year, and scenes of 'Ionych', especially the moonlit wait in a cemetery at night, follow on from 'A Visit to Friends', whose hero, the lawyer Podgorin, reluctantly accepts an invitation to stay with the Losevs. He knows they hope he will bail them from their financial mess by marrying Tatiana Loseva's sister, Nadezhda.

The Losevs' bankruptcy and the auction arranged that summer for their estate make the background less simple than that of 'Verochka', linking the story instead with the irresponsibility and doom that overhang Gaev and Ranevskaia's cherry orchard. Expected to give money and advice, Podgorin is inhibited, just as Lopakhin, the play implies, realises that by marrying Varia he will have to bail out the orchard's owners. In the story the mood of love is spoilt not only by this ill-concealed imminence of disaster; another guest, Varia, once close to Podgorin, casually recites poems she used to know. Quotation is common in all Chekhov's work; here the poetry is disturbing. Varia speaks Nekrasov's lines about the railway, for Nekrasov and Chekhov a double-edged symbol of linking and breaking, of progress and oppression:

> Straight is the track: the embankments are narrow,
> There are poles and rails and bridges,
> And by the sides, nothing but Russian bones?
> The Russian people have borne enough,
> They've borne this iron road as well –
> They'll bear the lot – and lay out for themselves
> A broad clear road with their chests . . .[10]

Nekrasov is just as disturbing in Act Two of *The Cherry Orchard*: a beggar, with his verses about 'your suffering brother', makes Ranevskaia spill her purse. With lines from Nekrasov, likewise, the marching workers of 'On Official Business', the oppressed of 'In the Ravine', burst into the gentry's nightmares. In 'A Visit to Friends' Podgorin cannot respond to the allurements of Nadezhda, just as Lopakhin is morally paralysed when shut into the nursery with Varia. There is a nocturnal scene in the garden, one of Chekhov's finest evocations of moonlight (like the moonlit end of Act Two of *The Cherry Orchard*) as Nadezhda waits. The black shadow of a statue contrasts with her white figure and creates an illusion of peace and melancholy. The birds – corncrakes, quail and cuckoo – make the same call to life as they do in 'Peasants' and 'In the Ravine'. But Podgorin feels only his 'inability to take' – the weakness of the Chekhovian hero. He longs for a woman who will fit in with the ideas of the Nekrasov poem, offering not love but 'new, high, rational forms of life', promising something of the dream-world 'on the eve of which we are perhaps now living and of which we sometimes have a premonition'. The dream of the future, which captivates Podgorin as it does Trofimov in *The Cherry Orchard*, blinds this hero as well to the present and makes him impotent. He is not saved by prescience of 'new forms'; he is damned by his 'inability to take'. Podgorin thus combines the caution of Lopakhin with the puritanical idealism of Trofimov.

Ranevskaia even achieves tragic grandeur when she echoes the words of the heroine of 'A Visit to Friends' by appealing to the memory of the dead, from her grandfather to her son. She declares to Trofimov: 'I was born here, my father and mother lived here, my grandfather? I love this house. Without the cherry orchard I can't make sense of my life.' Likewise, Tania Loseva declares to Podgorin: 'I swear to you by all that is sacred, by the happiness of my children, I can't live without Kuzminki! I was born here, this is my nest, and if they take it from me, I shan't survive, I'll die of despair.' And to this plea both males offer the same trite consolation of 'a new life'. Even more than Chekhov's other plays, *The Cherry Orchard* synthesises the predicaments of every story of loss and disillusion into one final black comedy, whose solution for a lost cause are the blows of the axe.

NOTES

The transliteration used is the British one, as used in *The Slavonic and East European Review*. The stories discussed are to be found in Hingley's *The Oxford Chekhov*, Wilks' four-volume collection for Penguin, and the revised translation of Constance Garnett's stories, by the author of this chapter. Details of these collections may be found in the Bibliography. See Appendix 1 for variations of translation and titles.

1 A. P. Chekhov, *Polnoe sobranie sochinenii i pisem* Moscow, 1974–87: *sochine-niia, Works* (henceforth: *Soch.*) XII, 385.
2 *Ivanov*, Act One, Scene IV (*Soch.* xii, 14).
3 See *Rossiiskaia gosudarstvennaia biblioteka: fond 331 opis' 59 item 71a–b* (letters from A. A. Suvorin to A. P. Chekhov), Autumn 1888, p. 21.
4 See *Perepiska A. P. Chekhova i O. L. Knipper* vol. I, Moscow, 1934, p. 211. Newspaper cutting attached to Chekhov's letter of 14 October 1900.
5 *Soch.* VI, 277.
6 *The Wood-Demon*, Act Three, Scene XII, (*Soch.* XII, 177).
7 *The Steppe*, ch. I (*Soch.* VII, 14).
8 *Soch.* VI, 215.
9 *Soch.* VI, 260.
10 *Soch.* X, 13. Quoted from Nekrasov's poem *Zheleznaia doroga*.

17

CYNTHIA MARSH

The stage representation of Chekhov's women

This is not the innocuous subject it may seem at first glance. Representation in art has a long and debated history; representation in the theatre is complex and is now being systematised by performance theory. Moreover, isolating women characters entails another specialised area of criticism. Feminist approaches to literature and the theatre have ensured closely argued views from both male and female critics, who have been made wary of gender-centred interests and judgements. I find myself in the position of a woman scholar writing about women. It is almost certain that I will fail to meet the expectations, whether negative or positive, of at least some sections of the readership of this book. I shall approach this topic wishing neither to engage with the heavily jargonised language used in performance theory, nor to assume a stance which is feminist or anti-feminist, but to acknowledge and to have learnt from each one.

In its essence, representation encompasses notions of mimesis (imitation of reality), comprehensiveness in relation to existing social norms, and formal issues. Did Chekhov's representation of his women characters conform with these existing norms? Did his representing process conform with existing theatrical convention? Or did he offer a radical alternative in both areas? The approach here rests on a concept of representation which covers the whole process from creation through to perception. In the representing process the creative part is separate from perception in that the agent of each is separate. The artist creates (and in so doing represents), the receiver perceives (and in so doing tests and completes the representation). The 'gap' which results from this division (or as the language of semiotics views it, the difference between *signifier* and *signified*), it is argued, ensures the endless variety of interpretation to which art is subject.[1] Did Chekhov utilise this 'gap' to mould audience perception?

The genre and period of his plays offer the major determining factor in an analysis of Chekhov's representation of his women characters. Chekhov's plays are generally regarded as realist with some naturalist influence. The latent implication of representation to be comprehensive of different social types is as important as mimesis of contemporary reality. We need, therefore, firstly to categorise the women characters to test the comprehensiveness of the representation; secondly, in response to our gender-driven theme, we need to examine how the determining characteristic of femaleness, sexuality, is dealt with in the plays. For our third point we turn to formal issues: realist/naturalist theatre at the end of the last century rested on a paradox which frequently drew audience attention to itself, the need to appear real within a patently artificial environment. We need, then, to explore how the women characters participate in this self-reflection, particularly examining that 'gap' in the representing process between creation and perception. Fourthly, we shall discuss, again for the reason that we are in a gender-determined category, whether there is significant function ascribed to gender in the representing process and whether we arrive at a different reading of the plays if we locate gender at the centre of our analysis. In conclusion, we shall consider whether the stage representation of the women characters was used by Chekhov as part of a radical agenda not so much to make a social point, as to change the form of his plays.

For present purposes we shall concentrate on Chekhov's four major plays: *The Seagull* (*Chaika*), *Uncle Vania* (*Diadia Vania*), *Three Sisters* (*Tri sestry*) and *The Cherry Orchard* (*Vishnevyi sad*). After a disastrous performance at the Aleksandrinskii Theatre in St Petersburg in 1896, the first was revived in the opening season of the Moscow Art Theatre (MAT) in 1898–9. The other three were all given premières at the MAT, and the final two were written for the MAT, often with specific performers in mind. These factors are important to the representational process for the particular slant they have on the *mise-en-scène*.[2] The MAT was admired for the thorough attempts at authenticity of its productions, based on extensive research into period, locale and manners for determining design and presentation. This artistic agenda has tended to affect perception not only of Chekhov's plays but also his approach to theatre. Their radical aspects have been masked.

The first step in our assessment of the women characters, then, is to establish what kind of categorisation is possible and appropriate. There is a wide range of age, and differing sociological types among the women in the four major plays. The youngest are Nina (*The Seagull*), Irina (*Three Sisters*), Ania and Duniasha (*The Cherry Orchard*), while the oldest are Mariia Vasil'evna and Marina (*Uncle Vania*) and Anfisa (*Three Sisters*), and there are two middle-aged heroines, Arkadina (*The Seagull*) and Ranevskaia (*The Cherry Orchard*). The other women are all in their twenties: Masha (*The Seagull*); Elena and Sonia (*Uncle Vania*); Olga Prozorov, Masha Kuligina and Natasha (*Three Sisters*) and Varia (*The Cherry Orchard*). Polina (*The Seagull*) and Charlotta (*The Cherry Orchard*) are of indeterminate age, except that Polina has a grown-up daughter. In terms of sociological type we have servants (Marina, Anfisa, arguably Varia) and some of these serving women are non-speaking parts (*The Seagull, Three Sisters*: Natasha's nursemaid and maid). There are estate holders (Arkadina, Ranevskaia, Sonia), daughters of the military (the three sisters), an estate manager's wife (Polina), provincial teachers' wives (Masha Medvedenko, Masha Kuligina) and a provincial miss (*baryshnia*, Natasha). Finally, there are teachers: Olga and then Irina, who aspires to become a teacher (*Three Sisters*, Act Four) whilst working as a clerk in a telegraph office (Irina – *Three Sisters*, Act Two), a governess (Charlotta), actresses (Arkadina, Nina) and a passing street entertainer (*Three Sisters*). These last five categories are the only ones who could be said to earn their living.

Chekhov's representation of women is problematised here since few of these sociological niches sum up the type of person involved. In most cases there is a discrepancy; the person is ill-suited to the job she holds or is thirsting to free herself from the relationship implied. Thus both Mashas hate their status as teachers' wives, and both Olga and Irina find the work of a teacher and telegraph office clerk, respectively, onerous and unfulfilling. Only the servants and actresses seem satisfied! There may be a deeper point to this general dissatisfaction which would raise a question of comparison: are the women more dissatisfied in general than the men? There are potent examples of male dissatisfaction in Konstantin (*The Seagull*), Vania (*Uncle Vania*), Tuzenbach and Chebutykin (*Three Sisters*), but notably it is the men who are driven to acts of violence against themselves in reaction to their situation.[3] The sociological picture appears to reflect the times in that women are more economically dependent than their male counterparts. Chekhov, however, asks his audience to admire the actresses and entertainers, the teachers, the governess and the telegraph clerk by making clear the fact that they are forced into low-paid or low-esteem occupations if they need or seek financial independence. In this view of women Chekhov denies existing norms of representation. We might also add that while age range seems comprehensive, the sociological range is restricted to the relatively well heeled, their associates and their servants.

With family roles, the representation appears as comprehensive as that of age and is not dictated by convention or prejudice. There are grandmothers, mothers, wives, aunts, nieces, sisters and daughters, granddaughters and stepmothers. There are faithful and unfaithful wives and mistresses, few good mothers but prominent bad ones – for example, Arkadina (*Seagull*), Mariia Vasil'evna (*Uncle Vania*) and Ranevskaia (*The Cherry Orchard*) – and grandmothers, substitute mothers, but notably no bad daughters. Good mothers tend to inhabit the off-stage world, or perhaps are idolised because of this – such as Sonia's mother, the three sisters' mother, Ranevskaia's mother or Iasha's mother (*The Cherry Orchard*); Natasha in *Three Sisters* seems a good mother but her solicitude usually has other motives. Fathers and husbands tend to be absent such as Konstantin's father, also Arkadina's husband; the sisters' father, Prozorov; Ania's father, also Ranevskaia's husband, and her Parisian lover (*The Cherry Orchard*); or remote – Sonia's father, Serebriakov, in *Uncle Vania*.

We have chosen next to consider female sexuality since the fact that most of the narratives are, at their simplest level, about love makes sexuality germane to the representation of the women. We find their sexuality treated with insight and exhibiting some difference from the expected norms. As we might suspect, however, of a male writer of this period in a genre as public as theatre, the sexuality of women is mostly explored through their relationships with men or through the absence of such relationships. There are a number of different levels of sexuality which seem to be determined by age: the range includes unawareness, unfulfilment, manipulation and negation. To begin with we find, as we might also expect from a late nineteenth-century writer, a range of innocents, or sexually unaware: Nina, Sonia, Irina, Olga, Ania and Varia. Each of them experiences trauma because of her gender but to a varying degree. The major difference from the expected norm comes in Chekhov's ironic treatment of the outcome of the trauma. Nina becomes the fallen woman (but regenerates herself); Sonia loves but is not loved in return; Irina is loved but does not love (and loses the person she might have loved, namely Tuzenbach); Olga would like to love (but becomes a headmistress); Ania loves (but is denied love and told she must be 'above love').[4] Varia is expected to love but lacks sexual attraction and fails to elicit a proposal. At the next level the women are sexually aware but their desires remain unfulfilled or are not recognised: Masha, Polina, Elena, Masha Kuligina and Duniasha. Both Mashas are married to the wrong person – both teachers, Polina to an estate manager. They each love another man but it is unclear whether they are all unfaithful. Duniasha loves Iasha in vain. Elena, perhaps the most perceptive and modern study, knows the power of her sexuality to attract and is angered that this seems to be the only way she is perceived by men. She refuses to be unfaithful, even though unhappily married.[5]

Beyond this level come the sexually active women who are clearly shown to manipulate others to achieve their desires: Arkadina, Natasha and

Ranevskaia. They are all mothers, but regarded as poor or at least not ideal mothers – particularly Natasha. Lovers are part of the normal course of events for these women. Arkadina and Natasha are condemned, but Ranevskaia is largely condoned. In her the norm is overturned as she is presented as a victim of her inability to control her sexuality: her lover has spent all her money, she loses the orchard to Lopakhin because he loves her and had possibly thought to control her by its purchase. She is amazed when she finds Trofimov impervious to her sexual advances.[6] She is undoubtedly placed at the centre of the play while she is in the grip of a dilemma. There is a clearly marked turning point, however, in the final act when she remarks that her health has improved and she is sleeping better. She is back in control, no longer a victim, and much less interesting to the audience.

Finally, there are the elderly, Mariia Vasil'evna, Marina and Anfisa, whose sexuality has been negated. Mariia Vasil'evna's sexuality is ironised in her unquestioning devotion to Serebriakov whom the play unmasks as a fraud; the other two are represented as in an apparently sexless old age.

The remaining woman character in this category is the most challenging, and provides the major variation from the predictability we foresaw about women characters' relationships. Charlotta is as uncertain of her sexuality as she is of her origins. She acts the siren with Pishchik in Act One of *The Cherry Orchard* but she is clearly unimpressed by his reaction, or she can masquerade as male by sporting hunting gear and gun in Act Two, and in the brief sequence in the ball scene of Act Three where she appears in male attire and undertakes a carnivalesque, male role as magician. She parodies motherhood by dumping her imaginary crying baby in Act Four, and by having apparently transferred her affections to her dog. There is no exploration of her feelings for other women. She is presented as remote from them as she is from the male characters.

The representation of female sexuality, then, is unconventional for the period. Our third point of discussion is whether the women characters contribute to and reference the artificiality of the theatrical exercise common in realist and naturalist theatre, given their range *and* the dramatic treatment of female sexuality. If they do, there is a direct point of contact with the formal aspects of the plays. One particular technique used by Chekhov invites his audience to challenge the characterisation. He sets up his characters in parallel. The implied counterpoint is often ironic and invites audience interrogation of the behaviour of the individuals involved. For example, among the women characters Arkadina is paired with Nina, as Masha is with Polina (*The Seagull*); Elena and Sonia form a parallel, as do Mariia Vasil'evna and Marina (*Uncle Vania*); Natasha is juxtaposed with Masha (and possibly, as we shall argue, with Olga and Irina); Anfisa is counterpointed to the dead sisters' mother (*Three Sisters*); Ranevskaia is paired with Duniasha, and Ania with Varia, leaving Charlotta out on a limb, though there are possibly implied comparisons with Ranevskaia (*The Cherry Orchard*). Such neat pairings also operate among the male characters, Konstantin and Trigorin (*The Seagull*), Astrov and Vania (*Uncle Vania*), for example. Grounds are usually provided to draw the paired characters together, and the irony stems from differences in personality and destiny. For example, Duniasha's ladylike behaviour is seen as a parody of Ranevskaia's, but her attempt to gain a lover fails miserably; or take Sonia and Elena, who are drawn together by age and location, but Elena defends herself from love while Sonia desperately seeks it. This kind of treatment invites the audience to isolate each character. Perception of this artifice leads to a questioning of the representation.

The interesting parallel set-up between Natasha and the three sisters is a strong indication of Chekhov's awareness of the complexity of female sexuality as well as a device to indicate the artificiality of the theatrical exercise. Even if we find the crudeness of the approach disappointing (preferring perhaps to see the complexity explored within the parameters of one individual), the presentation of *three* sisters seems an attempt to capture the multifacetedness of this complexity and of the roles women play. Nowhere is this paralleled in the treatment of the men. The sisters are united by familial bonds, by their orphaned state, by their commonly held dream of Moscow, by their general togetherness in the action and in the relationships that have developed as a result of their mutual unhappiness. Denying her sexual attractiveness, Olga has assumed the maternal role, while having no children of her own, and acknowledging that there is little likelihood she ever will. Her teaching of young people enables her to sublimate her sexuality, but she finds teaching burdensome. Masha is discovering the power of her physical attractiveness and the emotions of real love. She is also discovering that this experience when found with a lover who will leave her will only intensify her unhappiness and her sense of entrapment. Irina (in denial of the potency of her sexuality after her brush with Solenyi) has chosen marriage to a man she does not love in order to achieve safety and independence. But she is denied even that difficult solution by Tuzenbach's untimely death.

Together the three make a potent study of different aspects of female sexuality and social roles in their subjugation of real feelings and search for surrogate forms of fulfilment. This powerful interrelation among the sisters may also provide a reason for the exaggeration of Natasha. Not only is she exaggerated to counterbalance the integrated strength of the sisters, but in direct contrast to them she represents the type of woman who is willing to exploit her sexuality to achieve her mostly material aims. She gains from inhabiting a male world which will happily respond to her desires. Her assertiveness leads her to victimise those who do not exploit their sexuality, something she, and perhaps the male society she inhabits, despises. Chekhov's exploration of the sexuality of the three sisters reveals the limitations placed on those who find no means, or desire, to integrate with a successful thrusting male world. Those who read the sisters' state as undermined by their apparent inability to buy a train ticket and move to Moscow are missing the point. Those who reject this successful thrusting male world know that the path to female fulfilment does not lie in escape to Moscow or wherever. The play does not suggest where it does lie, but the reassertion of the sisters' dream of Moscow against the diminishing possibility of realisation emphasises it as a conscious metaphor for their longing for fulfilment. Thus the manner in which female sexuality is treated through the representation of the three sisters invites the audience not only to challenge contemporary views and expectations of women but also affects the formal aspects of the play.

We should examine whether Chekhov's treatment of male sexuality is any different. While there is no obvious parallel to the three sisters, certain of the male characters pose questions for a patriarchal society. Konstantin (*The Seagull*), Vania (*Uncle Vania*), Andrei, Chebutykin, Tuzenbach (*Three Sisters*), Gaev and Trofimov (*The Cherry Orchard*) could all be said to fit this framework for their denial of contemporary values. Thus this aspect of the stage representation of Chekhov's women, challenging current norms of female behaviour, may be seen as prophetic of change that may well come, and more surprisingly, perhaps, may lead to a reconsideration of some of the male characters.[7]

It is no less significant that Chekhov began his mature exploration of the female psyche with two actresses, Arkadina and Nina. Any representation in the theatre has to be viewed in relation to the physicality (use of the body for characterisation and to affect the audience) of the person playing the role. Chekhov is toying with spectacle and physicality in *The Seagull* when he counterpoints the established, mature Arkadina with the aspiring, youthful Nina, and then juxtaposes this Nina with the older and wiser but none the less still aspiring Nina at the end of the play. In addition, Arkadina directly foregrounds her physicality by comparing her apparent youth with the seeming age of Masha at the beginning of Act Two of *The Seagull*.[8] The words are addressed to Dorn as the on-stage audience. Is Chekhov titillating or challenging the male gaze by this gesture? On one level, staging the competitive spirit between the two women is titillation, but this invitation to gaze is subverted by the clarity with which in its final scenes the play condemns the theatre for its treatment of Nina.

In *Uncle Vania* the point is more obviously made. Elena's great beauty (or should we say potent sexual awareness and inactivity) is contrasted with Sonia's plainness (or should we say sexual innocence and activity). By this, the audience is invited to focus on the physicality of the two actresses playing the roles. Beauty attracts the male: Elena attracts Vania and Astrov, but Sonia fails to attract Astrov. The interesting point being made is that in this case the female (Elena) repulses advances, but through a clever trick almost falls prey to the male in Act Three.[9] Looked at in this light, the play is a challenge to male demands for beauty in women. But as a tragedy, *Uncle Vania* asks the audience equally to condemn the view that the plain woman has her faith and should endure (and support the men in their grief). It is no accident that the play's title *Uncle Vania* implies the voice of Sonia, since she is the only one who has the right to refer to Vania as uncle. There is, however, a double edge: not only does the word 'uncle' imply the displacement from being an individual in his own right of the eponymous hero, but it also denies to the equally suffering Sonia any claim to centre stage in the family or the theatrical event. Their two tragedies are played out side by side.

To stay with Sonia for a moment, a recent reviewer asserted with reference to her that 'no actress will convincingly play the part of an ugly girl'.[10] Not only is there an in-built assumption that female performers are not, or cannot be, ugly, but that it is ugliness which drives the characterisation of Sonia. Chekhov's implied invitation to separate the actress from the role leads to interrogation of the validity of a naturalist oriented theatre. It is possible that Chekhov knew the members of the theatre audiences of his own day too well. He challenged the male gaze and its obsession with beauty, but equally the challenge was thrown to female vanity. Perceiving the women characters as objects of the male gaze, desirable or otherwise, and as objects likely to cause women to dissociate from them, offers the audience a moment in which to question the reality of what is presented. By providing such moments Chekhov was bringing the whole process of representation within a naturalist and realist framework into question, distancing his audience from the given performance and allowing them to engage their critical judgement. The male characters are subject to similar moments, but these opportunities stem rarely from male *physicality*, but from dwindling economic resources and diminishing status, both at odds with society's concept of masculinity. However, that is material for a separate study.

Physicality of the actresses is focussed upon in another way. Chekhov was already beginning to disturb the conventions of realist representation in *Three Sisters*. The obvious sculpting of the sisters at the end of the play raises issues about the physicality of the actresses, and the relationship between them as actresses and the characters being created. Some see this sculpting as a deliberate classical reference.[11] However, if we view this posing as statues through the prism of representation then it becomes an ironising of the vicarious, the 'standing for' inherent to drama, rather than a presentation of the real. On the one hand, Chekhov could be seen to be divorcing the signifier from the signified, as actress ceases to be the character already created in the play; on the other, in posing them he reaches for a moment of petrification where signifier is only what is signified. In both cases Chekhov is manipulating the 'gap' in the representing process between presentation and perception. What is noteworthy is that in both approaches the artificiality of the theatrical process is clearly perceptible. At this point in any performance the play breaks away from its present fictional world since the sisters are attempting to penetrate the mystery of the future. As a finale this is a stroke of genius: the fictional world created by the play is questioned, and beyond that, the audience is invited to question the values attached to women (and actresses) in the real world it inhabits.

Similar reference to the artificiality of the theatrical undertaking is found with increased frequency in Chekhov's final play, *The Cherry Orchard*. Previously Chekhov had subscribed overtly to a realist and naturalist theatre. In *The Cherry Orchard* imitation of reality is put under pressure, an approach in which the women characters play a seminal role. Firstly, as already noted, there is the engagement of sympathy for Ranevskaia whose actions are reprehensible but condoned. She is a bad mother; a woman who allows her sexuality to lead her into problems which cause her to lose control of the situation; the woman with a lover who deceives her, whom she loves but has tried to leave; the seducer of students, the liar and cheat, who disappears to Paris with the aunt's money (and the residue of Lopakhin's payment from the sale of the beloved orchard) at the end of the play; the social snob unable to respond to the plain affection of her former serf; the woman employer who has not organised a position for her destitute governess; and the mother who is probably deserting her teenage daughter. Is the audience really meant to accept that these negative traits are countermanded or excused by her nostalgia for her childhood and grief for a son drowned years before? At the very least, these two contrasting emotions should make her feel ambivalent in her nostalgia, if not confused. And are these negative traits compensated by the fact that for three quarters of the play she is presented as a victim of circumstances beyond her control? Surely Ranevskaia raises a question mark over conventional characterisation of women and conventional attitudes to women.

Secondly, again as noted above, there is Charlotta, whose cross-dressing makes us question not only her sexuality, but even her reality. What is Charlotta's representative function within a realist theatre? She can be dismissed as a comic addition, an entertainer, but these descriptions hardly contain her eccentricity. Her function is to raise a question mark over realist theatre as much as over femaleness. Her cross-dressing, her uncertainty as to who she is, her rootlessness (even at the end of the play her future remains the most uncertain), all threaten the stability of the realist, and more especially the naturalist framework, where character is deeply dependent upon environment and women regarded as particularly contained within it. Of all the women characters, possibly of all the characters, Charlotta is the one who most forces the play to regard itself, and to exploit that gap in the representation between the creative process and the perception. The points about these two women characters are part of a series of others which increasingly threaten the stability of the fictional and stage worlds of *The Cherry Orchard*. Just as the sociological picture is fragmenting so the stage world questions the desirability of the photographic representation of reality implied by closed sets and proscenium arch frames. Open landscapes, absent cherry orchards, breaking strings and the abandonment and imminent destruction of the orchard and the house raise endless question marks. The gap between signifier and signified has begun to widen.

We have already implied responses to the fourth question we wish to raise. If we locate gender at the centre of our analysis of Chekhov's major plays do we reach interpretations which disturb the apparent verisimilitude of the representation? Firstly, we have commented that the characters (female) who are forced into low-paid, low-esteem employment should engage our admiration and thus raise questions about the patriarchal society of the time and the limitations it imposed. Secondly, it is apparent that some of the male characters might also be seen to be rejecting the values of the patriarchal society they inhabit. Resignation, despair and/or suicide are frequently symptoms associated with this rejection. Certainly the audience is invited to despise the thrusting male or those who believe themselves so to be: such as the Trigorins, Serebriakovs, Protopopovs, Vershinins (possibly) and Lopakhins of Chekhov's fictional play worlds. Therefore, it seems, Chekhov enables his audience to take a critical view of the gender-prescribed values of his day. In these respects the representation of the women characters plays a radical role at odds with the norms of imitation and verisimilitude.

My conclusion is, therefore, that through the women characters, as well as raising some questions of sociological and political importance, Chekhov invites interrogation of existing theatrical practice. Chekhov was writing at a period when melodrama was a popular form. Much of his theatre was aimed at rethinking melodramatic content and the melodramatic mode of performance. The stereotypical view of women proposed in melodrama was interrogated through the women characters he included in his plays. It is also notable that he used a woman character, Charlotta, to take the questioning further and interrogate the realist and naturalist theatre to which he had himself subscribed. It would be inappropriate to claim Chekhov as a writer with an understanding of feminist issues. What we can claim is that the treatment of the women characters contributes significantly to a wider theatrical agenda addressed in the major plays. He brought his audiences face to face with a paradox, the paradox of realist and naturalist 'representation'. Chekhov's attention to the form of his theatre is his most underrated and unexplored quality, and yet by confronting this paradox, exemplified here in the representation of his women characters, he opened theatre to Modernism and to the experimentation that has marked and thrilled the twentieth century.

NOTES

Unless otherwise attributed, translations are my own, and from N. F. Belchikov and others, eds., *Anton Chekhov, Polnoe sobranie sochinenii i pisem v 30 tomakh*, Moscow, 1974–83 (*Anton Chekhov, Collected Works and Letters in 30 volumes*, Moscow, 1974–83). This system of transliteration is that of System IV, The Library of Congress.

1 Stephen J. Greenblatt, ed, *Allegory and Representation*, Baltimore and London, 1981, p. ix; see Elaine Aston, George Savona, *Theatre as Sign System: A Semiotics of Text and Performance*, London and New York, 1991, pp. 5–10, for discussion of semiotic terminology in relation to theatre.

2 For discussion of this term, see Patrice Pavis, 'Towards a Semiology of the *Mise-en-scène*' (1980), *Languages of the Stage*, New York, 1993, p. 134.

3 Carolina De Maegd-Soep, *Chekhov and Women: Women in the Life and Work of Chekhov*, Columbus, Ohio, 1987, p. 77.

4 *The Cherry Orchard*, A. P. Chekhov, *'Vishnevy sad'*, *Works, Letters 1974–83*, *Polnoe sobranie sochinenii i pisem*, vol. XII, Moscow, 1978, p. 227.

5 Elena to Vania after he has expressed his desire to speak of his love at the end of Act One: 'This is unbearable', p. 74; Elena to Astrov in Act Four: 'All I ask is one thing: think better of me. I want you to respect me', *Uncle Vania*, *Works*, vol. XIII, p. 110.

6 Ranevskaia to Trofimov: 'You're not above love, just green behind the gills as old Firs would say. Fancy not having a mistress at your age!', *The Cherry Orchard*, *Works*, vol. XIII, p. 235.

7 For the sexual connotations of the song 'Tarara-boom-deay' in *Three Sisters*, see chapter 16 in this volume.

8 Arkadina to Masha and Dorn: 'Let's stand side by side. You're twenty-two. I'm nearly double that. Evgenii Sergeich, who looks the younger of us two?', *The Seagull*, *Works*, vol. XIII, p. 21.

9 Astrov suddenly turns the tables on Elena in their scene in Act Three by accusing her of mounting a cunning plan to catch *him*. He classifies her as a 'bird of prey', then even more demeaningly as a 'beautiful fluffy weasel'. He sees himself as a 'wise old sparrow' for having guessed her plan! (*Uncle Vania*, *Works*, vol. XIII, p. 96).

10 D. Rayfield, Review of film *Vanya on 42nd Street*, *The Slavonic and East European Review*, 74, 2, 1996, p. 395.

11 R. Peace, 'Chekhov's "Modern Classicism"', *The Slavonic and East European Review*, 65, 1, 1987, pp. 22–3.

18

VERA GOTTLIEB

Chekhov's comedy

'First of all I'd get my patients in a laughing mood – and only then would I begin to treat them.'[1]

Chekhov's words sum up the motivation for his comedy: laughter as medicine, and a vital prerequisite for any treatment of his fellow human beings. Implicit is the sense that laughter – and comedy – are restorative, and that the objectivity and detachment which laughter may produce could inoculate us against such human diseases as pomposity, hypocrisy, self-centredness, laziness, *or* – the worst of all – wasting life.

It is *Doctor* Chekhov who wrote those words, and beneath them lies a serious but non-judgemental sense that laughter is curative and healthy. Chekhov's comedy is therefore not only a stylistic feature in his works, but is also a vital part of his philosophy. It is the point where content and form meet, the one usually inseparable from the other. And this, in turn, relates to the subject matter of his works – not the artificial and complex, though enjoyable, plot lines of farces by Labiche or Feydeau, or their third-rate imitators, but the daily lives of ordinary people. As he put it himself in a much-quoted letter:

> Why write that a person gets into a submarine and goes to the North Pole to find some kind of reconciliation with humanity, while at the same time the woman he loves hurls herself off the nearest belfry with a theatrical shriek? All this is untrue and does not happen in real life. One must write simply – about how Pyotr Semyonovich got married to Marya Ivanovna. That's all.[2]

This approach informed all of his work, and is particularly evident in a series of newspaper articles he wrote over 1883–5, called *Fragments of Moscow Life (Oskolki)*, in which he dealt with every possible aspect of life in Moscow whether:

> the position of shop assistants and factory workers, the high death-rate amongst the poor, the insanitary conditions of the houses and streets, the

unsatisfactory state of the cobbled roads, the high-handed attitudes of the water-carriers, the extortion of the undertakers, the uncivilised manners of the merchants, the absurd customs of the middle classes, the vulgarity of the popular press, the villainy of the professional men who won't repay their debts to the Society for Aiding Needy Students, the craze for champion runners, hypnotists, mediums and 'thought-readers', the lamentable state of the theatre and actors . . .[3]

– a 'sociological survey' perhaps equalled only by Zola in France, and Dickens in England. And the point where fact and fiction blend to produce the particular kind of 'heightened realism' which was characteristic of Chekhov's writings.

My use of the phrase 'non-judgemental' above must be contrasted with the moral purpose which pervades the works of Tolstoy, and motivates writing as seemingly diverse as *Anna Karenina* (1873–77) – and his stories for children. As Tolstoy wrote in the preface to his *Improving Stories for Children* (1887): 'a writer does not write the truth who describes only what has happened and what this or that man has done, but he who shows what people do that is *right* – that is, in accord with God's will, and what people do wrong – that is, contrary to God's will'.

Chekhov's approach, clarified after his journey in 1890 to the penal colony of Sakhalin, was a rebuttal of Tolstoy's philosophy. In 1894 he crystallised the differences not only between himself and Tolstoy – but between his own writing and that of the majority of Russian classical literature from Pushkin and Lermontov onwards, where literature and art had, to varying degrees, been the means of carrying a 'message', *and* of expressing the writer's own commitment. Thus in another often quoted letter, Chekhov wrote:

> Tolstoy's philosophy moved me deeply and possessed me for six or seven years. It was not so much his basic ideas which had an effect on me . . . it was his way of expressing himself, his common sense, and probably a kind of hypnotism too. But now something in me protests. Prudence and justice tell me there is more love for mankind in electricity and steam, than in chastity and vegetarianism.[4]

In this sense, Chekhov was more 'in tune' with Ibsen, who wrote: 'I only ask. My task is not to answer' (*Letter in Rhyme*).[5]

The 'morality' implicit in comedy is a complex area, and one which is not altogether clarified by Henri Bergson's *Laughter* or George Meredith's *An Essay on Comedy*.[6] Instead, it must be seen within the context of Russian literature and the arts in general – a context which placed on the artist a particular responsibility. As Chekhov said about the writings of Gogol: 'It is essential that Gogol is not brought down to the level of the people – but that the people are brought up to the level of Gogol.'[7] This sense of obligation informs almost all Russian literature of the eighteenth and nineteenth centuries, a result of the vast disparity between the aristocracy and landowning classes – and the peasants, only released from serfdom in 1861. In some instances, writers suffered imprisonment and exile (a fate not invented by the Stalinist regime); in other cases, such as that of Maxim Gorky, there was constant police surveillance. Although he had been nominated, the Tsar refused to authorise Gorky's membership of the Academy of Sciences, causing both Chekhov and Korolenko to resign in protest. This was one of several major disagreements between Chekhov and his publisher and friend, A. S. Suvorin. The other row concerned Zola's defence of Alfred Dreyfus, the French Jewish army officer accused of treason and sent to Devil's Island – the French equivalent of Sakhalin. The issue was one which separated the reactionaries from the progressives throughout Europe – and the fact that Chekhov came out publicly in support of both Gorky and Zola illustrates clearly his political stance *and* belief in protest, a factor which in turn relates to his philosophy.

The relevance of this, in a chapter on comedy, is to set the context of social and even political thought which informed Chekhov's writings – though equally, it is evident that at no time did he lose the detachment and objectivity either of a doctor – a man of science – or of a detached observer and analyst of his contemporary Russia. It is almost impossible to detect Chekhov's dislike of a character in his plays – except, perhaps, of Ivanov, Natasha in *Three Sisters* and Yasha in *The Cherry Orchard*. With most of his characters, their three-dimensionality results in a 'realistic' perspective, with decent and weak aspects to each character, and no sense of the 'black and white' which informed the stereotypic characters and plots of many of the contemporary popular comedies.

But the significance here is that Chekhov was not writing 'popular comedies' – a factor which goes some way to explaining the negative reactions to the first performances of some of his plays. Accustomed to the stereotypic, audiences found depth and dimensionality of character; looking for conventional plots, his audiences often found plays which seemed to have no plot at all (although this was less true of the one-act vaudevilles); expecting the physicality *and* escapism of farce, Chekhov's audience found themselves required to observe people very much like themselves. Thus, to turn round a quotation originally applied to Beckett: 'Chekhov's audience are Chekhov characters in a Chekhov situation.' And seeking escapism, the audience often found themselves viewing characters who themselves were longing for 'escape'. This is true of Nyukhin in *On the Harmfulness of Tobacco*; of Vanya, Astrov and Sonya in *Uncle Vanya*;

of Andrey in *Three Sisters* - and the whole concept of 'to Moscow' as an image of escape in the sisters' longing for another and better life. It is also true of Nina and Konstantin in *The Seagull*, and even Masha and Medvedenko, while it is a major leitmotif in *The Cherry Orchard*, with variations on the theme from Charlotta Ivanovna, Dunyasha, Varya and Lopakhin, albeit differently, and from Anya and Trofimov, again individually motivated and treated.

All of this may not immediately seem to relate to the question of comedy. But the 'comedy' lies in the disparity between aspiration and reality, or between desire and fulfilment. In most cases, there is little to stop the characters from doing what they want – except themselves. And this, centrally, is where the keynote of Chekhov's comedy lies. Thus, in one of the many disagreements between Chekhov and Stanislavsky over interpretation, Chekhov reportedly said:

> Take my *Cherry Orchard*. – *Is it* my *Cherry Orchard?* Apart from two or three parts, nothing in it is mine. I am describing life, ordinary life, and not blank depression. They either turn me into a cry-baby or into a bore. They invent something about me out of their own heads, whatever they like, something I never thought or dreamed about. This is beginning to make me angry.[8]

Or to quote perhaps the most significant comment Chekhov made about comedy and his theatre work:

> You tell me that people cry at my plays. I've heard others say this too. But that is not why I wrote them. It is Alexeyev [Stanislavsky] who made my characters into cry-babies. All *I* wanted was to say truthfully to people: 'Have a look at yourselves and see how bad and dreary your lives are!' – The important point is that people should realise that since when they do, they will most certainly create another, a better, life for themselves. I shall not live to see it, but I know that it will be quite different, quite unlike our present life. And as long as this different life does not exist, I shall continue to say to people again and again: 'Please, understand that your life is bad and dreary!' – What is there to cry about in this?[9]

These words sound like Vershinin or Astrov. For Chekhov, the philosophical core of his 'comedy' is that of a doctor who knows there is a cure – yet everyone is sitting and wailing about the disease. To this, however, as ordinary mortals we might well protest a fear of death. But it is not the fear of death which concerns Chekhov (except in the manner and timing of it): it is the *fear of life* which he exposes, and presents as 'comic' in that the cure potentially lies in our own hands.

When Nemirovich-Danchenko wrote to Chekhov that 'there are too many tearful characters in the play [*The Cherry Orchard*]', Chekhov replied:

> Where are they? There is only one such character – Varya, but that is because she is a cry-baby by nature, and her tears should not arouse any sense of gloom in the audience. I often put down 'through tears' in my stage directions, but that shows only the mood of the characters and *not* the tears.[10]

If one looks more closely at the 'deaths' in the plays, there are a number of facets which clarify Chekhov's philosophy. At the end of *The Seagull*, a gifted young man commits suicide – yet the play is called 'a comedy'. According to David Magarshack, Chekhov's response to this was that 'a failure who runs away from life is not the subject of a tragedy'.[11] This may seem somewhat harsh, but it does relate to Chekhov's endless plea that we should improve our lives ourselves, and that there is much to be done. And to ensure that we are properly – dramatically – prepared, Chekhov's directions state that Konstantin tears up his manuscripts 'for two minutes': a long time in stage terms – and in real time, melodramatic. In the same play we have the dying Sorin:

> SORIN.   You're spoilt, that's why you talk like this. You've always had what you wanted, so life doesn't matter to you, you just don't bother. But even you'll be afraid of dying.
>
> DORN.   Fear of death's an animal thing. You must get over it. It only makes sense to fear death if you believe in immortality and are scared because you've sinned. But you aren't a Christian for a start, and then – what sins have you committed? You've worked for the Department of Justice[12] for twenty-five years, that's all.
>
> SORIN.   [laughs] Twenty-eight.[13]

In *Uncle Vanya* there is Professor Serebriakov whose supposed ill-health has caused Dr Astrov to ride some distance in haste, leaving his wretchedly poor peasant patients. Serebriakov is clearly a hypochondriac, but what emerges is Astrov's tormented memory of a patient's death he was unable to avoid – and horror at the conditions of the patients he normally treats, the peasants and workers. This is contrasted on the one hand with Serebriakov's self-centredness - and Vanya's depression on the other, a melancholy or depression arising from the sense of a wasted life. Again, Dr Astrov is quite acerbic with Vanya, not merely to get back the morphine Vanya stole and so stop a suicide, but because *in contrast* with most of his patients, the landowning gentry live rather well. This is not to minimise or deflect the real unhappiness of the characters but, as Astrov puts it to Vanya:

Those who live a century or two after us and despise us for leading lives so stupid and tasteless, perhaps they'll find a way to be happy, but as for us . . . In our whole district there were only two decent, civilised people – you and I. But ten years or so of this contemptible, parochial existence have completely got us down. This filthy atmosphere has poisoned our blood and we've become as second-rate as the rest of them.[14]

The evidence of the plays, the stories and Chekhov's letters suggests again and again that what he called 'the sad comicality of everyday life' was the subject, while the treatment was a strong dose of comedy or sense of proportion – and with that, the hope of a better future. This, another leitmotif in the works, is articulated by Vershinin and Tuzenbach in *Three Sisters*, by Trofimov and, albeit differently, by Lopakhin in *The Cherry Orchard*.

Death itself is the subtext of his short play *Tatyana Repina*, a work which remains rather a mystery within the Chekhov canon. Using the conventional theme of the discarded mistress committing suicide in front of her lover and his bride (this time in the church), Chekhov, it seems, intended it as a private joke between himself and Suvorin, who had written a mediocre four-act play called *Tatyana Repina*, both based initially on a true story.[15] What seems clear, however, is that Chekhov wrote it as a supposed 'fifth' act to Suvorin's play. Written in 1889, it exposes on the one hand Chekhov's attitude to melodramatic gestures, and on the other demonstrates in a way that the conventional dramas and operas do not, that taking poison is extremely unpleasant and painful. Whether a parody of Suvorin's play or (to name the best example of the formula) Dumas' *The Lady of the Camellias*, or of a romance by Turgenev on the same theme, *Clara Milich* (1882), the main point may be summarised thus: 'Chekhov wrote that neither Adashev (a character in Suvorin's play, missing from Chekhov's, whose sole function seems to be making long speeches) nor anyone else should pronounce long monologues on the necessity of living – in front of someone who is dying of poison, and therefore suffering from dreadful stomach pains.'[16] Chekhov's criticism was of excess, of melo-drama, and the manner of dying – particularly given the social and theatrical custom of the time which demanded that the sinful *woman* be punished, whether through Dumas' tuberculosis or – in Wilde's hands – by leaving for America! Thus the convention is evident in work as diverse as the ending of *Anna Karenina*, or the plays of Scribe, Sardou or Pinero and, of course, Shaw and Wilde, both of whom, like Chekhov, also used the convention to invert and so subvert a theme by then so well-worn that it could, particularly in opera, become almost comically unreal if 'willing belief' is suspended. Its relevance here, however, is Chekhov's use of comedy to make a serious point, *and* as a different perspective on death.

The other theme which relates to comedy in the plays (and the stories), is the constant refrain of 'I could have . . .'- and this too becomes both a philosophical statement *and* a comic technique. Perhaps one of the clearest examples is in Chekhov's story 'In Moscow' ('V Moskve'). In *Tatyana Repina*, written two years earlier, Chekhov debunked the myth of people 'doing a Tatyana Repina' – here, he presents for critical appraisal people who see themselves as Hamlet. This is not Shakespeare's Hamlet, but the popular nineteenth-century Russian idea of Hamlet which Turgenev analysed in his lecture of 1858, *Hamlet and Don Quixote*: Hamlet was viewed as passive, resigned, incapable of action and typifying people, like Chekhov's Ivanov, who 'don't solve problems' but 'cave in under the weight'.[17] Such characters are aimless, exhausted from doing nothing – and useless. As the Moscow Hamlet says of himself:

> I am a Moscow Hamlet. Yes. I go to houses, theatres, restaurants, and editorial offices in Moscow, and everywhere I say the same thing:
> 'God, how boring it is, how ghastly boring!'
> And the sympathetic reply comes:
> 'Yes, indeed, it is terribly boring.'

But then he says himself:

> And yet I could have learned anything. If I could have got the Asiatic out of myself, I could have studied and loved European culture, trade, crafts, agriculture, literature, music, painting, architecture, hygiene. I could have had superb roads in Moscow, begun trade with China and Persia, brought down the death-rate, fought ignorance, corruption and all the abominations which hold us back from living . . . Yes, I could have! I could have! But I'm a rotten rag, useless rubbish. I am a Moscow Hamlet . . .[18]

Such characters, for Chekhov, were not the subject of tragedy but of comedy. Again and again it is the characters themselves who usually provide the only major obstacle to self-fulfilment or enjoyment, to living as distinct from merely existing, and in this way the tragedy is usually presented as either avoidable – or not 'tragic' in the first place.[19]

In *The Empty Space*, Peter Brook writes: 'Brecht and Beckett are both contained in Shakespeare unreconciled. We identify emotionally, subjectively – and yet at one and the same time we evaluate politically, objectively in relation to society.'[20] The same is true of Chekhov – or, as Trevor Griffiths put it, Chekhov's plays 'are both subjectively painful and objectively comic'.[21] This is partly the philosophical motivation for the comedy, while the *nature* of the comedy, or the comic effects, are designed to take the spectator from close-up to long-shot, or vice versa. It is this which creates the contrapuntal nature of Chekhov's structure, where one conversation with one group on stage *counterpoints* another, with the action overlapping but the dialogue precisely harmonised to 'interrupt' one conversation from which at times only a laugh or sound may be heard – as at the end of *The Seagull*, where there are two distinct groups: two overlapping actions, but contrapuntal speech or sound when Arkadina and the others play lotto – while Dorn takes Trigorin to one side (or – more exactly – downstage) to say: '[Dropping his voice in an undertone.] "Get Irina out of here somehow. The fact is, Constantine has shot himself." – Curtain.'[22]

Examples of this technique are manifold, and used to different effect – sometimes working to deflate, as in *Three Sisters* when Olga, at the beginning of Act One, says to Irina: 'I felt so happy and excited, I felt I just had to go back home to Moscow' – after which, from the group comprising Tuzenbakh, Chebutykin and Soliony, Chebutykin says, with reference to something quite different: 'Not a chance in hell', and Tuzenbakh replies, 'Absolute nonsense of course.' The effect is virtually musical – a leitmotif counterpointed by another theme, and in this way it acts as an unconscious commentary on the aspiration, expressed virtually at the opening of the play, to go to Moscow – and lead a different life.

This is partly what Peter Brook means when he writes in *The Empty Space*:

> Any page of *The Three Sisters* gives the impression of life unfolding as though a tape-recorder had been left running. If examined carefully it will be seen to be built of coincidences as great as in Feydeau – the vase of flowers that overturns, the fire-engine that passes at just the right moment; the word, the interruption, the distant music, the sound in the wings, the entrance, the farewell – touch by touch, they create through the language of illusions an overall illusion of a slice of life. This series of impressions is equally a series of alienations: each rupture is a subtle provocation and a call to thought.[23]

There is, however, a major difference not only in philosophy but consequently also in the function of the comedy in Feydeau or Beckett – or, indeed, in Michael Frayn, some plays by Alan Ayckbourn, or other writers of comedy where the mechanistic results in a much more physical kind of farce and where the fatalistic destroys free will.[24] The point is really made by Ionesco in his essay *Experience of the Theatre*:

> The tragedy of man is pure derision ... I have never understood the difference people make between the comic and the tragic. As the 'comic' is an intuitive perception of the absurd, it seems to me more hopeless than the 'tragic'. The 'comic' offers no escape.

And Ionesco – author of what he named 'tragic farces' – presents a world, for example, in *The Chairs*, where 'life is nightmarish, painful and unbearable, like a bad dream', and in which frenzied action is performed by mechanical beings.[25] In this philosophical and theatrical world there is no such possibility as free will, no question of choice and, ultimately, no real danger of human responsibility and culpability. This is not Chekhov's farce, or comedy - or philosophy. So the mechanistic chaos of, for example, Michael Frayn's film script of *Clockwise*, or his highly successful farce, *Noises Off* (1982), has more to do with the dehumanisation and heartlessness of the farce vehemently attacked by Shaw, reacting to the flood of French farces on the English stage from the 1870s onwards. As Shaw put it: 'To laugh without sympathy is a ruinous abuse of a noble function . . .' We rarely laugh *at* Chekhov's characters; usually, we laugh *with* them. Even in *Jubilee* (*The Anniversary*), the chaos, physicality and farcical tableau – has been created by humans, not mechanical beings. Again, it was the mechanistic, highly physical and often brilliantly timed farces originating with Scribe, Labiche and Feydeau, which grew into a philosophy increasingly opposed to Chekhov's. This philosophy and this theatre were aptly analysed by Kenneth Tynan in his celebrated attack on Ionesco in 1958, in which he described Ionesco's landscape as 'that bleak new world from which the humanist heresies of faith in logic and belief in man will forever be banished'.[26]

Ionesco's view is completely opposite to Chekhov's. In Chekhov's works, whether plays or stories, there is no sense of an overriding 'fate' or 'God' or 'power' superior to his characters and what they may be capable of; equally, there is nothing mechanistic or automaton-like about the characters: it is up to Nyukhin in *On the Harmfulness of Tobacco* whether he rebels – or continues to live miserably. Vanya and Sonya are both disillusioned and hurt at the end of *Uncle Vanya* – but they settle down to make the best of what they have, and *to work!* While the end of *The Cherry Orchard* still poses the director the most profound *philosophical* decision: do we see a forgotten Firs locked in to an empty boarded-up house, and left to die? What is the theme and 'tone' of the final musical motif at the end, punctuated by the sound of chopping?

Perhaps two quotations, neither of which may safely be identified with Chekhov's own views, illustrate the difference between the two kinds of farce, the two kinds of comedy – and the very different philosophical bases for comedy. In the story 'Three Years', Chekhov's character Yartsev says: 'Life, my friends, is very short – and we must make the most of it.' And in *The Cherry Orchard*, Chekhov as always avoids the stereotype and 'gives' to the 'new man', Lopakhin, the sensitive and responsible line: 'the Lord gave us these huge forests, these boundless plains, these vast horizons, and we who live among them ought to be real giants'.[27]

Chekhov illuminates and demonstrates human absurdity – but in an essentially realistic context in which human behaviour struggles with itself in a defined society, not with an undefined, hostile, 'mechanised' force, like the suffocating growth in Ionesco's *Amédée – Or How To Get Rid of It*. There *is*, however, a 'nightmarish' reality for Chekhov's characters (see chapter 8, Leonid Heifetz on *Uncle Vanya*), and few would now argue with Ionesco's basic premise: 'No society has been able to abolish human sadness, no political system can deliver us from the pain of living, from our fear of death, our thirst for the absolute; it is the human condition that directs the social condition, not vice versa.'[28]

The philosophical argument rests on definitions of 'the human condition': determined, inevitable and hence impotent – or subject in some areas to human control, however fallible, and to the changeable human organisation of the social condition, and hence potentially potent.

The techniques work through the relationship of one component or organic element with another; through antithesis, parody, farce, the use or reversal of conventions, the incongruous or the grotesque, the deflation of character at a moment of 'drama' or self-dramatisation, through the undercutting or defusing of atmosphere and the acceleration – or more frequently – the *deceleration* of rhythm and pace. And more often than not, a Chekhov character turns out to be not Hamlet, but Tartuffe.

NOTES

Translations are the author's and quotations from the letters are from *Anton Chekhov, Polnoe sobranie sochinenii i pisem v 30 tomakh*, Moscow, 1974–83, (*Anton Chekhov, Collected Works and Letters in 30 volumes*, Moscow, 1974–83), unless otherwise indicated.

1 Letter to Nikolai Leykin, 20 May 1884.
2 Quoted in A. S. Dolinin, '*Parodiya li, 'Tatyana Repina' Chekhova?*', an article in A. P. Chekhov, *Zateryannye proizvedeniya*, Leningrad, 1925, p. 60. (See Vera Gottlieb, *Chekhov and the Vaudeville*, Cambridge, 1982, p. 212, notes 30–1).
3 From *Fragments – (Splinters) – of Moscow Life*, 1883–5; *Oskolki, Anton Chekhov, Polnoe sobranie sochinenii i pisem v 30i tomakh*, Moscow, 1974–1983.
4 Letter to A. S. Suvorin, 27 March 1894.
5 Trans. Michael Meyer, *Henrik Ibsen*, vol. II, *A Farewell to Poetry*, London, 1971, p. 210.
6 *Laughter* by Henri Bergson and *An Essay on Comedy* by George Meredith are to be found in one volume: *Comedy*, intro. Wylie Sypher, New York, 1956.
7 Letter to Nemirovich-Danchenko, 2 November 1903.
8 *Works/Letters, Polnoe sobranie sochinenii i pisem A. P. Chekhova, v 20i*

tomakh, ed. S. D. Balukhaty and others, Moscow, 1944–51, vol. XIX, pp. 257–8. Quoted in David Magarshack, *Chekhov the Dramatist*, New York, 1960, p. 14.

9 Reported by the writer Alexander Tikhonov in 1902, in *Chekhov v neizdannykh dnevnikakh sovremennikov*, in *Literaturnoe nasledstvo* 68, Moscow, 1960, pp. 479–80.

10 Letter to Nemirovich-Danchenko, 23 October 1903.

11 Quotation from Chekhov's notebooks in Magarshack, *Chekhov the Dramatist*, pp. 193–4.

12 From what historians of the period have written about Tsarist autocracy, police surveillance, the legal and penal systems, it may be that Sorin is not completely without culpability in his job at the Department of Justice, a point perhaps more immediate for Chekhov's contemporary audiences. See Bibliography for the historical context of the plays.

13 *The Seagull*, trans. and ed. Ronald Hingley, *The Oxford Chekhov*, vol. II, Oxford, 1967, Act Four, p. 271.

14 *Uncle Vanya*, trans. and ed. Ronald Hingley, *The Oxford Chekhov*, vol. III, Oxford, 1964, Act Four, p. 60.

15 See Gottlieb, *Chekhov and the Vaudeville*, pp. 133–46.

16 Ibid., p. 136.

17 Letter to A. S. Suvorin, 30 December 1888.

18 The translation of *A Moscow Hamlet (V Moskve)* (1891) is my own, and from *Anton Chekhov, Collected Works/Letters, Polnoe sobranie sochinenii i pisem v 30i tomakh*, vol. II, pp. 500–7.

19 The title character in *Platonov* (otherwise known as *Fatherlessness* – see *The Oxford Chekhov*, Hingley, vol II, Appendix 1, pp. 282–3) is the earliest example of the 'type' in Chekhov's plays.

20 Peter Brook, *The Empty Space*, Harmondsworth, 1968, p. 98.

21 *The Cherry Orchard – A New English Version*, Trevor Griffiths, London, 1978, p. vi. and see chapter 10 in this volume.

22 *The Seagull*, ed., and trans. Hingley, p. 281.

23 Peter Brook, *The Empty Space*, p. 89.

24 Discussed at greater length in Vera Gottlieb, *Why this Farce?* in *New Theatre Quarterly* 7, 27, August 1991, pp. 217–28.

25 Eugene Ionesco, *Notes and Counter-Notes*, trans. Donald Watson, London, 1964, p. 113.

26 Ibid., p. 92.

27 *The Cherry Orchard*, trans. and ed. Ronald Hingley, *The Oxford Chekhov*, Vol. III, Oxford, 1964, p. 170.

28 Ionesco, *Notes and Counter-Notes*, p. 95.

Chekhov's works: primary sources from the Russian – Variations of English Titles from the Russian

The Oxford Chekhov, trans. Ronald Hingley:

  vol. 1 (1968) *Short Plays*;

  vol. 11 (1967) *Platonov, Ivanov, The Seagull*;

  vol. 111 (1964) *Uncle Vanya, Three Sisters, The Cherry Orchard, The Wood-Demon;*

  vol. 1V (1980) *Stories:* 'The Steppe', 'An Awkward Business', 'The Beauties', 'The Party', 'A Nervous Breakdown', 'The Cobbler and the Devil', 'The Bet', 'Lights';

  vol. V (1970) *Stories 1889–1891:* 'The Princess', 'A Dreary Story', 'Thieves', 'Gusev', 'Peasant Women', 'The Duel';

  vol. VI (1971) *Stories 1892–1893:* 'My Wife', 'The Butterfly', 'After the Theatre', 'In Exile', 'Neighbours', 'Ward Number Six', 'Terror', 'An Anonymous Story', 'Fragments', 'The Story of a Commercial Venture', 'From a Retired Teacher's Notebook', 'A Fishy Affair';

  vol. VII (1978) *Stories 1893–1895:* 'The Two Volodyas', 'The Black Monk', 'A Woman's Kingdom', 'Rothschild's Fiddle', 'The Student', 'The Russian Master', 'At a Country House', 'The Head Gardener's Story', 'Three Years';

  vol. VIII (1965) *Stories 1895–1897:* 'His Wife', 'Patch', 'The Order of St Anne', 'Murder', 'Ariadne', 'The Artist's Story', 'My Life', 'Peasants', 'The Savage', 'Home', 'In the Cart';

  vol. IX (1975) *Stories 1898–1904:* 'A Hard Case', 'Gooseberries', 'Concerning Love', 'Doctor Startsev', 'A Case History', 'Angel', 'New Villa', 'On Official Business', 'A Lady with a Dog', 'At Christmas', 'In the Hollow', 'The Bishop', 'A Marriageable Girl', 'All Friends Together', 'The Cripple', 'Poor Compensation', 'A Letter'.

Chekhov Stories, trans. Ronald Wilks:

  'The Kiss and Other Stories' (1982) (and 'Peasants', 'The Bishop', 'The Russian Master', 'Man in a Case', 'Gooseberries', 'Concerning Love', 'A Case History', 'In the Gully', 'Anna Round the Neck');

  'The Duel and Other Stories' (1984) (and 'My Wife', 'Murder', 'The Black Monk', 'Terror', 'The Two Volodyas');

'*The Party and Other Stories*' (1985) (and 'A Woman's Kingdom', 'My Life', 'A Provincial Story', 'An Unpleasant Business', 'A Nervous Breakdown');
'*The Fiancée and Other Stories*' (1986) (and 'On Official Business', 'Rothschild's Fiddle', 'Peasant Women', 'Three Years', 'With Friends', 'The Bet', 'New Villa', 'At A Country House', 'Beauties', 'His Wife', 'The Student').

Some of the early stories may be found in:

Constance Garnett, trans. *The Tales of Anton Tchekhov* (in 13 vols.), London, 1916–22

Nora Gottlieb, *Early Stories*, London, 1960, and New York, 1961

Patrick Miles and Harvey Pitcher, *Anton Chekhov, Early Stories*, London, 1994

Constance Garnett, trans. (revised D. Rayfield), *The Chekhov Omnibus*, London, 1994.

For further titles of translations of primary sources in English, see select bibliography.

This is not intended as a definitive list of Chekhov's stories but includes some of the major ones mentioned in this *Companion*. Given the disparate English and American translations of the titles, and bearing in mind the requirements of the non-Russian reader, the editors decided a chronological order would provide the most coherent method of locating a particular story. The Russian reader is served by the original Russian title in brackets with the date of a particular story.

* denotes available in Hingley, *The Oxford Chekhov*, and Hingley's title/translation.

W. year of publication denotes available in Wilks, Penguin, e.g. Story W. 1986.

F denotes either filmed or part of a film script (see chapter 13 in this volume and Appendix 3).

'Belated Flowers/The Flowers are Late' F/'Tardy Flowers/Belated Blossom'* ('Tsvety zapozdalyye', 1882) and F

'The Butterfly*/ The Grasshopper' ('Poprygunya', 1882) and F

'A Live Chattel/A Living Chattel'* ('Zhivoy tovar', 1882)

'The Mistress' ('Barynya', 1882)

'29 June' ('Dvadstat devyatoye iyunya', 1882)

'An Unwanted Victory/Unnecessary Victory'* ('Nenuzhnaya pobeda', 1882)

'The Daughter of Albion' ('Doch Albiona', 1883) and F

'The Death of a Clerk/Death of a Petty Official/The Death of a Government Clerk'* ('Smert chinovnika', 1883) and F

'Fat and Thin' ('Tolsty i tonky', 1883)

'In Autumn'* ('Osenyu', 1883). See the play 'On the High Road' (1885)

'On Christmas Night' ('V rozhdestvenskyu noch', 1883)

'A Tragic Actor' ('Tragik', 1883)

'A Chameleon' ('Khameleon', 1884) and F

'Romance with Double-Bass' ('Roman s kontrabasom', 1886) and F

'The Shooting Party'* ('Drama na okhote', 1884–85) (F = 'Summer Storm')

'The Burbot' ('Nalim', 1885)

'A Christmas Dream' ('Son svyatochnyy', 1885)

'A/The Dead Body' ('Myortvoye telo', 1885)

'Grief/Sorrow'* ('Gore', 1885)

'A Horse's Name/A Horsey Name'* ('Loshadinaya familiya', 1885)

'The Huntsman' ('Yeger', 1885)

'The Mirror' ('Zerkalo', 1885)

'On the Road/On the High Road'* ('Na bolshoy doroge', 1885) and see under plays

'The Wallet' ('Bumazhnik', 1885)

'Warrant Officer Prishibeyev/NCO Prishibeyev/Sergeant Prishibeyev'* ('Unter Prishibeyev', 1885)

'A Cure for Hangovers/A Means of Sobering Up' (Sredstvo ot zapoiya', 1885)

'Agafiya' ('Agafya', 1886)

'Calchas'* ('Kalchas', 1886), and see Swan Song (Lebedinaya pesnya, 1887–8)

'The Chorus Girl' ('Khoristka', 1886)

'Easter Eve' ('Svyatoy nochyu', 1886)

'A Man's Friend/A Gentleman Friend/A Man Friend' ('Znakomy muzhchina', 1886)

'Misery*/Unhappiness/Heartache' ('Toska', 1886)

'Motley Tales/Stories' ('Pyostryye rasskazy', 1886)

'The Night Before the Trial' ('Noch pered sudom', 1886). See play of the same name, 1890s

'The Nightmare/A Nightmare'* ('Koshmar', 1886)

'On the Way' ('Na puti', 1886)

'Practical Jokes' ('Shyutochki', 1886)

'The Schoolmaster' ('Uchitel', 1886)

'The Slough/The Quagmire' ('Tina', 1886)

'The Witch' ('Vedma', 1886)

'The Wolf' ('Volk', 1886)

'In the Twilight/In the Dusk/At Dusk'* ('V sumerkakh', 1886–7)

'The Enemies/Enemies'* ('Vragi', 1887)

'Fortune' ('Schastye', 1887)

'The Kiss' ('Potseluy', 1887) and W. 1982

'One Among Many' ('Odin iz mnogikh', 1887). See the play A Tragic Role

'Tumbleweed/Thistledown/Uprooted'* ('Perekati-pole', 1887)

'Rusty/Kashtanka' ('Kashtanka', 1887) and F

'Illegal*/Lawlessness' ('Nazakonnyi*/Bezzakonie', 1887) and F

'Typhus'* ('Tif', 1887)

'An Unpleasant Business/A Bad Business' ('Nedobroye delo', 1887) and W. 1985

'Verochka' ('Verochka', 1887)

'Volodia/Volodya' ('Volodya', 1887)

'Panpipes' ('Svirel', 1887–88)

'An Awkward Business/An Unpleasantness'* ('Nepriyatnost', 1888)

'Beauties/The'* ('Krasavitsy', 1888) and W. 1986

'The Bet'* ('Pari', 1888) and W. 1986

'The Cobbler and the Devil' ('Sapozhnik i nechistaya sila', 1888)

'Lights'* ('Ogni', 1888)

'A Nervous Breakdown*/The Seizure' ('Pripadok', 1888) and W. 1985

'The Party'* ('Imeniny', 1888) and W. 1985

'The Steppe'* ('Step', 1888)

'Children' ('Detvora', 1889 – a collection)

'A Dreary Story*/The Ordinary Story/A Boring Story' ('Skuchnaya istoriya', 1889)

'The Princess'* ('Knyaginya', 1889)

'Gusev'* ('Gusev', 1890)

'Gloomy People'* ('Khmuryye lyudi', 1890)

'Thieves'* ('Vory', 1890)

'The Duel'* ('Duel', 1891) and W. 1984

'Peasant Women'* ('Baby', 1891) and W. 1986

'After the Theatre'* ('Posle teatra', 1892)

'In Exile'* ('V ssylke', 1892)

'My Wife'* ('Zhena', 1892)

'Neighbours'* ('Sosedi', 1892)

'Terror/The Terror'* ('Strakh', 1892) and W. 1984

'Ward No 6'* ('Palata No.6', 1892)

'An Anonymous Story'* ('Rasskaz neizvestnogo cheloveka', 1893)

'Two Volodyas*/Big Volodya and Little Volodya' ('Volodya bolshoy i Volodya malenky', 1893) and W. 1984

'At a Country House'* ('V usadbe', 1894) and W. 1986

'The Black Monk'* ('Chorny monakh', 1894) and W. 1984

'The Head Gardener's Story'* ('Rasskaz starshego sadovnika', 1894)

'Rothschild's Fiddle/Rothschild's Violin'* ('Skripka Rotshilda', 1894) and W. 1986

'The Russian Master/The Teacher of Literature'* ('Uchitel slovesnosti', 1894) and W. 1982

'The Student'* ('Student', 1894) and W. 1986

'A Woman's Kingdom'* ('Babye tsarstvo', 1894) and W. 1985

'Anna Round the Neck/Anna on my Neck/The Order of St Anne/Ranks and People' ('Anna na sheye', 1895), W. 1982 and F

'Ariadne'* ('Ariadna', 1895)

'His Wife'* ('Supruga' 1895) and W. 1986

'The Murder/Murder'* ('Ubiystvo', 1895) and W. 1984

'Patch'* ('Beloloby', 1895)

'Three Years' ('Tri goda', 1895) and W. 1986

'The Artist's Story*/The House with a Mezzanine' ('Dom s mezoninom', 1896)

'My Life: A Provincial Story'* ('Moya zhizn', 1896) and W. 1985

'Home/In the Home-stead'* ('V rodnom uglu', 1897)

'Peasants* /The Peasants' ('Muzhiki', 1897) and W. 1982

'In the Cart'* ('Na podvode', 1897)

'All Friends Together*/A Visit to Friends/With Friends' ('U Znakomykh', 1898) and W. 1986

'A Case History*/An Incident in Practice' ('Sluchay iz praktiki', 1898) and W. 1982

'Concerning Love' ('O lyubvi', 1898), and W. 1982

'Gooseberries'* ('Kryzhovnik', 1898), and W. 1982

'A Hard Case*/A Man in a Case' ('Chelovek v futlyare', 1898) and W. 1982 and F

'Ionytch/In the Town of S. (F) /Doctor Startsev'* ('Ionych', 1898) and F

'Lady with a Little Dog/A Lady with a Dog'* ('Dama s sobachkoy', 1899) and F

'Matter of Service/On Official Business'* ('Po delam sluzhby', 1899) and W. 1986

'The New Villa/New Villa'* ('Novaya dacha', 1899) and W. 1986

'The Cripple' ('Kaleka', 1900)

'In the Ravine /In the Hollow*/In the Gully' ('Vovrage', 1900) and W. 1982

'The Bishop'* ('Arkhierey', 1902) and W. 1982

'The/A Marriageable Girl*/The Bride/The Fiancée' (Nevesta, 1903) and W. 1986

'Poor Compensation'* ('Rasstroystvo kompensatsii', 1902–3) fragment

Plays

Four-act: *The Oxford Chekhov*, trans. Hingley, vols. II and III

Fatherless (Bezottsovshchina, 1877–8?)/Platonov (Platonov, 1880–1?). H.Vol. II

The Wood-Demon (Leshy, 1889). H.Vol. III

Ivanov (Ivanov, 1887–9). H.Vol. II

The Seagull/Seagull (Chayka, 1896)*. H.Vol. II

Uncle Vanya (Dyadya Vanya, 1890–6). H.Vol. III

Three Sisters (Tri sestry, 1900–1). H.Vol. III

The Cherry Orchard (Vishnyovy sad, 1903–4). H.Vol. III

One-Act: Hingley, Vol. I

The Bear/The Boor/The Brute (Medved, 1888)*

The Proposal (Predlozheniye, 1888–9)

On the High Road (Na bolshoy doroge, 1885). Based on the story 'In Autumn' ('Osenyu'), 1883

Swan Song (Calchas) (Lebedinaya pesnya – Kalkhas, 1887–8) Based on story 'Kalchas', 1886

Tatyana Repin (Tatyana Repina, 1889)

A Tragic Role*/The Reluctant Tragedian/A Tragedian In Spite of Himself – subtitled *A Holiday Episode (Tragik po nevole – Iz dachnoy zhizni,* 1889–90). Based on story 'One among Many', ('Odin iz mnogikh', 1887)

The Wedding (Svadba, 1889–90). Based on stories 'The Wedding Season', 1881; 'Marrying for Money', and 'A Wedding with a General', both 1884

The Anniversary*/Jubilee (Yubiley, 1891). Based on story 'A Defenceless Creature' ('Bezzashchitnoye sushchestvo', 1887)

Smoking is Bad for You*/On the Harmfulness of Tobacco/The Evils of Tobacco (O vrede tabaka, 1903)

The Night Before the Trial (Noch pered sudom, 1890s). Based on story of same name, 1886.

Other versions/translations of the plays may be found in Michael Frayn ed.
Chekhov Plays: The Seagull, Uncle Vanya, Three Sisters, The Cherry Orchard, The Evils of Tobacco, Swan Song, The Bear, The Proposal, London, 1988.

See also
The Wood-Demon in translation by S. S. Koteliansky, London, 1926,

and
David Magarshack, ed. and trans. *The Seagull,* London, 1952; *Platonov,* New York, 1964; *Four Plays: The Seagull, Uncle Vanya, Three Sisters, The Cherry Orchard,* New York, 1969.

French versions by Patrice Pavis with notes/introduction, *Le Livre de Poche*:
La Mouette (The Seagull), Paris, 1985.
Oncle Vania (Uncle Vanya), Paris, 1986.
La Cérisaie (The Cherry Orchard), Paris, 1988.
Les Trois soeurs (Three Sisters), Paris, 1991.
M(o)uettes, The Seagull (contemporary version of *The Seagull*), Brussels, 1999.

For other translations/versions/adaptations see selected bibliography.

Selected non-fiction

The Island of Sakhalin* /Sakhalin (Ostrov Sakhalin, 1891–4).
Chekhov, A. P., 'Things Most Frequently Encountered in Novels, Stories and Other Such Things' ('Chto chashche vsego vstrechayetsya . . .', 1880, in *Collected Works/Letters,* 1944–51, *Polnoe sobranie sochinenii i pisem A. P. Chekhova v 20i tomakh,* ed. S. D. Balukhaty and others, Moscow 1944–51, vol. I, 1880–2, pp. 17–18.

Selected stage productions

The following is a selected list of some of the major international productions of Chekhov, including British and Russian premières. A more detailed production history is given by R. Hingley in *The Oxford Chekhov*, vols. I, II, and III, L. Senelick in *The Chekhov Theatre*, N. I. Gitovich in *Letopis zhizni i tvorchestva, A. P. Chekhova*, and in the Glossary after chapter 15 in this volume. Directors and designers are given for most productions, though the absence of a director sometimes indicates how the significance of their contribution was still being defined at the beginning of the twentieth century. Central roles and the actors who played them are given in brackets for most performances, and venues are occasionally supplemented by the name of the theatre company performing, if it differs from the resident company. Guest productions which visited Britain are also indicated. Transliteration follows that of each particular production. Many of these productions are referred to in the following chapters in this volume: 3, 4, 5, 7, 8, 9, 10, 11, 12, 14, 15, 18.

Notation: Dir./s. denotes director/s; des. denotes designer; trans. denotes translator; adapt. denotes adaptation/version; rep. denotes repertoire; ed./s. denotes editor/s. NT/RNT is short for the National Theatre/Royal National Theatre (the name changed with the Royal Charter granted in 1988) and RSC is short for the Royal Shakespeare Company. MAT denotes Moscow Art Theatre/MXAT in Russian (MKhAT Moskovskii Khudozhestvennyi Akademicheskii Teatr/Moscow Art Academic Theatre).
* denotes a British première
+ denotes Russian première.

1886 + *O vrede tabaka* (*On the Harmfulness of Tobacco*), Korsh Theatre, Moscow, written for the comic actor L. I.Gradov-Sokolov (1845–90). This was a private theatre owned by F. A. Korsh (1852–1923), which opened after the abolition of the monopoly of the Imperial Theatres. It was run as a commercial rather than an artistic enterprise. Chekhov wrote six distinct versions of this play over the period 1886–1903.

1887 + *Ivanov* (first version), first performance at Saratov, between 10 and 19 November. First major production at Korsh Theatre, Moscow, 19 November, dir. M. V. Agramov, V. N. Davydov (Ivanov).

1888 + *Lebedinaya pesnya* (*Swan Song*), Korsh Theatre, Moscow, 19 February, for the comic actor V. N. Davydov (1849–1925).

1888 + *Predlozheniye* (*The Proposal*), Krasnoye Selo Theatre, St Petersburg, 9 August, written for and dir. I. L. Leontyev, M. Ilinskaya (Natasha), P. Svobodin (Lomov), K. Varlamov (1848–1915) (Chubukov).

1888 + *Medved* (*The Bear*), Korsh Theatre, Moscow, 28 October, dir. and acted by N. N. Solovtsov (1856–1902) (Smirnov), Natalya Rybchinskaya (Popova).

1889 *Ivanov*, Imperial Alexandrinsky Theatre, St Petersburg, 31 January, V. N. Davydov (Ivanov), M. G. Savina (1854–1915) (Sasha).

1889 *Tragik po nevole* (*A Tragic Role/A Tragedian in Spite of Himself*), 4 May, amateur production written for K. Varlamov; this role was also played by M. I. Bibikov at the Petersburg German Club, 1 October.

1889 *Leshy* (*The Wood-Demon*), Abramov Theatre, Moscow, 27 December, another private theatre, as the play had been rejected by the Imperial Alexandrinsky Theatre, St Petersburg.

1891 *Predlozheniye* (*The Proposal*), Imperial Maly (Little) Theatre, Moscow, 20 February.

1896 + *Chaika* (*The Seagull*), Imperial Alexandrinsky Theatre, St Petersburg, 17 October, dir. E. P. Karpov (1857–1926), des. A. Yanov, A. Diuzhikova (Arkadina), Vera Komissarzhevskaya (Nina), N. F. Sazonov (Trigorin), K. Varlamov (Shamrayev) and Davydov (Sorin). This production was a failure but was followed by successful performances in Kiev, Taganrog, Astrakhan and other provincial cities.

1898 *Chaika* (*The Seagull*), MAT, Moscow, 17 December, dir. K. S. Stanislavsky, des. V. A. Simov, O. L. Knipper (Arkadina), V. E. Meyerhold (Treplev), K. S. Stanislavsky (Trigorin).

1898 + *Dyadya Vanya* (*Uncle Vanya*), Nizhny Novgorod Dramatic Theatre, October–November, and other Russian theatres, e.g. in Odessa, Kiev, Tiflis, Saratov.

1899 *Dyadya Vanya (Uncle Vanya)* MAT, Moscow, 26 October, dir. K. S. Stanislavsky, des. V. A. Simov, O. L. Knipper (Yeliena Andreyeevna), K. S. Stanislavsky (Astrov), A. L. Vishnevsky (Vanya).

1900 *Yubiley (Jubilee/The Anniversary)*, amateur production for a 'Chekhov Evening' at the Moscow Hunt Club.

1901 + *Tri sestry (Three Sisters)*, MAT, Moscow, 31 January, dir. K. S. Stanislavsky, V. V. Luzhsky, des. V. A. Simov, O. L. Knipper (Masha), K. S. Stanislavsky (Vershinin).

1902 *Tri sestry (Three Sisters)*, *Ivanov*, *Chaika (The Seagull)*, *Dyadya Vanya (Uncle Vanya)*, Kherson, September–October season, dir. V. Meyerhold.

1902 *Chaika (The Seagull)*, Imperial Alexandrinsky Theatre, Moscow, 16 November, dir. Mikhail Yegorovich Darsky, Khodotov (Konstantin), M. G. Savina (Arkadina), L. V. Selivanova (Nina), I. Shuvalov (Trigorin), K. Varlamov (Sorin).

1903 + *Yubiley (Jubilee/The Anniversary)*, Imperial Alexandrinsky Theatre, St Petersburg, November, one night only as a curtain-raiser for a benefit performance, E. I. Levkeyeva (Merchutkina), K. Varlamov (Khirin).

1904 *Yubiley (Jubilee/The Anniversary)*, Maly (Little) Theatre, Moscow, December. Benefit for Olga Ossipovna Sadovskaya for one night only, playing with a repertory Gogol production.

1904 + *Vishnyovy sad (The Cherry Orchard)*, MAT, Moscow, 17 January, dir. K. S. Stanislavsky, des. V. A. Simov, O. L. Knipper (Ranyevskaya), K. S. Stanislavsky (Gayev).

1904 *Vishnyovy sad (The Cherry Orchard)*, Kherson, 4 February, dir. V. Meyerhold, V. Meyerhold (Trofimov).

1904 *Ivanov*, MAT, Moscow, 19 October, dir. V. I. Nemirovich-Danchenko, des. V. A. Simov, V. I. Kachalov (Ivanov), O. L. Knipper (Anna Petrovna), K. S. Stanislavsky (Shabyelsky).

1904 *Svadba (The Wedding)*, Komissarzhevskaya Theatre, St Petersburg, dir. Nikolai Arbatov (given name Arkhipov), des. Vrachev.

1904 *Tri sestry (Three Sisters)*, Artistic Society's Theatre, Tiflis, Fellowship of New Drama, 26 September, dir V. Meyerhold (revival of 1902 production).

1904/5 *Chaika (The Seagull)*, revival at Komissarzhevskaya Theatre, St Petersburg, dir. Molchanov, Vera Komissarzhevskaya (Nina).

1905 *Vishnyovy sad* (*The Cherry Orchard*), Imperial Alexandrinsky Theatre, Moscow, dir. Yuri Ozarovsky.

1909 **The Seagull*, Royalty Theatre, Glasgow, 2 November, dir. George Calderon.

1910 *Tri sestry* (*Three Sisters*), Imperial Alexandrinsky Theatre, Moscow, dir. Yuri Ozarovsky.

1911 **The Bear*, Kingsway Theatre, London, 13 May, dir. Lydia Yavorskaya, trans. Arthur A. Sykes.

1911 **The Cherry Orchard*, Aldwych Theatre, London, 29 May, dir. Kenelm Foss, trans. Constance Garnett.

1912 *The Seagull*, Little Theatre, London, 31 March, trans. and dir. George Calderon, des. Maurice Elvey.

1914 **Uncle Vanya*, Aldwych Theatre, London, 11 May, dir. Guy Rathbone, trans. R. S. Townsend.

1916 **The Proposal*, Birmingham Repertory Theatre, Birmingham, 18 March, dir. John Drinkwater.

1916 *The Seagull*, Bandbox Theatre, New York, 22 May, Washington Square Players, trans. Marian Fell, des. Lee Simonson.

1917 **The Wedding*, trans. Julius West, and **Swan Song*, trans. Marian Fell, Grafton Galleries, London, 14 May, dir. Nigel Playfair, des. Michel Sevier.

1920 *A Triple Bill: The Bear, *On the High Road* and *The Wedding*, dir. Edith Craig, St Martin's Theatre, London, 25 January, Dorothy Massingham (Popova), Joseph A. Dodd (Smirnov). (Edith Craig was the daughter of Ellen Terry and Edward William Godwin, sister of Edward Gordon Craig who had designed *Hamlet* for the MAT – and a leading feminist theatre manager and director.)

1920 **Three Sisters*, Royal Court Theatre, London, 8 March, dir. and des. Mme Vera Donnet (dir. of Art Theatre), trans. Harold Bowen, Felix Aylmer (Solyony), Harcourt Williams (Vershinin).

1920 **The Cherry Orchard*, St Martin's Theatre, London, 12 July, dir. Mme Vera Donnet, Edith Evans (Charlotta), Hesketh Pearson (Trofimov), Felix Aylmer (Semyonov-Pishchik).

1921 + *Chekhovsky vecher* (*Chekhov Evening: The Wedding, The Anniversary; Thieves*), Third Studio of the MAT, Moscow, 15 November, dir. Yevgeny Vakhtangov, des. Isaac Rabinovich.

1921 *Uncle Vanya*, Court Theatre, London, 27 November, dir. Fyodor Komissarzhevsky/Theodore Komisarjevsky, 'Komis', (brother of Vera Komissarzhevskya, he emigrated from Russia in 1919 and was briefly married to Peggy Ashcroft). Cathleen Nesbitt (Helena), Irene Rathbone (Sonya), Leon Quartermaine (Vanya). He anglicised his name, as above.

1925 *The Cherry Orchard*, Lyric Theatre, Hammersmith, London, 25 May, dir. J. B. Fagan, des. Edgar Brickell, trans. George Calderon, John Gielgud (Trofimov).

1925 *The Seagull*, Little Theatre, London, 19 October, dir. and des. Fyodor Komisarjevsky (Theodore), John Gielgud (Treplev).

1925 **Ivanov*, Incorporated Stage Society, Duke of York's Theatre, London, 6 December, dir. and des. Theodore Komisarjevsky (as he was now known, though many called him 'Komis'), trans. Marian Fell, Robert Farquharson (Ivanov).

1926 *Uncle Vanya*, Barnes Theatre, London, 16 January, dir. Theodore Komisarjevsky, trans. Constance Garnett, John Gielgud (Tusenbach).

1926 *Three Sisters*, 14th Street Theatre, New York, 26 October, dir. Eva Le Gallienne, des. G. E. Calthrop, Eva Le Gallienne (Masha). US première.

1927 *Uncle Vanya*, Birmingham Repertory Theatre, Birmingham, 2 April, dir. W. G. Fay, des. Hugh Owen, Laurence Olivier (Vanya).

1927 *Dyadya Vanya* (*Uncle Vanya*), MAT, Moscow, dir. V. I. Nemirovich-Danchenko.

1928 *The Cherry Orchard*, Bijou Theatre, New York, 5 March, James Fagin (Gaev), Glen-Byam Shaw (Trofimov).

1928 *The Cherry Orchard*, Garrick Theatre, London, Prague Group of MKAT, 11 April, dir. M. N. Germanova. Guest production.

1928 *Uncle Vanya*, Garrick Theatre, London, Prague Group of MKAT (Moscow Art Theatre), 30 April, dir. M. N. Germanova. Guest production.

1928 *The Cherry Orchard*, Barnes Theatre, London, 28 September, Martita Hunt (Carlotta), Charles Laughton (Epihodov).

1928 *The Cherry Orchard*, Civic Repertory Theatre, New York, 14 October, dir. Eva Le Gallienne, des. Aline Bernstein, Eva Le Gallienne (Varya), Alla Nazimova (Ranevskaya).

1928 world première of Chekhov's untitled play (generally known as *Platonov* or *Fatherlessness*) in a version by René Fülop-Miller entitled *Der unnützige Mensch Platonoff* (*That Useless Person Platonov*), Preussisches Theater, Gera, south-east Germany, dir. Helmut Ebbs.

1929 *The Seagull*, Arts Theatre, London, 16 January, dir. A. E. Filmer, trans. Constance Garnett, des. James Whale, John Gielgud (Konstantin), Miriam Lewes (Arkadina), Valerie Taylor (Nina).

1929 *Les trois soeurs* (*Three Sisters*), Théâtre des Arts, Paris, 3 February, dir. and des. Georges Pitoëff.

1929 *Three Sisters*, Fortune Theatre, London, 23rd October, dir. and des. Theodore Komisarjevsky, trans. Constance Garnett, Glen-Byam Shaw (Tusenbach).

1930 *Uncle Vanya*, Cort Theatre, New York, 15 April, dir. Jed Harris, des. Jo Mielziner.

1930 *The Seagull*, Fortune Theatre, London, 25 September, dir. Philip Ridgeway, trans. Constance Garnett, Miriam Lewes (Arkadina), Glen-Byam Shaw (Konstantin).

1931 *The Proposal* and **The Anniversary*, Kingsway Theatre, London, 7 December, Prague Group of MKAT, (MAT), dir. P. Pavlov. Guest production.

1931 *The Cherry Orchard*, Kingsway Theatre, London, 21 December, Prague Group of MKAT, dir. P. Pavlov. Guest production.

1933 *The Cherry Orchard*, Civic Repertory Theatre, New York, 6 March, dir. Eva Le Gallienne, des. Aline Bernstein, Eva Le Gallienne (Varya), Alla Nazimova (Ranevskaya). This was a revival of the 1928 production.

1933 *The Cherry Orchard*, Old Vic Theatre, London, 9 October, dir. Tyrone Guthrie, des. Frederick Crooke and Sophia Harris, Marius Goring (Epihodov), Elsa Lanchester (Carlotta), Charles Laughton (Lopakhin), Roger Livesey (Simionov-Pischik), Flora Robson (Varia).

1935 *Three Sisters*, Old Vic, London, 12 November, dir. Henry Cass.

1935 *33 Obmoroka* (*33 Fainting Fits: The Proposal, The Bear, Jubilee*), Meyerhold Theatre, Moscow, 25 March, dir. V. E. Meyerhold, des. V. A. Shestakov.

1936 *The Seagull*, New Theatre, London, 20 May, dir. and des. Theodore

Komisarjevsky, Peggy Ashcroft (Nina), Edith Evans (Arkadina), John Gielgud (Trigorin), Martita Hunt (Masha).

1937 *Uncle Vanya*, Westminster Theatre, London, 5 February, dir. Michael Macowan, trans. Constance Garnett, des. Peter Goffin, Alexis France (Sonya), Lydia Sherwood (Yelena), Cecil Trouncer (Astrov), Harcourt Williams (Vanya).

1938 *Three Sisters*, Queen's Theatre, London, 28 January, dir. Michel Saint-Denis, des. Motley (a design trio consisting of Margaret ('Percy') Harris, her sister Sophie and Elizabeth Montgomery), lighting des. George Devine, Peggy Ashcroft (Irina), George Devine (Andrey), John Gielgud (Vershinin), Alec Guinness (Fedotik), Michael Redgrave (Tusenbach), Glen-Byam Shaw (Soliony).

1938 *The Seagull*, Shubert Theatre, New York, 28 March, dir. Robert Milton, des. Robert Edmond Jones, Lynn Fontaine (Arkadina), Sydney Greenstreet (Sorin), Uta Hagen (Nina), Alfred Lunt (Trigorin).

1939 *La Mouette (The Seagull)*, Théâtre des Mathurins, Paris, 17 January, dir. and des. Georges Pitoëff.

1939 *Three Sisters*, Longacre, New York, 14 October, dir. Dwight Wiman.

1940 *Tri sestry (Three Sisters)*, MAT, Moscow, 24 April, dir. V. I. Nemirovich-Danchenko, des. V. V. Dmitriev.

1940 First performance of *Platonov* in English, entitled *Fireworks on the James*, Provincetown Playhouse, Massachusetts, USA, dir. McCormick.

1941 *The Cherry Orchard*, New Theatre, London, 28 August, The Surrey Players, dir. Tyrone Guthrie, des. Frederick Cooke, James Dale (Lopakhin), Nicholas Hannen (Gaev), Athene Saylor (Ranevskaya).

1942 *The Three Sisters*, Barrymore Theatre, New York, 21 December, dir. Guthrie McClintic, des. Motley, Judith Anderson (Olga), Ruth Gordon (Natasha), Alexander Knox (Tusenbach).

1944 *Chaika (The Seagull)*, Kamerny (Chamber) Theatre, Moscow, January–February, dir. Alexander Tairov (1885–1950), des. E. Kovalenko and V. Krivosheina (Act One), Alisa Koonen (1889–1974) (Nina).

1945 *Uncle Vanya*, New Theatre, London, Old Vic Company, 16 January, dir. John Burrell, des. Tanya Moiseiwitsch, Margaret Leighton (Helena), Laurence Olivier (Astrov), Joyce Redman (Sonia), Ralph Richardson (Vanya), Sybil Thorndike (Marina), Harcourt Williams (Serebryakov).

1948 *Il Gabbiano* (*The Seagull*), Piccolo Theatre, Milan, 24 November, dir. Giorgio Strehler, des. Gianni Ratto, trans. Enzo Ferrieri.

1949 *The Proposal*, Old Vic, London, 28 February, dir. Laurence Olivier, des. Roger Furse, trans. Constance Garnett, Peter Cushing (Lomov), Peggy Simpson (Natasha).

1954 *The Cherry Orchard*, Lyric Theatre, Hammersmith, London, 21 May, dir. John Gielgud, des. Richard Lake, trans. Ariadne Nicolaeff and John Gielgud.

1954 *La Cérisaie* (*The Cherry Orchard*), Théâtre de Marigny, Paris, 7 October, dir. Jean-Louis Barrault, des. Wakhevitch, Jean-Louis Barrault (Trofimov), Marie-Helene Daste (Charlotta).

1955 *Il Giardino dei Ciliegi* (*The Cherry Orchard*), Piccolo Theatre, Milan, 13 January, dir. Giorgio Strehler, des. Tanya Moiseiwitsch, trans. Virginia Puecher and Barbara Parfiliev.

1956 *Ce Fou de Platonov* [*Platonov*], Bordeaux Festival, May, dir. Jean Vilar, Jean Vilar (Platonov).

1958 *A Tragedian in Spite of Himself*, Toynbee Theatre, London, 12 April, dir. Dmitri Makaroff.

1958 *The Cherry Orchard*, Sadlers Wells, London, 15 May, MAT, dir. V. Ya. Stanitsyn. Guest production.

1958 *Uncle Vanya*, Sadlers Wells, London, 20 May, MAT, dir. M. M. Kedrov. Guest production.

1958 *Three Sisters*, Sadlers Wells, London, 16 June, MAT, original dirs. V. I. Nemirovich-Danchenko and I. M. Rayevsky. Guest production from rep.

1959 *Don Juan* (*in the Russian Manner*) [*Platonov*], Nottingham Playhouse, Nottingham, 6 April, dir. Val May, des. Marsh King, trans. Basil Ashmore.

1959 *Platonov e altri* [*Platonov*], Piccolo Theatre, Milan, 27 April, dir. Giorgio Strehler, des. Luciano Damiani, trans. Ettore Lo Gatto.

1960 *Platonov*, Royal Court Theatre, 13 October, dir. George Devine and John Blatchley, des. Richard Negri, lighting Richard Pilbrow, trans. Dmitri Makaroff, Rex Harrison (Platonov), Rachel Roberts (Anna Petrovna).

1961 *The Seagull*, Malmo City Theatre, Sweden, 6 January, dir. Ingmar Bergman.

1961 *The Cherry Orchard*, Aldwych Theatre, London, 14 December, dir. Michel Saint-Denis, des. Abd'Elkader Farrah, trans. Ariadne Nicolaeff and John Gielgud, Peggy Ashcroft (Ranyevskaya), Judi Dench (Ania), John Gielgud (Gayev), Ian Holm (Trofimov), George Murcell (Lopakhin), Dorothy Tutin (Varia).

1962 *Uncle Vanya*, Chichester Festival Theatre, Chichester, 16 July, dir. Laurence Olivier, des. Sean Kenny and Beatrice Dawson, Sybil Thorndike (Marina), Laurence Olivier (Astrov), Michael Redgrave (Vanya), Joan Plowright (Sonia).

1963 *Uncle Vanya*, Old Vic, London, National Theatre, 19 November, dir. Laurence Olivier, des. Sean Kenny, trans. Constance Garnett, Michael Redgrave (Vanya), Laurence Olivier (Astrov), Joan Plowright (Sonia).

1964 **On the Harmfulness of Tobacco*, The Little Theatre, London, 28 April, dir. Ralph Wilton.

1964 *The Cherry Orchard*, Aldwych Theatre, London, 29 May, MAT, dir. V. Ya. Stanitsyn. World Theatre Season guest production.

1965 *Tri sestry* (*Three Sisters*), Gorki Theatre, Bolshoi Drama (BDT), Leningrad, 23 January, dir. Georgi Tovstonogov, des. Sofia Yunovich.

1965 *Three Sisters*, Aldwych Theatre, London, Actors Studio Theatre (USA), 13 May, dir. Lee Strasberg. Guest production.

1965 *Ivanov*, Phoenix Theatre, London, 30 September, dir. John Gielgud, des. Rouben Ter-Arutunian, John Gielgud (Ivanov).

1966 *Chaika* (*The Seagull*), Lenin Komsomol Theatre, Moscow, dir. Anatoly Efros, des. V. Lalevich and N. Sosunov.

1967 *Three Sisters*, Old Vic, London, NT, 4 July, dir. Laurence Olivier, des. Josef Svoboda, trans. Moura Budberg, Anthony Hopkins (Andrey), Joan Plowright (Masha), Robert Stephens (Vershinin).

1967 *Tri sestry* (*Three Sisters*), Malaya Bronnaya (Moscow Drama) Theatre, Moscow, dir. Anatoly Efros, des. Diukgin and Chernova.

1969 *Dyadya Vanya* (*Uncle Vanya*), Central Soviet Army Theatre (now the Russian Army Theatre), Moscow, dir. J. Heifetz. See chapter 8 in this volume.

1969 *Three Sisters*, Aldwych Theatre, London, 28 April, Otomar Krejča's Theatre Behind the Gate, dir. Otomar Krejča. World Theatre Season.

1970 *Chaika* (*The Seagull*), Aldwych Theatre, London, 5 May, MAT, dir. Boris Livanov, des. E. Stenberg. World Theatre Season guest production, originally produced at MAT in 1968.

1970 *Chaika* (*The Seagull*), Sovremennik (Contemporary) Theatre, Moscow, June–July, dir. Oleg Yefremov, des. Sergei Barkhin.

1970 *The Seagull*, Arts Theatre, Cambridge, 21 July, dir. Richard Cottrell, des. Keith Norman, trans. Richard Cottrell, Lila Kedrova (Arkadina).

1973 *The Seagull*, Chichester Festival Theatre, Chichester, 23 May, dir. Jonathan Miller, trans. Elisaveta Fen, des. Patrick Robertson.

1973 *Uncle Vanya*, Joseph E. Levine Theatre, New York, June 1973, dir. Mike Nichols, trans. Albert Todd, Julie Christie (Yelena), Lillian Gish (Marina), George C. Scott (Astrov), Nicol Williamson (Vanya).

1973 *The Wood-Demon*, Arts Theatre, Cambridge, 10 September, dir. David Giles, des. Kenneth Mellor, trans. Ronald Hingley, Ian McKellen (Khruschov).

1974 **Tatyana Repina*, Mull Little Theatre, Scotland, dirs. Barrie and Marianne Hesketh, des. Barrie Hesketh, trans. Ronald Hingley.

1974 *Il giardino de ciliegi* (*The Cherry Orchard*), Piccolo Theatre, Milan, 21 May, dir Giorgio Strehler, des. Luciano Damiani, trans. Luigi Lunari and Giorgio Strehler.

1975 *Vishnyovy sad* (*The Cherry Orchard*), Taganka Theatre, Moscow, 30 June, dir. Anatoly Efros, des. Valery Levental, Alla Demidova (Ranevskaya), Vladimir Vysotsky (Lopakhin).

1975 *Vishnyovy sad* (*The Cherry Orchard*), Sovremennik (Contemporary) Theatre, Moscow, dir. Oleg Yefremov, des. Sergei Barkhin.

1976 *Ivanov*, MAT, Moscow, December, dir. Oleg Yefremov, des. David Borovsky, Innokenty Smoktunovsky (Ivanov). See Appendix 4.

1976 *Three Sisters*, Yvonne Arnaud Theatre, Guildford, 20 April, dir Jonathan Miller, des. Patrick Robertson, trans. Elisaveta Fen.

1977 *The Cherry Orchard*, Vivian Beaumont Theatre, New York, 17 February, dir. Andrei Serban, des. Santo Loquasto, Meryl Streep (Duniasha), Irene Worth (Ranevskaya). (See p. 143).

1977 *The Cherry Orchard*, a new English version by Trevor Griffiths, Nottingham Playhouse, Nottingham, 10 March, dir. Richard Eyre, des. John Gunter, from a trans. by Helen Rappaport, Brian Glover (Simeonov-Pischik), Dave Hill (Lopakhin), Antony Sher (Epikhodov), Bridget Turner (Ranevsky). This production was reproduced for BBC television in 1981.

1978 *The Cherry Orchard*, in a version by Peter Gill, from a literal translation by Ted Braun, Riverside Studios, Hammersmith, London, 6 January, dir. Peter Gill, des. William Dudley.

1978 *The Cherry Orchard*, NT, 14 February, dir. Peter Hall, des. John Bury, trans. Michael Frayn, Albert Finney (Lopakhin), Ben Kingsley (Trofimov), Robert Stephens (Gayev).

1978 *Three Sisters*, Residenztheater, Munich, 22 June, dir. Ingmar Bergman. Guest production.

1979 *Three Sisters*, The Other Place, Stratford-upon-Avon, RSC, 29 September , dir. Trevor Nunn, des. John Napier, trans. Richard Cottrell, Suzanne Bertish (Masha), Janet Dale (Olga), Edward Petherbridge (Vershinin), Emily Richard (Irina), Timothy Spall (Andrey), Susan Tracy (Natasha). (See chapters 9 and 11.)

1979 *Uncle Vanya*, a new version by Pam Gems, Hampstead Theatre, London, 22 November, dir. Nancy Meckler, des. Alison Chitty, Maurice Denham (Serebryakov), Nigel Hawthorne (Vanya), Ian Holm (Astrov), Susan Littler (Yelena), Alison Steadman (Sonya).

1980 *Chaika (The Seagull)*, MAT, Moscow, July, dir. Oleg Yefremov, des. Valery Levental, (restaging of 1970 Sovremennik production). See Appendix 4.

1981 *The Seagull*, Shared Experience Company, Oxford, Crucible Studio, Sheffield, 12 September, dir. Mike Alfreds, Gillian Barge (Arkadina), Philip Osment (Konstantin), Philip Voss (Dorn).

1981–83 *La Cérisaie (The Cherry Orchard)*, Les Bouffes du Nord (1983), Paris, 12 March, dir. Peter Brook, des. Chloe Obolensky, from a literal trans. by Lusia Lavrova, adapt. Jean-Claude Carrière, Niels Arestrup (Lopakhin), Maurice Bénichou (Trofimov), Irina Brook (Ania), Natasha Parry (Ranevskaya), Michel Piccoli (Gaev). Toured internationally for several years, including to Moscow and New York.

1981 *The Seagull*, Royal Court, London, 8 April, dir. Max Stafford-Clark, des. Gemma Jackson, adapt. Thomas Kilroy, Anton Lesser (Konstantin),

Anna Massey (Arkadina), Alan Rickman (Trigorin), Harriet Walter (Nina). (See chapter 7.)

1981 *Die Drei Schwestern* (*Three Sisters*), Berlin Schaubühne, West Berlin, dir. Peter Stein, des. Karl Ernst Herrman.

1981 *Three Sisters* (*Tri sestri*), Taganka Theatre, Moscow, dir. Yuri Lyubimov, des. Yuri Konenko, Alla Demidova (Masha). (See chapters 12, 14, 15 and Appendix 4).

1982 *The Cherry Orchard*, Round House, London (Oxford Playhouse), 5 August, dir. Mike Alfreds, des. Nadine Baylis, trans. Lilia Sokolova and Mike Alfreds, Alison Fiske (Ranevskaya).

1984 *The Seagull*, Tyl Theatre, Prague, dir. Otomar Krejča, des. Josef Svoboda. (See chapter 12 and Appendix 4.)

1984 *Wild Honey* [version of *Platonov*], trans. and adapt. Michael Frayn, NT, London, 19 July, dir. Christopher Morahan, des. John Gunter, Ian McKellen (Platonov). (See chapter 11.)

1984 *La Mouette* (*The Seagull*). Théâtre National de Chaillot, Paris, 9 February, dir. and trans. Antoine Vitez, des. Yannis Kokkos. (See chapter 12 and Appendix 4.)

1985 *Dyadya Vanya* (*Uncle Vanya*), MAT, Moscow, February, dir. Oleg Yefremov.

1985 *The Seagull*, a new English version by Tania Alexander and Charles Sturridge, Oxford Playhouse Company, Oxford and then Lyric Theatre, Hammersmith, London, 22 April, dir. Charles Sturridge, des. Eileen Diss, transferred to Queen's Theatre, London, 2 August, Vanessa Redgrave (Arkadina), Jonathan Pryce (Trigorin).

1985 *The Cherry Orchard*, NT, London, 16 December, dir. Mike Alfreds, des. Paul Dart, trans. Lilia Sokolova and Mike Alfreds, Sheila Hancock (Ranevskaya), Ian McKellen (Lopakhin), Laurence Rudic (Trofimov). (See chapter 11.)

1986 *Three Sisters*, Shared Experience Theatre Company, Bloomsbury Theatre, London, 1 April, dir. Mike Alfreds, trans. Mike Alfreds with Nikita Stavisky, des. Paul Dart, Chloe Salaman (Irina), Leslee Udwin (Masha), Philip Voss (Chebutykin), Holly Wilson (Olga).

1987 *Uncle Vanya*, King's Theatre, Edinburgh, 12–13 August, (BDT), Leningrad, dir. Georgi Tovstonogov. Edinburgh Festival guest production.

1988 *Trinidad Sisters* (version *Three Sisters*), Donmar Warehouse, London, 9 February, dir. Nicholas Kent, des. Poppy Mitchell, trans. Mustapha Matura.

1988 *The Sneeze*, plays and stories by Anton Chekhov, trans. and adapt. by Michael Frayn, Aldwych Theatre, London, 27 September, which consisted of *Drama* (the story of 1887), *The Alien Corn* (story 'In a Foreign Land', 1885), *The Sneeze* (story 'Death of a Government Clerk/Official', 1883), *The Bear*, *The Evils of Tobacco*, *The Inspector General* (from the story 'An Awl in a Sack', 1885); Michael Codron Production at the Theatre Royal, Newcastle, 23 August, and Aldwych Theatre, London, with Rowan Atkinson, Cheryl Campbell, Timothy West, dir. Ronald Eyre, des. Mark Thompson.

1989 *Three Sisters*, Old Vic, London, Katona Jozsef Theatre, Budapest, 13 July, dir. Tomas Ascher. Guest production.

1989 *Dyadya Vanya* (*Uncle Vanya*), RNT, London, MAT, 14 September, dir. Oleg Yefremov, des. Valery Levental. Guest production.

1989 *Ivanov*, in a version by Ronald Harwood, Yvonne Arnaud Theatre, 7 February, transferred to The Strand Theatre, London, 10 April, dir. Elijah Moshinsky, des. Mark Thompson, Alan Bates (Ivanov), Felicity Kendall (Anna Petrovna).

1990 *Three Sisters*, Royal Court, London, 24 July, dir. Adrian Noble, des. Bob Crowley, trans. Rose Cullen and Frank Guinness, Sorcha Cusack (Olga), Sinead Cusack (Masha), Niamh Cusack (Irena).

1990 *Piano*, after Chekhov and based on the original film *An Unfinished Piece for Mechanical Piano* by N. Mikhalkov and A. Adabashian, Cottesloe Theatre, RNT, London, 8 August, a new play by Trevor Griffiths, dir. Howard Davies, des. Ashley Martin-Davis. Cast included Penelope Wilton, Stephen Moore and Stephen Rea. (See chapters 4 and 13)

1990 *Three Sisters*, Queen's Theatre, London, 11 December, Rustaveli Company, Georgia, USSR, guest dir. Robert Sturua, des. Giorgi Meskhishvili, adapt. Nikolas Simmonds from a translation by Helen Molchanoff, Jeremy Northam (Andrey), Vanessa Redgrave (Olga), Lynn Redgrave (Masha), Jemma Redgrave (Irena). Guest direction and design.

1991 *The Seagull*, Barbican, London, RSC, 1 July, dir. Terry Hands, des. Johan Engels, Simon Russell Beale (Konstantin), Susan Fleetwood (Arkadina).

1992 *Cherry Orchard*, Berlin Schaubühne, West Berlin, dir. Peter Stein, des. Christopher Shubiger.

1992 *The Cherry Orchard*, BDT, St Petersburg, dir. Adolphe Shapiro, des. Eduard Kochergin.

1993 *Uncle Vanya*, Cottesloe Theatre, London, RNT, 25 February, dir. Sean Mathias, des. Stephen Brimson Lewis, Ian McKellen (Vanya).

1994 *The Cherry Orchard*, premièred at Odéon-Théâtre de L'Europe for the International Workshop, the Borders, Paris, April, dir. Lev Dodin, des. Eduard Kochergin.

1994 *August*, an adaptation of *Uncle Vanya*, Theatre Clwyd, Mold, 25 October, dir. Anthony Hopkins, des. Eileen Diss.

1995 *The Cherry Orchard*, version by Peter Gill from an original translation by Ted Braun, Swan Theatre, Stratford-upon-Avon, RSC, 28 June, dir. Adrian Noble, des. Richard Hudson.

1996 *Three Sisters*, Lyric Theatre, Hammersmith, London, 7 May, Out of Joint Company, dir. Max Stafford-Clark, des. Julian McGowan.

1996 *(Uncle) Vanya*, Almeida, London, The Wrestling School, 19 June, in a version by Howard Barker, dir. Howard Barker, des. Robin Don.

1997 *A Play without a Title* [*Platonov*], Maly (Little) Theatre, St Petersburg, Weimar Theatre, Germany, dir. Lev Dodin, des. Alexei Porai-Koshits. Played at London's Barbican Theatre, 1998.

1997 *Ivanov*, Almeida, London, 19 February, dir. Jonathan Kent, des. Tobias Hoheisel, trans. David Hare, Ralph Fiennes (Ivanov), Ian McDiarmaid (Kosykh), Harriet Walter (Anna Petrovna).

1997 *The Seagull*, The Old Vic, London, Peter Hall Company, 9 May, dir. Peter Hall, des. John Gunter, trans. Tom Stoppard, Felicity Kendall (Arkadina), Michael Pennington (Trigorin), David Yelland (Dorn), Dominic West (Konstantin).

1997 *The Wood-Demon*, Playhouse, London, 18 June, dir. Anthony Clark, des. Joel Froomkin, Abigail Cruttenden (Yelena), Brian Protheroe (Uncle Zhorzh), Philip Voss (Serebryakov).

1998 *Uncle Vanya*, Young Vic, London, RSC/Young Vic co-production, 1 April, dir. Katie Mitchell, des. Rae Smith, trans. David Lan, Stephen Dillane (Vanya).

1998 *The Seagull*, West Yorkshire Playhouse, Leeds, 29 October, dir. Jude Kelly, des. Robert Innes-Hopkins, Ian McKellen (Dorn). (See p. 132.)

2000 *The Cherry Orchard*, September, RNT, dir. Trevor Nunn. (See chapter 9).

2000 *The Cherry Orchard*, dir. Steve Unwin, des. Pamela Howard, Prunella Scales (Ranevskaya), English Touring Company.

Selected screen versions

(See also chapter 13 in this volume, and Jay Leyda, *Kino, A History of the Russian Film*, Allen and Unwin, London, 1973.)
photo. denotes cinematic photographer.
* denotes title and further details including dates of publication in Appendix 1.

1911 *Romance with Double Bass** (*Roman s kontrabasom*), prod. Pathé Frères, France, dir. Kai Hansen, des. Sabiwsky, photo. Georges Meyer.

1912 *Ward No. 6** (*Palata No. 6*), prod. Stern and Co., and Varyag, Russia, dir. Boris Chaikovsky, photo. Ivan Frolov.

1914 *The Daughter of Albion** (*Doch Albiona*), prod. Russian Ribbon, dir. Boris Glagolin, photo. A. Pechkovsky.
*Illegal (Bezzakonie**), prod. Russian Ribbon, dir. Boris Glagolin, photo. A. Pechkovsky.

1917 *The Flowers are Late** (*Tsveti zapozdaliye*), prod. Vengerov and Gardin, Russia, dir. Boris Sushkevich, des. Sergei Kozlovsky, photo. A. Stanke.

1929 *Ranks and people* (*Chiny i liudi*), from three stories by Chekhov, prod. Mezhrabpomfilm, USSR, dir. Yakov Protazanov, co-dir. Mikhail Doller, des. Vladimir Yegorov, photo. Konstantin Kuznetsov, with Ivan Moskvin.

1938 *The Bear** (*Medved*), prod. Belgoskino, USSR, dir. Isidor Annensky, des. L. Putiyevskaya, photo. Y. Shapiro.

1939 *The/A Man in the Case** (*Chelovek v futlyare*), prod. Sovietskaya Belorus, USSR, dir. Isidor Annensky, des. L. Putiyevskaya, photo. Y. Shapiro.

1944 *The Anniversary (Yubiley)*, prod. Mosfilm, USSR, dir. Vladimir Petrov, photo. Vladimir Yakovlev.
The Wedding* (Svadba), prod. Tbilisi Studios, Georgia, dir. Isidor Annensky, photo. Yuri Yekelchik.
The Bear*, prod. Dynamic Films Inc., USA, dir. Nathan Zucker.

1955 *The Gadfly/The Butterfly*/ The Grasshopper (Poprygunya)*, prod. Mosfilm, USSR, dir. Samson Samsonov, photo. F. Dobronravov and V. Monakhov.

1959 *A Work of Art (Khudozhestvo)*, prod. Mosfilm, USSR, dir. M. Kovalev.

1960 *The Lady with the Little Dog* (Dama s sobachkoi)*, prod. Lenfilm, USSR, dir. Joseph Heifetz, with Alexei Batalov and Iya Savvina.

1964 *Three Sisters (Tri sestry)*, prod. Mosfilm, USSR, dir. Samson Samsonov.
Three Sisters, prod. Ely Landau-Actors Studio Inc., USA, dir. Paul Bogart.

1968 *The Seagull**, prod. Warner Bros, USA, dir. Sidney Lumet, with James Mason, Vanessa Redgrave, Simone Signoret, David Warner.

1970 *Three Sisters**, prod. Ely Landau Organization Inc., USA, dir. Laurence Olivier, with Alan Bates, Derek Jacobi, Sheila Reid, Joan Plowright, Louise Purnell, Laurence Olivier.
The Seagull* (Chaika), prod. Mosfilm, USSR, dir. Juli Karasik.

1972 *Uncle Vanya* (Dyadya Vanya)*, prod. Mosfilm, USSR, dir. Andrei Konchalovsky.
Belated flowers* (Tzvety zapozdalye), prod. Mosfilm, USSR, dir. Abram Room.

1976 *An Unfinished Piece for Mechanical Piano (Mekhanicheskoe pianino)*, prod. Mosfilm, USSR, dir. Nikita Mikhalkov, with Alexander Kaliagin, Elena Solovei, Oleg Tabakov.

1977 *The Shooting Party (Drama na okhote)*, prod. Mosfilm, USSR, dir. Emil Loteanu.

1983 *The Cherry Orchard**, Trevor Griffiths' version, prod. BBC TV, dir. Richard Eyre, des. Susan Spence, with some of cast from 1977 Nottingham Playhouse production (see Appendix 2).

1990 *Uncle Vanya**, prod. BBC/WNET, UK/USA, adapt. David Mamet, dir. Gregory Mosher, with Ian Bannen, Ian Holm.

1992 *Three Sisters*,* prod. Hunnia Játekfilmsstudio, Hungary, dir. Andor Lukats.

1994 *Vanya on 42nd Street*, prod. Mayfair Entertainment, UK, dir. Louis Malle, original stage production directed by André Gregory, screenplay adapt. David Mamet, with André Gregory, Madhur Jaffrey, Julianne Moore, Wallace Shawm, Brooke Smith.

1996 *August*, adapt. from *Uncle Vanya**, prod. Granada Films/Majestic Films, UK, dir. Anthony Hopkins, written by Julian Mitchell, with Anthony Hopkins and Leslie Phillips.

Illustrations

Model for *Ivanov*, designer David Borovsky, director Oleg Yefremov,
Moscow Art Theatre, 1976.

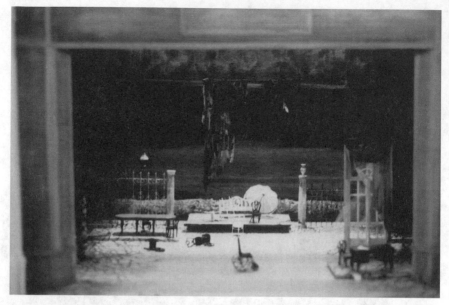

Model for *The Seagull*, designer Valery Levental, director Oleg Yefremov,
Moscow Art Theatre, 1980

The Seagull, designer Josef Svoboda, director Otomar Krejča, Tyl Theatre, Prague, 1984.
From the Czech Theatre Institute: catalogue *In Search of Light*, 1995.

The Seagull, Act 1, designer Yannis Kokkos, Théâtre de Chaillot, Paris, 1984.
'Impressionism was the aesthetic starting point for *The Seagull*. I did not want to work in the outdated, stereotypical cameo style which is associated with Chekhov and which would have drowned the design in nostalgia . . . The design for *The Seagull* comes from two sources: first, French Impressionism – though more realistic, like the Russian painter Levitan, a friend of Chekhov; and on the other hand, the colored light compositions made of grains of primary colors as in the first color photographs.' – Yannis Kokkos.

SELECTED BIBLIOGRAPHY

This has been compiled with the emphasis on the dramatic works. For Russian and other critical sources on Chekhov, see endnotes to chapters. Transliteration follows that of the given title.

Chekhov's Russia: social/historical context

Bruford, Walter H., *Chekhov and His Russia, A Sociological Study*, 2nd edn, Routledge and Kegan Paul, London, 1948; reprinted Archon Books, Hamden, Conn., 1971.

Charques, Richard, *The Twilight of Imperial Russia*, Oxford University Press, Oxford, 1958.

Figes, Orlando, *A People's Tragedy: The Russian Revolution 1891–1924*, Jonathan Cape, London, 1996; Pimlico, Random House, London, 1997.

Fitzlyon, Kryil, and Tatiana Browning, *Before the Revolution, A View of Russia under the Last Tsar*, Allen Lane, London, 1977.

Katkov, George, Erwin Oberlander, Nikolaus Poppe, Georg Von Rauch, eds., *Russia Enters the Twentieth Century*, Methuen, London, 1973.

Obolensky, Chloe, *The Russian Empire, A Portrait in Photographs*, Jonathan Cape, London, 1979.

Roosevelt, Priscilla, *Life on the Russian Country Estate, A Social and Cultural History*, Yale University Press, New Haven and London, 1995.

Seton-Watson, H., *The Decline of Imperial Russia*, Methuen, London, 1952.

Turkov, Andrei, ed., *Anton Chekhov and His Times*, trans. Cynthia Carlile and Sharon McKee, University of Arkansas Press, Fayetteville, 1995.

Chekhov's Russia: theatre context

Amiard-Chevrel, Claudine, *Le Théâtre Artistique de Moscou (1898–1917)*, Editions du Centre National de la Recherche Scientifique, Paris, 1979.

Bakshy, Alexander, *The Path of the Modern Russian Stage and other Essays*, Cecil Palmer and Hayward, London, 1916.

Bassekhes, A., *Khodozhniki na stene MXAT*, Vserossiyskoe teatralnoe obshchestvo, Moscow, 1960.

Benedetti, Jean, *Stanislavski: A Biography*, Methuen, London, 1990.

Braun, E., *Meyerhold, A Revolution in Theatre*, Methuen, London, 1995.

Brodsky, A., ed., *Moskovskii Khodozhestvennyi teatr vtoroi*, Moscow, 1925.

Davydova, M., *Ocherki istorii russkogo teatralno-dekoratsionnogo iskusstvo* XVIII-*nachala* XX *vekov*, Moscow, 1974.

Freidkina, L., *Dni i gody Vl. I. Nemirovicho-Danchenko*, Moscow, 1962.

Gitovich, N. I., *Letopis Zhizni i tvorchestva, A. P. Chekhova*, Gos. Izd. Khudozhestvennoy literatury, Moscow, 1955.

Gortchakov, N., *Vakhtangov, Metteur en scène*, Moscow, n.d.

Hapgood, E., trans. and ed., *Stanislavsky's Legacy*, Theatre Arts Book, New York, 1958; reprint Methuen, London, 1981.

Knipper-Chekhova, Olga Leonardovna, *Correspondence: 1896–1959*, Moscow, 1972.

Leyda, J., *Kino, A History of the Russian Film*, Allen and Unwin, London, 1973.

Lunacharsky, A., *O teatre i dramaturgii*, vol I, Moscow, 1958.

Markarova, M., T. Modestova, eds., *Pesi A. P. Chekhova v Moskovskom khodozhestvennom teatre*, Moscow, 1961.

Markov, P., ed., *A. Ya.Tairov*, VTO Moskva, Moscow, 1967.

Marshall, H., *The Pictorial History of the Russian Theatre*, Crown Publishers Inc., New York, 1977.

Meyerhold, Vsevolod, *Théâtre naturaliste et théâtre d'atmosphere*, in his *Ecrits sur le théâtre, L'Age d'homme*, trans. Béatrice Piçon-Vallin, POK, Lausanne, 1973–92.

Mikhalsky, F., ed., *Moskovskii khodozhestvennyi teatr v sovetskoi epokhe*, Moscow, 1974.

Moser, Charles A., ed., *The Cambridge History of Russian Literature*, Cambridge University Press, Cambridge, 1989.

Nemirovich-Danchenko, V. I., *My Life in the Russian Theatre*, trans. J. Cournos, Bles, London, 1937; reprint London, 1968.

V. I. Nemirovich-Danchenko – Teatralnoe nasledie, Moscow, 1954.

Pichkhadze, L., ed., *Moskovskii khodozhestvennyi teatr*, Moscow, 1978.

Polyakova, E., ed., *Stanislavskii*, Moscow, 1977; English edition Foreign Language Publishing House, Progress Publishers, Moscow, 1977.

Pozharskaya, M., *Russkoe teatralno-dekoratsionnoe iskusstvo kontsa* XIX, *nachala* XX *vekov*, Moscow, 1970.

Rudnitsky, K., *Meyerhold the Director*, ed. S. Schultze, trans. G. Petrov, Ann Arbor, Mich., USA, 1981.

Russian and Soviet Theatre, Tradition and the Avant-Garde, trans. Roxane Permar and ed. Lesley Milne, Thames and Hudson, London, 1988.

Russkoe rezhisserskoe iskusstvo 1898–1907, Moscow, 1989.

Sayler, Oliver M., *Inside the Moscow Art Theatre*, first published Brentano's, New York, 1925; reprinted and facsimile edition Greenwood Press, Westport, Conn., 1970.

Schuler, Catherine A., *Women in Russian Theatre, the Actress in the Silver Age*, Routledge, London and New York, 1996.

Senelick, Laurence, ed., *National Theatre in Northern and Eastern Europe, 1746–1900*, Cambridge University Press Series *Theatre in Europe: A Documentary History*, Cambridge University Press, Cambridge 1991.

Shakh-Azizova, T. K., *Chekhov i zapadno-yevropeyskaya drama yego vremeni*, Nauka, Moscow, 1966.

Simonov, Ruben, *Stanislavsky's Protégé, Eugene Vakhtangov*, trans. M. Goldina, DBS Publications Inc., New York, 1969.

Sokolova, N., V. Ryndin, B. Volkov, eds., *50 let khodozhniki teatra*, Moscow, 1969.

Solovyeva, Inna, ed., *Rezhisserskie ekzemplyary K. S. Stanislavskogo*, vol. III, 1901–4, Isskustvo, Moscow, 1983.

Stanislavski, C., *My Life in Art*, trans. J. J. Robbins, Bles, London, 1962.

Stanislavsky, K., *Sobranie sochinenii v vosmi tomakh*, Moscow, 1969.

Stroeva, M. N., *Rezhisserskiye iskaniya Stanislavskogo 1898–1917*, Moscow, 1973. *Rezhisserskiye iskaniya Stanislavskogo 1917–1938*, Moscow, 1977.

Svobodin, A. P., ed., *Teatr 'Sovremennik'*, Moscow, 1973.

Toporkov, V. O., *Stanislavski in Rehearsal*, trans. C. Edwards, Routledge, New York, 1979; reprint 1998.

Tovstonogov, G., *Quarante ans de mise en scène*, Foreign Languages Publishing House, Les Éditions du Progrès, Progress Publishers, Moscow, 1976.

Van Gyseghem, A., *Theatre in Soviet Russia*, Faber and Faber, London, 1943.

Varneke, B.V., *History of the Russian Theatre, Seventeenth through Nineteenth Century*, trans. Boris Brasol, reprint edn. Belle Martin (fascimile of 1951 edition), Hafner Publishing Company, New York, 1971.

Vendrovskaya, L., G. Kaptereva, eds., *Evgeny Vakhtangov*, trans. D. Bradbury, Foreign Languages Publishing House, Progress Publishers, Moscow, 1982.

Voitsekhovskaya, N. K., D. M. Shvarts, eds., *Teatr imeni Gorkogo*, Leningrad, 1968.

Worrall, Nick, *The Moscow Art Theatre*, Routledge, London, 1996.

Yuzovsky, Yu., *Razgovor zatianulsia za polnoch*, Moscow, 1966.

Znosko-Borovsky, E., *Russkii teatr nachala XX veka*, Prague, 1925.

Selected primary sources in Russian

Balukhaty, S. D., and others, eds., *Collected Works/Letters, Polnoe sobranie sochinenii i pisem A. P. Chekhova v 20i tomakh*, Moscow, 1944–51.

Belchikov, N. F., and others, eds., *Anton Chekhov, Polnoe sobranie sochinenii i pisem v 30i tomakh*, Moscow, 1974–83.

Chekhov, Anton, *Chto chashche vsego vstrechayetsya . . .* , 1880 (*A. P. Chekhov, Things Most Frequently Encountered in Novels, Stories and Other Such Things*), Works/Letters, *Polnoe sobranie sochinenii i pisem v 30i tomakh*, Moscow, 1974–83, vol. I, 1880–2.

Yelpatyevsky, S. Y., and others, eds., *Chekhov in the Memoirs of his Contemporaries, Chekhov v vospominaniiakh sovremennikov*, Moscow, 1954.

Yermilov, V. V., and others, eds., *Collected Works/Letters, Anton Chekhov, Sobranie sochinenii i pisem v 12i tomakh*, Moscow, 1960–4.

Selected primary sources in Russian: letters and other works

Chekhov, M. P., *Anton Chekhov i yego syuzhety*, Moscow, 1923.
Vokrug Chekhova. Vstrechi i vpechatleniya, Moskovsky rabochy, Moscow, 1980.

Chekhov, Al. P., *Pisma A. P. Chekhovu yego brata Aleksandra Chekhova*, ed. I. S.
    Yezhov, Moscow, 1939.
Chekhova, Maria P., *Iz dalyokogo proshlogo*, Moscow, 1960.
Derman, A. B., ed., *Perepiska A. P. Chekhova i O. L. Knipper*, vol. I, 1934, vol. II,
    1936, Moscow.
Surkov, Ye. D., ed., *Chekhov i teatr: pisma, felyetony, sovremenniki o Chekhove-
    dramaturge*, Isskustvo, Moscow, 1961.
Vinogradov, V. V. and others, ed., *Literaturnoye nasledstvo: Chekhov*, Moscow,
    1960.

Selected primary sources in English: plays

Alexander, Tania, and Charles Sturridge, eds., trans. *The Seagull*, Amber Lane Press
    Ltd., Oxford, 1986.
Ashmore, Basil, ed., *Don Juan (in the Russian Manner)*, P. Nevil, London, 1952.
Baukhage, Hilmar, ed., *The Boor* [*sic. The Bear*], Samuel French, New York, 1915.
Baukhage, Hilmar, and Barrett H. Clark, eds., *A Marriage Proposal* [*The Proposal*],
    Samuel French, New York, 1914.
Bentley, Eric, and Theodore Hoffman, eds., trans., *The Brute, and Other Farces*
    (*The Harmfulness of Tobacco, Swan Song, The Brute, A Marriage Proposal,
    Summer in the Country* (eds. note: more usually known as *The Reluctant
    Tragedian* or *A Tragic Role*), *A Wedding, The Celebration* (more usually
    Jubilee or *The Anniversary*)), Grove Press, New York, 1958.
Bristow, Eugene K., ed., *Anton Chekhov's Plays*, Norton Critical Edition, Norton,
    New York, 1977.
Butler, Hubert, ed., *The Cherry Orchard*, Baker International Play Bureau, Boston,
    1934.
Calderon, George, ed., trans., *Two Plays by Tchekhof*, London, 1912; Cape,
    London, 1928.
Caylor, Rose, ed., *Uncle Vanya*, Covici, Friede, New York, 1930.
Cournos, John, *That Worthless Fellow Platonov*, Dutton, New York, 1920.
Covan, Jenny, ed., *The Cherry Orchard*, Brentano's, New York, 1922.
    The Moscow Art Theatre Series of Russian Plays, Brentano's, New York, 1922.
    Uncle Vanya, Brentano's, New York, 1922.
Dunnigan, Ann, ed., *The Major Plays* (*Ivanov, The Sea Gull, Uncle Vanya, The
    Three Sisters, The Cherry Orchard*), Signet, New York, 1964.
Fell, Marian, ed., *Plays by Anton Tchekoff*, Scribner's Sons, New York, 1912–16;
    Duckworth, London, 1913.
    Ivanoff, Brentano's, New York, 1923.
    Five Famous Plays, Duckworth, London, 1939.
    Six Famous Plays, Duckworth, London, 1949.
Fen, Elisaveta, ed., trans., *Three Plays, The Cherry Orchard, Three Sisters, Ivanov*,
    Penguin, Harmondsworth, 1951.
    Chekhov Plays, Penguin, Harmondsworth, 1954.
Frayn, Michael, *Wild Honey, the untitled play by Anton Chekhov* [*Platonov*] in a
    version by Michael Frayn, post-production edition, Methuen, London and
    New York, 1985.
Frayn, Michael, ed., trans., *Chekhov Plays: The Seagull, Uncle Vanya, Three Sisters*,

The Cherry Orchard, The Evils of Tobacco, Swan Song, The Bear, The Proposal, Methuen, London, 1988.

The Sneeze, translated and adapted by Michael Frayn, contains the plays *The Bear, The Evils of Tobacco, Swan Song, The Proposal*, and dramatisations of the stories 'Drama' (1887), *The Alien Corn* (story 'In a Foreign Land', 1885), *The Sneeze* (from the story 'Death of a Government Clerk', 1883), *The Inspector General* (from the story 'An Awl in a Sack', 1885), Methuen, London, 1989.

Garnett, Constance, ed., trans., *The Cherry Orchard, and Other Plays*, Chatto and Windus, London, 1923; Seltzer, New York, 1924.

Plays, Chatto and Windus, London, 1925–1928.

Plays, Modern Library, New York, 1930.

The Three Sisters, and Other Plays, Chatto and Windus, London, 1923.

Gems, Pam, *Uncle Vanya*, A New Version, Eyre Methuen, London, 1979.

Gielgud, John, version of *Ivanov* from a literal translation by Ariadne Nicolaeff, Heinemann, London,1966.

Gill, Peter, version of *The Cherry Orchard* from a literal translation by Ted Braun, Oberon, London, 1995.

Gottlieb, Vera, trans. and adapt. *A Chekhov Quartet, two plays and two short stories*, dramatised version of 'A Moscow Hamlet', from the story 'V Moskve', 1891, and 'Accounts', from the story 'Razmaznya', 1883, with *Swan Song* and *On the Harmfulness of Tobacco*, Harwood Academic, GMBH., Amsterdam, 1995.

Griffiths, Trevor, ed., *The Cherry Orchard*, Pluto Press Limited, London, 1978.

Piano, Faber and Faber, London, 1990.

Guthrie, Tyrone, and Leonid Kipnis, eds., *The Cherry Orchard*, Minnesota Drama Editions, University of Minnesota Press, Minn., 1965.

The Three Sisters, The Avon Theater Library, Avon, New York, 1965.

Uncle Vanya, Minnesota Drama Editions, University of Minnesota Press, Minn., 1969.

Harwood, Ronald, version of *Ivanov*, Amber Lane Press Ltd., Oxford, 1989.

Hingley, Ronald, ed., trans., *The Oxford Chekhov in 9 Vols.*, vols. I–III, The Plays; vols. IV–IX, The Selected Stories 1889–1904 (excludes early stories), Oxford University Press, Oxford/New York/ Toronto/Melbourne, 1965–80. See Appendix 1.

Twelve Plays, Oxford University Press, New York, 1992.

Iliffe, David, ed., *The Seagull*, Samuel French, London, 1953.

Jarrel, Randall, ed., *The Three Sisters*, Macmillan, New York, 1969.

Kilroy, Thomas, adapt., *The Seagull*, The Gallery Press, Loughcrew, Meath, Ireland, 1993.

Koteliansky, S. S., ed., *Tchekoff's Plays and Stories*, introduction David Magarshack (*The Cherry Orchard, The Seagull, The Wood-Demon, Tatyana Repina, On the Harmfulness of Tobacco*, and stories include: 'My Life', 'The House with the Mezzanine', 'Typhus', 'Gooseberries', 'In Exile', 'The Lady with the Toy Dog', 'Goussiev', 'A Moscow Hamlet', 'At the Cemetery', 'At the Post Office', 'Schulz', 'Life is Wonderful', 'A Fairy Tale'), J. M. Dent, London, 1937, reprinted 1946.

The Wood-Demon, Chatto and Windus, London, 1926.

Magarshack, David, ed., trans., *The Seagull*, D. Dobson, London, 1952.

Platonov, Hill and Wang, New York, 1964.

Four Plays: Seagull, Uncle Vanya, Three Sisters, The Cherry Orchard, Hill and Wang, New York, 1969.

Mamet, David, adapt., *The Cherry Orchard*, Grove, New York, 1985.

adapt. *Uncle Vanya*, Grove, New York, 1985.

Mandell, M. S., ed., *The Cherry Garden*, Yale Courant, New Haven, Conn., 1908.

Mitchell, Julian, *August* (adaptation of *Uncle Vanya*), Amber Lane, Oxford, 1994.

Nicolaeff, Ariadne, and John Gielgud, eds., trans., *Chekhov Plays*, Hartsdale House, New York, 1935.

Nine Plays by Anton Chekhov, Caxton House, New York, 1946.

Senelick, Laurence, ed., trans., *The Cherry Orchard*, Arlington House Memorial, Arlington Heights, Ill., 1977.

The Cherry Orchard and *The Seagull*, Arlington House Memorial, Arlington Heights, Ill., 1977.

Szogy, Alex, ed., *Ten Early Plays*, Bantam, New York, 1965.

West, Julius, ed., *The Seagull*, Hendersons, London, 1915.

Four Short Plays, Duckworth, London, 1915, reprinted 1950.

Plays by Anton Tchekoff, Duckworth, London, 1916; Scribner's Sons, New York, 1916.

Five Famous Plays, Duckworth, London, 1939.

Yarmolinsky, Avrahm, ed., trans., *The Cherry Orchard*, The Avon Theater Library, Avon, New York, 1965.

The Portable Chekhov, Viking, New York, 1947; 2nd edn, 1968.

Young, Stark, *The Seagull*, Scribner's Sons, London and New York, 1939.

Three Sisters, Samuel French, New York and Los Angeles, 1941.

The Cherry Orchard, Samuel French, New York, 1947.

Best Plays, Modern Library, New York, 1956.

For French editions with information and commentary by Patrice Pavis see:

Pavis, Patrice, ed., *La Mouette (The Seagull)*, traduction d'Antoine Vitez, commentaires et notes de Patrice Pavis, Actes Sud, Le Livre de Poche, Paris, 1985.

Oncle Vania (Uncle Vanya), traduction et préface de Tonia Galievsky et Bruno Sermonne, commentaires et notes de Patrice Pavis, Le Livre de Poche, Paris, 1986.

La Cérisaie (The Cherry Orchard), traduction d'Elena Pavis-Zahradnikova et Patrice Pavis, Le Livre de Poche, Paris, 1988.

Les trois soeurs (Three Sisters), traduction de Jean-Claude Huens, Karel Kraus et Ludmilla Okuniéva, introduction et notes de Patrice Pavis, Le Livre de Poche, Paris, 1991.

M(o)uettes, The Seagull, a contemporary version written by Pavis, Degres, Brussels, 1999.

Selected primary sources in English: stories

Garnett, Constance, trans. *The Tales of Anton Tchechov* (in 13 vols.), Chatto and Windus, London, 1926.

(revised Rayfield, D.,) *The Chekhov Omnibus*, Everyman, London, 1994 (but not

'Panpipes', 'Fortune', 'Tumbleweed', 'The Kiss', 'Neighbours', 'The Grass-hopper', 'Big Volodia and Little Volodia', and 'Ariadna').

Gottlieb, Nora, *Chekhov: The Early Stories*, The Bodley Head, London, 1960; Anchor Books, Doubleday & Company, Inc., Garden City, N.Y, 1961.

Hingley, Ronald, *The Oxford Chekhov in 9 Vols.*, vol IV–IX, The Selected Stories 1889–1904 (excludes early stories), Oxford University Press, Oxford/New York/Toronto/Melbourne, 1965–80.

Miles, Patrick, and Harvey Pitcher, *Anton Chekhov Early Stories*, Oxford's World Classics, Oxford University Press, Oxford, 1999.

Wilks, Ronald, *The Kiss and Other Stories*, Penguin, Harmondsworth, 1982.
The Duel and Other Stories, Penguin, Harmondsworth, 1984.
The Party and Other Stories, Penguin, Harmondsworth, 1985.
The Fiancée and Other Stories, Penguin, Harmondsworth, 1986.
See Appendix 1 for full list of stories.

Selected primary sources in English: letters and other works

Benedetti, Jean, trans. and ed., *Dear Writer – Dear Actress: the Love Letters of Anton Chekhov and Olga Knipper*, Methuen, London, 1996.
The Moscow Art Theatre Letters, Methuen, London, 1991.

Chekhov, Anton P., *The Island: A Journey to Sakhalin*, introduction by Irena Ratushinskaya, trans. Luba and Michael Terpak, Century Hutchinson, London, 1987.

Friedland, Louis S., selected, trans., ed., *Letters on the Short Story, the Drama and Other Literary Topics by Anton Chekhov*, 2nd edn, reprinted Dover Publications, New York, 1966.

Hellman, L., ed. and introduction, *The Selected Letters of Anton Chekhov*, trans. S. K. Lederer, Hamish Hamilton, London, 1955, reprinted 1984.

Karlinsky, Simon, selection, commentary and introduction, *The Letters of Anton Chekhov*, trans. Michael Henry Heim in collaboration with Simon Karlinsky, Harper and Row, New York, 1973.

Koteliansky, S. S., and Philip Tomlinson, trans. and ed., *The Life and Letters of Anton Tchekhov*, 2nd edn, 1925; reprinted Benjamin Blom, New York, 1965.

Yarmolinsky, A., selected, trans., ed., *Letters of Anton Chekhov*, Viking Press, New York, 1973.

Secondary sources in English: biographies and memoirs

Avilova, Lidiya, *Chekhov in My Life: A Love Story*, trans. D. Magarshack, Greenwood Press, Westport, Conn., 1971.

Callow, Philip, *Chekhov – The Hidden Ground*, Constable, London, 1998.

Chukovsky, Kornei, trans. Pauline Rose, *Chekhov the Man*, Hutchinson and Co., London, 1945.

Elton, Oliver, *Chekhov (The Taylorian Lecture)*, Clarendon Press, Oxford, 1929.

Garnett, Edward, *Chekhov and his Art*, London, 1929.

Hingley, Ronald, *Chekhov, A Biographical and Critical Study*, George Allen and Unwin, London, 1966.
A New Life of Anton Chekhov, Oxford University Press, Oxford, 1976.

Koteliansky, S. S., trans. and ed., *Anton Tchekhov, Literary and Theatrical Reminiscences*, 2nd edn, 1927; reprinted Benjamin Blom, New York, 1965.

Koteliansky, S. S., and L. Woolf, trans., *Reminiscences of Anton Chekhov by M. Gorky, A. Kuprin, and I. A. Bunin*, B. W. Huebsh, New York, 1921.

Lafitte, Sophie, *Chekhov 1860–1904*, trans. M. Budberg and G. Latta, Angus and Robertson, London, 1974.

Magarshack, David, *Chekhov: A Life*, Faber, London, 1952; reprinted Greenwood Press, Westport, Conn., 1970.

Melchinger, Siegfried, *Anton Chekhov*, Frederick Ungar, New York, 1972.

Nemirovsky, Irene, *A Life of Chekhov*, trans. E. de Mauny, Grey Walls Press, London, 1950.

Priestley, John B., *Anton Chekhov*, International Textbooks, London, 1970.

Pritchett, V. S., *Chekhov: A Spirit Set Free*, Hodder and Stoughton, London, 1988.

Rayfield, Donald, *Anton Chekhov: A Life*, Harper Collins, London, 1997.

Saunders, Beatrice, *Tchehov the Man*, Centaur Press, London, 1960.

Senelick, Laurence, *Anton Chekhov*, Macmillan, Basingstoke and London, 1985.

Simmons, Ernest J., *Chekhov, A Biography*, The University of Chicago Press, Chicago and London, 1962.

Toumanova, Princess Nina Andronikova, *Anton Chekhov: The Voice of Twilight Russia*, Columbia University Press, New York, *c.* 1937; reprint 1960.

Troyat, Henri, *Chekhov*, trans. from the French by Michael Henry Heim, Dutton, New York, 1986.

Yermilov, Vladimir, *Anton Pavlovich Chekhov 1860–1904*, Foreign Languages Publishing House, Progress Publishers, Moscow, 1956.

Authored/edited critical books on Chekhov

Allen, David, *Performing Chekhov*, Routledge, London, 1999.

Balukhaty, Sergei, ed., *'The Seagull', produced by Stanislavsky*, trans. David Magarshack, Dennis Dobson Ltd., London, n.d.

Balukhaty, S. D., *Problema dramaticheskogo analiza: Chekhov*, Academia, Leningrad, 1927.

Balukhaty, S. D., and N. V. Petrov, *Dramaturgiya Chekhova*, Kharkov, 1935.

Berdnikov, G. P., *A. P. Chekhov: ideynye i tvorcheskie iskaniya*, Moscow, 1970.

   Chekhov-dramaturg: traditsii i novatorstvo v dramaturgii A. P. Chekhova, Isskustvo, Moscow, 3rd revised reprint, 1972.

Barricelli, Jean-Pierre, ed., *Chekhov's Great Plays, a Critical Anthology*, New York University Press, New York, 1981.

Brahms, Caryl, *Reflections in a Lake, A Study of Chekhov's Four Greatest Plays*, Weidenfeld and Nicholson, London, 1976.

Bruford, W. H., *Anton Chekhov*, Yale University Press, New Haven, Conn., 1957.

Bunin, I. A., *O Chekhove (Concerning Chekhov)*, trans. M. A. Aldanova, Chekhov Publishing House, New York, 1955.

Chudakov, Alexander P., *Chekhov's Poetics*, trans. E. Cruise and D. Dragt, Ardis Publishers, Ann Arbor, Mich., 1983.

Clyman, Toby W., ed., *A Chekhov Companion*, Greenwood Press, Westport, Conn., 1985.

Debreczeny, Paul, and Thomas Eekman, eds., *Chekhov's Art of Writing, A Collection of Critical Essays*, Slavica Publishers, Columbus, Ohio, 1977.

Eekman, T., ed., *Anton Cechov, 1860–1960, Some Essays*, E. J. Brill, Leiden, 1960.

Efros, Nikolai, *'Tri sestri' i 'Vishnevy sad' v postanovke Moskovskam Khudozhestvennom teatra*, Svetozar, Petrograd, 1919.

Ehrenbourg, Ilya, *A la rencontre de Tchekhov*, Didier-Forum, Paris, 1969.

Emeljanow, Victor, ed., *Chekhov, The Critical Heritage*, Boston and Henley, London, 1981.

Erlich, V., ed., *Twentieth-Century Russian Literary Criticism*, Yale University Press, New Haven, Conn., 1975.

Gerhardi, William, *Anton Chekhov, A Critical Study*, Macdonald, London, 1923; reprinted with preface by Michael Holroyd, 1974.

Gottlieb, Vera, *Chekhov and the Vaudeville, A Study of Chekhov's One-Act Plays*, Cambridge University Press, Cambridge, 1982.
  Chekhov in Performance in Russia and Soviet Russia, Chadwyck-Healey, Cambridge, 1984.

Hahn, Beverly, *Chekhov, A Study of the Major Stories and Plays*, Cambridge University Press, Cambridge, 1977.

Hulanicki, L., and D. Savignac, eds. and trans., *Anton Cexov As a Master of Story-Telling*, Mouton, The Hague, 1976.

Jackson, Robert Louis, ed., *Chekhov, A Collection of Critical Essays*, Englewood Cliffs, New Jersey, 1967.

Katzer, J., ed., *A. P. Chekhov, 1850–1960*, including Maxim Gorky and Olga Knipper-Chekhova, Foreign Languages Publishing House, Progress Publishers, Moscow, 1960.

Lantz, K. A., *Anton Chekhov, A Reference Guide to Literature*, G. K. Hall & Co., Boston, 1985.

Lakshin, V. Ya., E. A. Polotskaya, T. K. Shakh-Azizova, and others, eds., *Chekhoviana: statyi, publikatsii, esse*, Nauka, Moscow, 1990.

Llewellyn Smith, Virginia, *Anton Chekhov and the Lady with the Dog*, Oxford University Press, Oxford, 1973.

Lucas, F. L., *The Drama of Chekhov, Synge, Yeats and Pirandello*, Cassell, London, 1963.

de Maegd-Soep, Carolina, *Chekhov and Women, Women in the Life and Work of Chekhov*, Slavica Publishers Inc., Columbus, Ohio, 1987.

Magarshack, David, *Chekhov the Dramatist*, New York, Hill and Wang, 1960.
  The Real Chekhov, An Introduction to Chekhov's Last Plays, George Allen and Unwin, London, 1972.

Meister, Charles W., *Chekhov Bibliography. Works in English by and about Anton Chekhov; American, British, and Canadian Performances*, McFarland & Co., Jefferson, North Carolina, 1985.
  Chekhov Criticism, 1880 through 1986, McFarland & Co., Jefferson, North Carolina, 1988.

Miles, Patrick, *Chekhov on the British Stage 1909–1987 (An Essay in Cultural Exchange)*, Sam and Sam, England, 1987.

Miles, Patrick, ed. *Chekhov on the British Stage. Includes Appendix compiled by editor: A Chronology of British Professional Productions of Chekhov's Plays 1909–1991*, Cambridge University Press, Cambridge, New York, 1993.

Nilsson, Nils Ake, *Studies in Chekhov's Narrative Technique*, Stockholm, 1968.

Paperny, Z. S., *'Chayka' A. P. Chekhova*, Khudozhestvennaya literatura, Moscow, 1980.

Vopreki vsem pravilam: pyesy i vodevili Chekhova, Iskusstvo, Moscow, 1982.

Paperny, Z. S., and E. A. Polotskaya, and others, eds., *Chekhov i mirovaya literatura*, vol. I: *Chekhov in France; Chekhov in Germany; Chekhov in Austria; Chekhov in England; Chekhov in Ireland; Chekhov in Belgium*, Moscow 1997.

Peace, Richard A., *Chekhov, A Study of the Major Plays*, Yale University Press, New Haven, Conn., 1983.

Pitcher, Harvey, *The Chekhov Play, A New Interpretation*, Chatto and Windus, London, 1973.

Chekhov's Leading Lady, John Murray, London, 1979.

Rayfield, Donald, *Chekhov: The Evolution of His Art*, Barnes and Noble, New York, 1975.

The Cherry Orchard: Catastrophe and Comedy, Twayne Publishers, New York, 1994.

Senelick, Laurence, *The Chekhov Theatre – a Century of the Plays in Performance*, Cambridge University Press, Cambridge, 1997.

Shestov, L., *Anton Chekhov and Other Essays*, Ann Arbor, Mich., 1966.

Speirs, Logan, *Tolstoy and Chekhov*, Cambridge University Press, Cambridge, 1971.

Stroyeva, M., *Chekhov i Khudozhestvenny teatr*, Iskusstvo, Moscow, 1955.

Styan, J. L., *Chekhov in Performance, A Commentary on the Major Plays*, Cambridge University Press, Cambridge, 1971.

Trudeau, Lawrence J., ed., *Drama Criticism, Criticism of the Most Significant and Widely Studied Works from all the World's Literatures*, vol. IX, *A Special Volume Devoted to Anton Pavlovich Chekhov 1860–1904*, Gale Research, Detroit and London, 1999.

Tulloch, John, *Chekhov, A Structuralist Study*, Macmillan, New York, 1980.

Valency, Maurice, *The Breaking String, The Plays of Anton Chekhov*, Oxford University Press, New York, 1966.

Vilenkin, V. L., ed., *Stanislavsky, K. S., A. P. Chekhov v Moskovskom Khudozhest-vennom teatre*, Izd. Muzeya MKhATa, Moscow, 1947.

Wellek, René, and D. Nonn, eds., *Chekhov: New Perspectives*, Prentice-Hall, Englewood Cliffs, New Jersey, 1984.

Winner, Thomas, *Chekhov and His Prose*, Holt, Rinehart and Winston, New York, 1966.

Worrall, Nick, *File on Chekhov*, Methuen, London, 1986.

Yermilov, V., *Dramaturgiya Chekhova*, Sovetskiy pisatel, extended from 1948, Moscow, 1954.

Essays and chapters in collections

Barrault, Jean-Louis, *'Pourquoi "La Cérisaie,"'*, Cahiers Renaud-Barrault, Paris, 1954.

Bely, Andrey, *'The Cherry Orchard'*, in Laurence Senelick, ed. *Russian Dramatic Theory from Pushkin to the Symbolists*, University of Texas Press, Austin, 1981.

Bentley, Eric, 'Craftsmanship in *Uncle Vanya*', in his *In Search of Theater*, Alfred A. Knopf, New York, 1953.

Braun, Edward, 'Stanislavsky and Chekhov', in his *The Director and the Stage*, Methuen, London, 1982.

Brustein, Robert, 'Anton Chekhov', in his *The Theatre of Revolt, An Approach to the Modern Drama*, Little, Brown, Boston, 1964.

Corrigan, Robert W., 'The Drama of Anton Chekhov', in T. Bogard and W. I. Oliver eds., *Modern Drama, Essays in Criticism*, Oxford University Press, New York, 1965.

'The Plays of Chekhov', in his *The Theatre in Search of a Fix*, Delacorte Press, New York, 1973.

Gassner, John, 'Chekhov and the Russian Realists', in his *Masters of the Drama*, Random House, New York, 1940.

Gilman, Richard, 'Chekhov', in his *The Making of Modern Drama*, Farrar, Strauss, and Giroux, New York, 1975.

Golumb, Harai, *A Badenweiler View of Chekhov's End(ings): Beyond the Final Point*, Proceedings of the Chekhov International Symposium, October 1985.

Gottlieb, Vera, 'The "dwindling scale": the Politics of British Chekhov', in Patrick Miles, ed., and trans., *Chekhov on the British Stage*, Cambridge University Press, Cambridge, 1993.

'Chekhov in Limbo: British Productions of the Plays of Chekhov', in Hanna Scolnikov and Peter Holland, eds., *The Play Out of Context, Transferring Plays from Culture to Culture*, Cambridge University Press, Cambridge, 1989.

Guthrie, Tyrone, 'A Director's View of *The Cherry Orchard*', in T. Guthrie and L. Kipnis, eds., *The Cherry Orchard*, University of Minnesota Press, Minneapolis, 1965.

Holland, Peter, 'Chekhov and the Resistant Symbol', in J. Redmond, ed., *Drama and Symbolism*, Cambridge University Press, Cambridge, 1982 (Themes in Drama Series).

Knipper-Chekhova, Olga, 'The Last Years', in J. Katzer, ed., *A. P. Chekhov, 1860–1960*, Foreign Languages Publishing House, Progress Publishers, Moscow, n.d.

Lewis, Allan, 'The Comedy of Frustration – Chekhov, "*The Cherry Orchard*"', in his *The Contemporary Theatre: The Significant Playwrights of Our Time*, Crown Publishers, New York, 1962.

Mann, Thomas, 'Chekhov', in Donald Davie ed., *Russian Literature and Modern English Fiction, A Collection of Critical Essays*, University of Chicago Press, Chicago and London, 1965.

'Essai sur Tchékhov', in his *Esquisse de ma vie*, Gallimard, Paris, 1967 (1956).

Maurois, André, 'The Art and Philosophy of Anton Tchekov', in his *The Art of Writing*, trans. from the French by Gerard Hopkins, The Bodley Head, London, 1960.

Meyerhold, Vsevolod, 'Naturalistic Theater of Mood', in Edward Braun, ed., *Meyerhold on Theatre*, Methuen, London, 1969.

Moravčevich, Nicholas, 'Women in Chekhov's Plays', in J. P. Barricelli ed., *Chekhov's Great Plays, a Critical Anthology*, New York University Press, New York, 1981.

Shevtsova, M., 'Chekhov in France, 1976–79: Productions by Strehler, Miquel and

Pintilé', in Ian Donaldson, ed., *Transformations in Modern European Drama*, Macmillan, London, 1983.

'*The Three Sisters* in French and Russian (Théâtre de l'Enfumeraie and Teatr Tembr)', in her own *Theatre and Cultural Interaction*, Sydney Studies, University of Sydney, 1993.

Strehler, Giorgio, *Notes de mise-en-scène sur 'La Cérisaie' de Tchekhov*, Un Théâtre Pour la Vie, Fayard, Paris, 1980.

Styan, J. L., 'Naturalistic Shading', in his *The Dark Comedy: The Development of Modern Comic Tragedy*, Cambridge University Press, Cambridge, 1968.

Tynan, Kenneth, 'Theatre in Moscow'; '*The Cherry Orchard*', '*Three Sisters*', '*Uncle Vanya*' and '*The Troubled Past*' in his *Tynan on Theatre*, Penguin, Harmondsworth, 1964.

Williams, Raymond, 'Anton Chekhov', in his *Drama from Ibsen to Brecht*, Hogarth Press, London, 1968; revised paperback 1987.

Winner, Thomas G., 'Myth as a Device in the Works of Chekhov', in B. Slote, ed., *Myth and Symbol, Critical Approaches and Applications*, University of Nebraska Press, Lincoln, 1963.

Worrall, Nick, 'Stanislavsky's Production of Chekhov's *Three Sisters*', in Robert Russell and Andrew Barratt eds., *Russian Theatre in the Age of Modernism*, Macmillan, Houndsmills, Basingstoke, 1990.

Journal articles

Allen, David, 'Exploring the Limitless Depths: Mike Alfreds Directs Chekhov', *New Theatre Quarterly* 8, 2, Cambridge University Press, Cambridge, November 1986, pp. 320–35.

'David Jones Directs Chekhov's *Ivanov*', *New Theatre Quarterly* 15, August 1988, pp. 232–46 [Reconstruction of RSC production].

'Jonathan Miller Directs Chekhov', *New Theatre Quarterly* 17, February 1989, pp. 52–66 [Reconstruction of Miller's *Three Sisters*].

Bentley, Eric, 'Chekhov As Playwright', *Kenyon Review* 7, 1949, pp. 226–50.

Bunin, Ivan, 'Chekhov', *Atlantic Monthly* 188, 1951, pp. 59–63 .

Chudakov, Alexander P., 'Newly-Discovered Works by the Young Chekhov', *Soviet Literature* 10, 1975, pp. 134–42.

Clayton, J. Douglas, 'Cexov's *Djadja Vanja* and Traditional Comic Structure', *Russian Language Journal* 40, 136–7, Spring–Fall 1986, pp. 103–10.

Clyman, Toby W., 'Chekhov's Victimized Women', *Russian Language Journal* 28, 1974, pp. 26–31.

Conrad, Joseph L., 'Sensuality in Cexov's Prose', *Slavic and East European Journal* 24, 1980, pp. 103–17.

'Unresolved Tension in Cexov's Stories, 1886–1888', *Slavic and East European Journal* 16, 1972, pp. 55–64.

Corrigan, Robert W., 'Some Aspects of Chekhov's Dramaturgy', *Educational Theatre Journal* 7, 1955, pp. 107–14.

Cousin, Geraldine, 'Revisiting the Prozorovs', *Modern Drama* 40, 3, Fall 1997, pp. 325–33.

Efros, Anatolij, 'Energy, Enervation, and the Mathematics of Intrigue', Anatolij Efros in discussion with Spencer Golub, *Theatre Quarterly*, 7, 26, Summer 1977, pp. 28–33.

Fodor, A., 'In Search of a Soviet Chekhov', *Journal of Russian Studies* 21, 1971, pp. 9–19.

Gerould, Daniel C., '*The Cherry Orchard* as a Comedy', *Journal of General Education* 11, 1958, pp. 109–22.

Gilman, Richard, '*Ivanov*, Prologue to a Revolution', *Theatre* 22, 2, Spring 1991, pp. 14–27.

'Broadway Critics meet *Uncle Vanya*, *Theatre Quarterly* 13, February 1974, pp. 67–72 [American critics' mistaken reviews of Mike Nichol's *Uncle Vanya*].

Glenny, M., 'Tovstonogov in The Soviet Theatre', *Bulletin of the Great Britain–USSR Association* 14, Autumn 1966.

Golub, S., 'Acting on the Run: Efros and the Contemporary Soviet Theatre', *Theatre Quarterly*, 7, 26, Summer 1977, pp. 18–28.

Gorky, Maxim, 'What Chekhov Thought of It', *English Review* 8, 1911, pp. 256–66.

Gottlieb, Vera, *Why This Farce?*, *New Theatre Quarterly* 27, 7, August 1991, pp. 217–28

Hahn, Beverly, 'Chekhov's *The Cherry Orchard*', *Critical Review* 16, 1973, pp. 56–72.

Hristic, Jovan '"Thinking with Chekhov", the Evidence of Stanislavsky's Notebooks', *New Theatre Quarterly* 42, 11, May 1995, pp. 175–83.

'Time in Chekhov: the Inexorable and the Ironic', *New Theatre Quarterly* 3, August 1985, pp. 271–82.

Kramer, Karl D., 'Chekhov at the End of the Eighties, The Question of Identity', *Études Slaves et Est-Européennes* 11, 1966, pp. 3–18.

Lahr, John, 'Pinter and Chekhov, The Bond of Naturalism', *Drama Review* 13, 1968, pp. 137–45.

Mann, Thomas, 'Anton Chekhov', *Mainstream* 12, 1959, pp. 2–21.

McDonald, Jan, 'Production of Chekhov's Plays in Britain Before 1914', *Theatre Notebook* 34, 1980, pp. 25–36.

Merlin, Bella, 'Which Came First: the System or *The Seagull?*', *New Theatre Quarterly* 59, August 1999, pp. 218–27.

Saint-Denis, Michel, 'Chekhov and the Modern Stage', *Drama Survey* 3, 1965, pp. 77–81.

Senelick, Laurence, 'Lake-Shore Bohemia, *The Seagull*'s Theatrical Context', *Educational Theatre Journal* 29, 1977, pp. 199–213.

Shakh-Azizova, Tatiana, 'A Russian Hamlet, *Ivanov* and His Age', *Soviet Literature*, 1980, pp. 157–63.

Shevtsova, Maria, 'Resistance and Resilience: an Overview of the Maly Theatre of St Petersburg', *New Theatre Quarterly* 52, November 1997, pp. 299–317.

'Drowning in Dixie: The Maly Drama Theatre Plays Chekhov Untitled', *Theatre Forum* 13, 1998, pp. 46–53.

Silverstein, Norman, 'Chekhov's Comic Spirit and *The Cherry Orchard*', *Modern Drama* 1, 2, September 1958, pp. 91–100.

Smith, J. Oates, 'Chekhov and the "Theater of the Absurd"', *Bucknell Review* 14, 1966, pp. 44–58.

States, Bert O., 'Chekhov's Dramatic Strategy', *Yale Review* 56, 1967, pp. 212–24.

Styan, J. L., 'The Idea of a Definitive Production, Chekhov In and Out of Period', *Comparative Drama* 4, 1970, pp. 177–96.

'The Delicate Balance, Audience Ambivalence in the Comedy of Shakespeare and Chekhov', *Costerus* 2, 1972, pp. 159–84.

Szewcow, Maria (Shertsova, Maria), 'Anatolij Efros directs Chekhov's *The Cherry Orchard* and Gogol's *The Marriage*, *Theatre Quarterly*, 26, 1977, pp. 34–46.

Tulloch, J., T. Borvill and Andrew Hood, 'Re-inhabiting "*The Cherry Orchard*", Class and History in Performing Chekhov', *New Theatre Quarterly* 52, Vol 13, November 1997, pp. 318–28.

Vickers, Sylvia 'Space, Genre and Methodology in Max Stafford-Clark's Touring Production of Chekhov's *Three Sisters*', *New Theatre Quarterly* 57, 15, February 1999, pp. 45–57.

Wilson, Edmund, 'Seeing Chekhov Plain', *New Yorker* 22, November 1952, pp. 180–98.

Winner, Thomas G., 'The Chekhov Centennial Productions in the Moscow Theatres', *Slavic and East European Journal* 5, 1961, pp. 255–62.

INDEX OF WORKS BY CHEKHOV

GENERAL INDEX